RAISING THE BANNER
OF FREEDOM

Raising the Banner of Freedom

The 25th Ohio Volunteer Infantry in the War for the Union

Bvt. Col. Edward C. Culp
Edited by Tom J. Edwards

iUniverse, Inc.

New York Lincoln Shanghai

Raising the Banner of Freedom
The 25th Ohio Volunteer Infantry in the War for the Union

iUniverse, Inc.

For information address:
iUniverse
2021 Pine Lake Road, Suite 100
Lincoln, NE 68512
www.iuniverse.com

ISBN: 0-595-27608-3

Printed in the United States of America

For the Boys of the 25th Ohio

About the Cover

The background photo is a copy of the original newspaper *"The Banner of Freedom,"* published April 10, 1865 by the printers of the 25th Ohio Volunteer Infantry regiment in Sumter, South Carolina. It is provided courtesy of the University of South Carolina, Caroliniana Library, Columbia, South Carolina. The newspaper was taken over by occupying Union forces just prior to press time and afforded these soldiers the opportunity to re-set the paper and distribute it as a propaganda tool. On April 9, members of the 107th Ohio Volunteer Infantry had assisted the printers of the 25th in publishing their first edition of this paper, the *"Clarendon—Banner of Freedom*, in Manning, South Carolina. The photograph of Edward C. Culp is courtesy of the Firelands Historical Society, Norwalk, Ohio. Major Culp was the last regimental commander of the 25th Ohio. He was breveted twice for bravery, as Lt. Colonel and as Colonel and is the author of the original book.

Acknowledgments

In preparing this edited version of Col. Culp's book, I have benefited from the assistance of a great many people through shared archives, photographs, publishing tips, and continued encouragement. My early incentive for pursuing this project came from Dr. Phillip Shriver, President Emeritus of Miami University and a eminent Ohio historian. Dr. Shriver reviewed my initial work and set me on a proper path toward publication. I particularly wish to express my appreciation to Mrs. Beth Bigelow for her hours of proof reading and her unwavering support of this project. This book was a technological challenge, using desktop publishing to prepare this document. I wish to thank Florence-Darlington Technical College and Mr. Pat Sowell, in particular, for my training and assistance in world of computer tech and online education. The marvel of the world wide web for research and communication resulted in meaningful contacts throughout the country. Through the assistance of a web site for the 25th Ohio Volunteer Infantry, I have been contacted by nearly one hundred persons who are directly descended from veterans of this regiment (www.geocities.com/pentagon/barracks/3727). This would not have been possible without the technical assistance of my son, U.S. Army Major T. J. Edwards.

Others were instrumental in the development of this book. Mr. Mike Musik, of the National Archives and Records Administration, made it possible for me to review their entire collection of 25th Ohio records, reports, descriptive books, and muster rolls. History came to life as I sorted through documents unseen in more than a century. The Ohio Historical Society staff was consistently helpful, whether that assistance was on their premises or long distance. I am indebted to Dr. Allen Stokes, Director of the Caroliniana Library, the University of South Carolina, and Brian Cuthrill for providing valuable assistance in locating records related to the 25th Ohio's occupation of the campus including an original copy of the "Banner of Freedom" produced by the printers of the 25th OVI. Thanks, too, go to Randy Hackenburg, U.S. Army Military History Institute, Carlisle Barracks, Pennsylvania. I am grateful to Mr. Jim Leeke, of Worthington, Ohio. His book "A Hundred Days to Richmond," provided an excellent format which was adopted to my editing of Col Culp's book.

Richard A. Baumgartner's book, "Buckeye Blood: Ohio at Gettysburg" provided a valuable resource and I appreciate Mr. Baumgartner's assistance in locating further photographic evidence of the 25th Ohio. He led me to Mr. Dennis Keese, author of "Too Young to Die: Boy Soldiers of the Union Army, 1861-1865," who generously provided copies of his fine collection of 25th OVI officer and enlisted images.

Sincere appreciation also goes to the following people and institutions for their contributions to the publication of this book: The University of Toledo (OH), University of Missouri (Kansas City, Mo. Western Manuscript Collection), Charleston Library Society (SC), Indiana State Library, Brooklyn (NY) Public Library, Puskarich Public Library (Cadiz, OH), Clarendon County Historical Society (SC), Firelands Historical Society (Norwalk, OH), Norwalk Public Library, Isis Temple (Salina, Kansas), National Museum of Civil War Medicine (Frederick, Md.), Eric Barkhurst, Katherine Dhalle, Donald Dunn, Mark Haselberger, Ron Mesnard, Dan Rivera, and Dr. Adrian Wheat.

Contents

Illustrations

Pictures

Maps

Foreword
(Original Author's Preface)

Courtesy of Firelands Historical Society
Bvt. Colonel Edward C. Culp

The matter contained in the following pages was prepared while we were yet in the field, upon the days immediately following our marches and battles, while in camp or bivouac, or during the long season of rest upon Folly and Hilton Head Islands.

I have revised it twice since the war, but still feel as if I was giving a very unsatisfactory history of the gallant old Regiment, and regret that its preparation has not fallen into abler hands.

Our Regiment was raised from so many portions of the State, that we have been unable to meet in annual reunions, which would have been the means of correcting many errors, especially in names.

Our members are now scattered over the Western States to the Pacific coast, but I have endeavored to get as many names as possible, with the present postoffice address, and will have them added in an appendix to this volume.

I am indebted to many of the old comrades for information asked for at different times during the past two years, and still ask for correction in names and dates, which will be noted for a second edition.

This book is only a plain record of events, with no attempt at humor, and will only be of interest to those who participated in the changing fortunes of the

Regiment, or those others whose sons and brothers went out with us, never to return in this life.

E.C.C.

Salina, Kansas, March 10, 1885

Introduction

Ohio Historical Society, Artist Rob Neeham.
25th Ohio Volunteer Infantry State Colors

In 1885, Brevet Colonel Edward C. Culp set into print his recollections of the American Civil War as seen through his experiences with the 25th Ohio Volunteer Infantry. He titled his book, *The 25th Ohio Veteran Volunteer Infantry in the War for the Union*. Col. Culp answered his country's call from the opening days of the war in 1861 at the age of 18, and served through and beyond its conclusion in 1866. During this time he rose rapidly through the ranks. His rising position of leadership in the regiment gave him unique perspective on the activities and engagements of this veteran Ohio unit. Enlisting June 8,1861, he was elected as a Sergeant in Company D. By November of that year, he was promoted to Sergeant Major of the regiment. In May 1862, Sgt. Major Culp was commissioned as a Second Lieutenant and by September 1862 promoted to 1st Lieutenant. In March of the following year, Lt. Culp was promoted to the rank of Captain and received the command of Company A. By January 1865, he had earned the rank of Major and served as a staff officer for the 25th Ohio. In October 1865, Major Culp assumed command of the entire regiment, at the age of 23. Major Culp served in this capacity until the final muster of the unit in 1866, more than a year after the war had ended. On the eve of the regiment finally returning home, Major Culp was promoted to the rank of Lt. Colonel. In 1867, the Adjutant General of the US War Department recognized Col. Culp's record of service over five years, awarding him a brevet rank of Lieutenant Colonel for "long and faithful services with his regiment" and Colonel for "gallant conduct on many battle-fields." Edward Culp had been captured near Brooks Station, Virginia in June,1862 and subsequently exchanged the following September. He was also wounded in the arm July 1,

1863 at the Battle of Gettysburg while servicing as aide-de-camp for General Francis Barlow.

As a part of the Army of the Potomac and the Coastal Division of the Department of the South, Col. Culp and the 25th Ohio played integral roles in well-known conflicts such as Cross Keys (Virginia), Second Bull Run (Virginia), Chancellorsville (Virginia), Gettysburg (Pennsylvania), and Honey Hill (South Carolina). Culp's writings reflect a clear, collective dedication to preserving the Union and to ending slavery; a dedication that paid a dear price in life and limb. At the start of the war, the 25th Ohio boasted more than 1100 effective troops. By day two of the Battle of Gettysburg, July 2, 1863, fewer than 60 men remained standing. Col. Culp spares no words but shares his feelings and insights as an officer in exciting, graphic detail.

A Latin phrase is found on the cover page of Col. Culp's book, "*Quaeque ipse vidi et quorum pars fui.*" A translation reflects Col. Culp's inner feelings and inspiration for his writings. "*That which I have seen…and…of this I am a part.*"

The editing of Edward Culp's fine book is intended to be a tribute to his memory and to those brave veterans with whom he served. Every effort has been made to maintain the integrity of Col. Culp's manuscript. It is the foundation of a fascinating story best told by those who were present for duty with Col. Culp. Through years of research, I have been quite fortunate to uncover accounts of other soldiers of the 25th Ohio who served with Col. Culp. Letters, diaries, photographs and regimental reports add a meaningful dimension to Culp's writings. This new material adds to and enhances the reader's knowledge and understanding of the American Civil War from the personal viewpoint of both officers and enlisted men in the Union Army.

To assist in following the format of this book, the reader is advised that, while the majority of what follows is an exact reprint of Col. Culp's own words, the supplemental accounts of other veterans which are integrated throughout the text are separated by astrick notations. Editorial notes provide continuity of thought and a smooth transition between Col. Culp and his contemporaries' writings.

I am indebted to my mother, Elizabeth Anderson Edwards, formerly of Woodsfield, Ohio, for introducing me to the 25th Ohio Volunteer Infantry. When I was a small boy, she took me by the hand into the rotunda of the Ohio State Capitol, Columbus, Ohio. Encircling the center chamber was a glass-encased collection of flags from all Ohio regiments which served in the American Civil War. We found our way to the flag of the 25th Ohio and she proceeded to tell me about my great grandfather (Lt.) James A. Driggs serving honorably with that regiment. Upon our return home, she shared with me his veteran's medal, buttons from his uniform and his Bible carried throughout the war. These artifacts of the past were but a precursor to my lifelong interest and journey toward uncovering the history and legacy of the 25th Ohio Volunteer Infantry and the brave souls who served their state and nation so nobly. It is my sincere hope that the reader will find this composite of history as fascinating and inspirational as it has been for me.

Thomas J. Edwards
Lakeside, Ohio
2003

Chapter 1

Organization of the Regiment—Assignment of Companies

When the President's call for "three years men" was issued, in the early part of May, 1861, many of the "three months" companies still remained in various camps throughout the State with no prospect of assignment to duty in the field.

These companies were given the privilege of re-enlisting for "three years, or during the war," and such as accepted the offer were immediately consolidated into regiments, placed in camp, and drilled and disciplined for active service.

*   *   *   *

Editor's Note: Among the regiments thus organized was the 25th Ohio Infantry, which, with the 23rd, 24th, and 26th Ohio, formed the brigade in Camp Chase, Columbus, Ohio, early in June, 1861. Some of the companies, as before mentioned, had originally enlisted for three months, and had at first gone into camp in Camp Taylor, Cleveland, Ohio. (Advertisement for Recruits in <u>Spirit of Democracy</u>, Woodsfield, Ohio, to help find replacements for those whose three year enlistments were running out is seen on next page)

*   *   *   *

When the 25th Ohio was organized, offers of companies poured in so fast that none but the very largest were accepted; and, frequently, the captain of one company would think himself fortunate in securing the position of first lieutenant by fusing his company with another—thus bringing the number to the maximum (101) which warranted a speedier muster in and consequently an earlier assignment to a regiment and active service.

VOLUNTEERS WANTED FOR THE
25TH REGT. O. V. I. V.

The undersigned, under orders, has
opened a Recruiting Office, one door
south of Walton's Store. The term of
enlistmen will be for three years, pay
from $30 to $20 per month, $3½ per
month for clothing and rations.

Recruits, — — $302
Veteran Volunteers, — $402
N. J. MANNING.
Capt. & Recruitting Officer
Feb. 10 1864.—tf.

Ohio Historical Society
Recruitment Notice, 25th O.V.I., <u>Spirit of Democracy</u>, Woodsfield,
Ohio, posted by Captain N. J. Manning, February, 1864.

Owing to this patriotic "rush to arms," regiments were now raised from one section of the State, but were composed of men from all parts, as many as sixty counties being represented in a single regiment. This was the condition of affairs in the 25th which was, however, remarkably fortunate in its assignment of companies and the character of its officers who were, as a rule, gentlemen of culture and some of them of considerable experience in army matters having creditably served in the war with Mexico. The enlisted men of the regiment were above the average in intelligence and social standing. The majority were young men and it is safe to say that the average age of the Regiment was not over twenty-one. Ninety percent of the occupations were embraced in teaching, farming, book-keeping and clerks.

On the 28th of June, 1861, the last company required to complete the regimental organization was mustered into service, when the regiment presented the following roster:

Editor's Note: Col. Culp had intended to make name spelling corrections in a second edition. I have attempted to include as accurately as I can an alphabetical listing of regimental members, along with brief service records. It is recommended that readers wishing more complete and accurate military service and pension records contact the National Archives and Records Administration directly (http://www.nara.gov).

Colonel—James A. Jones, Norwalk
Lieut. Colonel—Wm. P. Richardson, Woodsfield
Major—George Webster, Steubenville
Surgeon—Louis G. Meyer, Cleveland
Asst. Surgeon—Lawrence G. Andrews, Toledo
Chaplain—Zachariah Ragan, Steubenville
Adjutant—Wm. L. Hoyt, Norwalk
Quartermaster—Andrew J. Hale, Fremont
Sergeant Major—Robert F. Jackson, New London
Q.M. Sergeant—Abner J. Phelps, Mansfield
Com. Sergeant—Samuel P. Houston, Summerfield
Hospital Steward—Oliver W. Williams, Tiffin
Prin. Musician—Ad. J. Hess
Sutlers—Wm Jordon and Wilson Askew

Company A—St. Clairsville

Captain: James F. Charlesworth
First Lieut: Wm. Askew
Second Lieut: Arthur Higgins
First Sergeant: John D. Koontz
Sergeants: Wm. B. Wright, Zenas Smith, Henry Johnson, Israel White
Corporals: Burget McConnaughy, Wm. H. Spear, James Mellor, Thomas W. Fowler, Abram Heed, Robert Kennedy, Hiram Nicholl, Thomas. H. Ferrel
Privates: William Allum, Joseph Acres, George W. Bayless, William F. Bloor,

The Spirit of Democracy, June 12, 1861
Woodsfield, Ohio

Departure of Our Volunteers
A very large crowd was assembled in Woodsfield on Saturday morning last to see Capt. Washburn's and Williams' Companies take their departure for Camp Jackson at Columbus where they have been ordered. We regret that we have not time to give more detailed accounts of the journey of the soldiers from here to Barnesville or to mention specially some of the incidents on the way.

The citizens of the town and surrounding country having furnished an abundance of vehicles to convey the soldiers to Barnesville, which being drawn up in line ready for starting; the soldiers and their friends commenced taking leave of each other, perhaps forever, and many and sad were the partings between husbands and wives, mothers and sons, brothers and sisters and soldiers and their friends; and but few dry eyes were seen on the streets as the long line of wagons took their departure conveying the soldiers from Woodsfield.

The soldiers were accompanied from here by the Brass Band and by quite a number of other citizens, and all along the road from here to Barnesville they were greeted with enthusiastic demonstrations of welcome by the people.

They were escorted into the town of Malaga by a military company belonging to that place and upon their arrival to town, the soldiers were drawn up into line and were welcomed in a neat, appropriate, and patriotic address by the Rev. Logan, which was responded to by Maj. Wm. P. Richardson of this place. The citizens of Malaga having provided an abundance of good cheer which was spread out on long tables under the shade of the trees with which the town is amply provided, the soldiers after the speaking were marched to the table and then did ample justice to the good cheer provided for them. There was a large number of persons present at Malaga to welcome and take leave of the soldiers, who also partook of the dinner provided.

The soldiers then gave three rousing cheers in testimony of their appreciation of the hospitality of the citizens of Malaga and vicinity and then took up their line of March for Somerton where in like manner they were welcomed and where they halted to partake of the abundant refreshments prepared for them by the citizens of the town. The soldiers and others were quartered around at the different houses and if it would not be considered invidious to particularize where everybody did everything just as near right as they could, we would like to state what we had for dinner at Somerton and who furnished the dinner. Anyhow the gentleman who furnished that dinner is entitled to our hat and we wish it was a newer one.

With three rousing cheers for the citizens of Somerton, the soldiers took up their line of march and in due time arrived in the vicinity of Barnesville where they were received and escorted into town by the Barnesville Cavalry Company and Home Guard and also a number of citizens of the area. Every preparation that was possible was made in Barnesville for the comfortable quartering of the soldiers during the time they had to remain. On Sunday the soldiers attended church...[1]

*   *   *   *

Dennis Keese Collection
**George W. McBride, Company A
Principal Musician**

Alexander Barrett, Joseph Boggs, Levi Butler, Elias Baile, James C. Bolan, Joshua Burkhead, Lleander J. Beall, Samuel Beall, Daniel J. Crooks, Wm. H. Criswell, George Coss, John Conaway, James E. Clifford, Robert Creighton, John T. Crowe, Hugh Donally, Reuben Donnelly, Robert M. Fulton, Robert A. Flowler, Samuel Glasgow, Phillip Gable, Joseph Gallagher, John W. Holland, Eli Hawker, Samuel Henry, John R. Hedge, Charles Hoober, William Harrison, Hiram J. Hahn, George W. Iden, Drewer C. Iverson, Benjamin R. Johnson, Andrew M. Jeffers, James Justus, Charles H. King, James Kelley, John W. Kent, Dewitt C. Kinney, Josephus I. Kinney, Patrick Kaine, Wm. Linden, Wm. T. Lockwood, Henry Lambert, John Lebold. John McMillen, John McConnell, George D. W. McPherson, James McMullen, Samuel McCrumb, Jacob McCabe, John

McKirahan, Thomas McBride, George W. McBride, Michael Murray, Robert H. Miller, Henry Meek, Jesse C. Patterson, Levi Ryan, James Russell, John Richards, Emanuel L. Riley, Josephus I. Riol, Wm. C. Rankin, Nathaniel Sutton, Charles Smith, Samuel R. Stewart, Ignatius Tillett, Wm. F. Tolbert, Samuel Tolbert, Hezehiah Thomas, George W. Verbeck, Simon L. Voorheis, John Weyer, Robert Wright, James G. Whittle, Henry C. White, Wm. H. White, Wm. A. Whitcraft, John Zane.

Company B—Woodsfield

Captain—James Washburn
First Lieut—Charles B. Jones
Second Lieut—John D. Merryman
First Sergeant—Alston C. Archbold
Sergeants—George W. Martin, James I. Carrothers, Slater B. Brock, Thomas A. Masters
Corporals—James D. McMunn, James A. Driggs, Hugh McConville, Henry H. Moose, Samuel Trigg, John E. Hill, Elias Hoffman, Barney Powell
Musicians—Wm. S. Shaner, John A. Hoffman
Wagoner—Appolo Wells

Privates—John O. Archbold, Michael Archer, Isaac Beaver, Daniel Berry, John Brown, Ebenezer L. Boughner, Charles Beck, Fred J. Beck, Elijah Brown, Joseph Brown, Mark Brown, James M.

United States Army Military History Institute
**Sgt. William M. Lowther, Co. B,
25th Ohio Volunteer Infantry**

Bowman, Wm. R. Bowman, Joshua Brown, Charles T. Chase, Thomas Cain, Stephen Conger, James D. Coffman, John B. Driggs, Peter Dailey, John W. Doherty, John C. Duff, Wm. Elliger, John Easthorn, Martin L. Folwell, Augustus Fierhelder, Henry H. Ford, Phineas Gano, Wm. M. Green, Reason House, Samuel B. Hurd, Joseph J. Hopten, Abram Hayden, Duncan Highman, John M. Hinds, Patrick L. Hamilton, David A. Hollingsworth, Cornelius N. Jones, Henry Jones, Ralph T. Jefferey, Benjamin Keene, Levi Keadle, Andrew J. Lloyd, Garwood P. Lacy, Benton Longwell, Mark Lawerence, David Lowe, Elias Lowther, Wm. M. Lowther, Wm. N. Long, Robert Marriner.

Nathan Morris, Wm. Moffatt, Thomas Moffatt, Perry Moffatt, Newlin C. Mercer, John J. Moose, Daniel Norfolk, John Osborn, Samuel Prescott, John L. Patten, John L. Pratt, Samuel Rhynard, Frederick Rose, Robert Rutherford, Isaac Rucker, Oliver P. Smith, James Snyder, Wesley B. Sultzer, Sylvester Sultzer, James Sultzer, Wm. H. Stine, Joseph Stewart, Wm. Smith, Harrison Stilt, Charles Twinum, James Trigg, John H. Twaddle, Charles G. Troy, Sylvanus Ullum, Joshua B. Vaughn, Anthony Wheeler, Samuel White, John White

Company C—Woodsfield

Captain—Jeremiah Williams
First Lieut—William P. Richner
Second Lieut—Francis M. Sinclair
First Sergeant—Nathaniel J. Manning
Sergeants—William J. Akers, William Craig, Alexander Sinclair, William Kast
Corporals—Oscar F. Little, Abraham Tisher, Wm. Henthorn, John W. Harrison, James M. Barker, Alexander Drum, James M. Cunningham, Wm. G. Tesse.
Musicians—Ad. J. Hess, John Walton
Wagoner—George W. Henderson

Privates—Francis Armstrong, Henry Armway, Herman Buckleman, Andrew Boston, Ellijah Becket, George Beach, Martin V. Barnes, Jacob H. Bailey, Thomas Batton, William H. Bodkins, Smith Bodkins, Benoni Bennett, Albert Cavanaugh, Jesse Campbell, Samuel Coppersmith, John T. Cunningham, Jonathan Dunn, Wm. R. Drum, Joseph Dixon, John Frey, George Frick, August Fisher, John W. Fisher, Christian Frankhauser, Wm. Fallon, Thomas Grisell, Alonzo P. Henthorn, Lafayette Henthorn, James B. Henthorn, Wm. J. Henthrorn, Samuel Hutchison, Isaac Hutchison, Jeremiah Hicks, William Hamilton, Alexander E. Holland, Thomas B. Hudson, Isaac N. Headley, John Hall, John W. Haskins, James L. Hopper, Isaac Johnson, Harvey L. Jeffereys, Wm. J. Kelley, Franklin Long, Henry M. Link, Jacob H. Lorcall, Robert Longwell, John A. Luke, Alexander W. Lowe, Lewis Mason, John McCollister, Isaiah Masters, James B. McPeek, Aaron Noland, Joseph P. Noll, Henry Nunn, John W. Pearce, Uriah Province, James Province, Amida Province, Albert Pratt, Christian Resecker, Charles T. Riley, Peter Ryan, James L. Richardson, Mortimer Smith, Francis Schonhart, Joseph Sill, Washington Swallow, Solomon Suter, Charles W. Terry, John Tisher, John F. Thonen, Marion Y. Thornberry, Sylvanus Williams, George W. Wisiner, Lewis E. Wilson, Frederick Woodtler, Peter Yohe.

Company D—Richland,Huron&FayetteCounties

Captain—Aaron C. Johnson
First Lieut—Darius Dirlam
Secont Lieut—Archibald McClellen
First Sergeant—Robert F. Jackson
Sergeants—Edward C. Culp, Ami P. Fairbanks, Wm. B. Flemming, Hiram Ward
Corporals—Levi D. Vinson, Daniel S. Coe, Henry Stedwell, Myron Webber, W. W. Banning, Flavius J. Heller, Benjamin S. Mallory, John B. Ward
Musicians—John B. Wells, Benjamin Harrison
Wagoner—George Dunks
Privates—George W. Armstrong, Charles Alvine, Anderson Blue, George Bracey, John M. Beelman, Albert Bradley, Theodore Brown, Newton A. Briggs, Wm. H. Brown, Frank Bisel, Cicereo H. Boden, Otho W. Byrood, William D. Banks, George W. Crawford, Robert B. Cumpton, Wesley B. Cummings, Warren Collins, James L. Clark, John Crawford, George H. Clock, Clark O. Childs, Calvin A. Day, Wm. Duff, Nathaniel S. Davis, Wm. F. Fisher, Samuel Fleck, Joseph Ferguson, Lewis Ferman, Alponzo E. Gregory, Thomas Grimes, Frederick Henick, David Houghtlin, Edward D. Hubbell, Benjamin F. Jones,

Thomas Jones, Charles Jesson, John E. Jameson, Samuel Keifer, George Kester, Frank B. Lockwood, Lewis M. Lewis, H. Lickliter, George Logan, Morris McGregor, Lyman May, James McBride, Alfred Meeker, James Nesbit, Alfred Noacker, Nathaniel O. Osborn, James N. Pulver, Emanual Ribblets, Charles C. Rodier, Samuel Reed, George Rumsey, Wm. Roberts, Fred Schnauffer, Jeremiah Snyder, Samuel Sutler, John M. Sparks, John H. Sharrett, Jesse Sharrett, John R. Smithson, Wm. S. Straley, John Truxell, William Underwood, John Vaughn, Clark F. Wright, Wm. White

Company E—Fremont

Captain—Moses I. Crowell
First Lieut—John W. Bowlus
Second Lieut—Andrew J. Hale
First Sergeant—Elisha Biggerstaff
Sergeants—Chas. Ladd, David R. Hunt, Carrington E. Randall, George N. Holcomb
Corporals—Lewis H. Bowlus, Cyrus Odell, John A. Stump, William Herring, Howard Carmon, Daniel Hubble, James Clark, Jacob P. Thomas
Musicians—Robert H. Culley, Benj. S. Gilmore
Wagoner—Clinton Walters
Privates—George W. Alger, George F. Alfred, John Bigley, James W. Barnes, Charles Cimmerer, Elbridge Comstock, Frederick Cannell, Charles Caul, George W. Cleland, Thomas E. Coalwell, Samuel H. Deselems, Andrew J. Davis, George Dugan, Samuel Edgar, John Everingham, Isaiah Eastlick, George C. Edgerton, Josiah Fought, Samuel Frontz, August Freet, John Ferrell, Frederick Guilger, Joseph Hess, Monta Heath, Harvey N. Hall, Thomas C. Hemmiger, Wm. L. Hutton, Thomas Howell, John Q. Hutchins, Frederick Halderman, Oliver P. Hershey, Virgil Jacobs, John Jell, George Kesseler, John Knappenberger, Jesse Little John Leary, John Loose, Lawrison Marsh, Joseph Mitchell, Wm. Mensor, Lucius Marsh, Darius Minnier, Hohn Minnier, Peter Molyet, Wm. H. Mackey, John P. Merris, Lewis Moorer, Michael Mulgrove, Orlando L. Mills, Harrison J. Meyers, Peter Miller, Isaac Nye, Hiram Odell, Hiram Ostrander, Richard D. Phelps, Alexander Pemberton, John E. Rearick, Joseph Riddle, Lewis Robber, Frederick Schultz, Wm. R. Stump, Alfred F. Stump, Abednego Stevens, Norton G. Skinner, Joel Sphon, Levi S. Stewart, Hemry Smuck, Florence Smith, Alexander Scott, Benjamin Stahley, Charles Slaughterbeck, Edward J. Teeples, Christopher J. Thayer, John Tweedle, Decatur Whitney, George D. Wormwood, Joseph Wright, Lewis Zeigler.

Company F—Steubenville

Captain—John F. Oliver
First Lieut—John W. Ross
Second Lieut—James Templeton
First Sergeant—Joseph Hollis
Sergeants—Peter Yarnell, John F. Thompson, James M. Jones, Wm. Maloney
Corporals—William Bougher, Samuel P. Huston, William M. Stager, Wm. Gassaway, George A. Aubert, David C. Zugler, Wilson H. Peterson, Emile A. Huston
Musicians—Jacob A. Crabill, Benjamin F. Crabill
Wagoner—Israel Brown
Privates—Florence Ariman, Geo. M. Aulter, John Armstrong, John Barrett, John Brownlee, Patrick Burke, David Casteel, Michael Cantwell, Albert V. H. Clark, Charles L. Collin, Wm. L. Cooper, James Collins, Samuel Crawford, Josiah O. Curl, James Conroy, Emanuel P Dotson, Edward Dunn, Frederick Eberheart, Solomon Ebersole, Samuel M. Forrester, Edwin O. Forrester, Jonathan C. Fuller, John A. Garrison, John F. Grange, Henry Greer, John T. Hancock, Geo. Harmon, George W. Horner, Wm. H. Irwine, Gustav Kolby, John Larkins, Theodore E. Lodge, Thomas Long, John C. Maxwell, John Meeker, Jerome P. Miller, Israel Miller, Josiah H. Meredith, Andrew Moffat, James Mooney, Barnard McLaferty, Thomas Nolen, John O. Neal, Wm. P. Parrish, John P. Parrish, Samuel Price, Leander Proviner, Stephen Point, John Pool, John I. Roberts, John Ruddicks, John H. Saunders, David P. Scott, James Schallett, John Serrels, James S. Shannon, Wm. F. Shannon, Alexander Shannon, Basil C. Shields, Isaac H. Smith, Moses Sweeney, Franklin D. Steetson, John Tucker, John H. Veite, Levi M. Wells, Joseph H. White, Hugh Wilson.

Company G—Seneca, Muskingum & Jefferson Counties

Private William Pancost, Co. G
25th **Ohio Volunteer Infantry**

Captain—Asa Way
First Lieut—Wesley Chamberlain
Second Lieut—Benjamin W. Blandy
First Sergeant—John A. Perky
Sergeants—John H. Milliman, John Fenton, Omer P. Norris, Alfred A. Lampkin

Corporals—Herbert G. Ogden, Wesley Milliman, Blydon H. Boyce, Edward P. Wilcox, Samuel Baughman, Andrew D. Stewart, John C. Livensparger, Geo. S. Ogden
Privates—Moses Cram, Amender Eaton, Eli F. Beard, Rush P. Baldwin, Irwin W. Bergerstresser, Andrew J. Ames, William Burgess, John Benny, George Blair, Joseph Bush, John J. Cummings, Edward Considine, Andrew J. Crosley, William W. Chamberlain, Thomas Cuthbertson, John Cole, Josiah Downs, John N. Dickin, Joseph Dyerman, William H, Ephraim, John Ewalt, John D. Fisher, John Gallagher, Wm. H. Gulick, Geo. W. Greeling, Leander W. Gaddis, Charles V. Harrison, Geo. Hany, Isaac S. Hill, John R. Hill, Michael Harris, James C. Houston, William Jackson, John C. Kirley, Elijah S. Karns, Wm. J. Kyle, Noah Kensor, Joseph Kuldenbach, Simon L. Kahn, Francis A. Lumbar, Jacob Lips, Robert Langmore, Thomas Lotz, George Longstreet, Oliver C. Langmore, Adolphus Meyer, William T. Maher, William Miller, James Mackey, George W. McVicar, Wm. McMillen, Uriah Magee, James Male, Thomas J. Meyers, James T. Moore, Martin Miller, Daniel Metzer, Leonard K. Nye, Charles Norple, Samuel Ogbern, Gilbert T. Ogden, Wm. Pancost, Charles T. Robinson, Melvin O. Robinson, William Robinson, John W. Smith, Conrad Smith, John G. Sparks, John Steel, Charles Silcox, Wm. H. Swigert, William Steel, Silas Sturkey, James W. Simpkins, Isaac Troxel, George Taylor, Matthew Teach, John Troutfelter, John Veurick, Wm.. Walker, Martin V.

F. Wolf, James T. Williams, George White, Edgar A. Way, George Whitson, Oliver W. Williams, John W. Wallace

Company H—McConnelsville

Captain—Lewis R. Green
First Lieut—Francis A. Davis
Second Lieut—John T. Wood
First Sergeant—George Newmand
Sergeants—Samuel McCaslin, John L. Cox, Michael F. Danfort, Wm. M. Metcalf
Corporals—Robert S. Russell, Wm. Barrell, James S. Wiley, Luther Flagg, Wm. D. Davis, Wm. H. Bundy, Zachariah T. Roach
Musician—Lewis R. Brent Wagoner—Eli Pyle
Privates—John Burral, Cornelius Burral, Dempsey Boswal, Grifett Butler, Alvin N. Burlingham, Wm. Chadwick, Alfred G. Cornelius, George Clements, David Craig, Thomas J. Cooper, James Castor, Wm. Camden, John S. Dunn, Oscar J. Dunn, Jesse M. Davis, John F. Davis, Benjamin Dawson, John Darnel, Zeno F. Davis, Barzelia F. Eavaland, John C. Edwards, Jefferson Fouts, Thomas Foster, Wm. L. Fouts, William Gellespie, John W. Grier, Samuel M. Gordon, Levi Golden, Joseph Harkins, Cyrus Harman, David Hartley, John W. Horseman, Isaac P. M. Kean, Blair Kincaid, George W; Lochner, James Martin, William H. Menderhall, Samuel Mason, Levi McLaughlin, Silas Noland, Henry W. Outcalt, John T. Painter, Greenberry Penn, Cyrus Police, Jacob Palmer, James A. Roland, George W. Spurrier, Thomas Sheets, Peter Smith, William L. Smoot, William Pedro, Franklin Thompson, John Timberlake, Theodore Timberlake, Oran Wheeler, John Woodward, Amos Wilcox, James S. Welch, John D. Wizner, Philip D. Wizner, James T., Woodman, Isaac N. Young, Wm. T. Yeaton

Company I—Summerfield

Captain—John M. Moseley
First Lieut—James A. Pettay
Second Lieut—Joseph L. Ball
First Sergeant—Edward Ellis
Sergeants—William A. Allen, Thomas H. Timberlake, John S. Snyder, Samuel G. Shirk
Corporals—Harrison Wilson, Francis M. Sheckle, Jacob L. Barnett, Andrew J. Collins, Joseph S. Perry, Samuel T. Calland, John Harlam, Wesley McConnell

Privates—Howard Atherton, John M. Ashfield, George W. Altop, Wm. H. Brown, Wm. J. Brown, Jenney Beach, Samuel J. Brooks, Benjamin Barlow, William C. Barlow, James C. Bassford, John W. Bunting, Thomas Bunting, John W. Beall, Thomas Barnes, Wallace H. Colley, John W. Calvert, Samuel Clary, Joseph Cunningham, Zachariah Dailey, Elisha Dunn, George W. Dobbins, Kins. Davis, Emanuel DeNoon, Merace T. Floyd, Reuben E. Gant, William Gant, Francis R. Gant, Isaac Harper, Hollis Hutchins, John H. Houston, Samuel W. Houston, Lorenzo D. Hill, Howard Hallett, Jonathan Hayden, William A. Johnson, John H. Johnson, Philip M. Jones, Nelson C. Lovett, Edward T. Lovett, Noah H. Lindsay, Archeleus Lingo, Stephen Loveall, David Logan, Isaac M. Kirk, Wm. McBride, James H. McBride, David McConnell, James W. McWilliams, David McCollock, James McKitrick, Adam S. Ninicle, Henry Miller, Joseph P. Oliver, Isaac Powell, Seneca C. Rogers, John T. Rhodes, Jube M. Rhodes, Benjamin F. Rickey, James Rutherford, John W. Rucker, Harrison Shaw, Wm. H. Shaw, Aspberry Stephens, Chester Still, John J. Smith, Wm. S. Smith, Thomas Smartwood, George Shaffer, Henson W. True, McDonald Thorley, Wilbert B. Teters, Joseph Wilson, Isaac Wilson, Friend P. Wilson, Archibald Wiley, Wm. F. Wiley. Arthur Wharton, Wm. Wharton, Charles Weinstein

Company K—Toledo

Captain—Jonathan Brown
First Lieut—Nathaniel Haughton
Second Lieut—Harlow Milliken
First Sergeant—Edward H. Severence
Sergeants—Erwin F. Carver, Wm. F. Scott, John J. Worts, John H. Kehn
Corporals—Lewis F. Shannon, Joseph Houston, John W. Forbs, Wm. H. Fenton, Charles Oeckel, Marcus L. Decker, Edwin B. Buckner, Wm. Hadnett
Musician—Wm. H. Ritch
Wagoner—Austin Haughton
Privates—John H. Brisco, James Benway, Martin Bender, George Brown, James E. Bridge, John Baker, Charles O. Baker, John H. Bolesmeyer, Lawrence Burns, Christ. Bauman, Lewis C. Boegholt, Calvin A. Carpenter, Westley H. Cooper, Charles M. Cass, George T. Copeland, Charles H. Conger, Reginald Crawford, Niel Cameron, William Carroll, John A. Church, Charles Chollette, Thomas Dunn, Maynard H. Dean, Thomas Delvin, Charles H. DeBolt, Reuben Drippard, Conrad Daum, Lewis Emery, Christian E. Evans, John H. Flinn, Charles Ferrenbock, Chauncey M. Griffith, James D. Groff, Orlando Gray, Daniel D. Grover, Burton S. Hayes, George A. Hyck, Andrew J. Hutchins, James

W. Hall, Michael Hurlbert, Wm. S. Halloway, Anthony Jeremy, James Jones, August Knack, William T. Ketchum, Enos Kameron, Clark Kelley, John Klinck, Shepherd Lewis, Frederick Lang, Peter Matthews, Charles T. Millhollin, Emil L. Marx, Lewis Miller, John Mortal, James Moran, James W. Metzger, Joseph Millett, Enos W. Miner, Deville Nelson, Thomas O'Neal, George W. Page, George H. Palmer, Harlem Page, John Patton, Edward Peck, Thomas Rose, James R. Smith, Charles A. Smith, Richard M. Sherman, John Segrist, John Stoker, Wester H. Shaffer, Lyman B. Stone, Lemuel E. Viers, David S. Viers, William Vickery, Henry J. Welling, George Wenzle.

Lieut. A. J. Hale of Company E was appointed Quartermaster and Benjamin F. Hawks was appointed by the Governor to fill the vacancy. Although the Regiment was only a few days in service, its organization had been complete, and the appointment of Hawks to the vacancy in Company E was looked upon with much disfavor in that company, and feeling largely sympathized with the balance of the Regiment.

Lieut. Hawks was an excellent officer and well qualified, as he afterwards proved, to fill any position in the Regiment; but the feeling against his appointment was so marked that he shortly afterwards was detailed from the Regiment, at his request, and soon resigned. He afterwards served in the Adjutant General's Department and was at one time Lieut. Colonel of the 78th Ohio.

Chapter 2

Preparations—Off for the War: Guarding the B. & O. R.R.— First March—Cheat Mountain—Green Briar

The Regiment remained in Camp Chase daily improving in drill and discipline until the 27th of July, 1861, when, having secured arms, smooth-bore muskets, excepting the flank companies, which were armed with Enfield rifles, it marched from camp to the union depot at Columbus and took the cars for Virginia.

The 23rd and 24th left on the two preceding days and the 26th followed the next day. The 25th made a handsome appearance, being uniformed in gray jackets and trousers, and, already well advanced in regimental drill, attracted very favorable attention as it marched through the streets of Columbus.

During the entire service of the Regiment, one of its distinguishing features was its easy, regular step with a slight swinging motion of the body that always attracted favorable comment from reviewing officers. This peculiarity is thought by many to have been acquired from Company A, commanded by Capt. Charlesworth, an old soldier, and one of the best drill masters in the Regiment. From whatever source derived, it remained with the Regiment through all its vicissitudes.

* * * *

Editor's Note: The Twenty-fifth was composed of men from almost every section of the State, and was organized at Camp Chase on the 28th of June, 1861. On the 29th of July it proceeded to Western Virginia, and was stationed along the Baltimore and Ohio Railroad from Oakland to the Ohio River. [1]

* * * *

Grafton, Virginia, was reached on the afternoon of the 25th and Col. Jones was given command of the Grafton District with headquarters at that place and the Regiment distributed along the Baltimore & Ohio Railroad as follows:

Companies A, F, and C—Camp Battery, Grafton
Company E—Fetterman
Company E—Iron R.R. Bridge and Fairmont
Company D—Fairmont and Barracksville
Company K—Farmington and Burnt Bridge
Company H—Mannington and Burton
Company G—Littleton and Belton
Company B—Cameron
Company A was afterwards sent to Rowelsburg & Oakland.

The duties performed along the railroad were not particularly arduous and much time was, therefore, given to drill which afterwards proved of great benefit. Several scouting parties were sent out from different posts and quite a number of bushwhacking gangs broken up without the loss of a man to the Regiment, and to the great relief of the loyal people of that section. The constant drills and rapid marches made after bushwackers gradually inured the men to army life and, undoubtedly, saved the lives of many for during the entire war, the deaths from disease were trifling compared to other regiments.

On the 21st of August, 1861, the 8th Ohio was ordered to relieve the 25th which was ordered to report to Brig. Gen. Reynolds at Huttonsville, fifty-eight miles southwest of Grafton. It left on the same day, going by cars to Philippi, where it remained all night. The next morning early, the Regiment started on its first real march and made eighteen miles with ease, although a drenching rain fell almost the entire day rendering the roads heavy and making necessary the fording of several streams where the water was waist deep. It was five o'clock when the Regiment went into camp at Bealington and very soon tents were pitched, fire built, and active preparations for supper being made when a courier came galloping into camp, his horse covered with foam and himself with mud, and with orders for Lieut. Col. Richardson (commanding in absence of Col. Jones, who remained in command at Grafton) to push on with the Regiment to Beverly where an attack was threatened. The sight of galloping courier had already quickened the blood and, when the bugle immediately sounded the officers' call, everyone knew it meant a night march. Six months afterward the coffee, under like circumstances, would have been drank and the sow belly and hard tack eaten; but, upon this occasion, the fear was the war would soon be over and such a lucky chance to engage the enemy might not again occur. It was a cash prize to be seized at once; the partly made coffee was thrown upon the ground, frying pans turned upside down and before the orders were really issued by the regimental commander, the tents were being struck; in five minutes' time the Regiment had resumed its march to the tune of "Old John Brown." We were going over historic ground where we were marching, the 14th Ohio, a few weeks previous, had an engagement with the rebels. This was early in the war so it was called the battle of Laurel Hill. But the idea helped and although rain was coming down steadily, there never were one thousand happier boys than started out on that night march over the mountain range. The mountain streams became foaming torrents, making the fords deep and dangerous. The night set in black as ink and still the rain poured down. The cheerful laugh and reckless song gradually died out, excepting from a few fellows with an extra quality of grit, and they, getting fewer responses, finally lapsed into sobriety. On and on marched the Regiment, every man settling into a dogged determination to last it through. Beverly was reached some time in the early morning and the boys, completely exhausted, did not wait for the wagons to come up with the tents, but threw themselves upon the ground in the rain and mud, and sank into forgetfulness.

It was the first march of the Regiment, and it made forty miles in a little over fifteen hours, over mountains, through gorges and ravines, fording deep streams and with rain constantly falling. Considering the circumstances attending this march, it is justly claimed by the members of the Regiment to have been the severest march of the war made by either side and that history does not furnish a parallel. After all, the march was useless; the enemy did not put in an appearance and, two days after reaching Beverly, the Regiment marched to Cheat Mountain pass. The regimental records do not show that a single death resulted from the march to Beverly. This good fortune may be attributed to the hardening process experience along the Baltimore & Ohio R.R.

On the morning of the 25th of August, the right wing of the Regiment marched to the summit of Cheat Mountain, followed the next day by the left, and a camping place was selected. It was indeed a dismal outlook. The 24th Ohio and the 14th Indiana were already in camp on the summit on the right of the pike. The 25th's camp was on the left and near the fort then being laid out, afterwards completed and known as Fort Gilbert.

The history of the Rebellion furnishes no instances of greater suffering, except-ing in rebel prisons, than that experienced by the troops on the summit of Cheat Mountain in the fall and winter of 1861. One-half the force was daily engaged at work upon the fort or upon picket duty; for three months rain or snow fell almost daily and, as the men of the 25th were totally unprovided with overcoats and with one thin blanket each, their sufferings can hardly be imag-ined. Horses were chilled to death, and one man froze to death while on picket. While deaths were occurring every day in the 14th Indiana and 24th Ohio, the 25th had its usual good fortune and lost no member from disease.

Cheat Mountain camp remained comparatively quiet until the morning of the 12th of September when a wagon train on its way to the valley for supplies was surprised and captured by a body of rebels. John Truxell, private, of Company D, was driving one of the wagons; he fired twice, killing one man and severely wounding another, when he fell mortally wounded being the first man in the Regiment killed in an engagement with the enemy. One of the teamsters escap-ing brought news of the attack and Companies H and D were immediately sent in pursuit of the rebels and were soon engaged skirmishing and, upon being re-enforced by companies of the 24th Ohio and 14th Indiana, drove the enemy to the main body, which was in position between the summit and the valley. About this time, another attack was made from the Green Briar road and appearances soon indicated that the camp was entirely surrounded. Prisoners brought in during the afternoon by Company D stated that the enemy num-bered 10,000 and were under the command of General Robert E. Lee. Col. Kimball, of the 14th Indiana, commanding the brigade, immediately made preparations for a most vigorous defense. All men not capable of the most arduous duties were placed in the defenses; the tents and standing obstructions removed, and all available men thrown as skirmishers in the dense growth of pines and laurels. For eight days, skirmishing was almost continuous and the enemy appeared surprised at the apparent strength of the position. On the eighth day, re-enforcements arrived from the valley bringing supplies of provi-sions, by that time very much needed. For two days more the rebel commander made some feeble attacks, but quickly was repulsed and the next day withdrew his forces to Green Briar, greatly discomfited. For this failure, General Lee was relieved from command in Western Virginia, and, some time afterwards, held an unimportant command in South Carolina. Before the close of the war, he became known throughout the world as the great rebel general.

In this affair on Cheat Mountain, Company H, Second Lieut. John T. Wood commanding, was the first company in the Regiment to actually confront rebels and, both officer and men, laid the foundation for steadiness which was not impaired during the war. Detachments of K, under Lt. Nathaniel Haughton, and E, under Lieut. John W. Bowlus, were sent on independent expeditions and both were successful in unmasking strong positions of the enemy. The expedition under Lieut. Bowlus was a remarkable one. Selecting sixty men, all dressed in the grey uniform of the Regiment, he managed, during the dusk of the evening, to enter and pass through the rebel lines; meeting at daylight a large detachment of rebels, he secured a good position in the mountains and kept the rebels back from 7 until 11 a.m. The rebel force was under Col. John A. Washington who fell in the engagement with over sixty of his men. Bowlus escaped with trifling injury.

The casualties in the Regiment were very light, being John Pratt, Company B, Charles Ferenbeck, Company K, and John Truxell, Company D, killed; and Noah Stump and Henry Barnup, Company E, wounded and captured.

During the balance of the stay of the Regiment on Cheat Mountain, several expeditions were sent out, commanded variously by Major George Webster, Lieutenants Nathaniel Haughton, and John W. Bowlus. The country was decidedly poor and, as the great art of subsisting upon the enemy had not yet become popular, these expeditions were without much profit excepting as educators.

On the 27th of September, a promising young officer of the Regiment, Capt. John M. Moseley, of Company I, died of typhoid fever.

Nothing of importance occurred upon the mountain until the 3rd of October when an expedition against the rebel camp on the Green Briar was undertaken under the direct command of General Reynolds, The troops composing the expedition were the 24th, 25th and 32nd Ohio regiments (the latter regiment, under Col. Tom Ford, having recently arrived), the 14th, 9th, 13th, and 17th Indiana regiments, and Daums', Howes' and Loomis' batteries.

This rather formidable forced march from the summit before daylight and, at 8 o'clock in the morning, the advance drove in the rebel pickets, killing and wounding several and taking a few prisoners. The Confederate troops retired in good order to their fortifications which were well calculated for a good defense occupying, as they did, the range of hills south of the river and with an open valley in front extending well on both flanks. Our troops were, after considerable artillery firing, placed in position under the direct fire of rebel batteries and ordered to remain steady until orders were given to charge. For two hours the troops were maintained in this position and, although it was the first time they were under an artillery fire, they behaved fully as well as at any later period of the war, perhaps better. It is true, that the rebel guns were wretchedly served, and but few shells were fired, as they seemed to have a limited number. But they kept up a pretty lively noise and threw a good many solid shot, nearly every one going over the heads of the men into the side of the hill.

General Reynolds finally made up his mind that the position was too strong to carry and withdrew his forces to Cheat Mountain, "the main object of the expedition having been accomplished." What the main object of the expedition really was will now never be known. We had enough material, eager for a fight, to have easily taken the position and, in either regiment, there were half a dozen subaltern officers who, with the next two years' experience, would unhesitatingly have attacked and carried such works with half the number of troops we had on the field. It was early in the war and the fruit had not yet matured.

Dennis Keese Collection
**Lt. Col. William P. Richardson,
commanding,
25th Ohio Volunteer Infantry**

Lieut. Colonel Wm. P. Richardson commanded the Regiment, and the following is an extract from his official report:

"When the order to retire was given, my Regiment remained drawn up in line of battle under a heavy fire from the enemy's guns, until all the regiments had passed, when we followed, bringing up the rear in good order. We brought off all the wounded, and buried all the dead. Colonel Jones was prevented by severe illness from taking command of his Regiment. Wounded: John Everingham, Alex. Pemberton and Michael Mulgrove, all of Company E."

*   *   *   *

Editor's Note: Lt. Col. Richardson possessed the confidence and esteem of his men and was bold in action, having come into the Army as an experienced military man. Prior to the Civil War, he had served in the Third Ohio Infantry in the Mexican War and at the outbreak of the rebellion he was a Brigadier General in the Ohio Militia. Immediately upon the attack on Fort Sumter, he raised two companies, but Ohio's quota was filled before he could get them accepted. The companies, however, were able to change their enlistments from three months to three years and became assigned to the Twenty-fifth Ohio Volunteer Infantry. Col. Richardson would eventually receive a severe right should wound in the Battle of Chancellorsville, Virginia, May 2, 1863 which would deprive him of the use of his right arm, from which he never fully recovered. He was subsequently detailed as commandant of the Camp Chase (Ohio) prison in 1864, during which time he also was elected Attorney General of the State of Ohio. He remained in that capacity until August, 1865. In recognition of his distinguished service, Col. Richardson was breveted Brigadier General in December, 1865. Thereafter, General Richardson re-joined his command in South Carolina where he was placed over a sub-district with headquarters in Columbia and later placed in command of the District of East South Carolina, at Darlington. Following the war, General Richardson returned to his profession as an attorney in southeastern Ohio and for some time in Indiana. Prior to entering the war effort in 1861, he had been elected prosecuting attorney in Monroe County serving continuously for six years.[2]

An incident occurred at the Battle of Green Briar which is worthy of note. During the heat of battle, the color sergeant Elenander Pemberton fell and private Joseph A. Palmer of Company E rushed forward to pick up the colors. For his act of bravery, General Milroy recommended him for promotion, However, it was subsequently learned that private Palmer was a mulatto. At that time, it was against the law for blacks to serve in all white Union regiments. Company commander Captain Moses Crowell had no choice but to drop private Palmer from the regimental rolls. Private Palmer returned to his home in Dayton, Ohio where he learned through reading a rebel published newspaper about the formation of an all black Union regiment, the 54th Massachusetts.
Ironically, the 54th Massachusetts found its way to South Carolina where it fought side by side with the 25th OVI at the Battle of Honey Hill. The following are exerpts from Palmer's correspondence to the government in his attempt to establish his military service record for pension eligibility; his spelling has not been changed.

Private Joseph A. Palmer, Company E:

...Yours received and in answer will say I inlisted in co. E 25 Ohio, Capt. M. H. Crowel comd...and it was at the fight of Green river the collor Sergt fell and I pick up the color and general milroy recommended me for Promotion....I used the name of Joseph a. Palm as it sounded more Spanish my mother was full bloded German Born in Germany my father was three quarters Spanish and one quarter collord so you see it was no trubel for me to pass...I do not rember the Date of the fight at green Brier (.) it has Been a long time ago and after I left the regt I thought no more of it—But I think it was in the midle of october 61 as we was surounded on cheat mountain on sept 12 and in a short time after that We Went to green Briere (.) the law Was again inlisting collored men in andy Way.

When the War first Brake out (.)....I never was cold beefore any cort of any kind in my life military of P(p)rivate (,) Burte I tried to be a soldier and tueur american...[3]

*　　　*　　　*　　　*

The above engagement was called the Battle of Green Briar. A rather amusing experience will be remembered by the boys. They had not yet received their overcoats and had suffered severely in consequence. The 25th was the last regiment to leave the summit and, when they reached the valley, the sun came out very warm. The 24th Ohio had preceded our Regiment and, their overcoats becoming burdensome as their patriotism warmed, they threw them away and for miles they were scattered along the road. The 25th boys were in a condition to appreciate the overcoats and gathered them up. All day long, through the sweltering heat, the boys clung to the coats and carried them back to camp with the idea that they were appropriating abandoned property which really was the case; but the next day Col. Kimball issued an order for the coats to be turned over to the 24th. It raised quite a row and, some of them at least, still lie buried on the mountain. It seemed to us that the 24th Ohio pleaded the baby act in the overcoat business and, from that time on, there never was any real warm friendship between the two regiments.

Chapter 3

Cheat Mountain to Huttonsville—Camp Alleghany— Huntersville Expedition—Co. D transferred to 12th Ohio Battery

Nothing of importance occurred on the mountain after the Battle of Green Briar. Several scouting parties were sent out, but nothing was accomplished worthy of note. On the 15th of October clothing was received by the Regiment. The suffering among the men from lack of sufficient clothing had been very great.

On the 24th of November, 1861, the Regiment received marching orders and on the morning of the 25th, left Cheat Mountain camp for the valley. A halt was made in the pass at the foot of the mountain for three days when the command was moved three miles farther to Huttonsville, where it went into camp. A portion of the Regiment under Capt. Washburn was sent to Elkwater, eight miles southwest of the main camp. The duty at these two camps was quite light, giving the men a chance to recruit after the arduous duty on the mountain (*Editor's Note: and a chance to recover from exposure on the mountain*).

On the morning of the 11th of December, detachments from the Regiment, numbering in all four hundred and sixty men and officers, under command of Col. James A. Jones, left Huttonsville to take part in the attack on Camp Alleghany. The forces intended for the expedition were assembled on Cheat Mountain and were composed of the detachment spoken of from the 25th Ohio, the 9th Indiana, 2d Virginia, and small detachments from the 32d Ohio and 13th Indiana.

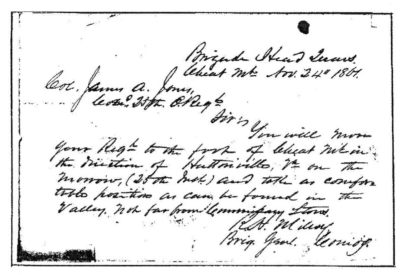

Gen. Milroy Orders 25th OVI to Cheat Mountain

On the afternoon of the 12th, the column left Cheat Mountain and arrived in the evening at Green Briar, the battleground of the 3rd of October. The camp had been abandoned by the rebels for several days and, anticipating a visit from the Federal troops, they had left several amusing sentences written upon the walls for our edification. After viewing their works it was rather humiliating to think that we did not even try to capture them.

The plan of attack upon Camp Alleghany was as follows: Col. Jones, with his Regiment and the detachments from 32d Ohio and 13th Indiana, was ordered to advance to the right and rear of the enemy's camp and there to await the attack in front by the 9th Indiana and 2d Virginia under the immediate command of General Milroy, but, owing to a succession of blunders, the attack was not made in front at the proper time and the enemy, discovering the position taken by Col. Jones, was forced to make an immediate attack or retire. He chose the former course, trusting that the sound of his firing would hasten the attack by Milroy and advancing his lines just at daylight became immediately engaged. He pushed bravely forward, driving the enemy before him, expecting every moment to hear Milroy's guns in front, until being heavily re-enforced, the enemy made a desperate and gallant stand. Here the battle raged furiously for three hours, each side being repeatedly driven back, only to gain fresh courage for a new attack. Every man on both sides was engaged in the action and few engagements of the war show as stubborn a contest. Twice were the rebels driven into their cabins and compelled to fire from the windows and loop holes. Finally, finding that his ammunition was nearly exhausted, Col. Jones ordered his command to retire, and they drew off in perfect order not even being followed by the enemy. Many amusing incidents took place between individual combatants. Not the least amusing incident was a body of the 25th giving three cheers to a squad of rebels fully protected in a log cabin into which the boys had driven them.

The following is Col. Jones official report:

SIR: In compliance with your order, I have the honor to inform you of the movements and conduct of my Regiment, and a portion of the 32d Ohio and 13th Indiana, which were temporarily attached to my command, on the 13th inst. at Camp Baldwin on the summit of the Alleghany Mountains.

After leaving the pike, we advanced up the mountain which was very steep and rock, for about one mile, to the summit, on the right and rear of the enemy's camp, there to await the attack of the 9th Indiana and 2d Virginia as you directed. But, as we approached the top of the hill, we discovered the enemy's pickets who immediately retreated. I gave the order to pursue them in double quick as the enemy would be informed of our advance. One company of the 13th Indiana, being in advance, was conducted by Lieut. McDonald of Gen. Reynolds' staff, until we arrived at the edge of the woods, in full view of the enemy's camp. Finding them already formed and, with a large force to attack us, Lieut. McDonald halted the company of the 13th and ordered it to deploy into line. I immediately formed the 25th on his right, and the other two companies of the 13th on his left, and the 32d Ohio detachment on their left. The fire was immediately opened on the right and carried through the line. After a few rounds, the enemy retreated in great confusion and slaughter, leaving the dead and wounded on the field. They rallied, however, and commenced to advance, returning our fire with vigor. In a few minutes the enemy fell back and attempted to turn our right flank, but were immediately met and repulsed. After making several attempts to drive us from the woods, they deployed to our left. I ordered a portion of my command to advance and attack them, which was done in a gallant manner the enemy retreating to their cabins, but soon again appearing. Some of the men along the entire line, finding they were not receiving the expected support, disgracefully left the field. The remainder of the command fought like veteran soldiers driving the enemy again into the cabins; but, being soon rallied by their officers, they again renewed the attack with a large re-enforcement and poured a galling fire into our thinned ranks, our men holding their position and returning the fire with great effect. Many of the men had left the field with wounded, and others without cause, which had much reduced our numbers. Our ammunition was almost exhausted. At this time the enemy was re-enforced with artillery and opened upon us with shot and shell, but without much effect. A third time we drove them to their quarters, but having no ammunition left. I thought it prudent to fall back to the headquarters of the commanding general which was done in good order. The enemy's force, as near as I could ascertain, was about 2,500 with nine pieces of artillery. The force under my command numbered 700.

*   *   *   *

Editor's Note: Col. Culp stated in the Preface to his book that he had prepared the first draft of his regimental history while still on duty in the field in South Carolina. Col. Culp was relying upon his unit's collection of regimental reports and correspondence which had not yet seen publication in The War of the Rebellion: A Compilation of the Official Records of the Union and Confederate Armies, *1880-1901. A review of these records now on file in Record Group 94, at the National Archives, reveals some discrepancies between the official reports quoted by Col. Culp and the final version printed in the "Official Records." Reference, for instance, to the "Second Virginia" regiment is more accurately the "Second West Virginia." Errors in transposition are not unusual, as original hand-written copies prepared by the reporting commander, found in the 25th OVI Record Group, contain insertions, strikeovers, corrections and editing which makes reading difficult. In keeping with Col. Culp's wish to make corrections his book's second edition, the following addendum is added to the conclusion of Col. Jones' December 13, 1861 report to Brigadier General Milroy.*

Col. James A. Jones, commanding, 25th OVI:

....Many of the men had left the field with the wounded, and some without cause, which had much reduced our number, and our ammunition was almost exhausted. The artillery was turned upon us with shot and shell, but without any effect, and the enemy was again compelled to retire to their cabins with great slaughter, as usual. Our ammunition being exhausted, I thought it prudent to fall back to the headquarters of the commanding general, which was done in good order.[4]

I am sorry to be compelled to say some of the men behaved very badly, but it was not confined to any one regiment. I cannot close this report without expressing my entire approbation if the conduct of the officers of the different detachments. Captains Charlesworth, Crowell, Johnson, Askey; Lieutenants Dirlam, Bowlus, Merryman, Wood, and Haughton, of the twenty-firth Ohio; Lieutenant McDonald of General Reynolds' staff, hile there; Major Dobbs, Captais Myers and Newland, and Lieutenants Kirpatrick,
Bailey (?), Harrington (?), and Jones (who was killed), of the Thirteenth Indiana; Captain Hamilton and other officers of the Thirty-second Ohio, whose names I did not learn, rendered me efficient service by their cool and gallant bearing throughout the engagement which lasted about three hours. The enemy's force, as near as I could ascertain, was about 2,500, with nine pieces of artillery. The force under my command was about 700. Lieutenant Colonel Richardson and Major Webster were absent. Captain Brown received an injury on the evening before, and was not able to be in the engagement.

Very respectfully, your obedient servant,
J.A. JONES[5]

EDITOR'S NOTE: The leadership of the 25th Ohio Volunteer Infantry initially fell to Col. James A. Jones, of Norwalk, Ohio, a seasoned war veteran of the late Mexican War. He served during that war as a Captain of the 15th U.S. Infantry. On August 20, 1847, he was promoted to the rank of Major for gallant and meritorious conduct in the battles of Contreras and Cherubusco. When the Civil War broke out in 1861, the old military spirit again rose within him and he offered his services to his government and was made colonel of the 25th OVI. His hometown newspaper "The Norwalk Daily Reflector" referred to Col. Jones as a "born soldier" and maintained the characteristics of a true soldier throughout his life, "being tall, erect and of fine military carriage." His father before him, Amos Jones, was also a soldier and was killed at the Battle of Lundy Lane in the War of 1812. He was with the 25th Ohio but a year and a half and was forced to resign due to ill health. However, Col. Jones left an indelible mark on the molding of this new Union regiment. He was regarded by his officers and men as a strict and thorough disciplinarian and his orders were always understood to be fully obeyed. Col. Nathaniel Haughton, subsequent commander of the regiment, said of Col. Jones, "He was my ideal of a thorough military man." Col. Jones died May 20, 1893, at the age of eighty-one. The respect held by his community is reflected in his obituary which, in part, concluded "He has responded to the last bugle call and answered to the last roll call. The last enemy charged upon his works and he sur-

rendered unconditionally. With his face to the foe he sleeps the sleep of one who went forth to battle and who returned crowned with honors and laurels."

*   *   *   *

Report of Casualties

KILLED—Charles Latham (D); Corporal Levi S. Stewart (E); Isaac Nigh (E); Christopher J. Thayer (C); John C. Fuller (F); Sergeant Hiram Ward (D); Wm. T. Mather (G).

WOUNDED—Co. A—Sergeant Hezekiah Thomas; Privates Jno. W. Holland, Clark H, King, Levi Butler, Henry Meekl, Daniel J. Crooks, James C. Bolan. Co. B Lieut. John D. Merriman; Sergeant Geo. W. Martin; Corporal Charles Beck; Private Joseph I. Hopton. Co. D Lieut. Darius Durkan; Privates Wm. Jones, Jonathan Ward, Wm. White, Daniel Coe, Benjamin B. Compton, Wm. H. Brown, Charles C. Rodier. Co. C Sergeant Wm. Henthorn (mortally); Privates Jonathan Dunn, Wm. J. Henthorn, Eligah Becket (mortally). Co. E Privates John E. Rearick, Richard D. Phelps, August Freet. Co. F Corporal Emile A. Huston; Privates Thomas Jones, Asa Meredith, George M. Aulter, John McKinley, Hugh Wilson. Co. G Privates George Haney (mortally), Michael Harris; John D. Fisher, Gilbert J. Ogden, John Ewalt. Co. H Corporal Cornelius Burral; Privates John S. Dunn, Wm. Chadwick, Blair Kincaid, Wm. Work, George W. Reed. Co. I Privates Archeleus Lingo, Wm. Barlow, N.C. Lovett, Isaac M. Kirk, Jenney Breach. Co. K Privates Shepherd Lewis (mortally), Harlan Page, Andrew Hutchins.

MISSING—Private John Richards (A), Lorenzo Shackle, Jonathan Hayden (I), Marcus L. Decker and John H. Brisco (K).

Very respectfully, your obedient servant,

James A. Jones
Col. 25th Reg't O.V.I.

The Regiment returned to Cheat Mountain camp that evening, having marched sixty miles, and fought four hours, within a space of forty hours. The next day it returned to Huttonsville. From this time until the latter days of December, nothing of importance occurred. Upon the last day of December, the Huntersville expedition, under Major Webster, left camp at Huttonsville.

The account of the expedition is best given in the following report of Major Webster.

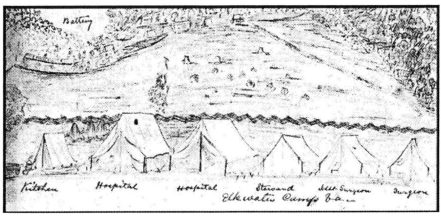

Courtesy of the National Museum of Civil War Medicine
Encampment of the 25th OVI regiment at Camp Elkwater, Virginia

Huttonsville, Va., Jan. 6th, 1862

Brig. Gen. R. H. Milroy—

SIR: I have the honor to report that, in obedience to your orders on the 31st day of December last at 10 o'clock P.M., I left this place with a detachment of four hundred men of the 25th Ohio for Huntersville, Pocahontas Co., Va. At Elkwood I was joined by a detachment of four hundred men of the 2d Virginia, under Major Owens, and at Big Springs by a detachment of 28 cavalry, of the Bracken Cavalry, under Lieut. Dalzell. I appointed Lieut. C. B. Jones of the 25th Ohio, acting adjutant.

On the morning of the 3rd of January, finding the road at the base of Elk Mountain, and for the distance of one mile, so obstructed by felled trees as to render the passage of teams impossible, I left my own wagons and detached Captain Johnson, of the 25th, with fifty of the most disabled men, to guard them.

Avoiding the obstructions by a detour to the left, I pushed forward to Green Briar River and ascertained that a considerable number of militia were gathered at the bridge, one mile below, on their way to Huntersville. I directed Lieut. Dazell with his detachment of cavalry to ford the river and, by a rapid movement across the River Mountain, to gain possession of the road in rear of the bridge. This he did in most gallant style and, cut off from Huntersville the entire militia at the bridge, excepting a few mounted scouts. The balance fled back into the country evidently in great confusion and dismay. Hastily detaching Capt. Williams of the 25th with fifty men to hold the bridge, I pushed forward and, when two miles form town, I discovered the enemy's cavalry at the extreme of a level bottom field, dismounted, and posted over the brow of a hilly spur which jutted out into the field from the right with Knapp's Creek on their left. I immediately deployed a part of the 25th up the hill to our left, to turn the enemy's right, and with the balance of our force, moved up in front. The enemy at once opened on us and their fire became general which was vigorously responded to by our men. They soon discovered my flank movement and falling back to their horses, hastily mounted and fled.

I again moved the column forward, crossed Knapp's Creek, and found the enemy posted upon a second bottom extending from our right nearly across the valley and half a mile in front of town.

I deployed Companies A and B of the 25th into line to our right, at the base of the hill, to attack the enemy's left, and directed Major Owens of the 2d Virginia, and Bracken Cavalry, to make a considerable detour, turn the enemy's right, and take them in rear. The balance of the 25th I formed to attack in front. This disposition made and, in the way of rapid execution under the enemy's fire, and Companies A and B having opened up on his left, the enemy again retreated, mounted, and retired into town. After a few minutes rest, I formed my command into two columns, the 25th to move upon the right, and the 2d Virginia and cavalry upon the left of town. In this order, the troops rushed forward, cheering, into the streets, as the enemy, after a few ineffectual shots, fled in confusion to the country.

We found the place deserted, houses broken open and goods scattered, the cause of which was soon stated by a returned citizen. The rebel commander had ordered all the citizens to remove their valuable property, as he intended, if beaten, to burn the town. We found large quantities of rebel stores, consisting in part of 350 barrels of flour, 150,000 lbs. salt meal, 30,000 lbs. salt pork, and large quantities of sugar, coffee, rice, bacon, clothing, and etc., all of which I caused to be destroyed, by burning the building in which they were stored, having no means of bringing them off. The value of the property thus

destroyed, I estimated at $30,000. Our forces captured and brought back a large number of Sharp's carbines, sabers, horse pistols and some army clothing. The enemy had in the action 400 regular cavalry armed with Sharp's carbines and several hundred mounted militiamen assembled from Pocahontas country the night before. There were also two companies of Infantry in the village, but they fled without making a stand.

Private Oliver P. Hersey, Co. E, was severely wounded in the arm. No other casualty occurred on our side. I nailed the stars and stripes to the top of the court house and left them flying.

U.S. Army Military History Institute
**Lt. Oliver P. Hershey, Co. E,
25th Ohio Volunteer Infantry**

After remaining in town two hours, I marched back to Edry through a drenching rain and sleet, having made twenty-five miles that day. Today I returned to Huttonsville, having made a winter march of one hundred and two miles in less than six days, and penetrated into the enemy's country thirty miles farther than any body of our troops had before gone.

I have the honor to be, very respectfully, your obedient servant,

George Webster
Major 25th O.V.I.
Commanding

*   *   *   *

Editor's Note: The Official Records January 6, 1862 report of Major Webster indicates the opening of Maj. Webster's report made reference to Camp Elk Water (not Elkwood), a detachment of 300 men (not 400) from the Second West Virginia Regiment (not 3d Virginia), and 38 cavalry (not 28 cavalry). In addition, the final paragraph of Maj. Webster's report is missing in Col. Culp's book and is as follows.

Major George Webster, commanding, Huntersville Expedition, 25th OVI:

Today I returned to Huttonsville with the detachment from the Twenty-fifth Ohio, having made a winter march of 102 miles in a little less than six days, and penetrated into the enemy's country 30 miles farther than any body of troops had before gone. The men are in good condition, considering the march, and are in excellent spirits. To my second in command, Major Owens, of the Second West Virginia; Captains Washburn, Williams, Johnson, Crowell, Green, and Askew; Lieutenants Higgins, Bowlus, Haughton, Blandy, and Ball and __bson, and McNally; Lieutenants West, Eckeer, Day, Hunter, Smyth, Huggins, and Weaver, of the Second West Virginia, and to Lieutenants __elzell and Bassett, of the Bracken Cavalry, I desire to tender my acknowledgements for the prompt, efficient and gallant manner in which they performed their respective duties on the march and in the action. To the men composing my command generally too much praise cannot be awarded. During the long and weary march their spirits never dragged. They at all times cheerfully submitted to necessary discipline. For one hour and a half in which they were engaged in driving the enemy from cover to cover, a distance of 2 miles, not a man flinched. My self and comrades of the Twenty-fifth Ohio to the officers and men of the Second West Virginia for the very hospitable manner in which we were entertained at Camp Elk Water last night, and thereby saved a night's exposure to a storm of rain, hail and snow.

I have the honor to be, very respectfully, yours, & c.
GEO WEBSTER [7]

*   *   *   *

While at Huttonsville, Company D, Capt. Johnson, was permanently detached as a battery of artillery and armed with steel guns. It was afterward known as the 12th Ohio battery and achieved an enviable reputation in the different campaigns of Virginia and the Southwest. Edward C. Culp, one of the sergeants of Co. D, had been, previous to the detachment of his company, appointed Sergeant Major of the Regiment and remained with it.

Chapter 4

Bull Pasture Mountain—Cross Keyes— Strausberg

On the 27th of February, 1862, the Regiment left Huttonsville, and marched to Beverly, where it remained in camp until the following April. Here the old "smooth-bores" were turned over to the ordinance officer, and the men armed with Vincennes rifles, splendid guns, carrying two-ounce balls, and having saber bayonets. They proved very effective pieces, but were too heavy and gradually were exchanged for regulation Springfield rifles.

On the first day of April, the Regiment, under command of Major George Webster, proceeded on the Seneca scout, and going via Ludesville, crossed the Cheat and Alleghany Mountains, passed through Circleville, and arrived at Monterey April 10th having marched over almost impassable roads one hundred and twenty-five miles and through a country entirely new to Union troops. At Monterey the 25th Ohio was joined by a similar expedition sent via Camp Alleghany. On the 12th of April, Gen. Ben Johnson (rebel), who had retired from Monterey upon the Federal approach, made upon the Union troops. He was gallantly repulsed, and Gen. Milroy's arrival with re-enforcements, compelled him to fall back to McDowell, thirteen miles south of Monterey.

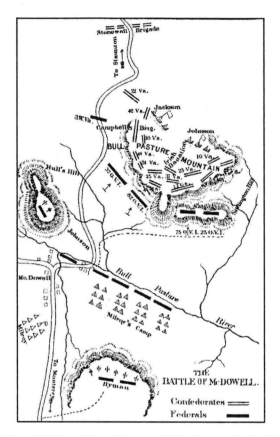

U.S. Army Military History Institute, Ohio Commandry. MOLLUS
The Battle Map of McDowell,
or Bull Pasture Mountain,
May 8, 1862

On the morning of the 18th of April, Gen. Milroy advanced his command to McDowell, without serious opposition, the enemy retreating towards Staunton.

The troops went into camp at McDowell. Everything remained quiet until the 7th of May, when a large rebel force under Gen. Johnson appeared in front of McDowell. Heavy forces of skirmishers were sent forward and held their ground gallantly, against heavy odds, preventing a general engagement until the arrival of Gen. Schenck with his excellent brigade of Ohio troops, when it was decided by the Union generals to attack the rebels who were advantageously posted on the summit of Bull Pasture Mountain.

*　　　*　　　*　　　*

Editor's Note: General Robert H. Milroy reconnaissance brigade commander, for Mountain Department Major General John C. Fremont, gives an excellent overview of the McDowell (Bull Pasture Mountain) engagement in his official report. General Milroy's assignment was to assess the enemy strength in the Shenandoah valley and Bull Pasture Mountain, in particular. He encountered the strong forces of Confederate Generals Jackson and Johnson and a sharp engagement ensued. Portions of his report follow.

Brigadier General Robert H. Milroy:

The Soldier in Our Civil War, A Pictorial History of the Conflict, 1861-1865, 1888
Brigadier General Robert Milroy, Brigade Commander, Mountain Department

Upon May 7 I was first advised by my scouts and spies that a junction had been effected between the armies of the rebel Generals Jackson and Johnson, and that they were advancing to attack me at McDowell. Having the day previous sent a large portion of the Third West Virginia and Thirty-second and Seventy-fifth Ohio Regiments to Shaw's Ridge and upon Shenandoah for the purpose of protecting my foraging and reconnoitering parties, I immediately ordered my whole command to concentrate at McDowell, and, expecting re-enforcements, prepared for defense there.

In the afternoon of the 7th instant a large force of the rebel was discovered descending the west side of the Shenandoah Mountain along the Staunton and Parkersburg turnpike. I ordered a section of the Ninth Ohio Battery (Captain Hyman) on Shaw's Ridge to shell them and endeavor to retard their progress. This they did with such effect as to cause the enemy to retire beyond the Shenandoah Mountain; but observing another force crossing the mountain on our right, some 2 miles distant, I deemed it prudent to fall back and concentrate at McDowell.[8]

The next morning (8th instant) the enemy was seen upon the Bull Pasture Mountain, about 1 1/2 miles distant from McDowell, on my right and front. I commenced shelling them and sent out parties of skirmishers to endeavor to ascertain their numbers. At about 10 a.m. your brigade arrived. Desultory firing of a section of Hyman's battery and occasional skirmishing engaged the attention of the enemy during the morning. Major Long, of the Seventy-third Ohio Volunteer Infantry, with a party of skirmishers, rendered a good service by his efforts in ascertaining the position of the enemy. In the afternoon, at about 3 o'clock, being informed by Captain George R. Latham of the Second West Virginia Volunteer Infantry, who, with his company, was engaged in skirmishing, that the rebels were endeavoring to plan a battery upon the mountain which would command our whole encampment., with your permission I made a reconnaissance for the purpose of obtaining accurate information of their strength and position. For this purpose the following troops were placed at my disposal: The Twenty-fifth Ohio Volunteer Infantry, Seventy-fifth Ohio Volunteer Infantry, Thirty-second Ohio Volunteer Infantry, Eighty-second Ohio Volunteer Infantry, Third West Virginia Volunteer Infantry. These regiments were by no means full, various companies of each being detailed for special duty. The number of privates, non-commissioned officers, and officers actually engaged are reported to me as follows:

25th Ohio Volunteer Infantry	469
75th Ohio Volunteer Infantry	444
32nd Ohio Volunteer Infantry	416
3rd West Virginia Volunteer Infantry	438
Total	1,768

Which is the entire number of field officers, company officers, and privates of this brigade engaged. The exact number of the Eighty-second Ohio Volunteer Infantry engaged is not known to me, but has doubtless been reported to you.

Under my order the Twenty-fifty Ohio and Seventy-fifth Ohio Regiments (the former under command of Lieutenant Colonel W.P. Richardson and the latter under the command of Colonel N.C. McLean and Major Robert Reily) advanced in the most gallant manner up the face of the hill and attacked the enemy in their front. Numbering less than 1,000 men, unprotected by any natural or artificial shelter, they advanced up a precipitous mountain side upon an adversary protected by entrenchments and the natural formations of the mountain, and unsupported drove them (being at least twice their numerical strength) over the crest of the mountain, and for one and a half hours maintained unaided, while exposed to a deadly fire, the position from which they had so bravely driven the foe.

Too much praise cannot be awarded to the officers or men of these regiments. The Twenty-fifth Ohio led the advance, and were rapidly followed and supported by the Seventy-fifth, both acting with the coolness of veterans and the determination of patriot soldiers, willing to sacrifice their lives for the good of the Republic.[9]

＊   ＊   ＊   ＊

Editor's Note: Brigade commander Brigadier General Robert C. Schenck was assigned by General Fremont as a relief brigade to General Milroy's reconnaissance mission. His official report of the Bull Pasture Mountain engagement spells out the military strategy under trying circumstances.

Brigadier General Robert C. Schenck, Relief Brigade commander:

A little observation served to show at once that McDowell, as a defensive position, was entirely untenable and especially against the largely outnumbering force that was ascertained to be advancing; and if it had been otherwise there was no choice left on account of an entire destitution of forage. I determined to obey, with as little delay as possible your orders to fall back with the force of our two brigades to this place. Such a movement, however, could not with any safety or propriety be commenced before night, nor did it seem advisable to undertake it without first ascertaining of feeling the actual strength of the rebel force before us, and also, perhaps, taking some step that would serve to check or disable him from full power or disposition to pursue. This was effectively done by our attack of his position on the mountain in the afternoon, and in the night following I was enabled to withdraw our whole little army along the road through the narrow gorge, which afforded only agrees from the valley in which McDowell is situated, in the direction of Franklin. This withdrawal we effected without the loss of a man and without the loss or destruction of any article of public property, except some stores, for which General Milroy was entirely without the means of transportation.....

At 3 o'clock, General Milroy, having reported to me that his scouts informed him of re-enforcements continually arriving tot he support of the enemy, concealed among the woods on the mountain, and that they were evidently making preparations to get artillery in position for sweeping the valley, I consented to his request to be permitted to make a reconnaissance. The force detailed for the purpose consisted of portions of four regiments of this brigade—the Seventy-fifth, Twenty-fifth, and Thirty-second Ohio and the Third West Virginia and the Eighty-second Ohio, of mine, the latter regiment gladly receiving the order to join the enterprise, although the men were exhausted with the long march from which they had just arrived, with want of food, sleep, and rest. The infantry was supported in a degree also by a 6-pounder of Johnson's battery, which General Milroy had succeeded in conveying to the top of one of the mountain ridges on his left. This movement resulted in a very sharp encounter with the rebels…

As evening closed in, and it was ascertained that, from the unexpected severity and protraction of the fight, the ammunition of some of the regiments was almost completely exhausted. I endeavored in person to get a supply of cartridges to the men, and had three wagon loads taken some distance up the Saunton road for that purpose, but the only way it could reach them up the steep mountain side was to be carried by hand or haversacks….The troops that were engaged, after fighting with a coolness and order and bravery which it is impossible to excel, and after pressing back the enemy over the mountain crest and maintaining unflinchingly and under the most galling and constant fire their ground until darkness set in, were then withdrawn under the immediate order of Colonel McLean, of the Seventy-fifth Ohio, leaving, as I believe, not a prisoner behind, for the 3 men reported missing are to be among the killed.[10]

Too much praise cannot be awarded to General Milroy himself, to Colonel McLean of the Seventy-firth Ohio; Colonel Cantwell, Eighty-second Ohio; Lieutenant Colonel Richardson, commanding the Twenty-fifty Ohio; Major Reily, Seventy-fifth Ohio; Lieutenant Colonel Swinney, commanding Thirty-second Ohio; Lieutenant Colonel Thompson, Third West Virginia Infantry, and the officer and men of their several commands for their steady gallantry and courage manifested through out the whole affair.

The attack was made late in the afternoon of the 8th, by the 25th, supported by the 75th Ohio. By a gallant charge, the enemy was driven from his first position. The Confederates made desperate attempts to regain the lost position, but each charge was repulsed with heavy loss. Re-enforcements were sent forward on both sides and very soon the engagement assumed a rather formidable character. On the Union side were engaged the 25th, 75th, 32d, and 82d Ohio regiments, and the 2d and 5th Virginia regiments, and the 12th Ohio battery. The battle raged until after dark with unremitted fury, and without apparent advantage to either side. Finally the Union troops were ordered to leave the field, bringing off all the wounded that had not previously been removed. It was claimed that this engagement had been brought in to cover the withdrawal of the division to Franklin that night. At least, while the battle was being fought, all the wagons were started to that place, followed the same night by the troops, without molestation from the enemy. The whole division was in camp at Franklin on the 11[th][11].

*   *   *   *

Editor's Note: In describing this engagement, E.R. Monfort, late Captain of the 75th Ohio Volunteer Infantry, quoted General Robert Milroy in his observation of troop movements at McDowell, in his 1888 article in the Ohio Commandry, Military Order of the Loyal Legion of the United States (MOLLUS).

E. R. Monfort, Captain, 75th Ohio Volunteer Infantry:

"From the top of a high peak I had full view of the splendid fight of the Twenty-fifth and Seventy-fifth Ohio Volunteer Infantry with the rebels across on the other side of the Pass, and I was perfectly delighted to see the steady, gallant and beautiful style with which these two regiments maintained the battle against a superior force during the hour and one-half I watched them."[12]

*   *   *   *

Editor's Note: Colonel Nathaniel C. McLean, commanding seven companies of his own regiment (75th Ohio) and nine companies of the (25th Ohio), reported the coordinated effort of the two regiments as they struggled up the mountain.

Colonel Nathaniel C. McLean, commanding the advanced order of battle:

As soon as these companies were deployed properly I ordered Lieutenant Colonel Richardson to support them with the whole of his regiment formed in line of battle, which order was executed with great promptness, and in a few moments the whole of the Twenty-fifth Ohio was advancing steadily to the front up the mountain, overcoming the difficult ascent with great labor. As soon as the Twenty-fifth Ohio had advanced so as to make room in the open ground for the movement, I formed my own regiment (Seventy-fifth Ohio) in line of battle and gave the order for the advance, so that the whole force under my command was within easy supporting distance. The enemy did not permit the skirmishers to advance far before a heavy fire was open upon them from the whole crest of the hill. The mountain was circular in its formation, so that when the whole line was engaged the flanks were in a manner concealed from each other. The enemy received us with so heavy and destructive a fire that I was compelled to bring forward as rapidly as possible the whole of the forces under my command.[13]

＊　　　　＊　　　　＊　　　　＊

The following extract from the official report of Lieut. Col. Richardson, commanding the 25th Ohio, gives a list of the casualties in the Battle of Bull Pasture Mountain or, as called by the rebels, Battle of McDowell:

Company G. was commanded by Serg't Milliman, in the absence of all commissioned officers of this company.

Every man in the Regiment seem inspired by the same resolution to do his whole duty and acted accordingly. I was under the immediate command of Col. N. C. McLean, of the 75th Ohio, a brave and efficient officer, who will probably report more at length. The engagement lasted about two hours, when night prevented further contest. The Regiment returned in good order to McDowell, bringing off their dead and wounded. The whole number engaged in my Regiment, 469.

KILLED—Wm. D. Driggs (B), James B, McPeek, Sylvanus S. Williams, Thomas E. Coalwell (C), Josiah Fought (E), Theodore E. Lodge (F), Brazelia M. Eveland (H), Thomas Smartwood (I), Neil Cameron (K).

WOUNDED—Co. A—Lieut. Arthur Higgins; Corporal Wm H. Spear; Privates Samuel Beall, Wm. R. Bloor, Hiram S. Hahn,Geo. W. Iden, Drewer C. Iverson, Henry Lambert, Samuel McCrum, Robert H. Miller, Henry Meek, James Russell, Geo. W. Verbeck, Henry C. White. Co B—Sergeants Geo. W. Martin. Slater B. Brock; Corporals Chas. G. Troy, Samuel Trigg, Chars. Twinum; Privates Wesley B. Sultzer,Nathan Morris. Co. C—Corporal Orlando L. Mills; Privates Geo. Algyer, John Schell, Fred. Gillyer, John Everingham. Co. F— Corporal Leander Provines; Private Samuel M. Forrester. Co. G—Private

Gilbert Ogden. Co. H—Privates Henry W. Outcalt, Wm. M. Metcalf, Geo. W. Reed, James Williams. Co. I—Sergeant Wm. Teters; Corporal James W. Houston; Privates Howard Hallett, Wm. H. McBride, Aspberry Stephens, Wm. West, Wm. H. Brown, Samuel J. Brooks. Co. K—Privates Wm Vickery, Christian E. Evans, Thomas O'Neal, Charles A. DeBolt.

Major General Fremont soon joined the forces at Franklin with re-enforcements and assumed command of the army.

On the 18th of May, 1862, the Regiment lost the services of an excellent officer by the resignation of Col. James A. Jones who for some time, had been too ill to attend to regimental duties. The command of the Regiment then devolved upon Lieut. Col. Richardson who was soon afterwards promoted to colonel. Major George Webster was made lieutenant colonel and Captain James F. Charlesworth, Company A, promoted to major.

On the 26th of May, the 25th Ohio accompanied the forces under Gen. Fremont on this march from Franklin to Strausburg and thence up the Shenandoah Valley in pursuit of Stonewall Jackson which ended in the Battle of Cross Keyes on the 8th of June.

The campaign in the valley will always be remembered by those who took part in it; the severe storms, cold weather, and lack of clothing and provisions make up a sad tale of suffering. The idiotic orders issued preventing the burning of fence rails, the killing of hogs, chickens and cattle, when the troops were absolutely without rations, will remain as wonderful specimens of the "kid glove policy" advocated during the early part of the Rebellion.

General Jackson was closely pursued by the army under Fremont to Cross Keyes where he was to cross the river to Port Republic. The indecisive engagement, known as the Battle of Cross Keyes, commenced about nine o'clock in the morning, and continued with unremitting fury until four o'clock in the afternoon; the balance of the day and early hours of the evening were taken up by skirmishing and artillery firing. The battle was fought without a plan and resulted in no advantage to the Union cause. The bivouac of our army on the battlefield, the retreat of Jackson during the night across the river, and his battle the next day with Shields, are well known to the students of history. The 25th was still in Milroy's brigade and behaved with its usual credit, receiving praise upon the field from the commanding general.

A severe loss to the Regiment was the wounding of Capt. Charlesworth who was shot through the bowels and, at the time, considered to be mortally wounded. He recovered in a measure and afterwards returned to his Regiment as Lieut. Col., but after a few days service was compelled to resign on account of disability. He was a brave and efficient officer.

*   *   *   *

CASUALTIES AT CROSS KEYES

KILLED—John Eastahorn (B), James L. Hopper (C), Frederick Woodtler (C), George Whitson (E), Friend J. Wilson (I), Reuben E. Gant (I), Conrad Daum (K).

MISSING—William Mackey (E), Andrew J. Collings (I)

WOUNDED—Co. A—Capt. James F. Charlesworth; Sergt. Israel White; Privates Joseph Acres, William Harrison. Co. B—Corporal James D. McMunn; Privates Samuel White. Co. C—Sergt. Alonzo P. Henthorn; Private Amida Provine. Co. E—Privates Joel Spohn, Charles Slaughterbeck. Co. F—Privates Joseph H. White, Michael Cantwell, Patrick Burke. Co. G—Sergt. Alfred A. Lamkin; Corporals herbert Ogden, Samuel Bughman, William J. Kyle; Privates Conrad Smith, Eli F. Beard, Geo. Longstreet, Leonard W. Gaddis, Melvin O. Robinson, Aldolphus Meyer, John N. Kline, Simon L. Kahn. Co. I—Sergt. Joseph Perry; Privates William H. Wharton, Seneca O. Rogers, Daniel McCullock, Samuel Calland, Ed. T. Lovett. Co. K—Charles A. Smith, Charles M. Cass, Michael Herbert, Wesley H. Cooper, Reginald Crawford, James Jones.

*   *   *   *

Editor's Note: Scanning through the archives of any state historical society can be quite revealing. While taking graduate courses at the Ohio State University, I visited the nearby Ohio Historical Society museum. I happened across a typed transcript of the diary of Sergeant Thomas C. Evans who served with the 25th OVI. His battle accounts were compelling, as evidenced in his description of his first experience in battle at Cross Keyes, Virginia.

Thomas C. Evans, Sergeant, Company K, 25th OVI:

June 8, 1862. Soon the skirmishers were engaged. On we rushed and soon we were met in force. The battle now became general. This was my first battle.

Imagine will you what were my feelings. Here I was rushing pell mell to probable destruction. I paused. I thought of all whomever I held dear—a mother and sister's tears will probably be poured out for my life. I may soon be in the eternal repose of death. I trembled with emotion. Then breathing a prayer to God for strength and protection, I commenced the work of Death.

The deafening roar of musketry and loud pealing of artillery. The bursting of shells, the whiz of grape and canister. The crushing of timber by the dread missiles mingled with the unearthly yells of opposing forces and the moaning of the dying and the screams of the wounded. O God, how terrible is war. How long must man thus strive with man? Here lies a dear comrade bleeding and dying at your side who can just breathe the name of Mother, sister or wife, and he is gone. Another in the prime of life is cut down without a second's warning. Think, O man, is not the thought of these moments enough to chill the blood in thy veins.

Such was the scene now enacting and such the horror of battle. We fought with but little success on either side and a night's coming on found us each occupying our relative positions. We had captured two pieces of artillery being the principal advantage gained. We must now withdraw and await the morning, which, accomplished, we began to count up the loss which I judge, from the loss in our own regiment, must be quite heavy. General Milroy had his horse shot from under him. Also the major's horse suffered a like fate together with the adjutant's horse.[14]

The Soldier in Our Civil War, A Pictorial History of the Conflict, 1861-1865, 1888
Battle of Cross Keys, Virginia Sunday, June 8, 1862, Center and Front of Federal Army Sketch by Edwin Forbes

*   *   *   *

After pursuing the enemy to Port Republic on the 9th, the army was halted, marched back to Harrisonburg, and thence to Strausburg, having marched during the campaign two hundred and fifty miles.

While lying at Strausburg some important changes took place in the Regiment. Lieut. Col. George Webster was promoted to the colonelcy of the 91st Ohio, and shortly afterwards, while commanding a brigade, was killed at the Battle of Perryville in Kentucky. He was a chivalrous gentleman and a natural soldier. Had he lived he would undoubtedly have taken high rank among the notable leaders of the war. Major Charlesworth was promoted to lieutenant colonel, but was still kept at home by the severe wounds received at Cross Keys. Capt. James Washburn, of Company B was promoted to the colonelcy of the 116th Ohio and served with credit, becoming a brigade commander. Capt. Jere. Williams, of Co. C, was commissioned major, vice Charlesworth, promoted. Capt. Lewis R. Green, a young and promising officer of Company H, died of typhoid fever after a short illness. Lieuts. Askew, Haughton, Bowlus and Jones were promoted to captains, and Sergeants N. J. Manning, C. E. Randall and Edward C. Culp were commissioned officers of the Regiment were given commissions in new regiments, and a large number of recruits from Ohio, and some from Virginia.

Chapter 5

Under Pope—Second Battle of Bull Run— Marching to Fredericksburg—Winter Quarters

The reorganization of the army took place on the 26th of June and was known as the Army of Virginia, and Major General John Pope assigned by the President to the chief command. The 25th, 75th,55th and 73d Ohio Regiments constituted the second brigade of the first division of the first corps. Col. N. C. McLean of the 75th Ohio was the brigade commander, Major General C. Schenck was the division commander, and Major General Franz Sigel corps commander.

The 25th remained at Strausburg until July 6th when, with its corps, it marched through Middleton, Front Royal and Lurray, via Thorton's Gap, to Sperryville, arriving there on the 10th.

On the evening of August 8th, the first corps left Sperryville, passed through Culpepper, and arrived on the battlefield of Slaughter Mountain August 10th. The corps was placed in position for the next day's fight, but during the night the enemy retreated. The corps moved forward to the Rapidan, where it was halted until the 15th, when it marched via Culpepper C. H. to White Sulphur Springs.

*   *   *   *

Editor's Note: Sometimes injuries occurred off the battlefield, in unusual ways, as illustrated in a letter from Pvt. James D. McMunn of Company B to his brother.

Pvt. James D. McMunn, Co. B, 25th OVI
Rapidan Station August 17th '62

Dear Brother,
.....I am well and able for my rations; but I received a slight wound yesterday—there are plenty of roasting ears here and the boys go down on it pretty heavy,

and the cobs they use to fight sham battles; and while some of them were throwing on yesterday evening I chanced to get in the way and was struck on the left cheek an cut slightly. The cut is painful but will I think heal up in a few days.... [15]

*   *   *   *

The Regiment took its full share in the various movements culminating in the second Battle of Bull Run, and the following official report of Col. Wm. P. Richardson carries the history of the Regiment to include that engagement:

Headquarters 25th Reg't O.V.I.
Upton Hill, Va. Sept. 19, 1862

Col. N. C. McLean, Comdg. 2d Brig., 1st Div., 1st Army Corps:

SIR: I beg to submit the following report of the part taken by my Regiment in the maneuvers and battles of Pope's army, from the 21st of August to the 31st of the same month.

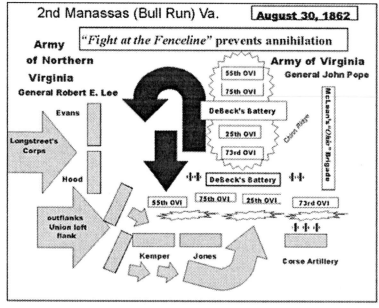

Overview Map, Second Battle of Bull Run

On the 21st day of August, we were at the White Sulphur Springs, in Fauquier County, Va., and received orders to send our baggage trains to Warrenton, taking with the Regiment four wagons, two for ammunition and two for supplies. Five days' rations were issued—that is, of hard tack, sugar and coffee—and we marched to the neighborhood of Rappahannock Station. In the evening we were moved farther up the river, and encamped for the night. Heavy cannonading had been kept up all day down the river on our left. On the morning of the 22d we moved up to Freeman's Ford and, immediately upon our arrival, our artillery became engaged. General Sigel himself came on the ground and superintended the planting of a battery of reserve artillery, in addition to the one of our brigade at that time engaged. After some two or three hour's heavy firing, the rebel batteries were silenced or withdrawn. Soon after, Bohlene brigade of Schenck's division was sent over to the river for some purpose unknown to me. They crossed the river near the left of our brigade. The ford was deep and the bank of difficult ascent. After they had penetrated some distance into the country on the opposite side of the river, heavy firing was heard and it presently became evident that our forces were falling back to the ford. By your direction my Regiment was placed as quickly as possible in a situation to command the ford and protect our troops in recrossing. The enemy advanced in heavy force, but upon receiving our third fire, retired, and all the troops on the south side passed safely over before dark. In this skirmish we had one man mortally wounded—George Ogden, corporal of Company G. We remained that night at Freeman's Ford. On the morning of the 23d, we received orders to march and, after considerable delay, we started on our return to the springs arriving in the neighborhood of them after sun down. A short skirmish occurred on our left, which was kept up some time after dark. I was informed it was Milroy's brigade that was engaged.

On the morning of the 24th, my Regiment and the 73d Ohio, with four pieces of artillery of DeBeck's battery, were sent on a reconnoissance and, after advancing two miles, it was ascertained that the rebels had recrossed the river and had some batteries in position on the opposite side. They were opened upon by our battery, but did not reply. Shortly afterwards we were joined by our brigade, marched to Waterloo bridge, and encamped for the night. We remained in the neighborhood of Waterloo bridge all day of the 25th. Nothing of importance occurred except that all day large bodies of rebel troops could be seen passing north and west at a distance of some four or five miles from the river and, about sun down, it was found they had crossed above us in force. About dark we received orders to march and proceeded in the direction of

Warrenton. The night was very dark, the roads miserable, the progress very slow and excessively fatiguing to the men. We arrived at Warrenton at 2 o'clock on the morning of the 26th and remained there all that day, starting on the morning of the 27th for Gainesville, which place we reached about dark. When within four miles of Gainesville, our advanced guard came up with the rear of some rebel force; skirmishing was kept up until we stopped.

*   *   *   *

Library of Congress, sketch by Edwin Forbes
John Bell Hood's Texas Brigade and Longstret's Corps crash into the Ohio Brigade holding Bald Hill near Chinn House, The Buckeyes make a stubborn stand and by valuable time for Pope to retreat.

*   *   *   *

Editors Note: At the site of the "Fight at the Fence Line," on Chinn Ridge of the Second Manassas battlefield stands a National Park Service marker which quotes 73rd Ohio Volunteer Infantry regimental historian Samuel B. Hurst, citing the onslaught of Longstreet's Corps falling on the Ohio Brigade, "The enemy in our front, moving in concert with those on our flank, came out of the woods—their lines masking and overlapping our own. The whole left of our brigade poured into them a murderous volley. The combat grew fierce indeed. But the contest was not long. On came the flanking column. We stood until the enemy had nearly gained our rear, and had opened fire on our flank. Then we retired."[16]

*   *   *   *

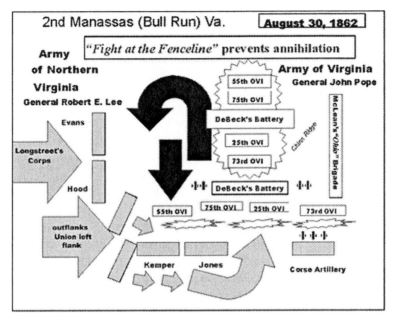

Ohio Brigade Stand at Chinn Ridge and Bald Hill Fenceline,
Battle of Second Manassas (Bull Run)

for the night and several prisoners taken. On the morning of the 28th we marched towards Manassas taking several prisoners along the road. When, within a short distance of Manassas, we turned around and marched towards Gainesville and, having proceeded in that direction some distance, were again countermarched towards Manassas and then turned to the left towards Bull Run. About sun down we came within sight of the rebel force and, after some skirmishing took up a position, and our battery opened upon a rebel battery in the edge of the woods. About dark a sharp engagement took place a mile or two to our left, the force upon our side engaged being under General King. Early on the morning of the 29th we were in motion and advanced on the south side of the road, in all perhaps two miles, and occupied during part of the day the ground upon which the battle had been fought by General King. We found some of his wounded who were cared for by your direction. In the afternoon the enemy appeared endeavoring to pass around our left and we were marched to the left and rear, and late in the evening were withdrawn to a position a short distance in advance of the one we had occupied in the morning. Although frequently under fire of the enemy's artillery, we had no opportunity of using our small arms and we had but two men wounded. After dark an attempt was made upon our lines by the enemy and a portion of the night was spent under arms. We remained in our position on the 30th until about four o'clock in the afternoon when the brigade was ordered to take up a position on Bald Hill to our left, to support General Reynolds. You placed your brigade in position and your battery as follows: the 25th and 73d Ohio regiments in line on the left of the battery.

A short time after we had taken our position, the troops on our left marched past us by the right flank and in our front, and disappeared to our right. The enemy soon appeared in our front, driving before them a regiment of Zouaves. You opened upon them as soon as they came within range, with grape and canister, and the infantry were soon after briskly engaged in firing. They were driven back by our fire in considerable confusion and unquestionably heavy loss. They made their appearance again directly in front of the 73d Ohio, in the edge of the woods, but were a second time driven back by our fire. Our men were in high spirits, feeling confident of their ability to maintain their position, when a large force of enemy were perceived advancing with artillery on our left and rear. They opened upon us at the same time, with grape, canister, and infantry. In a short time the regiment on my left, under a terrific fire, gave way. Shortly afterwards, an order was given to change front, which I attempted to execute, but the fire was so terrible and the noise of the battle so great, that it was impossible to be heard or do anything without confusion. We were forced from our position and retired to the woods in our rear. My men behaved well, indeed gallantly; but, by some blundering, we were left unprotected on our left and then came the murderous assault on three sides of us which resulted as I have stated.

I wish to state, before closing this report, that constant marching, both day and night, for the last twelve days previous to the 30th, and had reduced my number of effective men to two hundred and thirty on the day of the battle; and many of those bare-footed, and all of them exhausted. I further desire to protest against what I consider the injustice done to the troops of Sigel's corps by a published report of Major General Pope. From the 21st to the 31st of August, some portion of our corps was engaged every day, often fiercely; our marches have been extraordinary and our losses great. Yet we have been totally ignored. I am glad also to state that the officers and men of my command have every confidence in the ability, bravery, and patriotism of the commanding general of the corps and fully believe that no part of the disaster of Bull Run was produced by an act, neglect, or omission of his; but, on the other hand, that if he had had control of the army, it would not have happened.

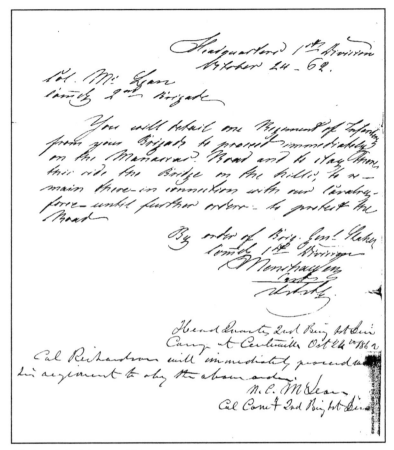

National Archives and Records Administration
2nd Brigade Commander Gen.
McLean's Order for the 25th OVI to reposition.

The following is a list of the casualties in my regiment:

KILLED—Private John Ferrel (E), Alvin N. Burlingham (H), Privates John Benny, Geo. W. McVicker (G), Sergt. Lewis F. Shannon (K), Privates Enos W. Miner, Edward D. Peck (K).

MISSING—Co. A. Privates Wm. T. Lockwood, James McMullen, George W. Iden, William T. Andrews; Co. B. Privates Newlin C. Mercer, Joseph Stewart, William Lowther, James Trigg. Co. E. Privates Jesse C. Chance, Hiram Odell. Co. G. Private Erwin M. Bergstresser. Co. H. Privates Thomas Cooper, J.N.

Stevens, O. J. Dunn. Co. K. Corporal Wm. T. Ketchum; Privates Charles Cholett, Lewis Miller, James Benway, John A. Church, Richard M. Sherman, William Vickery, David H. Linn.

WOUNDED—Co. A. Privates Drewer C. Iveson, William H. Crisswell, George Cass, Robert Creighton, John McKirahan, Robert A. Fowler, Reuben Donnally, Emanuel Riley, John Lebold. Co. B. Sergt. Hugh McConville; Privates Daniel Berry, Oliver P. Smith, John w. Doherty. Co. C. Corporals John Tisher, Thomas Batton; Privates Jacob H. Bailery, Joseph Sill, Francis Schonhart, John W. Hoskins, Robert Longwell, William Batton. Co. E. Sergeants Elisha Biggerstaff, and Charles Ladd; Corporal Cyrus Odell; Privates Lucius Marsh, John Leary, Elbridge Comstock, Franklin Wright, William Lowry, Flavius N. Lowry, Geo. Taylor, James Male, Ephraim H. Lewis, James C. Houston. Co. H. Private David Hartley. Co. I. First Lieut. John D. Merryman; Corporals Joseph Cunningham, Samuel Shirk, Emanuel DeNoon; Privates Benjamin F. Rickey. Wm. Gant, Charles Weinstein, Nelson C. Loveatt. Co. K. George Huyck (mortally), Thomas Rose, James Moran, Sergeant Peter Triquart.
Very respectfully, your obedient servant,

Wm. P. Richardson
Col. 25th Reg't. O.V.I.

At this late date (1883), over twenty years after the above report was written, it is gratifying to pick up a recently published volume and find justice at last done to the second brigade referred to in Richardson's report. The volume referred to is <u>The Army Under Pope</u>, by John Codman Ropes and contains the only reliable account of Pope's campaign in Virginia that has yet been published. Every soldier of the Army of the Potomac, at least, should read this excellent work. In speaking of the engagement on Bald Hill, where the 25th Ohio sustained its principal loss, the author says:

The struggle for the possession of Bald Hill was most obstinate and sanguinary. McLean's brigade of Schenck's division was first sent to hold it, and did hold it handsomely, repulsing several attacks both in front and rear, until the command was reduced to a skeleton. Schenck himself was severely wounded at the head of the reinforcements which he was leading to McLean's support. The two brigades of Koltes and Kryzanowski were put in, and for a time, stayed the advancing tide. The losses were very severe, as the enemy were in large force. The brave Colonel Koltes here fell, sword in hand, at the head of his men. In the conflict around this hill, General Tower was severely wounded at the head of two of Rickett's brigades and Col. Fletcher Webster of the 12th Massachusetts, a son of the great statesman, was killed while leading his regiment.

In their first attack on this strong position, even the impetuosity of Hood's Texans failed to make any impression. Hood was compelled to fall back and all that could be done, says Evans, who commanded the division, was to hold the enemy with the other brigade until Anderson's division came up. In one of his brigades, 631 officers and men were killed and wounded, probably one-fourth of the actual force present on the field. Two colonels were killed and one wounded.

D.R. Jones (Confederate) also found his way to the Chinn House, and the two brigades which he had with him "went in most gallantly, suffering severe loss." In one of these brigades, (Anderson's) consisting of five regiments, but one field officer was untouched. They had to fall back, however, and were evidently very severely handled. The account which Generals Benning and Anderson give of their experience with these two brigades is very interesting. It was evident that the troops who held the hill held it with obstinate courage and that they yielded only to the assaults of fresh troops. Jones' division got no farther than the Chinn House that day.

In spite, however, of this heroic resistance, the enemy carried the position by main force. They suffered heavily, but fresh relays pressed on with great enthusiasm and they finally drove our forces from Bald Hill.

Thus ended, so far as our brigade was concerned, the second battle of Bull Run or, as the rebels called it, the battle of Manassas. It was a severe defeat to the Union army and a humiliating one to Gen. Pope. Yet it was not a panic, nor did it partake of the nature of a rout. There were some stragglers hastening to the rear, as is always the case in a general engagement. But the army, as an army, retired under orders, and the retreat was conducted in good order with no pursuit. The army was really defeated when the engagement took place at Henry House Hill. The position was important and, if lost to Pope's army, might possibly turn the decent retreat into a disorderly panic. But the position was not lost and, after repeated charges of the most desperate character, the rebels were forced to give up the contest.

The history of the war does not furnish a single instance, upon either side, where the defeated army behaved as creditably as did Gen. Pope's army on this memorable day; and when, on the evening of the 30th, it arrived at Centreville, the organizations were perfectly preserved.

On the 3d of September the Regiment marched, via Fairfax C. H. and Vienna, to Upton Hill, having been under fire fourteen days in succession on the Rappahannock, and participated in the second battle for Bull Run.

The Regiment remained in camp at Upton Hill until September 25th when it was ordered to Centreville. On the 29th it was again on the march through Manassas Junction to Warrenton, and from there back to Centreville, where it remained until November 2d when the entire corps marched to Thoroughfare Gap remaining there until the 19th, and then returning to Chantilly.

About this time Capt. Asa Way, of Company G, resigned his commission on account of disability. Dr. William Walton of Woodsfield, Ohio, joined the Regiment as second assistant surgeon.

The Regiment remained at Chantilly until December 10, 1862, when its brigade was placed en route for Fredericksburg, but arrived there too late to participate in the battle and marched back to Stafford C. H.. It was at this place where, after much neglect, all the sutlers came in with loaded wagons. The men had not yet been paid, or not for some time at least, and many hungry eyes were fixed longingly upon the wagons. Private _____ (*Editor's note: name omitted in Col. Culp's book),* of Company K, was equal to the occasion—carefully noting the time at which the guard was to be relieved, and the number of the relief, he "borrowed" a sergeant's blouse and made a special detail of his own. About ten minutes before the regular relief was due, he made the rounds, relieving every man on guard around the wagons and, before the trick was discovered, there was only a "beggarly array" of empty wagons left. The peculiar facility with which the boys of the 25th could do up a job of that kind, merited and received, the appreciation of the balance of the division. The boys engaged in the fraudulent relief never were discovered.

We remained in camp at the Court House until January 20th, 1863, when the brigade marched to Belle Plains, but in a few days returned to the neighborhood of the old camp and built permanent winter quarters.

While the Regiment was at Belle Plains, Adjt. William L. Hoyt resigned his commission.

Chapter 6

Brooks' Station—Spring of 1863—
Chancellorsville

From January 20, 1863, until the latter part of the following April, the Regiment remained in camp at Brooks' Station, in the brigade temporarily under command of Col. J. C. Lee, of the 55th Ohio. The division was commanded by Gen. N. C. McLean. Battalion and brigade drills were had daily in preparation for the spring campaign which, under Major General Hooker, promised to be unusually active.

*   *   *   *

Editor's Note: Colonel William P. Richardson remained in command of the 25th Ohio Volunteer Infantry. While commanders in the field were faced with the arduous task of fighting the enemy, other battles loomed within their own ranks through disagreements between commanders and interference from politicians. We have already seen the result of higher echelon commanders not heeding the warnings of regimental commanders in the wake of Stonewall Jackson's crushing blow at Chancellorsville. Col. Richardson had been called a coward when reporting to Generals Devens and Howard the movement of the enemy on the Union right flank. And records in the National Archives reveal running problems between the 25th OVI commanders and the Ohio Governor's Office. In early 1863, Col. Richardson exchanged a series of communiqués with then Governor David Tod regarding the appointment of a private to the rank of Captain. Each regiment had a fixed number of officers and noncommissioned officers. Typically, regimental commanders would recommend promotions to the Governor and Adjutant General of Ohio, based upon demonstrated leadership skills and experience in the field. In some instances, the Governor would also recommend promotions based upon petitions from other politicians, local military committees, and even from troops in the field. The Governor was aware of vacancies within the ranks at any given point in time because of the troop strength reports submitted by the units to the Adjutant General's Office. This was usually done with the concurrence of regimental commanders.

In the case of private A. G. Cornelius, Col. Richardson was absent from his regiment when a petition was made to Gov. Tod. The Colonel was understandably angry when he discovered that the Governor had elevated a private to the rank of Captain within the 25th Ohio without his knowledge or consent. The following are brief excerpts from the correspondence which ensued between the 25th Ohio commander and the Governor:

Col. Richardson (to Gov. Tod, January 25, 1863):

Sir: It becomes my duty to call your attention to some extraordinary facts connected with the appointment and promotions in my regiment.....you have appointed Kirk, Maloney and Cornelius 2d Lieutenants without my knowledge or consent...Buy the most extraordinary fact is your extreme liberality in the number of officers with which you have from time to time supplied me....But sir, your liberality in this respect has become troublesome....on the 1st day of September you commissioned A. G. Cornelius (private of Comp A) 2d Lieut.....But on the 5th day of September you gave him a commission as Captain....Towards him I have no personal ill feeling. His military history makes it an injury and insult to many of the old and gallant officers over whom, without claim or merit, he as been unjustly promoted......He has never to my knowledge in any way distinguished himself or merited particular notice.[17]

Gov. Tod (to Col. Richardson, February 1st, 1863):

Dear Sir, Before proceeding to reply to your letter of the 25th Ult—the interest of service requires that I should notice the bad temper and taste of your communication. Officials should always use respectful language when communicating with each other on official business.....your next complaint is the appointment of Kirk, Maloney & Cornelius as 2d Lieutenants "without your knowledge or consent"...I have only time today to investigate the case of Kirk.....[18]

*   *   *   *

Editor's Note: Governor Tod, in his response to Col. Richardson's inquiry about several promotions, only responded to the case of Kirk who, the Governor was careful to note, "had" been recommended for promotion by the Colonel himself. But no mention was made of the accelerated promotion of private Cornelius. Col. Richardson was not content to leave the matter remain unaddressed.

Col. Richardson (to Gov. Tod, February 13, 1863):

Sir—I am compelled to acknowledge to some extent the justice of your stric-
tures upon the "temper and taste" of my communication of the 25th Ult., and
as far as the same was ill tempered in bad taste, I now apologize.......Do you
not truly think that the promotion of Alfred G. Cornelius from a private to a
Captain in such a short space of two months over the heads of all the old, tried,
brave, efficient, and ranking officers of a lower grade in the regiment sufficient
to excite some feelings for resentment?[19]

Col. Richardson (to Gov. Tod, March 8, 1863):

Sir......you predict harmony in our future relations and yet, your persistence
in the case of A. G. Cornelius whom you have appointed Capt. in my regiment
is enough to disturb the harmony of the relations between the persons of the
Trinity....I must and do believe that some mistake has again occurred and the
you do not mean him to retain his commission. Seven 1st Lieuts. Tendered
their resignations but I persuaded them to wait until I can hear from you....[20]

Gov. Tod (to Col. Richardson, March 15, 1863):

Dear Sir: Your letter of the 8th inst. is before me...The appointment of
Cornelius of which you complain was made upon the petition of 50 privates of
the Co. and 19 commissioned officers of the Regt. incl a statement from one of
the officers that you were absent from the Regt. at the time the petition was
prepared. He, of course, was a stranger to me, but the Military Committee of
the county in which he lives strongly recommend him as a worthy gentleman......I am aware of the absolute necessity of harmony between the
Command of a Regt. and all subordinates and to promote this harmony would
at once revoke Cornelius commission as Capt if I had the power so to do, but I
do not. If you can prevail upon him to return his commission, I will cancel it
thereby restoring him to this former position.[21]

*　　　*　　　*　　　*

*Editor's Note: Further evidence of promotions being given by both regiment com-
manders and Governors from their respective states is seen in the case of Sergeant
James A. Driggs, Co. B, 25th OVI. In the 25th Ohio records, Driggs is shown holding the rank of Sergeant from November 1, 1861 to March and April, 1864 when*

he received two promotions by the regimental commander as 2d and 1st Lieutenant, respectively. However, Sgt. Driggs was appointed by the same Governor David Tod as a 2d Lieutenant in April 24, 1863. Driggs, however, would not actually move into that position of rank for another year.

$*$ $*$ $*$ $*$

In the reorganization of the army we were placed in the eleventh corps which was formed mostly of troops that had been under the command of Gen. Franz Sigel. Gen. O. O. Howard was the corps commander. Some alterations had occurred in our brigade. The 73d Ohio had been transferred to another division, and the 107th Ohio and 17th Connecticut, a new regiment, just come to the front, had been added to the brigade; three of the old regiments remained, viz., 25th, 55th and 75th Ohio. Before the campaign fully opened, Col. J. C. Lee returned to the command of his regiment and Brig. Gen. N. C. McLean, late colonel of the 75th Ohio, to the brigade, leaving the division to the command of Major General Devens. As before stated, Gen. O. O. Howard commanded the corps. Some dissatisfaction existed among the German troops, occasioned by the removal of their favorite commander, Gen. Franz Sigel, and Howard was looked upon with considerable disfavor. The free-thinking element of the corps took but little stock in the ministerial reputation of the new commander. They felt that a representative countryman had been unjustly deprived of his command and, therefore, entered upon the campaign with less enthusiasm than would have been shown had Sigel occupied his old position as their leader. This feeling, however, occasioned no part of the disaster which befell the eleventh corps on the 2d of May, 1863. Twenty years have elapsed since the battle of Chancellorsville, during which time it has been convenient to attribute the result of that campaign to the demoralization of the corps. It is time justice should be done by calling attention to the actions of Generals Howard and Devens, and the position occupied by the first division, upon which the disastrous assault was made.

On the 27th of April, 1862, the corps marched toward Chancellorsville via Hartwood Church, Kelly's and Germania fords, and reached Chancellorsville April 30th, and was placed in position near Hatch's house.

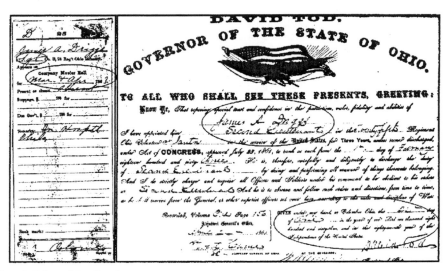

Tom J. Edwards' collection

Sergeant James A. Driggs served as a Sergeant in the field; however, Governor Tod promoted him to the rank of 2nd Lieutenant. Confusion arose in the field when the Governor granted commissions to soldiers in the ranks without regimental commander's consent. There was a officer quota for each company and field grade.

It is a remarkable incident that the 25th Ohio left camp at Brock's Station with 443 officers and men and, on the evening of the last day's march took, 444 men into camp, one man from the hospital, Oliver W. Williams, hospital steward, having joined the Regiment, and not one having straggled from the ranks during the march.

Devens' division formed the extreme right of the army with Von Gilsa's brigade on the right, two regiments facing west, and the other southwest. McLean's brigade was on the left about one mile from the Chancellorsville House; the 55th Ohio in line on the right of the brigade, the 107th Ohio in line in the center, and the 17th Connecticut in line on the left excepting that three companies, under Lieut. Col. Walter, of this regiment, were advanced a few yards, and occupied the garden east of Hatch's house with a picket fence against which they threw some brush and dirt to form slight breastworks.

These three regiments faced southwest and were on that side of the dirt road. A rail fence running along that side of the road was utilized as far as possible in making breastworks. The 75th Ohio was in rear of the 55th, formed in column by division, and the 25th Ohio occupying same formation in rear of the 107th, both facing southwest. In front of our brigade were open fields for half a mile extending to the wilderness to our right.

When the pickets, detailed the night before from the Regiment, were relieved in the morning, a sergeant of unusual intelligence in charge of them, Abe Heed, of Company A, reported to Colonel Richardson that large bodies of troops had passed in our front to the right during the night.

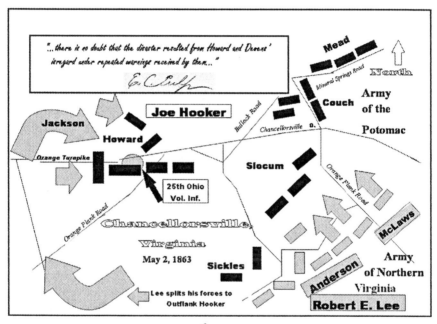

Jackson's Flank attack on the 11th Corps, Chancellorsville, May 2, 1863

Richardson reported this fact immediately to General McLean and, with the approval of that officer, sent out four scouts—Sergt. Abe Heed, privates James Justus, John T. Peck, and William Linder—of tried courage and fidelity, from in front of our picket line. They proceeded to our extreme right—until fired upon by the enemy's pickets, and returned with the astounding intelligence that the rebels were massing heavily on the right and rear of the division and not more than half a mile from the outer regiment, and not much over one mile from division headquarters. Colonel Richardson conveyed this intelligence to General McLean, who reported it to General Devens. An hour passed without any new disposition being made to meet the threatened attack, when Colonels Richardson and Lee both visited General McLean at his headquarters to ascertain if any order were to be issued. General McLean suggested that they, with him, go to General Devens and reiterate the information. The general, however, seemed utterly unable to appreciate the gravity of the situation and, in fact, treated the information with disrespect and suggested to General McLean that the proper place for his colonels were with their regiments. With such insulting neglect, Colonel Richardson returned to his regiment and, although it was early in the afternoon, he ordered the company cooks to immediately prepare supper, privately conversed with his officers as to what they should do under certain circumstances, and, in fact, prepared them for a surprise which he knew by four o'clock on the afternoon of May 2nd that his condition of affairs existed.

But this was not the only intelligence received of the movements of Stonewall Jackson. In spite of his precautions to conceal his march, it was observed by officers and men of General Birney's command and at once reported to General Hooker. Although Hooker did not regard it as a flanking movement on the part of the enemy, for the very audacity of such a step upon the part of Lee did not render it probable, he was compelled to believe that either the general was making a retreat, or adopting some new plan of attack or defense. But to provide against the contingency of a flank attack, at ten o'clock on the morning of 2d of May, he sent a written dispatch to General Howard directing him to examine the ground around his position, with a view of meeting a flank attack. He was told in the dispatch that the commanding general had good reason to suppose that the enemy was moving on his right, and that he should advance his pickets well for the purposes of observation. Not withstanding this dispatch, no precautions were taken against the impending danger. We now have the unpardonable stupidity of two general officers, a division and corps commander, absolutely ignoring—the one, positive intelligence of the immediate presence of a large body of enemy, the other a direct order from his superior officer to ascertain if such a condition of affairs did exist. The dispatch from Hooker to Howard was received by the latter not later than 10:30 a.m., while Devens received his information from Colonel Richardson the first time through General McLean at one o'clock, and again in the presence of McLean, Lee and Richardson, not later than three o'clock.

From 10:30 a.m. to 6 p.m., when the assault was made, there was more than enough time for Devens' position to have been made absolutely impregnable. The singular thing about this whole matter is that neither Devens or Howard seemed to have any curiosity to gratify. There is no proof on record that any attempt was made to ascertain the truth or falsity of the reports. The subsequent rout of the division was possible only from the grossest neglect of all military precautions, and there is no doubt that the disaster resulted from Howard's and Devens' disregard, under repeated warnings received by them during the eight hours preceding the assault. Howard scouted the reports and Devens insulted the informants.

The writer was present when Richardson informed Devens of the reports brought by his scouts and heard Devens say to McLean, "I guess Col. Richardson is somewhat scared; you had better order him to his regiment."

Fitz John Porter was dismissed from the army in disgrace and barely escaped death for less fault. Devens has since been Attorney General of the United States and now holds a high federal appointment in Massachusetts.

The first notice our troops had of the approach of the enemy was the rapid flight of a large herd of deer which came out of the wilderness and passed along the front of the second brigade, followed almost immediately by the overwhelming onslaught of Stonewall Jackson's veteran troops upon an unprepared division, occupying a weak line of defense, and facing in a different direction from which the attack was made. Some of the regiments had their guns stacked, and men were eating, making coffee, playing cards, cleaning guns, and engaged in the usual avocations of camp life when the enemy is a thousand miles away. This was the case in many of the regiments of the brigade on our right, Von Gilsa's, which received the first attack. But Cols. Lee and Richardson, knowing the deadly danger hovering over the division, had their regiments well in hand and were anxiously awaiting the expected attack. Several shells coming directly down the road followed almost immediately by canister and musketry, proclaimed the rapid advance of the enemy. The writer of this was an aide on the staff of Gen. McLean, and when the attack was made he was lying on the grass in front of Hatch's house holding his horse by the reins, in readiness for immediate use. Hearing cheers and laughter, he raised on his elbow to ascertain the cause and found it to be the frightened deer rushing in front of the brigade; while watching them, and dimly conscious of the cause, a solid shot came from the right and struck the body of the apple tree under which he was lying. Gen. McLean sprang on his horse and started down the road to the right of the brigade, accompanied by his staff officers, and almost immediately followed by Gen. Devens; the soldiers from the first brigade were coming to the rear in the utmost confusion, crushed by the first assault. After the first rush the enemy stopped for a minute or two to get in some kind of order and, in that interval, which was hardly distinguishable, Col.

Lee asked for permission to change front of his regiment saying that his men were being shot in the back; receiving no response, although McLean and Devens were within ten feet of him, he called out for his men to get up upon the other side of the light works they had thrown up.

The 75th Ohio was lying massed in column by division with its flanks exposed to the murderous fire and, in five minutes, had lost every field officer and two-thirds of the regiment lay dead or wounded.

By this time the first brigade was coming back in waves of panic-stricken men, not stopping to throw aside their equipment, but slashing the confining straps with their knives. To them, resistance was simply impracticable. The best and bravest troops that ever existed would, under the same circumstances, have been terrorized. The regiments of the second brigade opened their ranks for the fugitives. Amidst this dire confusion, an

Editor's Note: Brigidier General Nathaniel C. McLean, commanding the Second Brigade, commented in his official report regarding the disposition of the 25th Ohio and the wounding of its commander Colonel William P. Richardson. Command of the 25th then fell to then Major Jeremiah Williams.

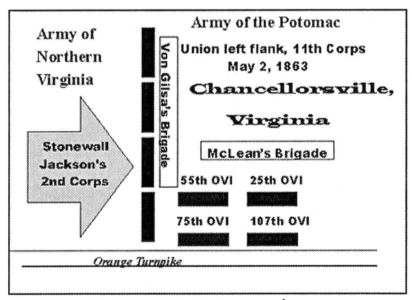

Position of McLean's Brigade, 11th Corps,
Union Right Wing, Chancellorsville

*   *   *   *

Brigadier General Nathaniel C. McLean, commanding Second Brigade:

...At this moment I found, from the rush of fugitives from the right flank, that the First Brigade had given way, and I immediately ordered the Twenty-fifth Ohio, under Colonel Richardson, to wheel to the right in column, and deploy on the double-quick into line facing the approaching enemy. This was done with as much precision as if on parade, and as soon as possible the regiment opened fire and remained firm until ordered back.

Its commander, Colonel Richardson, was severely wounded while leading his men with great gallantry. The regiment could not have done more against the greatly superior numbers of the enemy, and it was also prevented from doing as much execution as it might have done by the rush of fugitives through its lines. By the retreat of the First Brigade, the right flank of my regiments in the rifle-pits was exposed to a severe enfilading fire of artillery and musketry, which they bore in their positions until it was evident they must be totally destroyed if they remained. Under these circumstances, they left the rifle-pits and endeavored to form in the rear of the Twenty-fifth, but the rush was so great so as to prevent any effective organization for resistance....[22]

*　　　　*　　　　*　　　　*

Editor's Note: After Col. Richardson fell to enemy fire, Major Jeremiah Williams took command of the regiment in the thick of battle. Major Williams would continue as regimental commander of the 25th Ohio through the first day of Gettysburg at which time he, too, would fall prey to the enemy. His official report of the Battle of Chancellorsville further details the 25th attempt to stem the tide and hold the Union right flank against overwhelming odds.

Major Jeremiah Williams, Staff Officer, 25th OVI:

May 8, 1863

SIR: I have the honor to report the following as the operations of the Twenty-fifth Ohio Volunteer Infantry during the ten days commencing on April 27 and ending on May 6: We left our camp near Brooke's Station, Va., with (including non-combatants) 433 men, and 2 field, 2 commissioned staff, and 18 line officers, each of the men carrying eight days' rations (except five days' meat), and 60 rounds of cartridges.. We encamped the first night of our march near Hartwood Church. The next night crossed the Rappahonnock at Kelly's Ford.

The next we crossed the Rapidan, and the following day we reached Chancellorsville, where we remained until the engagement on the evening of the 2nd instant.

In this march, severe as it was, but one man straggled from our regiment, and he was present and wounded in the battle.

Our formation at the commencement of the engagement on the afternoon of the 2nd was in double column, about 100 paces in rear of the center of the left wing of the three regiments which were in line of battle, the direction of our column being parallel with their line.

The attack was made by the enemy with suddenness and great fury upon the right flank of our brigade. The enemy's balls were already reaching our regiment when we commenced forming our line of battle. We had first to change direction at right angles, and, while deploying the enemy had gained to within 200 paces, and was driving back through our lines the troops that were in advance of our new front.

The deployment was made under great difficulties. Fleeing men dashed through our lines, while the enemy's musketry and grape and canister killed and disabled many of our men before the formation was completed. It was, however, successfully accomplished, with nearly as much dispatch, and the line was nearly s good, as if no enemy had been present.[23]

The enemy was now within 150 paces, in very heavy column, and steadily advancing. The regiment opened fire with a coolness and deliberation highly commendable, in view of the general confusion with which it was surrounded. Our right wing rested among some scrubby bushes and saplings, while the left was in comparatively open ground. The fire of the enemy as they approached was murderous, and almost whole platoons of our were falling; but our men stood firmly. The enemy's left flank extended far beyond our right, and was being rapidly pushed farther. There was now of our forces none but broken and retreating, and the enemy were nearer our next line of breastworks than we were.

Fairwell Retreat Cemetery, Republic, Ohio
**Corporal Edgar Way, Co. G, killed
May 2, 1863 buried on the battlefield**

The men had fired here an average of 5 to 6 rounds when the enemy had approached to within 30 paces of our left wing, and perhaps 50 on our right wing, and was rushing upon us with redoubled speed and overwhelming numbers, when the order was given to about face.

We had in line of battle 333 men and 16 commissioned officers, of whom 5 officers (including the colonel) and over 130 men (including the missing last seen here) were killed and wounded at this point. Two companies were on picket, and escaped with 1 man wounded and 1 officer and 7 men missing.

The line of our retreat was through a dense thicket, from which the men emerged much shattered. A large portion of them were rallied at the breastworks near General Howard's headquarters. Some of them, however, joined with a German regiment (believed to be the Sixty-eighth New York), which was ordered by its colonel to about face and retreat, and all went off together. There was no further organized fighting by the regiment during the engagement...[24]

*　　　　*　　　　*　　　　*

Many of the 55th and 75th Ohio fell into the ranks of the 25th which remained in line, keeping up a stubborn fire, until the broken flying fragments of the first brigade had passed and the enemy had encircled it on three sides. Then the order to retreat was given and more than half the Regiment engaged left bleeding and dying on the ground where the line had been maintained. Darkness, fresh troops well handled, principally of the twelfth corps, and massed artillery, checked the rebel advance, and thus ended the first day's battle.

At the commencement of the assault, only 330 men were in line, two companies being on picket duty in front, and escaping with small loss.

That night the corps was re-organized and the next morning placed in the intrenchments where it remained until the morning of the 5th, when it was moved across the river, and the same day marched to its old camp at Brooks Station

∗   ∗   ∗   ∗

Editor's Note: The Colonel Lee referred to in Lt. Col. Culp's narrative of the meetings with Generals McLean and Deven is Col. John C. Lee, commander of the 55th Ohio Volunteer Infantry, which was holding the right flank reserve next to the 25th Ohio at the time of the attack. The following is a portion of Col. Lee's official report of the May 2d battle.

∗   ∗   ∗   ∗

Colonel John C. Lee, commanding, 55th OVI:

...At about 6 p.m. a heavy discharge of musketry on our right and rear announced the approach of the attacking column. Almost simultaneously, from artillery posted in the old Turnpike road on the right, and within short range, the enemy delivered an enfilading fire of grape and canister upon the men in the rifle-pit. There was no enemy in front, direct or obique, but the firing clearly told him to be in the rear and but little to the right.

Every officer and man remained at his post, including Lieutenant-Colonel Gambee, who was with the line at the pit.

At this juncture, I hastily rode to General Devens and yourself (*Editor's Note: 2nd Brigade commander General N. C. McLean*), reported the condition of affairs, and requested leave to change front. The general commanding the division answered, "Not yet," and I hastily returned to the regiment. Soon discovering that a part, if not all, of the First Brigade had confusedly given way, I again reported to yourself (*General McLean*) and General Devens that additional fact. Without receiving any orders whatever, I again rapidly returned to my command. A storm of fire from both the artillery and musketry was falling upon the helpless line, which yet was without an enemy upon whom to fire.

My horse, receiving a wound, dashed furiously with me toward the enemy's advancing left, carrying me beyond possibility of directly the movements of the battalion, partially for the time disabling me, and escaping to the rear.

That gallant regiment, the Twenty-fifth Ohio Volunteer Infantry, having deployed and presented a front to the advancing attack, with its left resting near the road, under the command of Lieutenant-Colonel Gambee, the companies successively from the right withdrew from the rifle-pit and form line in rear of the Twenty-fifth, where the fighting was maintained until both the regiments were swept from their position by the overwhelming force of the attack. As a regiment it could not again rally.[25]

…Allow me to insist that when the Eleventh Corps is charged with cowardice on the 2d instant, as is common, the Second Brigade, First division should not be included. The men did and will fight when they have opportunity, but a rifle-pit is useless when the enemy is on the same side and in rear of your line.[26]

*   *   *   *

Editor's Note: Sgt. Thomas Evans' (Company K), diary, reflects not only collaborative, supportive observations, but also the terrible consequences of himself and others resulting from the ignoring of repeated warnings by upper Union command.

Sgt. Thomas C. Evans, Company K, 25th OVI

April 28, 1863. Skirmishing commenced on our left about noon and at one o'clock there was a feint made on our right after which the band played us a national air. Thus, as we supposed, we were secure from danger, such was the near-sightedness of our commander. Our regiment was in reserve of the brigade. We had just drew a ration of fresh beef and was now cooking it. For my part I had a coffee pot full of beef on the fire cooking when all at once a terrible musketry opened on our right. We were ordered in line of battle in a minute and in another minute 20 thousand rebels rushed on us in mass with several pieces of artillery.

In 10 minutes the ground was literally covered with the dead and dying, our colonel wounded and we forced to give way for we were only about two thousand against 20 thousand. Old Stonewall Jackson had flanked us with his whole corps and now rained grape and canister and minnie balls in our ranks like hail. In 15 minutes we were all cut to pieces. There was no place left us but to flee for our lives which we did with a right good grace. We soon became scattered to the four winds every one for themselves.

Darkness was now on us and Jackson was on us and fear was on us. Jackson was now checked by the troops in reserve and soon a death silence ensued.

As for myself I ran into a dense wood and was soon lost. I had lost all but shirt, pants and gun and hat. I was very warm and I knew to lay down and sleep it might kill me. I walked on a little ways when I spied a dark object in the leaves which at first I took to be a dead man but on examination it proved to be a knapsack containing a blanket, overcoat and few articles belonging to a barber among which was a razor which I stored away for safe keeping. I knew I must be near the enemy and to undertake to go back I was open to be shot by our pickets.

So here I was not knowing what to do. Just then a whippoorwill came and lighted over my head and commenced to hollow very sympathetically. I was inclinded to think it was token of something so I resolved to lie down just where I was and wait for daylight. I was soon asleep. Just at the peep of day the sound of the whippoorwill awakened me. I was nowsure it meant something so I arose and mused on my condition. I listened to the bird with a kind of reverential awe. Just as my things was ready for me to move my bird set off in acertain direction and I concluded to take it as my guide. After following it about one hundred yards I found myself in a ravine with a dense laurel thicket.[27]

My bird now disappeared so I concluded to view my position. Crawling down in the laurel I discovered a kind of cave under the bank. I had now but one cracker left to eat so I set me down to think. It was now day and soon the battle opened with fury not being inclined to risk my life out of my own regiment I resolved to remain in this condition until providence showed me the way out since I was inclined to think the bird led me in there. For the most part of the day the battle raged, the earth shook with artillery and the elements resounded with the roar of musketry and the yells of the charging foe. But it is not so much the describing of battles I wish as the describing of my own condition and self.

During the day I was joined by 2 sergeants and two corporals and two privates out of a Pennsylvania regiment who had become worn down with the fight.

We soon joined our lots and became partners. Here we spent the night and in the morning we resolved to either reach our commands or be killed and captured. Accordingly, a part struck out one way and a part another. I and my party steered for the river toward which we believed our army was falling back. We had not proceeded far when we came into an opening and just beyond was a brigade of rebels moving along. They had skirmishers deployed who soon discovered us and resistance being vain we gave the signal of surrender which was answered by them sending a cavalry man after us who conducted us into their lines and thence back to a squadron of cavalry where we were treated very kindly and gave some hard tack which refreshed us not a little.

We was now conducted back to a place not far above Fredericksburg and delivered in the hands of the rebel provost guard numbering about 20. Here we was used well. I shaved nearly the whole crowd with my razor which I had captured. This had been a day of sighs. We saw thousands all mangled and torn laying all over the ground having their wounds dressed. All the houses and churches were filled and whole lots full of them. I soon became acquainted with the Lt. of the guard and him and I talked most of the night on various subjects.

The following morning we were marched down to a church above Fredericksburg. Here we joined many more Yanks who were as unlucky as ourselves. At this church had been some hard fighting the day previous and the slaves were now employed in burying the dead. They had our boys piled in a long windrow (?) and were digging a ditch alongside to tumble them into. We nearly all cried to witness these horrible sights, but to no avail. We were prisoners and would probably be tortured to death and in the long run be as they fit subjects for the ditch.

Oh, war! War! Who but those who have witnessed its atrocities can conceive of half? Pen cannot describe nor tongue declaim half nor will I attempt to say more on what I have seen save what particularly relates to myself individually.[28]

*   *   *   *

Every regiment in the brigade suffered the loss of one or more field officers. Col. Noble, of the 17th Connecticut, was severely wounded and Lieut. Col. Walter killed. Col. Riley, of the 75th, was killed and Col. Richardson was severely wounded in the shoulder and, for some time, the wound was considered a mortal one. He finally recovered with the loss of the use of his right arm, and until the close of the war had command of Camp Chase, Ohio.

$$*\qquad*\qquad*\qquad*$$

Editor's Note: 2d Lt. Joseph H. Hollis wrote to his younger brother, Thomas, shortly after the Battle of Chancellorsville and described the declining state of affairs and strength of his regiment.

2d Lt. Joseph H. Hollis, Company F, 25th OVI

May 12, 1863....I suppose you have seen an account of it (sic, Chancellorsville battle) in the papers but it is beyond discription (.) the roar of artillery and musketry is (was) beyond anything you can imagine. How little people at Home know about war. Our camp is more gloomy than it ever was known to be. Our Col waswoulded in the brest and passing into his arm. We will lose him....Two of our Captains of Co. I & H I hear have resigned and many a man left killed or wounded upon the battle field our ranks are thined by this wicked Rebellion, everything looks so very dull. We had Corps drill yesterday and our Regt. turned out about what we had in one company when we left Camp Chase. One more fight and we are all gone. No more of the 25th will be left. But we all wish to see the Rebellion finished. The Rebils all had their canteens full of whiskey and Gun powder and they fought walking up to the very cannon mouth. But what a sin it is to put men into battle in that way where they are like demons. I pray God may turn their hearts and that they may see the folly of their ways....[29]

$$*\qquad*\qquad*\qquad*$$

CASUALTIES IN THE BATTLE OF CHANCELLORSVILLE

KILLED—Co. A. Privates John Zane, William T. Lockwood, Levi Butler. Co. C. Privates Lafayette Henthorn, James Province, August Fisher, Isasac F. Hutchinson, Joseph P. Nell, John W. Harrison. Co. E. Private George F. Alford, Joseph C. Wright. Co. F. Private John T. Hancock. Co. G. Private Edgar A. Way. Co. H. Private James S. Wiley. Co. K. Lieut. Alex. Sinclair; Private Anthony Jeremy.
MISSING—Co. A. Lieut. William A. Whitcraft; Sergt. William B. Wright; Corporal Hiram Nichol; Privates Hiram S. Hahn, Benjamin R. Johnson, Willliam Linder. Co. B. Lieut. Isaac M. Kirk; Sergt. Hugh McConville; Privates

J. J. Hopton, James B. Trigg, A. J. Lloyd. Co. C. Privates Henry M. Link, John Tisher. Co. D. Privates Joseph Waters, Soloman, Christopher Hughes. Co. E. Private Henry Barnup. Co. F. Sergt. John McKinley; Corporal John C. Maxwell; Private Thomas Evans. Co. G. Private Charles F. Robinson. Co. H. Privates Samuel B. Marquis, George W. Reed, William H. Timberlake, T. Timberlake. Co. I. Privates William H. Beymer, John W. Beall, James W. Calvert, Samuel J. Davids, Joseph W. Monland, George W. Shafer. Co. K. Sergt. E. L. Viers; Privates Calvin Carpenter, William H. Dean, William S. Halloway, Werter H. Shaffer.

WOUNDED—Field and Staff. Col. William P. Richardson; Lieut. Col. Jere. Williams; Sergt. Major Hezekiah Thomas; Hospital Stewart Oliver W. Williams. Co. A. Lieut. Wm. A. Whitcraft (mortally), Second Lieut. Israel White; Sergts. Samuel R. Stewart, Abram Heed; Corporal William Peck; Privates Joseph Acres, James C. Bolan, Robert M. Fulton, John Wyer, William Simpson. Co. B. Lieut. George W. Martin; Sergt. F. A. Masters; Corporals John O. Archbold, H. N. Ford (mortally), Nathan Morris; Privates Joseph Brown, Henry Jones, Mark Lawrence. J. L. Patton, William H. Stine, J. B. Vaughn, John C. Duff, John M. Hinds, Frederick Rose, Israel Rucker. Co. C. Sergts. William H. Kast, Francis Armstrong; Corporals Thomas Batton, John Frey, George Beach; Privates Henry Armstrong, Jacob H. Bailey, William Craig, Alex. Dunn, George Trick, August Tisher (mortally), Israel N. Headley (mortally), Franklin Long, Alexander W. Lowe. Co. E. Sergt. John A. Stump; Privates Alfred T. Stump, Frederick T. Beagle, George Dugan, August Freet, Joel Spohn, James Bacon, Richard D. Phelps, Lewis Zeigler, Henry Smuck. Co. F. Privates John M. Kehr, George Harmon, David C. Ingles, David S. McKinley, Michael Cantwell, William H. Irwins, John Williams, James M. Jones. Co. G. Lieut. C. E. Randall; Sergts. J. C. Lininsparger, Blyden H. Boyce; Corporals A. J. Ames, F. A. Lumbar; Privates E. L. Karns, William McGee, H. Perkins, William R. Gray, J. W. Smith, George White, L.D. Fisher, Robert Longmore, John M. Dickie, George Taylor. Co. H. Sergts. John E. Timberlake, George Newman, James Hyler; Corporals Robert W. Spurrier, John T. Painter, John L. Dunn; Privates Michael F. Danforth, Zeno F. Davis, Jefferson Fouts, John Gellespie, William N. Mills, Thomas B. Sheets, Newton Livezey. Co. K. Sergt. William P. Scott; Corporals Lyman B. Stone, John Klinck; Privates George Brown, Martin Bender, Christ. Bowman, Lawerence Burnes, Sumner B. Felt, Shubert Hutchins, Andrew J. Hutchins, Michael Herbert, Enos Kameron, Morrison Lewis.

Many of the missing were killed and wounded. Company D, which took part in this battle, was a small company of recruits; it was not recognized as an organization and the men were shortly afterwards assigned to other companies in the Regiment.

Surgeon Louis G. Meyer remained upon the battlefield, purposely allowing himself to be captured in order to personally care for our wounded. He was exchanged in a few days. His action is deserving of the highest credit.

Chapter 7

Changes in Regiment—New Commander Presentation of Sword to Maj. Gen. R. H. Milroy

The Regiment remained in camp until June 12th following, during which time the brigade and division commanders were changed, the division being commanded by Brig. Gen. Francis C. Barlow, and the brigade by Brig. Gen. Adelbert Ames, both efficient and gallant officers. Col. Richardson being absent on account of wounds, the regiment was commanded by Lieut. Col. Jere. Williams.

Several changes also occurred among the officers of the Regiment. Lieut. Col. Charlesworth was discharged on account of wounds received. Major. Jere. Williams was promoted to Lieut. Col., Capt. John F. Oliver, Co. F, was promoted to major, but never served in that capacity with the Regiment, being appointed provost marshal of one of the districts of Ohio. Capt. John W. Bowlus, Company C, was commissioned major, but very soon afterwards discharged on account of disability. Capt. Askew, Co. I, Crowell, Co. E, Higgins, Co. H, Jones, Co. B, Lieut. Merryman, Co. I, and Quartermaster A. J. Hale, resigned, the latter being succeeded by Commissary Serg. David R. Hunt. Several new officers were promoted from the ranks. But four of the original officers remained with the regiment, and they had all received promotions, viz., Col. Richardson, Lieut. Col. Williams, Capts. Nat. Haughton and John T. Wood.

While the Regiment was lying at Brook's Station, the officers and enlisted men purchased a handsome sword and sash, and sent them by Lieut. Col. Charlesworth to Maj. Gen. R. H. Milroy, then commanding a division in the 8th army corps.

* * * *

Editor's Note: The good will gesture to present General Milroy with a presentation sword occurred shortly after the soldiers received their military pay. Diary notes written by 2d Lt. Alfred A. Lampkin reveal not only his contribution to General Milroy's gift, but also shed interesting light on the prices charged by sutlers.

2d. Lt. Alfred A. Lampkin, Company C, 25th OVI:

Tues April 14 Major Johnson's office to get pay....then I went to a clothing store and bought me a suit of cloaths that cost me 4 dollars and 1 shirt that cost 1.75.

Weds Apr 15th...I bought me a sword that cost 20.00 dollars and a belt 5.00, a Haversack 2.00, 1 shirt 1.75, 1 pair gloves 40.

Mon April 20th of 63......got my supper & then went over to the 25th Regt wheir the officers weir holding a meeting for the purpose of getting money to by a sword for Gen Milroy. I gave ten dollars and it will cost 100.00.[30]

*   *   *   *

The testimonial was an expression of esteem and affection toward a former commander. The following letter from Gen. Milroy acknowledges acceptance of the gift:

Headquarters 2d Division, 8th Army Corps
Winchester, Virginia, May 6th, 1863

Col. William P. Richardson, and Officers and Privates of the 25th Ohio Volunteer Infantry:

I was agreeably surprised today by the appearance of Lieut. Col. Charlesworth, of your Regiment, at my headquarters. Of course, being an old comrade-in-arms, and an honored and gallant member of your Regiment, he received at my hands a most cordial welcome. Before I had recovered from the agreeable recollection which his presence suggested, in your name he presented me with a sword, the dress and service scabbards of which are richly ornamented with jewels, and a sash and belt of corresponding elegance; and handed me your flattering and affectionate letter of presentation. This letter is signed by all the officers and men of your gallant Regiment that served under my command. You are all aware of my dearth of language, and will not, I am certain, judge of the emotions excited in my heart by this greatest surprise of my life, from the mode in which I may express them. Your Regiment was a part of the first brigade which I had the honor to command. You endured the rigors of a Cheat Mountain winter, participated in driving the rebels away from the territory now comprising West Virginia, across the Alleghenies and the Valley of Monterey, and gallantly led the Union forces in the battle of Bull Pasture Mountain. As a part of my command you served in the arduous campaigns under Fremont, in the Shenandoah Valley, and fought with unfaltering courage at Cross Keys. During the whole time you served under my command, you all officers and privates, conducted yourselves like men who had engaged in the struggle which now convulses our country from no venal motive, but from a conscientious conviction of duty. Shortly after the battle of Cross Keyes, against my wish, and greatly to my regret, you were to another command, but as you remained in the same army corps with my brigade, I was an eye-witness of your fidelity and courage in the campaign of the Rappahonnock, and at the last battle of Manassas. When your Regiment first became a part of my command, it was near a thousand strong. It has since been strengthened by recruits, as I have been informed, not less than three hundred. It now numbers about five hundred. The Regiment has not, to my knowledge, been disgraced by a single desertion, and has suffered, in consequence of its good discipline and strict attention of its officers, but little from the ordinary causes of morality. The great majority of the eight hundred missing from your ranks have been disabled in battle, or repose in honorable graves on the Alleghenies, Bull Pasture Mountain, Cross Keyes, along the lines of the Rappahanock, or on the plains of Manassas. As the sun of the Union rises with increased splendor above the storm of battle, it is consoling to hope that those who have been gathered to their fathers have not died in vain. The consideration that this present is made to me as their former commander, at the expiration of nearly a year after the severance of that relation, by the survivors of so many hard-contested fields, and of such a heroic band, invests it with a peculiar significance and value. I would have preferred that the gift had been less costly, for it derives none of its importance, in my estimation, from its intrinsic worth. The brief and affectionate letter of presentation, accompanied by the signatures of the donors, is as highly prized, and will be as carefully preserved by me, as the costly present which it represents. Rest assured, brother soldiers, of my heart-felt wish that you may survive to witness, in the restoration of the Union of your fathers, the fruition of your sacrifices and labors. With feelings of admiration, gratitude and respect, I am, fellow-soldiers,

Very truly your friend,
R.H. Milroy, Major General

Chapter 8

The Battle of Gettysburg

The movements of the army preceding the battle of Gettysburg need not be dwelt upon. Lee had invaded the North, a part of his command almost penetrating the suburbs of Harrisburg. Hooker was keeping a vigilant outlook and, while protecting Washington, was waiting for re-enforcements before striking a decisive blow. A force of over 10,000 men was in the garrison at Harper's Ferry. General Hooker asked that these passive troops be added to the command of General Slocum, in order that a large force might act directly against Lee's communications with Richmond. Halleck positively refused this request. Having before this refused to allow Heintzelman to report to Hooker, the latter finding himself thwarted in all his plans by the authorities in Washington, offered his resignation which was accepted and Major General George C. Meade was assigned to the command of the Army of the Potomac. The new commander was undoubtedly a favorite of General Halleck for when he, without any authority, ordered the troops from Harper's Ferry, he was not reprimanded, and in fact no notice taken of his action. In addition to these reinforcements, General Couch, who commanded the department of Susquehanna, was also placed under the order of Meade, a request which had been denied to Hooker. Had the latter remained in command of the army, Lee's army would never have recrossed the Potomac as an organization.

It was on the 12th of June, 1863, that the Regiment, with its corps, left camp to participate in the Gettysburg campaign, and the 29th of June found it at Emmitsburg, Pennsylvania. Both armies were being rapidly concentrated, Lee having issued orders for his corps commanders to unite at Gettysburg. On the date above given, the 1st and 11th corps were at Emmitsburg, the 3rd and 12th at Middleburg, the 6th at New Windsor. On the 30th the army advanced nearer the Susquehanna, the 11th corps still at Emmitsburg. The 1st corps had been ordered to Gettysburg, but General Reynolds, its commander, had halted it at Marsh Creek as the enemy were reported nearing his position on Pipe Creek, about 15 miles southeast of Gettysburg. In looking over the map of the country around Gettysburg, it is difficult to conceive what Meade's idea could have been in selecting this position. He could not have forced Lee to fight him on that line and, as it did not in any way interfere with the latter's communication, he might have kept up his depredations in Pennsylvania, retiring at his convenience across the Potomac. But fortunate blunders intervened in favor of the Union cause, and a gallant Pennsylvanian, General Reynolds, was fortunately near the rebel forces. Without orders from Meade, he determined to advance to Gettysburg, directing the 11th Corps to come to his support and, upon the morning of July 1st, our corps was marching rapidly towards Gettysburg, General Barlow's division in advance. Upon arriving at a church, four miles from Gettysburg, Barlow was to halt the head of the column and await orders.

Before reaching the church, heavy cannonading was heard in the direction of Gettysburg and Barlow ordered one of his aides, Lt. Culp, to ride ahead as rapidly as possible, to ascertain the cause of the firing, and to convey the information that he would not halt at the church. The aide rode rapidly as possible to Gettysburg and met Captain Pearson of General Howard's staff who directed him to return to Barlow at once and requested him to bring up the 11th corps with the utmost dispatch; that the 1st corps had been engaged for 3 hours with a greatly superior force; General Reynolds was killed, and half his corps line of the 1st corps to the right on Seminary Ridge. Steinwehr's division, with the reserve artillery, under Major Osborn, were placed on Cemetery Hill in the rear of Gettysburg. This disposition was made under the orders of General Howard who had preceded his corps to Gettysburg and, upon the of General Reynolds, assumed command of the two corps.

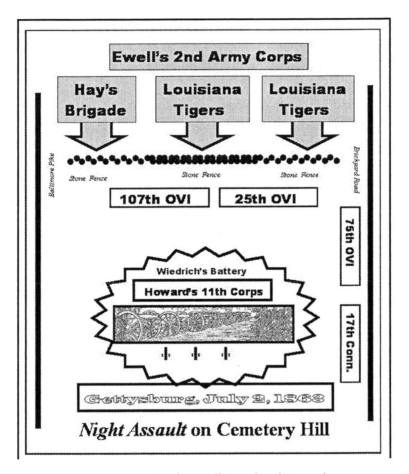

July 1, 1863, Barlow's Knoll, Battle of Gettysburg

It was evident that our forces were now engaged with over half of Lee's army and, unless help was soon at hand, would be compelled to fall back. Howard selected the position on Cemetery Hill as a rallying point and the next two days' fighting show the wisdom of the selection. It was well adapted for a defensive position. Its stone fences formed perfect works for infantry, while its gentle slopes were admirably adapted for artillery. Commanding eminences were on either flank, on which batteries could be posted to great advantage. Its convex shape allowed reinforcements to move with great celerity to any point of the line. Upon this hill General Howard made his headquarters during the afternoon.

*   *   *   *

Editor's Note: Controversy surrounds the leadership exhibited by 11th Corps Commander General O.O. Howard, particularly after the collapsing of the 11th Corps at Chancellorsville just two months prior to the Gettysburg engagement. Serving as an aid on both a brigade and division level, Lt. Edward Culp, author of this book, was in a particularly advantageous position to evaluate that leadership. And he did so objectively in an article subsequently published in the National Tribune *in 1885. His account accurately portrays the actions of the General officers present and the positioning of troops, leading up to the collision of Union and Confederate forces at Gettysburg on July 1, 1863.*

Lt. Edward C. Culp, Company D, 25th OVI:

So many articles have recently been published in THE TRIBUNE relating to Gettysburg—many of them containing criticisms upon Gen. Howard—that I hardly feel at liberty to take up your valuable space. I would like not to do so if I had not heretofore, in your columns, expressed my disapproval of Howard at Chancellorsville.

I am a sincere admirer of Gen. Howard, and, while I think he was at fault at Chancellorsville, I as clearly as possible, desire to give him great credit for his cool judgement at Gettysburg, which, backed by prompt action, gave us the position on Cemetery Ridge upon which to fight the great and decisive battle of the war.

I will pay no attention to the assaults upon the bravery of either of the Eleventh or the First Corps. I myself belonged to the Eleventh Corps both at Chancellorsville and Gettysburg, and ran about as fast as I could in both battles, and am glad that I had the nerve to do so. In fact, in nearly every engagement I was in up to the second day at Gettysburg, I had to do more or less running, and I have no use for a soldier of the last war who tells me he never was in retreat. It is a confession that he was always in the rear.[31]

The First Corps was as good as the Eleventh—no better. There were probably cowards in both. I saw stragglers from both corps and in about the same proportion. I saw officers of the First Corps running away from nothing and I saw an officer of the Eleventh Corps Judge C. P. Wickham, now upon the bench in Ohio, run his sword into an officer of the Eleventh Corps who was acting in a cowardly manner.

Is it not better to try and bring out facts for future history, and let up on this silly twaddle of cowardice? A man is a fool that assumes that 1,000 American boys between the ages of 18 and 25 raised in Central New York, Vermont or Main, could march farther, fight harder or run faster when occasion required, than the same number of boys raised in Massachusetts, Western New York or Ohio.

The date I give and language generally are taken from the regimental history of the 25th Ohio now before me, made up from memorandas written the day following the last day's battle. I will only add here that I served with Gen. Barlow [1st Division, Second Brigade,11th Corps] as Aid until he was wounded, and after that with Gen. Ames [1st Division, 11th Corps] and have visited the battlefield since the war.

It was on the 12th of June 1863, that our corps (Eleventh) left camp to participate in the Gettysburg campaign and the 29th of June found it at Emmittsburg, Md. Both armies were being rapidly concentrated—Lee having issued orders for his Corps Commanders to unite at Gettysburg. On the date above given the First and Eleventh Corps were at Emmittsburg, the Third and Twelfth at Middleburg, the Fifth at Taneytown, the Second at Union town, and the Sixth at New Windsor.

On the 30th the army advanced nearer the Susquehanna, the Eleventh remaining at Emmittsburg. The First Corps had been ordered to Gettysburg but Gen. Reynolds, it commander, had halted it at Marsh Creek, as the enemy were reported nearing his position.

At this time Gen. Meade determined to make his defensive position on Pipe Creek, about 15 miles southeast of Gettysburg....

General Barlow had been ordered to halt the head of the column and await orders when he reached a church four miles from Gettysburg.

Before reaching that place, however, heavy cannonading was heard in the direction of Gettysburg and Gen. Barlow directed me to ride ahead as rapidly as possible, ascertain the cause of the firing, and also to carry the information that he would not halt at the church.[32]

I rode with speed toward Gettysburg, but before reaching the town made up my mind that the heaviest fighting was going on the the left of the road, and I struck across the fields, but before reaching the battlefield I met Capt. Pearson of Gen. Howard's staff and repeated my order to him. Capt. Pearson replied: "I was just on my way to Gen. Barlow. Ride back and tell the General for God's sake to push on with the utmost speed. The First Corps has been engaged for three hours with a greatly superior force, which is being rapidly re-enforced. Gen. Reynolds and half his corps are killed and wounded, and Gen. Howard has assumed command."

This was about 11 o'clock a.m., not over five minutes either way and I have often wondered since whether Gen. Howard knew at that time of the death of Reynolds. I know as I rode back, my impression was that Capt. Pearson was carrying the intelligence to Gen. Howard of Reynolds death, and knowing Gen. Howard had reached Gettysburg and was the ranking officer, had of course, assumed command.

Gen. Barlow had become impatient and dispatched Capt. Wickham, on of his staff officers, for orders. I met Wickham, and we rode back meeting Gen. Barlow some distance ahead of his command, which was marching at almost a double-quick.

I repeated the information received from Pearson, and Gen. Barlow directed Capt. Wickham to return to the head of the column and urge the march as much as possible.

The battle was raging furiously, the whole of the First Corps being engaged and having suffered great loss. Gen. Barlow rode to the suburbs of Gettysburg, accompanied by myself, and there met a staff officer of Gen. Howard, who directed him where to take his division. The officer spoke of what a small reserve we would have on Cemetery Hill.

Our corps soon came in sight on the dusty road, and at 1 o'clock was in position on the right of Schimmelpfennig's Division, prolonging the line of the First Corps to the right on Seminary Ridge.

Steinwehr's Divison with the reserve artillery under Maj. Osborne was placed on Cemetery Hill in rear of Gettysburg.

This disposition, I am well satisfied, was made by the direct order of Gen. Howard who had preceded his corps to Gettysburg, reaching there in time to hear of Gen. Reynolds death. He knew that he had at best but a feeble force left.

The First Corps was being driven back and he could only hope to check the rebel advance with the remnant of the First Corps and two divisions he could spare from the Eleventh Corps, backed by the reserve artillery.

I understood from staff officers immediately after the battle, that while Gen. Howard was making his dispositions for holding Cemetery Hill, he receive five distinct orders from Gen. Meade to withdraw his forces and not attempt to hold the position he had chosen. To each dispatch he returned the reply that he could not withdraw his forces but would hold the position until re-enforced by the army; and that finally Gen. Hancock was sent forward by Gen. Meade to use his judgment and upon it the latter would act. Hancock recognized the value of the position and the balance of the army pushed rapidly forward.[33]

Gen. Howard does not mention this matter in his reminiscences but I know it was talked about and believed by nearly all the officers in the corps.

The two divisions of the Eleventh Corps were under severe fire before they were well in position, and the battle raged furiously and obstinately without one ray of hope that we could do any better than to finally fall back to the cemetery. I never saw as hopeless a battle as that afternoon's fighting, and I never saw as many individual actions of courage.[34]

*   *   *   *

The two divisions of the 11th corps were under the enemy's fire before they were well in position and, shortly afterwards, Colonel Williams received orders to support Battery G, 4th U.S. Artillery, and the 25th took its position under a most trying artillery fire. Soon, however, the entire division moved forward, but met a fresh division under Early, which had just arrived on the field. The battle waged fiercely and obstinately for an hour and two-thirds of Barlow's division were killed or wounded. Barlow himself was severely wounded, his horse killed, and all of his staff officers and orderlies but two dead or wounded.

*   *   *   *

Editor's Note: The official report of Lieutenant Israel White, the fourth commander of the 25th Ohio on July 1, gives a more detailed account of the disposition of his regiment.

1st Lieutenant Israel White, Company 1, 25th OVI:

…Upon the first day of the engagement, the regiment was taken to the extreme right, as a support to a section of the Fourth Regular Battery (G, Fourth Artillery), where it remained until the section of battery was withdrawn. The regiment then took position in the woods on the left of the position occupied by the above-mentioned battery. Upon the approach of the enemy, the regiment was placed in position, fronting upon a small stream of water. The first division, consisting of Companies A and F, were deployed as skirmishers. Skirmishing commenced and continued until they were compelled to retire by the advance of the enemy's line. The regiment engaged the enemy, and maintained its position until compelled to retire before the superior force of the enemy….the regiment was led into action by Lieutenant Colonel Jeremiah Williams, who is supposed to be a prisoner….[35]

*   *   *   *

Editor's Note: In 1880, Major Thomas Ward Osborn, former Chief of Artillery for General O.O. Howard, wrote an article relating his recollections of the three days' fighting at Gettysburg. Clearly he felt that the July 1 stubborn resistance of Schurtz, Barlow and Schimmelfennig's divisions on the Union right wing had won critical time in allowing General Howard to anchor his defenses on Cemetery Hill.

Major Thomas Ward Osborn, Chief of Artillery, 11th Army Corps:

…Howard ordered Schurz, with Barlow's and Schimmelfenning's divisions, through the town to the right to check the advance of Ewell's corps, then approaching the town from the north, while he withdrew the First Corps. Steinwehr's division was retained on Cemetery Hill to entrench while the other troops were being withdrawn. After I had Wheeler's and Dilger's batteries well at work, I rode back to town and from there took Battery G, 4th U.S. Artillery, commanded by First Lieutenant Wilkeson, to the front with Schurz's command. Schurz went into position on the bluff independent of, and to the right of, Doubleday's command and intercepted Ewell's advance to the town and the rear of the First Corps. I put Wilkeson's battery into position and remained with it until it was well at work.

Leaving Wilkeson, I rode quickly to Cemetery Hill to look after the position of Dilger's (Heckman's) and Wiedrich's batteries left on the Hill with Steinwehr's division, and from there again to Wheeler's and Dilger's batteries....

I again returned to Wilkeson's battery, where I met Wilkeson being carried to the rear by his men on a stretcher. One leg had been cut off at the knee by a cannon shot. He spoke to me and was cheerful and hopeful. I knew at a glance that the wound was fatal. There was no time for me to stop and, after talking with him, perhaps a quarter or half-minute, I left him. I never saw him again, as he died a few hours later. He was very young, less than twenty years of age, and of remarkable promise.

I soon hurried on to the front where I found the battery engaged in line with Barlow's division. The lines of battle were in the open field and very close together. The enemy's line overlapped ours to a considerable extent on both flanks. Lieutenant Bancroft was in command of Wilkeson's battery and doing good work. I knew that the two divisions must soon fall back or would be drawn back. I gave Bancroft what instructions were necessary and returned to get the other four batteries into satisfactory positions. A few moments after I left the line, General Barlow was seriously wounded and fell into the hands of the enemy...

...Howard, in person and through his aides, located the two corps along the crests of Cemetery and Culp's Hills. Colonel Wainwright, Chief of Artillery of the First Corps, retained command of the First Corps batteries upon Culp's Hill, while I retained command of the Eleventh Corps batteries on Cemetery Hill.[36]

*   *   *   *

The 1st corps had been fighting since 10 o'clock and was almost annihilated; the two divisions of the 11th corps were reduced to one-third their number, when a general retreat was ordered to the cemetery, which was rapidly accomplished.

*   *   *   *

Battles and Leaders of the Civil War

Lt. Bayard Wilkeson directs fire of Battery G, 4th US Artillery on Barlow's Knoll, facing heavy Rebel fire. It was reported that he gave the Confederates so much trouble on the first day, that Gen. John B. Gordon directed two of his batteries to fire at the young mounted officer. Wilkeson was struck by a shell that nearly severed his right leg. The Lieutenant coolly lay down, twisted his sash into a tourniquet and amputated his limb. The brave officer died a few hours later.

Editor's Note: Twenty year old 1st Lieutenant Edward Culp was sent by General Barlow during the height of the battle he was dispatched to Cemetery Hill. Culp's 1885 <u>National Tribune</u> article details his return to Blocher's Knoll where the 25th Ohio was supporting Battery G of the 4th U.S. Artillery.

1st Lieutenant Edward C. Culp, Company D, 25th OVI:

During the hottest of the fight I was returning to Gen. Barlow from executing an order, and in passing over the field I caught a glimpse through an opening in the woods of moving troops. I rode back to get a fresh look from a little eminence and became satisfied they were rebel reinforcements. As I reached Gen. Barlow he exclaimed: "What is that skirmish line stopping for?" The skirmishers, a very heavy line, had advanced to the edge of the woods into which I had seen the re-enforcements marching and of course had discovered them.

Barlow's Division was moving in rapid support of the cloud of skirmishers and he struck spurs into his horse and dashed forward to the skirmish line before I had time to give my information. I rode by his side, however, and told him what I had seen. By the time we had reached the skirmish line and one glance showed that I was correct. Thousands of fresh troops were hurled against our weakened lines.

General Barlow directed me to inform Gen. Howard and to request artillery support. Before I had ridden 20 rods Gen. Barlow was severely wounded, and all but one of his staff officers and orderlies killed or wounded.

I found Gen. Howard on Cemetery Hill; and now after nearly 22 years, I linger with pride upon that interview which in two or three minutes taught me what a cool and confident man could do. No hurry, no confusion in his mind. He knew that if he could get his troops in any kind of order back of those stone walls [Cemetery Hill] the country was safe, and that upon the succeeding days Lee would meet his great defeat.

While I was receiving instruction from Gen. Howard, Gen. Hancock rode up to the former—the first meeting they had that day. As near as I can remember it was a little after 4 o'clock and I am confident I am only a few minutes, if any, out of the way.

My message to Gen. Barlow was that orders had been issued for a retreat to Cemetery Hill. Before I could reach the position [Blocher's Knoll] occupied by Barlow's Division I met the retreating regiment of the First Corps and Schimmelpfennig's Division, followed by my own division. There was no organization so far as I could see, and I sat upon my horse and saw thousands of soldiers pass. Neither was there any great hurry. The army was defeated for the day, but in broken squads was moving leisurely back to Cemetery Hill.

I recall to mind one pleasing memory of Gettysburg: the noble women who stood upon their doorsteps and passed cups of cold water to the thirsty soldiers; and I recall many cheers that greeted their heroism. Soldiers that could stop to drink water, and then cheer benefactors, were not much frightened.

*   *   *   *

Lt. Culp, however, was not privileged to a leisurely retreat as the soldiers he described. For he was nearly captured by advancing Rebel forces in the town limits of Gettysburg. And in making his escape, he brought fear into a household of *the citizenry he had just praised. His March, 1885 <u>National Tribune</u> article related a very exciting moment and Culp's close encounter with captivity.*

*   *   *   *

1st Lieutenant Edward C. Culp, Company D, 25th OVI:

Noticing a familiar form clinging to a lamp-post, I rode up and discovered a Captain of my regiment badly wounded. [this would have been Capt. Nathaniel Manning one of the four commanding officers of the 25th Ohio that day]. In caring for him, I discovered that I was liable to become a prisoner. I dashing up a street to find it absolutely blocked with ambulances and abandoned wagons and caissons. I was still riding my horse, and too valuable a one to lose; besides, he had stood my friend in several hot places, and was reliable as steel. As a last resort, I rode up the steps of a veranda, opened the hall door and rode through the hall into a large sitting room in which the frightened family were gathered. I asked if there was a lane back of the lot I could get out through, and a young lady of perhaps 16 quickly opened the door, and requesting me to follow her tripped lightly through the house and to the back of the lot, where she commenced to let down some bars. Telling her not to mind (them), but get back and to the cellar as quickly as possible, I jumped my horse over the bars and just saved my self from a trip to Libby prison."³⁷

*   *   *   *

The official account of the battle shows that, on the first day, the 25th Ohio had four commanding officers, viz., Lieut. Col. Williams, Capt. Manning, Lieut. William Maloney, and Lieut. Israel White.

*   *   *   *

Editor's Note: Col. Jeremiah Williams had been in command of the 25th Ohio owing to the absence of Col. Jones and Col Richardson who had been forced to relinquish command of the regiment due to ill health and battle injury, respectively. Col. Williams' leadership of the regiment came to an end on the first day's engagement at Gettysburg when he was wounded and captured on Blocher's Knoll. His service is worthy of note.

In June 1861, Jeremiah Williams, age 29, of Monroe County, Ohio enlisted in the 25th Ohio Volunteer Infantry and was appointed Captain and commander of Company C, a company of men from his hometown of Woodsfield. Capt.

Williams answered his country's call, as did his fellow soldiers, by leaving his civilian life and work for military duties. Williams was one of two proprietors of the Woodsfield newspaper The Spirit of Democracy. *In assuming his new responsibilities he did not, however, remove himself entirely from the journalistic world. He would continue reporting on the movements of his regiment by sending reports to his newspaper and having them published under the title "Army Correspondence.". His articles chronicled the movements of the troops, encouraged families and fostered patriotic feelings in the community. All were all signed "JERE." This continued for more than two years until July 1, 1863. At a knoll of ground just north of the town of Gettysburg, Pennsylvania (Blocher's Knoll) Williams' regiment had been ordered to support Battery G of the 4th US Artillery. By this time Captain Williams had risen to the rank of Lt. Colonel and now commanded the 25th Ohio regiment. The right flank of the Union forces was outflanked and overrun by General Jubal Early's Confederate Division. In the retreat which ensued Col. Williams was reported as missing, He had been wounded and fallen into enemy hands Col. Williams was subsequently brought from Staunton, Virginia and imprisoned at Libby Prison, Richmond, Virginia. The conditions in which he lived resulted in ill health for which he later sought and received pension relief. On August 1, he wrote a letter to his wife, Flora. "I am still in this notorious prison, with the prospect for getting away but slightly improved. There is a report that the commissioners of exchange will meet next week, when something may be done....Our room is large and airy, but the water is wretched. I have heard nothing from the regiment since I left it.... You need feel no uneasiness about me. I am quite safe from disease here as in camp. We have become tolerably comfortable, but I am anxious t join my regiment again...." He was paroled at City Point, Virginia March 21, 1864, duly exchanged and ordered back to the field May 19, 1864, but resigned his commission and returned home. He was succeeded in command by Capt. Nathaniel Haughton. Col. Williams resumed his civilian publishing duties at* The Spirit of Democracy, *however, further information about his remaining life is sketchy. Pension records reflect that Col. Williams worked for thirteen years in the Office of the Secretary of the U.S. Senate and resided in Washington, D.C. for twenty years; also working in the Department of Interior. On May 19, 1915 his daughter Mrs. Daisy Williams Hartman informed the Commissioner of Pensions that her father had died May 11, 1915 at the age of 83 in Brooklyn New York. A second letter from the same New York address, this time from another daughter (Eloise Williams McGam), arrived at the Commissioner's office June 4 seeking final payment of his pension; implying that no spouse survived Col. Williams. A feeling of pride emanates from Col. Williams' record of service in the Civil War. This is reflected in his June 14, 1861* Spirit *report of the organization of Woodsfield's Companies B and C. "We* *were universally pronounced two of the finest looking companies in the camp, and when they heard where we were from, many a shout went up for "bully old Monroe."*

*　　　　*　　　　*　　　　*

Capt. Nathaniel Houghton was upon General Ames' staff and wounded severely. Capt. John T. Wood, Company E, was staff officer with General Barlow and severely wounded. Lieut. E.C. Culp was also with General Barlow. At daylight on the morning of July 4th, the 25th led the advance into Gettysburg. All of the officers had been killed or wounded and the regiment was commanded on the 4th by First Lieut. John H. Milliman who was wounded on the first day. The regiment went into battle on the first day with 220 officers and men and sustained a loss of 179, and had eight color sergeants killed or wounded.

Upon arriving at Cemetery Hill, the Regiment, then under command of Lieut. White and numbering only 60 men, was deployed as skirmishers in the outskirts of town. The regiment remained on the skirmish line all that night and until 2 p.m. the next day, sustaining an additional loss of fourteen men from rebel sharpshooters who were posted in houses fronting our position. At that hour, it was ordered to support a battery on the hill and remained exposed to a terrific artillery fire until evening, when the firing ceased and, under the cover of the smoke, the rebels made a desperate charge and succeeded in gaining the very crest of the hill. Among the batteries the fighting was hand-to-hand and, for a few minutes, it was the most sanguinary of the campaign. The rebel charge was led by Hays' and Hoke's brigades of Early's division, with Gordon's division in reserve. They first struck Von Gilsa's brigade which was posted behind the stone fence at the foot of the hill. Ames' brigade was driven back to the batteries where it made a stand with the artillery men, the latter fighting with hand-spikes, rammers, and staves. The smoke of the battle was so thick that with the increasing darkness it became difficult to distinguish friend from foe; at this junction Carroll's brigade came to Ames' relief and the enemy, finding they were about to be overwhelmed, retreated in confusion. Our guns opened a most destructive fire and the slaughter was terrific. Out of 1,750 men of an organization known as the "Louisiana Tigers," only 150 returned from the charge. Within thirty minutes from the time the charge was made, the smoke had cleared away and the moon had risen with great brilliancy, flooding the Battlefield with mellow light. General Ames reformed his lines and extended aid to the hundreds of rebel soldiers lying wounded inside our lines. It was a ghastly battlefield.

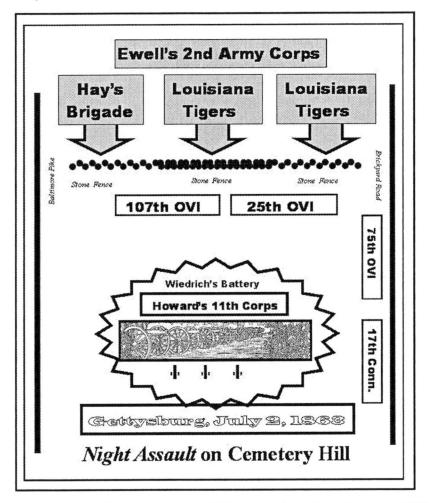

Hay's Brigade of Early's Division Night Assault on East Cemetery Hill

Editor's Note: An excellent account of the struggle for Cemetery Hill is found in <u>Gettysburg, Culp's Hill & Cemetery Hill,</u> *by Harry W. Pfanz, University of North Carolina Press, 1993.* [5] *In it, he refers to the assault on Cemetery Hill:*

"The Louisianans forced the Ohioans on the left back up the hill toward Weidrich's battery. Lieutenant Jackson of the 8th Louisiana wrote that they 'fotched up' at the stone wall manned by Yanks that did not wish to leave, but with bayonets and 'clubbed guns,' drove them back even though by this time it was so dark they could not tell whether they were shooting their own men or not. Sgt. George S. Clements of the 25th Ohio remembered the Jonnies charging down the hill from the left and toward him. They 'put their big feet on the stone wall and went over like deer, over the heads of the whole…regiment, the grade being steep and the wall no more than 20 inches high."[38]

Battles and Leaders of the Civil War
Hay's Louisiana Brigade assault upon East Cemetery Hill

* * * *

The history of the third day is well known; the terrific musketry, the deafening roar of artillery, the desperate assaults of the enemy, will never be forgotten by those on Cemetery Hill. The Regiment suffered severely from sharp-shooters, as it still occupied the advanced line.

* * * *

Editor's Note: In a letter from Edward C. Culp published in the summer of 1863 by the <u>Norwalk Reflector</u>, the young lieutenant who was serving as an aid to Gen. Ames gives a graphic description of the bombardment. The air "was resonant with the angry shrieks of shells. The battle of Chancellorsville was a mere skirmish compared to the scene which now took place. Gen. Hunt, chief of Artillery for the army said it was the heaviest cannonading that ever took place on this continent.

One shell burst within twelve feet of where Gen. Ames and staff were standing, killing four men and wounding eight."[38]

Colonel Andrew L. Harris, appointed 2d Brigade commander, 1st Division, 11th Corps following the July 1 disaster at Barlow's Knoll, presents an excellent overview of the disposition of his command during the three days of fighting at Gettysburg in his July 5, 1863 report. Col. Harris was also commander of the 75th Ohio Volunteer Infantry. On the eve of the second day of the battle, the troop strength of the 25th Ohio was less than sixty men.

*   *   *   *

Colonel Andrew L. Harris, 2d Brigade commander, 1st Division, 11th Army Corps:

SIR: In compliance with your request, I lay before you the following facts in regard to the different positions and the part taken by the Second Brigade, First Division, Eleventh Corps, in the battle of Gettysburg: I assumed command of the brigade in the afternoon of the 1st of July, and took my position, by order of General Ames, at the stone wall on the right, and nearly at right angles with the Baltimore road, throwing a heavy line of skirmishers into the edge of town. During the night a few random shots were fired; but early in the morning of the 2nd the enemy attacked my skirmishers, firing from behind the fences and the brick-kiln on the right, and from the houses on the left. This continued until near sundown, when the positions of the different regiments of the brigade were changed to that designated in the diagram yesterday. In moving the Seventeenth Connecticut Volunteers to the extreme right and front of my line, their place at the wall was left vacant, thus endangering the left flank of the Seventy-fifty Ohio Volunteer Infantry and the right flank of the Twenty-fifth Ohio Volunteer Infantry. Before I could make any arrangements to remedy this breach in the line, the attack of the enemy on Cemetery Hill was made, and I was forced back by superiority of numbers, with heavy loss. After the repulse of the enemy, I took up a position at the stone wall in the rear of and parallel with the one occupied the previous day, my left resting on the Baltimore road. Before day on the morning of the 3d, I was ordered to move to the right along the wall until I joined the First Brigade, and to throw a strong line of skirmishers to the front, which was done. At daylight my skirmishers commenced a heavy fire upon the skirmishers of the enemy, which \they replied to with vigor. This was kept up the entire day, in which my command suffered severely. Early on the morning of the 4th, I was ordered by General

Ames to throw my brigade forward into town, which I did, finding but few of the enemy remaining, who were easily made prisoners. I may safely add that the Second Brigade was the first to enter the town of Gettysburg after the battle. While in the town, Colonel Noble arrived, and assumed command of the brigade.[39]

*　　　*　　　*　　　*

The following is a list of the casualties during the three days fighting:

KILLED—Private James E. Clifford (A), Privates Wm. Elliger, Joshua t. Brown (B), First Sergt. John W. Pierce (C), Corporal John Frey (C), Private Martin V. Barnes (C), Sergeant Charles Ladd (E), Privates David Highman, Samuel Twaddle, John Tweedle (E), Charles V. Harrison, William H. Gulick (G), Hiram M. Hughes (E), Edward T. Lovett (I), Lieut. Lewis E. Wilson (K), Private Thomas Dunn (K).

MISSING—Lieut. Col. Jere. Williams, also wounded. *Co. A.* Sergt. James Melon; Privates Theodore Carter, William Gallaher, Thomas Gallaher, Joseph Gallaher, Wm. Hughes, John Kent, Elias Baile, Philip Gable, John McConnell, Wilson S. Colby, Issac C. Patterson. *Co. B.* Sergt. Slater B. Brock, Corporal John H. Twaddle; Privates John C. Duff, Abraham Hayden, William M. Lowther, Samuel Prescott, Augustus Fierhelder. *Co. C.* Privates Alex. E. Holland, Wm. Hamilton. *Co. E.* Sergts. Elisha Biggerstaff, Hiram Odell. *Co. F.* Sergts. John F. Thompson, Basil C. Shields, John H. Saunders; Corporals Thoms Nolan, John Tucker, Josiah O. Curl, Gustav Kolby; Privates Patrick Burk, Thomas Burchfield, Samuel Crawford, George W. Cooper, Henry Grier, James McConnell, Wilson H. Patterson, David P. Scott, James L. Shields. *Co. G.* Sergt. William J. Kyle; Privates Leonard W. Gaddis, Eli F. Beard, Hohn A. Perky, Ephraim H. Lewis, Jacob Lips, John J. Cummings.*Co. H.* Lieut. H. H. Moseley; Lieut. William Maloney; Corporals John T. Painter, William L. Smoot; Privates William Davis, William Chadwick, James A. Roland, Isaac N. Young, Oscar J. Dunn, Maurice Donahue, John W. Stephens. *Co. I.* Sergt. Howard Hallett; Corporal John Bunting; Privates William Shaw, John S. Rhodes, Kins. Davis, Reuben E. Gant. *Co. K.* Corporal John Baker; Privates George S. Frazier, Sumner B. Felt, Jonathan Raney, Thomas O'Neil.

WOUNDED—*Co. A.* Capt. Nat. Haughton; Privates James E. Clifford, Hohn Lebold, Simon L. Voorheis, Daniel L. Tyrrel, James G. Whittle, William White, James Russell, Samuel McCrumb, Robert Creighton, Nathaniel Wallace,

Adolph Weidebusch, John McKirahan, Thomas W. Fowler; Corporal Michael Murray; Sergt. Samuel R. Stewart. *Co. B.* Lieut. George M. Martin; Corporal Samuel B. Hurd; Privates Fred J. Bick, Duncan Highman, William N. Long, John J. Moore, Samuel N. Rhynard, James Snyder, William R. Bowman, Sylvnus Ullum, Anthony Wheeler. *Co. C.* Capt. Nat. J. Manning; Privates Joseph Dixon, Francis Schonhart, Jesse W. Campbell, Marion T. Thornlberry, James B. Henthorn. *Co. E.* Capt. Capt. John t. Wood; Sergts. Alex. Pemberton, Vincent Carroll; Privates William R. Stump, William R. Taylor,Bennager Odell, Richard D. Phelps, Abednego Stephens, Henry Smuck, Lewis Zeigler, Samuel H. Deselms, James Bacon, Samuel Edgar, Frederick Schultz, Peter Molyett, Thomas Howell. *Co. F.* Corporal Edward Barrett; Privates James Conway, James Saunders, Hugh Wilson, David Williams. *Co. G.* Lieut.. John H. Milliman; Sergt. Andrew D. Stewart, Adolphus Meyer, Thomas Cuthbertson, William Miller, Joseph Dyerman, Oliver C. Longmore, *Co. H.* Sergts. John Milton, James B. Hyler; Corporal John S. Dunn; Privates Levi McLaughlin, Newton Livezey, John Gellespie, Michae l Danforth. *Co. I.* Sergts. Samuel J. Brooks, Jacob L. Barnett, John H. Johnson; Corporals Joseph Cunningham, Samuel G. Shirk, Zachariah Dailey, John N. Rhodes; Privates James E. Bigford, Samuel T. Calland, William Gant, Lorenzo D. Hill, Archeleus Lingo, Stephen Loveall, Henson True, Archeleus Wiley, William F. Wiley, Harrison Shaw, Isaac M. Harper. Co. K. Sergt.G. H. Palmer; Corporal Reuben Drippard; Privates Charles T. Mehollen, Charles Chollette, Charles H. Conger.

Many of the missing were killed or afterwards died of wounds.

*   *   *   *

Editor's Note: The cost in human life and suffering was high for both Generals Meade and Lee, however the local citizenry expressed great relief when the Army of Northern Virginia began its withdrawal from Gettysburg. The 25th Ohio was the first regiment assigned to proceed cautiously into town on July 4th to assess the presence and strength of the Confederates. As Lt. Edward Culp was riding down York Street, he observed "The inhabitants were overwhelmed with joy at what they called their delivery...I found [Lieutenant John] Wood gazing out of a window and looking ridiculously happy. He is severly wounded in the arm. I went in the house and he introduced me to a Mrs. Culp. She was taking care of half a dozen of our wounded men in her own house."[40]

*   *   *   *

On the afternoon of July 5th, the Regiment with its division left Gettysburg in pursuit of the rebels and marched through Emmittsburg, Frederick City, Middletown, Boonboro, and Hagerstown to their main army.

From Hagerstown the Regiment marched to Williamsport and, from thence via Hagerstown to Berlin, where it crossed the Potomac on the 19th day of July and reached Warrenton Junction on the 25th, having marched 160 miles since leaving Gettysburg.

$*$ $*$ $*$ $*$

Editor's Note: The Spirit of Democracy, in the absence of it's war correspondent and editor, Major Jere Williams, published a brief report on the Gettysburg engagement which most certainly spread fear and apprehension in the local community. Companies B and C consisted of primarily of Monroe County residents. This was typical of Civil War enlistments. Friends, family and neighbors served together in the same regiments; however, when disaster struck, an entire community would go into mourning.

$*$ $*$ $*$ $*$

This gallant regiment which took part in the battles of Gettysburg, form the report which we have received, is nearly annihilated, being all killed, wounded or prisoners. The privates including one commissioned officer, to the number of 68 were taken prisoners and paroled. Lieutenant Col. Williams commanding the regiment and Lieut. Mosely are prisoners. Captain Manning is wounded in the thigh, Lieut. Martin had his arm shot off. Lieut. Wilson killed.

Although we ought to have had full particulars by this time, this is all the information we have received.[41]

We have received no list of killed and wounded in the 7th Virginia regiment.

Will war alone, unaccompanied by either moderation, wisdom or statesmanship restore the Union? It is so certain that in this land of liberty and free speech, no one can be permitted to doubt it without being arrested.

This is the position of John Brough.[42]

$*$ $*$ $*$ $*$

Chapter 9

Transferred to the Department of the South
Veteran Organization
Return of the Old Flags to Governor Brough

The Regiment remained in camp at Warrenton and vicinity until August 6th when, with its division, then under command of General Gordon, it was placed en route for the Department of the South and was disembarked at Pawnee Landing, Folly Island, South Carolina, the Regiment then numbering seventy-two men and commanded by Lieut. John H. Milliman.

The brigade, once more under General Ames, was placed in the entrenchments on Morris Island and took part in the siege of Fort Wagner. After that fort was captured, the brigade was moved to a healthy location on Folly Island and permitted to take the rest it so much needed.

The Regiment was rapidly recruited, many men having recovered from wounds received at Chancellorsville and Gettysburg rejoining their companies, and some new recruits were received. Captain Haughton returned on the 20th of August and took command of the Regiment, being soon afterwards promoted to major. Captains Wood, Manning, and Randall, having partially recovered from wounds, rejoined the Regiment about the same time; but the gallant and genial Lieutenant Martin lost his right arm with his fourth wound and was honorably discharged.

Head Quarters 25th Regt. O. V. I.
Folly Island, S. C.
Oct. 9. 1863.

Special Orders
No. 4.

All kinds of Gambling, or gaming for money, Treasury Notes, Sutlers' Tickets, or other thing of value, by any person connected with this regiment, is hereby strictly prohibited, and hereafter any one who shall be engaged in gambling will be severely punished.

Non-commissioned officers will report to their company commanders any violation of this order that may come to their knowledge in their respective companies, and failing to do so, they will be held equally guilty with the parties violating this order, and be subject to the same punishment.

Company Commanders will promulgate this order to their commands; and they are specially charged with its execution.

By order of
Nat Haughton, Major
Comdg 25th Ohio

National Archives and Records Administration

Major Haughton issues order, warning of improper use of off-duty hours

On the first of January, 1864, the Regiment re-enlisted as a veteran regiment. The original term of service would have retarded its muster-out until June 14th; but the patriotism which induced the men to enlist early in the war had not been dimmed by hard and continuous service. Indeed, several were rejected by the rigorous medical examination on account of wounds having been received which would have incapacitated them from another severe term of service.

The members of the Regiment who did not re-enlist were to be transferred temporarily to some other Ohio regiment serving in the department.

At the time considerable ill-feeling was manifested towards those who chose to serve out their original term of service before again enlisting. But want of patriotism could not properly be charged against those who had served faithfully nearly three years and many of whom had received wounds in their country's service, because they wanted a longer rest than the thirty days veteran furlough. Indeed the majority of them afterwards re-enlisted in the Regiment and others in regiments organized in Ohio before the close of the rebellion.

Before the Regiment left on its veteran furlough, some trouble arose regarding the terms of re-enlistment. The distinct understanding between the Government and the officers and men of the Regiment was that the latter should leave the department as a regimental organization, with its flags. After the muster-in was completed, the department commander issued an order for one-half of the Regiment to leave on furlough at a time, the organization to be retained in the department. Such an infamous violation of the agreement was received with surprise and anger. Major Haughton rode immediately to headquarters, and finding the muster-rolls still lying upon the table, seized them and, stepping to the fireplace, was upon point of throwing them into the fire when the department commander and mustering officer came into the room. In a few words he told them of the disreputable breaking of the agreement and insisted that, if the Government could not keep faith with its soldiers, he wanted nothing to do with it and would burn the papers. He left headquarters with transportation for the entire Regiment and, on the morning of the 15th of January, it left this old camp, and was escorted to the landing, three miles distant, by the 17th Connecticut, as fine and brave a regiment as there was in service, and between which (with) the 25th the utmost harmony and good feeling always existed.

After friendly greetings were exchanged between the two regiments, the 25th was embarked on the Mayflower and at 2 o'clock P.M., left the dock giving a farewell cheer to the 17th, which was heartily returned.

The Regiment arrived at Hilton Head on the morning of the 16th of January and, on the 17th the baggage and men were transferred to the Cambria, and at 4 o'clock on the same afternoon left the harbor of Hilton Head for New York City.

The passage was a stormy and dangerous one and, but for the admirable sea-going qualities of the ship, and the efficiency of its courteous commander, Capt. Sumner, we would have been lost off Hatteras. We reached New York in a badly shattered condition on Thursday evening, January 21st. On the next day we crossed to Jersey City and, on the same day, took a special train on the Atlantic & Great Western Railroad for Cleveland, Ohio, where Major Haughton was ordered to halt the Regiment.

The ride on the Atlantic & Great Western Railroad is a pleasant reminiscence in the history of the Regiment. Everything possible was done to insure comfort and, at the McHenry House in Meadville, a sumptuous and free dinner was provided for the entire Regiment.

The splendid treatment received in Pennsylvania prepared the Regiment for a hospitable reception in Cleveland; but the men were too sanguine, and either over-estimated the loyal impulses of its people, or they were poorly represented by the men in power.

The train was stopped some distance from the depot, and the Regiment disembarked in mud nearly knee deep. A staff officer of Colonel Center came to the train after some time and informed Major Haughton that good quarters had been prepared at the rendezvous camp, but a short distance from there.

With hopes somewhat revived, the Regiment waded through the slush and mud into the dismal camp where the "good quarters" were, and found a few miserably dirty cabins which had been used as depositories for filth of all kinds by occupants of other quarters near by. There were no stoves, no fire-places, no wood and no rations. We had nothing with us to eat and had tasted nothing since the late breakfast, or early dinner, at Meadville. The night was bitterly cold to add to the discomfort.

Captain Sanford of the 128th Ohio, himself a resident of Cleveland, came to see us and expressed surprise and regret at such treatment, condemning it in the strongest terms. He said that the services of his regiment had been tendered Colonel Center to assist in preparing quarters for us, and to receive the Regiment in a proper and cordial manner; but that officer (who, by the way, was only a political parasite of Governor Brough, and never saw any service in the field) pompously refused the offer, stating that he, as commanding officer of the camp, had made suitable provision for the reception and care of the Regiment.

Captain Sanford volunteered his services to pilot us to the Cleveland Grays' armory where, by his and Colonel Hayward's influence, good quarters were provide for and also an excellent supper at the principal hotels in the city. After the men had been provided for, the regimental officers were invited to Richards' restaurant where a game supper awaited them with a bountiful supply of champagne to wash it down. These two gentlemen were indefatigable in their efforts to sustain the hospitable character of the city and succeeded admirably.

The next day was rather more pleasant and the Regiment returned to camp where, after a hard day's work at cleaning up, passable quarters were secured.

On the 3d of February the Regiment was paid off and furloughed with orders to report at Camp Chase, Ohio, in thirty days.

The following is the roster of the Regiment upon its veteran organization:

Colonel—Wm. P. Richardson, commanding Camp Chase, O.
Major—Nathaniel Haughton, comd'g Regiment
Lt. Col.—Jere. Williams, prisoner in Libby prison
Surgeon—Louis G. Meyer
Asst. Surgeon—Wm. Walton
Adjutant—Edward C. Culp
Quartermaster—David R. Hunt
Sergeant Major—Hezehiah Thomas
Hospital Steward—Oliver W. Williams
Com. Sergeant—Joseph C. Coulter
M. Sergeant—Phineas Gano
Prin. Musician—Benjamin F. Gilmore

Company A

First Lieut.: Israel White
Second Lieut.: Wm. F. Bloor
Sergeants: Burget McConnaughy, Samuel R. Stewart, Thomas H. Ferrell
Corporals: Thomas W. Fowler, Wm. H. Criswell,
         Michael Murray, Geo. W. Iden, John McKirahan
Musician: Geo. W. McBride
Artificer: Henry Lambert

Privates:

Joseph Acres, Alexander Barrett, Andrew J. Beall, Joshua Burkhead, Daniel J. Crooks, John Conway, Theo. H. Carter, Robert M. Fulton, Andrew Fulton Charles Hoober, James Justus, John W. Kent Josephus S. Kinney, John McConnell, Thos. McBride, Emanuel L. Riley, Levi Ryan, Ignatius Tillett, Simon L. Vorhies, John Wyer

Company B

Sergeant: James A. Driggs
Corporals: John O. Archbold, Garwood P. Lacey, Samuel
Prescott, John H. Twaddle
Privates:
Isaac Beaver, Thomas Cain, John C. Duff, Augustus Fierhelder, John M. Hinds, Patrick L. Hamilton, Ralph T. Jeffrey, Wm. M. Lowther, Wm. N. Long, Newton Mercer, Samuel Rhynard, Sylvanus Ullum.

Collection of Tom J. Edwards
Sgt.JamesA.Drigg, Company B

Company C

Captain: Nathaniel J. Manning
Sergeants: Samuel T. Hutchinson, Uriah Province
Privates: Wm. H. Tatton, Benoni Bennett, Albert J.
Cavanaough, Wm. Fallan, George Henderson,
James B. Henthorn, Jeremiah Hicks, John Hull,
Isaac Johnson, Jacob H. Loveall, Isaiah Masters,
John Walton, Peter Yoho.

Company E

Captain: John T. Wood
Second Lieut.: Geo. N. Holcomb
Sergeants: Elisha Biggerstaff, Oliver P. Hershey
Corporals: Fred. Halderman, Wm. R. Stump, Thomas Howell
Wagoner: Joseph Hess

Privates: Henry Barnup, James Bacon, Howard Carmon, Samuel H.
Deselmns,Frederick Gillyer, Harvey N. Hall, Richard Kinney,
John Leary, Peter Molyett, Wm. Mackey, Peter Miller, Hiram
Odell, Richard Phelps, Alfred F. Stump, Fred. Schultz,
Edward J. Teeple.

Company F

Lieut. (1st): Edward C. Culp
Second Lieut.: Joseph H. Hollis
First Sergeant: Solomon Ebersole
Sergeants: John H. Sanders, John H. Viete
Corporal: Florence Ariman
Musicians: B. F. Crabill, Samuel M. Forrester
Privates: John Brownlee, Israel Brown, Geo. W. Cooper, James Conway,
Samuel Crawford, Thomas Evans, Thomas Long, Israel Miller,
Stephen Point, John Pool, John Sorrels, Wm. F. Shannon,
John Tucker, Hugh Wilson.

Company G

Captain: Carrington E. Randall
First Sergeant: John P. Lininsparger
Sergeant: Wm. F. Kyle
Corporals: Francis A. Lumbar, James F. Williams, Isaac Troxell.
Privates: Eli F. Beard, W,. Burgess, George Bare, John N. Cline, Joseph Dyerma,
Richard Farmer, Geo. W. Griling, Leonard W. Gaddis, John R. Hill,
Elijah S. Karns, Jacob Lips, Oliver O. Longmore, Ephraim H. Lewis,
Aldolphus Meyer, Thomas J. Meyers, John G. Sparks, John Steel,
Charles Silcox, Matthew Teach.

Company H

Second Lieut.: Wm Maloney
First Sergeant: Wm. L. Fouts
Sergeants: John S. Dunn, Geo. S. Clements, Thomas. J. Barclay
Corporals: Eli Pyle, Theodore Timberlake, John Gellespie,
Wm. Barrell
Musician: Wm. W. Fogle

Privates: Wm. Gellespie, John W. Grier, John Hiatt, Blair Kincaid, Lelvi
McLaughlin, Silas Noland, James A. Roland, Henry H. Sutton, Thomas
B. Sheets, Wm. Work.

Company I

First Lieut.: Isaac M. Kirk
Second Lieut.: Sam. W. Houston
First Sergeant: John S. Snyder
Sergeant: Samuel J. Brooks
Corporals: Samuel G. Shirk, Jehu M. Rhodes, Joseph H. Wilson, Zachariah
Dailey, John M. Bunting, Kins. Davis, Wm. H. Shaw
Privates: Benjamin Barlow, Thomas H. Bunting, Wm. C. Barlow, Wm. H.
Beymer, Charles A. Baker, James W. Calvert, Samuel T. Callin, Elisha
Dunn, George M. Dobbins, Reuben E. Gant, Hollis Hutchins, Noah H.
Lindsey, Archeleus Lingo, James W. McWilliams, James McBride, Joseph
S. Oliver, John S. Rhodes, Secenca C. Rogers, Harrison Shaw, Wm.
Smith, McDonald Thorla, Isaac Wilson, Wm. F. Wiley, Arthur
Wharton.

Company K

First Lieut.: John H. Milliman
First Sergeant: Wm P. Scott
Sergeant: Peter Triquart
Corporals: August Knack, James R. Smith
Wagoner: Austin Haughton
Privates: John Baker, Charles A. Debolt, Sumner B. Felt, George S. Frazier,
James W. Hall, ClarkKelley, Morrison, Lewis, Deville Nelson, Thomas
O'Neil, Charles A. Smith, Henry J. Willing

Most of the Regiment was in camp on the 5th of March and orders had already
been received to proceed to South Carolina which was a great disappointment
to the men as they had become disgusted with the red-tape ideas of the
Department of the South and wished to try their fortunes in the old Army of
the Potomac.

It was not until the 15th of March that the Regiment became perfectly organized, as many new recruits had joined, and one entire company from Norwalk

and Toledo. It was assigned as Company B, and the following is the roster of the company as mustered into service:

Captain, Luther B. Mesnard.
First Lieut., Charles W. Ferguson; Second Lieut., Alexander Mattison.
First Sergeant, Ethan W. Guthrie; Sergeants: David McGuckin, James McGuckin, B. Volney Howard.
Corporals: Moses D. Grandy, Lorenzo D. Haley, Benjamin F. Welch, Leander Taber, Dwight K. Smith, Theodore S. Williams, Henry Benson.
Musician, Quinby Batdorf
Wagoner, Bristol Haughton
Privates: George W. Smith, Charles H. Hastings, Samuel A. Wildman, Darius H. Odell, George Burke, Clayton T. Danforth, Wm. Holman, Ira B. Sturges, Lafayette Curtis, Sewel C. Briggs, D. W. Angel, Charles Andrews, Benjamin Benson, George Benson, Charles R. Benson, William Benson, Martin Brown, Charles R. Bailey, Reuben Bemis, John bowers, Joseph Barat, Wm. H. Cleveland, Victor Catlin, Wm. H. Coit, Noah Chriestlieb, Gaylord Cowles, David Cunningham, Levi H. Derby, Edmund C. Davis, Oscar Easterbrook, John Foughty, David, K. Gauff, Andrew J. Goodell, John H. Green, Jacob Hunt, Wm. Howard, Joel Hadley, Geo. Hastings, Gideon M. Jones, Gideon Kellogg, Franklin Keith, Edward Kelley, Porter Knight, James R. Knight, David Kinney, Geo. Lindeman, Albert Lockhart, Eugene Marsh, Hardin D. Marsh, Chas. McGuckin, John McLaughlin, Wm. R. Norton, Michael R. Newton, Gilbert Osborn, Geo. Osborn, John Perdu, Enock Porter, Geo. W. Plummer, Jeremiah O'Ragan, Isaac Reckner, Lowel Reese, Peter Roberts, Hiram S. Shuman, Nelson Shutt, Abram Starkey, John W. Starkey, Joseph Skinner, Geroge Stevens, Nathan Sturges, Edward Stebbins, Edward Soper, Geo. W. Tanksley, Levi Whiteman, John Wahl, Joseph N. Watros, John Wheeler, Elijah C. Walsworth.

On the morning of the 16th of March, 1864, the old flags of the Regiment, that had passed through the fiery ordeal of twenty battles, and under whose folds eighteen color bearers had been killed or wounded, were presented by Col. Richardson to Governor Brough to be placed in the flag room of the State capitol. In turn, the Governor presented the Regiment with a beautiful new stand of colors for future service in the field.

*   *   *   *

Editor's Note: In 1970, the Ohio Historical Society (OHS) began to restore and photograph its extensive collection of 500 battle flags used by Ohio troops in five

(5) wars. Color copies of these original flags may be obtained from OHS upon request at a modest fee. The OHS also accepts contributions in its continuing effort to restore regimental flags.

*   *   *   *

Chapter 10

Leaving for the Front—Disappointment— Once More in South Carolina—Along the Picket Line

**Lt. Col. Nathaniel Haughton
Commanding,
25th Ohio Volunteer Infantry**

Col. Richardson still remained in command of Camp Chase and Major Nat. Haughton retained command of the Regiment which left Columbus on the day of the presentation of the flags and arrived at New York via New York Central Railroad on the morning of the 19th.

In New York the Regiment was quartered in the city park and while there old Companies B and C were consolidated as "C" company, both being below the minimum.

While awaiting transportation to South Carolina, the orders were countermanded and the Regiment ordered to report immediately to Maj. Gen. Casey in Washington and, in compliance with that order, left New York on the morning of the 21st. Philadelphia, always among the foremost cities in patriotism, furnished the Regiment a royal meal at one of the soldiers' homes, and Baltimore did the same the next morning, near the place where the mob fired upon the Massachusetts soldiers, on the 19th of April, nearly three years previous.

The Regiment marched through Washington on the 23d of March, passed over Long Bridge, and was once more on the soil of old Virginia, and in great humor at escaping more service in South Carolina. This feeling was short lived, however, for without participating in any of the movements toward Richmond, orders were received to return to the Department of the South and, on the 22d of April, the Regiment was embarked at Alexandria on the "Admiral Dupont" and, after an unusually pleasant voyage, reached Hilton Head on the 26th, and the same day anchor was dropped in its capacious harbor.

After two or three days of delay and a variety of conflicting orders, the Regiment was taken to Seabrook Landing on Hilton Head island, and five miles from the Head, where it relieved the 52d Pennsylvania.

The headquarters of the Regiment were established at Seabrook Landing and in the house on the old Seabrook plantation. The picket line extended for nine miles along Skull Creek and Calibogue Sound. Those waters varied in width from seventy to three hundred yards and the immediate islands on the opposite side were considered neutral territory.

On the 29th of April the following disposition was made along the picket line: Companies A, I and C at Seabrook; Company E, Capt. John T. Wood at Fort Mitchell; Company H, Lieut. Wm. Mahoney, at Pope's Plantation; Companies F, K and G, Capt. C. E. Randall, at Jenkins Island; Company B, Capt. L. B. Mesnard, at Spanish Wells.

*   *   *   *

Editor's Note: At this point in the history of the 25th OVI, the regiment consisted of many veteran soldiers who re-enlisted rather than leaving the service at the end of their original three year enlistment; in addition to about 300 new recruits. The feeling of patriotism and camaraderie had not waned in spite of the terrible toll taken by the war. It is best expressed in the feelings of newly promoted Sgt. Samuel Shirk, of Company I, a twenty-three year old, 5' 11" red-headed blacksmith from Summerfield, Ohio. Records show that Sgt. Shirk was wounded at 2nd Bull Run, Gettysburg and Honey Hill, SC. On the eve of his venture into South Carolina, Sgt. Shirk expresses his feelings about his role in the Union cause to his friend, Morrie Danford.

Sgt. Samuel Shirk, Co. I,
(to friend Morrie Danford)
March the 14, 1864

...Give my respects to the family, also to all good union people that is true to their country and we will try and close this war this summer. I am willing to rune the risk of loosing my life. If <u>I do</u> I am noe better than <u>those</u> that has fell in defence of there country. I am now in favor of freeing eve culored man in the South. Makes noe difference what it cost. If it cost money and blod, let us wipe out Slavery and be done with such instiution fore all. I bleave we are reaping our reward fore what has bin Dunn....[43]

＊　　　　　＊　　　　　＊　　　　　＊

Seven companies of the 32d U.S. C. Troops were ordered to report to Major Haughton, and were placed in various detachments along the line to assist in the arduous duties.

During the hottest part of the summer, the 32d was removed and the heavy duties of the entire line devolved upon the 25th. Although the various posts were reduced to the least number, the men were on duty every other day, and frequently for several days in succession. This constant strain upon the nearly every member of the Regiment had been prostrated.

Lieut. Col. Jere. Williams, who had been taken prisoner at Gettysburg, returned to the Regiment, but almost immediately resigned and was succeeded by Major Haughton, who had well earned his promotion, having served with gallantry and distinction in the Regiment since its first organization, when he entered with Company K, being junior first lieutenant in the command.

On the 6th of May, Capts. N. J. Manning and E. C. Culp were sent to Florida for the members of the Regiment who did not re-enlist as veterans and were temporarily attached to the 75th Ohio. The men were found at Jacksonville, having just returned from a raid into the southern part of the State. They were anxious to rejoin the Regiment and meet their old comrades. They had seen some service and behaved creditably, always keeping up their identity as "25th Ohio men." The detachment did not reach the Regiment until the first of June and did not leave the Regiment for Columbus, Ohio, where they were to be mustered out, until the 17th of July, several weeks over their time.

Several officers went home with the detachment, being honorably mustered out of service. They were Surgeon Louis G. Meyer, Capts. N. J. Manning, and John H. Milliman, and Lieuts. Joseph H. Hollis, Samuel W. Houston, Wm. F. Floor, John S. Snyder and Wm. Maloney. They had all served honorably and with the exception of Surgeon Meyer had been promoted from the ranks. The loss of the latter officer was universally lamented by the entire Regiment. He came out as its first surgeon and remained faithfully at his post until the

Tom J. Edwards' collection
Ass't Surgeon Eli M. Wilson

expiration of his term of service, never having accepted a leave of absence. The self-denial he exhibited at Chancellorsville, when he allowed himself to be captured in order to take care of our wounded who were left upon the field, will never be forgotten by those whose lives he saved, or by the comrades who sorrowed for their wounds. After a few weeks vacation passed in traveling of the Pacific coast, he returned to the field with a new organization, and remained on duty until the close of the war.

He was succeeded by Assistant Surgeon Wm. Walton, who had joined the Regiment shortly after the second battle of Manassas; and E.M. Wilson came to us from Ohio as assistant surgeon.

Captain Manning also returned from the field, after a short vacation, as field officer in a new regiment, and served with credit until the close of the war.

On the 22d of August Lieut. Col. Haughton (*Editor's Note: Nathaniel Haughton held the rank of Major at that time*) went north after recruits and the command of the Regiment devolved upon Capt. John T. Wood. He retained command but a few days when a severe family affliction caused him to resign, and he left the Regiment on the 2d of September.

By Capt. Wood's resignation the Regiment suffered another severe loss. He entered the service as a second lieutenant of Co. H and was the only remaining line officer of the first organization. He afterwards entered the service as a major of the 180th Ohio and served with honor and promotion.

*   *   *   *

Editor's Note: A newspaper clipping in the Wood family records recorded, "...carried a shattered arm from the battle of Gettysburg, and died in Kansas City hospital in 1887, at the age of 55, after long suffering a victim of his wounds in battle." Captain Wood proudly bore his responsibility, re-enlisting as a Major in the 180th

OVI within days of his resignation from the 25th Ohio, in August, 1864. The 180th Ohio regiment was assigned to General Schofield's 23rd Corps was pushing it way west in North Carolina to provide supplies for General Sherman's exhausted troops. After the Battle of Wise Forks, NC Major Wood was promoted to Lt. Colonel, filling the vacancy of Lt. Col. Hiram McKay who died of wounds received in that battle. Col. Wood's strong commitment to preserving the Union, as well as his disenchantment with politicians and citizens who would not support the sacrifices of troops in the field, is best expressed in his letter to his mother November 24, 1862:

Captain John T. Wood, Company E, 25th OVI:

...The Rebels seem to think there is still hope for them as Van Buren and Seyman of New York are both in favor of a Separation. And I myself think that so long as such men are allowed to go at large, & make speeches in favor of traitors to the cowards and misers and weak kneaded men at home, who are all to do the voting. While the soldier in the field who is true to the union is disfranchised and looses his citizenship simply because he is a soldier & fighting the Rebels. I say that my opinion is, that as long as this is allowed there will be no prospect of a successful termination of this war. I am in favor of a Military Dictator instead of President & making an issue between the peace party & the war party but the whole country under Martial Law allow Soldiers the Elective franchise in its fullest sense, and the person who either by word or deed condemns the doings of the war party arrest them for treason & punish them accordingly. I am confident that as long as the Civilians at home have the views of government this war will not end, at least not while Lincoln is in power & if it lasts until his administration is out it will be a disgraceful peace...[44]

*   *   *   *

After Capt. Wood's resignation the Regiment passed under the command of Capt. C.E. Randall who was soon afterwards promoted to major.

*   *   *   *

Editor's Note: In the aftermath of heavy combat, there was a lull in hostilities and Major Haughton found it necessary to maintain discipline, since some of his soldiers were inclined to diversions which were not appropriate for military protocol. In September, 1863, Major Haughton issued Regimental Order No. 4 warning his men about the evils of gambling.

*   *   *   *

National Archives and Records Administration
Major Haughton's Regimental Order #4, *No Gambling or Gaming Allowed*

Major Nathaniel Haughton's Commanding, 25th OVI
Regimental Order #4 (transcript):

All kinds of gambling or gaming for money, Treasury Notes, sutler's tickets, or other things of value, by any person connected with this regiment is hereby strictly prohibited, and hereafter anyone who shall be engaged in gambling shall be severely punished.

Non-commissioned officers will report to their Company Commanders any violation of the order that may come to their knowledge in their respective companies, and, failing to do so, they will be held equally guilty with the parties violating this order, and subject to the same punishment.

Company Commanders will promulgate this order to their commands, and are especially charged with its execution.

By order of Nat. Haughton, Major, Comd'g 25th Ohio

*   *   *   *

On the 25th of September, Capt. E. C. Culp, Co. A, was ordered to Fort Pulaski with Companies A, K and G, and remained there until October 23d, when he was ordered to rejoin the Regiment with his detachment, and the next day the entire Regiment was relieved from duty on the picket line and ordered into camp a short distance from Hilton Head for the purpose of recuperation.

On the 2d of November Lieut. Col. Haughton returned to the Regiment bringing nearly 300 recruits, including one entire company, which was assigned as D. The following is its roster:

Captain, Wm. W. King.
First Lieut., Maurice S. Bell; Second Lieut., Wm. McFee
First Sergeant, David H. Connell; Sergeants: Robt. Thompson, Theo. Van Guntly,
George Wasoner, David M. Hammond.
Corporals: Oliver V. Haycock, Wm. S. Porter, Manuel Stevens, Jacob B. Keyser, James L. Kemper, Wm. Cornwell, Daniel Fox, Judson K. Taylor.
Musicians, James A. combs, Jefferson Schloott.
Wagoner, John E. Oyer.
Privates: Henry Bixler, Wm. Bixler, John Bixler, Benjamin F. Bixby, M. Walland Batty, Geo. M. Beaty, Samuel Baker, Wesley Baker, David Bandy, Geo. N. Borgart, Haynes Burkhart, James W. Barnhart, Album Cluff, Wm. A. Cluff, John Burns, Wm. Cook, Charley Coy, Amos. J. Connell, Frederick Corbian, Hiram C. Copper, Thomas S. Crawford, John Carrigan, John Carruthers, Ezekiel Eklerberry, John Evans, Jacob Eddy, Isaiah Edgey, David Flower, Joseph Faulk, George Fagen, Linford Fisher, Samuel Harley, Isaiah Harley, George Hardinger, John S. Hague, Barclay B. Haycock, David Henderson, Zacharias Harrison, Jacob Hoover, David S. Marsh, Wm. H. Jones, Tish Jackson, Alpheres Keller, Daniel Kramer, John E. Kobb, John Koonse, John Kauble, Joseph Love, James P. Legin, Geo. W. Long, James Langan, Julius H. Laughlin, Godfrey Myer, Joel Minlen, John Miller, James Martin, Thomas L. Manley, Richard B; Manley, Wm. H. Mann, John R.

Nelson, Louis Olovet, Emmit D. Porter, Harris Peters, Wm. Patterson, Geo. Peaver, Martin Perkins, Wm. Reading, Thomas Riddle, John Ralson, Matthew G. Ritchey, Benjamin Right, Olando Shine, Geo. Sunholder, Michael Shaffer, Levi R. Stump, Walter B. Taylor, Jonah Terflinger, Benjamin Walton, Wm. Weber, Thomas Northington, Newton Whetstone, Jacob Ziller.

By the energetic recruiting of Lieut.Col. Haughton, the Regiment once more presented a good line, and a systematic course of efficient drilling soon placed it in excellent condition. In addition to the regular camp duties, the Regiment furnished daily fatigue details to work on Fort Howell, which was situated a short distance from camp.

*   *   *   *

Editor's Note: Col. Nathaniel Haughton was appointed commander of Company C of the 25th Ohio Volunteer Infantry November, 1861 and served in this capacity until August 25, 1863 when he was promoted as commander of the 25th Ohio regiment. He served as regimental commander through October, 1865 at which time he assumed command (provost duty) of the 1st Sub District of Western South Carolina, a position he held until the muster out of the 25th Ohio regiment in 1866. In addition to earning promotions through the ranks, Col. Haughton distinguished himself as a "brave and efficient soldier" at the Battles of Boykin's Mills and Statesburg, SC in April, 1865 and for this was breveted as a full Colonel by Major General Quincy A. Gillmore, Headquarters, Department of the South. Then, June 24, 1867 the US War Department breveted Col. Haughton as Brigadier General "for gallant and meritorious services during the war." Col. Haughton was also wounded severely in the right arm on the first day's fighting in the Battle of Gettysburg, taking him out of action for thirty days. Adventures for Col. Haughton started early in life. A lifelong native of Toledo, Ohio, Haughton joined one of the first overland expedition to California in search of gold at the age of 16. Upon his return to Ohio, he attended college at Michigan State Normal School, returning to set up a dry goods business in Toledo before the outbreak of the Civil War. After his return to civilian life, Col. Haughton returned to Toledo and established the Haughton Foundry and Machine Company, pro-ducing steam engines, mill equipment, and general machinery. By 1880, Haughton became active in the manufacture of elevator equipment The firm became incorporated as Haughton Elevator and Machine Company, with control remaining in the Haughton family into the twentieth century until the passing of his son, Irving N. Haughton. The company became one of the largest of its type in the United States and was subsequently purchased as a subsidiary by Swiss-based

Tom J. Edwards' collection
1899 25th OVI Reunion, Haughton Memorial

Schindler Elevator Corporation in 1979, subsequently being renamed Millar Elevator Company in 1990. Col. Haughton also worked as a waterworks department inspector. He was active in local civic and political activities, often seen leading the old-time torchlight processions and was remembered as "always the moving spirit in the parades and always took charge of the marchers." Col. Haughton always held true to his roots of military leadership. He was the junior vice commander of the Toledo Post of the Grand Army of the Republic and a member of the Union Veterans Union. Col. Haughton died at the age of 65, following complications which set in from a severe fall on the icy pavement. He had just retired thirty days prior to his death. His "moving spirit" and "take charge" disposition characterized this dedicated man both in peace and at war. As noted in the headline of his January 31, 1899 obituary (Toledo Blade), "The Old Warrior passed to his reward." Tribute was paid to Col. Haughton's memory by the veterans of the 25th Ohio by placing his image on the Reunion ribbon at the regimental gathering September 21, 1899 in Col. Haughton's hometown of Toledo, Ohio.

✳　　　✳　　　✳　　　✳

Chapter 11

Honey Hill—Gregory's Landing—
Deveaux's Neck

Several expeditions had been organized during the summer, some of them in connection with the navy, but all of them had been attended with poor success. In fact, with the exception of the first expedition to the Sea Islands, and the rather barren honors resulting from the Morris Island campaign, the "Department of the South," from a military point of view, was a magnificent fraud and reflected no honor upon the commanding general of the troops.

However, with Sherman's grand army rapidly approaching the coast, it became necessary for a cooperation movement to take place from the seaboard with the Charleston & Savannah Railroad as an objective point. Accordingly, the "Coast Division" was organized and placed under the immediate command of Gen. John P. Hatch.

The expedition left Hilton Head on the 28th of November with the usual pomp attending all such movements in the department; but several steamers ran aground that night and it was not until the next afternoon that the troops were landed at Boyd's Neck on the mainland.

The same evening the column moved forward towards Grahamville, but became bewildered in the darkness and, at midnight, encamped near a church. The next morning the march was resumed, the 25th Ohio in advance, and the enemy early discovered. Companies A and B were deployed as skirmishers, and the Regiment placed in line of battle, with a wing on each side of the road. Col. Haughton, with the right wing, was directed to drive the enemy from their position by a flank movement. He succeeded in doing it and, returning to the line, the Regiment advanced steadily in support of its skirmishers.

The rebels retreated to their works on Honey Hill and the brigade, under Gen. E. E. Potter, moved forward to carry the position. The 25th was placed upon the extreme right of the second line, the formation being column by division.

Moving rapidly forward, the Regiment overtook the first line, and heavy firing commenced on the left. Colonel Haughton deployed his regiment in support of the 144th New York.

A charge was at this time ordered, but owing to a deep swamp in front, the first line was considerably broken up in crossing. Col. Haughton took his regiment through the swamp in perfect order and the sight of an unbroken front, backed by a well directed volley, caused the rebels to give way. At such a moment, prompt and efficient action from sell-drilled and willing troops means certain victory. Col. Haughton rapidly changed front forward on tenth company and understanding that the 144th New York would support him, moved up the hill, through an almost impenetrable thicket, and under a terrible fire formed his regiment within two hundred yards of the rebel works, for the purpose of charging their position which at that time was comparatively weak. But certain victory was lost by the eccentric movements of the 144th New York, which fell back to its line, a very safe place, leaving the 25th entirely without support.

The rebels, taking advantage of this grave blunder, to call it by no worse name, re-enforced their left and, under a murderous fire, the 25th sustained its position for nearly an hour, when a regiment of colored troops came up on its left and the 32d colored troops on the right.

Col. Haughton seeing the futility of maintaining the line at such a sacrifice, rode to the commanding officer of the regiment on his right, and urged him to swing his regiment around so as to face the enemy, and move forward to his (Col. H.) support, while he charged the enemy in front, and thus accomplished by desperation what might have been done at the commencement of the battle with but slight loss. But the department troops were unaccustomed to fighting in real engagements and the colonel commanding the 32d, with the excuse that he had received no orders for such a movement, refused to comply with Col. Haughton's suggestion.

With no one on the field to give orders, and no support whatever, the colonel knew that the day was lost; and recognizing the uselessness of longer maintaining his position with such heavy loss, he withdrew the Regiment in perfect order to the first line of battle. The Regiment was nearly out of ammunition, but received a supply in time to check an attempted flank attack. After dark the troops were withdrawn from the field, and to the cover of the gunboats.

Thus ended the battle of Honey Hill, fought without a plan, without commanding officers near enough to give intelligent orders, at the will of regimental commanders, and most of them too timid or cowardly to use decent judgment. Had the old "second brigade" been together, it would have been swept over Honey Hill and regarded it as a joke. At it was, the loss to the 25th was very severe, more than in all the other regiments combined and, without any compensation, excepting to show the department troops what an old "Army of the Potomac" regiment could do under fire.

Sixteen commissioned officers and one hundred and eleven enlisted men were killed or severely wounded. The names of those slightly wounded do not appear in this report; if so, it would swell the number to over two hundred.

KILLED—Major Carrington E. Randall; Adjt. John C. Archbold, Lieut. Austin Haughton (C). Lieut. Ethan W. Guthrre (mortally wounded), Color Sergt. August Knack (K), Co.. A—Privte Thomas G. White. Co. B. Sergts. Moses D. Grandy, Henry Benson; Private Michael R. Newton. Co. C—Corporal James Redgeway; Privates James M. Henthorn, J. E. Eastman, George Wright. Co. D. Two men, names unknown. Co. E—Jeremiah Mackey. Co. H—Corporals Eli Pyle, John Gellespie, Oscar J. Dunn. Co. K—Privates George Shuse, John Bowers.

WOUNDED—Co. A. Sergt. James Justus; Privates William T. Hughes, Samuel T. McClelland, Charles Kline, Eli Navarre, James McCormick. Co. B—Lieut. Alex. Mattison; Corporals Theodore S. Williams, Benjamin R. Welsh, Dennis H. Odell. Privates John Perdu (mortally), Lowell Martin Brown, Gideon M. Jones (mortally), Joseph N. Watrous, William Holman, Enoch Porter. Co. C— Lieut. Isaiah Masters, William H. Batton; Privates G. Clapper, J. Conolly, John Henderson, W. Louther, C. H. Lockwood, James W. Monroe, Dias Markee, Albert Reed, William Steed, Alfred Vance. Co. D—Lieut.M. S. Bell and seventeen enlisted men, names unknown. Co. E—Sergt. Thomas Howell (mortally); Corporals Harvey N. Hall, Edwards J. Teeples; Privates Howard Cameron, Oscar Cotant, Frederick Gilyer, Jeremiah Grant (mortally), John Miller, Daniel Potter, Daniel Kniceley, John Schoup. Co. F—Sergts. John Tucker, Hugh Wilson; Privates Eli Stiles, Frank B. Adams, Simon Keck, Hohn W. Shotwell, Spencer F. Andrews, James Wagner, NelsonThorp, Elbridge Scott, Jacob Crossley, Andrew J. Crossley, Lucius Moore. Co. H—Lieut. Hez. Thomas; Sergt. George S. Clements; Corporal Theodore Timerlake (mortally); Privates Artilus Musgrave, Ruel Noland, William A. Barell, Samuel M. Gillespie, Thomas J. Barclay, Thomas B. Sheets, John W. Grier. Co. I—Capt. Israel White; Sergts.

Samuel G. Shirk, Joseph H. Wilson; Corporal Benjamin F. Brown; Privates Michael Consadine, David McMeen, James N. Moore, Hugh Schullen (mortally), Charles R. Thompson, Arthur Wharton, Jacob Wanzel. Co. K—Capt. Charles W. Ferguson; Lieut. Peter Triquart; Corporal James S. Grim (mortally); Privates John P. Linden, Fred Conrad, Joseph Bierschmidt, Fred. Richards, Charles A. Smith, Charles W. Smith.

Eric Barkhurst collection
Cpl John Gilespie, Co. H
25th Ohio Volunteer Infantry,
killed in the Battle of Honey Hill

Although the 25th Ohio took the most prominent part of any regiment in the battle, and its losses exceeded that of all the other regiments combined, at least in its brigade, it was not mentioned in any of the dispatches or official accounts of the action. Lieut. Col. Haughton was the only regimental commander in the action in our brigade who showed himself capable of handling a regiment under fire and having absolute control of it. His name was not mentioned in the dispatches; yet the colonel of every other regiment in the brigade was breveted brigadier general, presumably for meritorious conduct in the battle. This was only a continuation of the petty jealousy against the "regiment from the Army of the Potomac."

*   *   *   *

Editor's Note: It is interesting to view the Honey Hill engagement from the perspective of different levels of command, beginning with the 25th Ohio's commanding officer, Lt. Col. Nathaniel Haughton's report on the November 30 action. Following this battle description will be that of Company B commander Capt. Luther Mesnard and Company B non-commissioned officer Corporal Samuel Wildman..

Lt. Col. Nathaniel Haughton, commanding, 25th OVI:
Regimental Report, December 3, 1864

...About 9 a.m. we left the White Church, the One hundred and twenty-seventh New York in advance, taking the road toward Grahamville; had moved but a short distance when the enemy opened with a battery in front. I formed my regiment on the right and left of the road in line of battle, to support the advance of the One hundred and twenty-seventh New York. Moved forward until the advance was checked and the long grass in front (fired) by the enemy. My regiment then moved forward the right wing farther to the right and the left wing farther to the left to avoid the burning grass—and met a division of the enemy on our right; the rebels soon fell back. I then moved to the road and advanced by the flank until their batteries opened from a second position; I then formed the right of a second line on the right of the road. Moved steadily forward by the right of companies until the first line—composed of the Thirty-second U.S. Colored Troops and part or all of the One hundred and forty-fourth New York—was fired upon with musketry. This caused the first line to waver, and the Thirty-second fell back in considerable confusion. I immediately formed line of battle, and charging through the Thirty-second and a portion of the right of the One hundred and forty-fourth New York, we drove the enemy from the cross-road in confusion, with, however, doing him much damage, as the wood and brush were so thick that we could not see him when within fifteen or twenty yards, and I did not venture to fire for fear some of our men might be in front. Unexpectedly we came out on the cross-roads, where I rapidly formed my men, the Thirty-second arriving and forming on our right, and a portion of the One hundred and forty-fourth New York on our left; there was no firing in our front, but I could still hear firing to the left. Thinking I had gained an advantage over the enemy, was anxious to profit by it. I immediately sent an officer with some men to learn his position and see if his flank could be pressed. Receiving a favorable answer, I at once made a half change of front on my left company and moved forward into the woods about 80 or 100 yards, where we met a strong line of rebels; here a severe fight took place. We held our line till our ammunition was completely exhausted, even stripping our dead and wounded of the contents of their cartridge-boxes and borrowing of the Thirty-second U.C. Colored Troops, which rather tardily came up on our right, but did not swing far enough to support me sufficiently to warrant my making another charge, as the fire was more severe on my left and center than on my right. Even had I been supplied with ammunition, I consider that it would have been imprudent to remain longer, as I found during the engagement that my immediate left was entirely unsupported. Under these circumstances, I thought it best to retire; and notifying Colonel Baird of my intention, I about-faced my regiment and moved slowly back to the cross-road, there receiving ammunition. The enemy showed little disposition to advance, and made no attack on our line while there. Soon after dark I received orders to fall back.[45]

*   *   *   *

Editor's Note: At the beginning of the Honey Hill engagement, the 25th Ohio Volunteer Infantry, the regiment consisted of 1,532 men; 1,164 seasoned veterans, 350 one-year enlistees and 18 draftees. It was one of the few experienced regiments among many newly formed Coastal Division units. The 25th experienced heavy casualties at Honey Hill. Their dedication and commitment to their mission is aptly demonstrated through the words of those who fought shoulder-to-shoulder under Lt. Col. Haughton's direction; Company B Captain Mesnard, 2d Lt. Hugh Ballantine, and Corporal Samuel Wildman.

Diary Excerpt from Capt, Mesnard's diary, 1864:

Tom J. Edwards' collection
Capt. Luther B. Mesnard, commanding, Company B 25th Ohio Volunteer Infantry

....I had carried a musket over 3000 miles, and felt ready for a commission...went to Columbus, was assigned to the 25th Ohio Veteran Volunteer Infantry. Was commissioned and mustered as Captain of Company B, therein March 16th, 1864. Sent to Washington via New York City. Was at Camp Distribution a few days, then by board went to Hilton Head, S. C., where the regiment was stationed at the inland side of the island. My Company was first at Pope Plantation for a few days, then stationed at the "upper" post, Spanish Wells, opposite May river, and in sight of the spires of Savannah.....

I had at first a company of 101 green men, in a veteran regiment, noted as hard fighters, and a tough lot of fellow and I was very anxious about the standing of my company in the regiment.

Taught my boys from the first to keep their places, mind their P's and Q's and allow no one to tread on their toes. That they might better be in Purgatory, than become the butt of that regiment. I drilled the men very little—very few hours—compared with the drilling I had in my early service. I had non commissioned offers schools, etc.. The drills were short and sharp—the boys young, intelligent and quick to learn.[46]

Toward fall we were inspected by a regular army captain and surgeon, General Hammond. The Colonel, Nat. Haughton, had been up to see me twice about my preparing for this. I said little but made sure that everything was right. When the day came the 1ˢᵗ Sergeant detailed for guard the awkward or ill shaped men, and about nine o'clock some half dozen officers rode into camp in style. The Colonel thought I should go out and see to the Company, but I was quiet, saying to the inspecting officers, wheresoever they wished it the Company would be formed. At the orders of the first Sergeant the Company fell in a way I was proud of, and as the Sergeant saluted—"Sir the Company is formed," I took charge, and put them in shape for inspection. The first two files were six feet two inches in height, and models of perfection. The Captain as he took the gun of the first man never looked at it, but admiringly ran his eye over the man, <u>Henry</u> <u>Benson,</u> one of the finest men physically, I ever saw and every inch a soldier. Well he examined every man, every gun, every button in the company, but not a speck of dirt or dust, not a button or thread was wrong and the way the boys handled those guns and themselves made me feel proud of them. Then the Doctor or Surgeon inspected them, and when the boys "unslung knapsacks" and opened them up it was like a machine, every man rose or straightened up at the same time, I never saw another company that could do it as they did that day. And those knapsacks! Every one had the same clothing in sight, clean shirt, drawers and socks, nothing else. The blankets all rolled the same, and all in alignment. All the men had their hair cut, ears and neck clean and answered all questions about rations, camp equipage and duties, right up plain. While the officers looking on said "That's fine," "I never saw it done better" At dinner later, the old surgeon say's to me, "Captain I have a compliment for you. You can feel proud of it as long as you live." I said "I shall be glad to receive it Sir." He said "I have been in the regular army many years and inspected many thousand men, and I say to you, you have the finest company of men, I ever saw I want to know where they raise such men." I said, "Up in the northern Ohio on the western reserve." The Inspecting officer spoke, "I think General there is much in the way those men have been handled I said, "Thank you." And now after nearly forty years I still feel proud of those boys. The Colonel was greatly surprised and pleased.[47]

All the forces on the Island were soon after assembled at Hilton Head, where we had battalion drill and my boys were among the best, and at officers school, evenings, the Colonel was greatly pleased to find me "up" on everything. We had a grand review of all the forces and soon started on a campaign leaving tents, etc., behind. Were to have left the harbor at daylight to go up Broad

River. At nine o'clock we were still in the harbor, on transports mostly aground as the tide was out, but finally got off and just before dusk landed a few miles up the river and marched some six miles inland, camping near a church. Some firing in front. Next morning turned to the right past the church toward Honey Hill, went a mile or more. Some firing in the front all the time. Some artillery shot coming down the road as we march along the side in the open timber. Soon four guns of ours whirl past us, and a few rods ahead unlimber and open on the rebs. A shot takes the captain's leg off, and knocks a wheel off one of our guns. The Captain is carried back past us, his leg dangling by a chord, his life blood spurting in jets as we cross to the other side of the road. My boys had been under fire but once before and then at long range when at Spanish Wells, and not worth mentioning, and <u>now</u>, they were much affected. Two or three vomited from sheer fright, while all, even the old veterans, looked very solemn. We deployed and were in the second line of battle, as we advanced. It soon became hot and the colored regiment in front hesitated, and I suggested to Colonel Haughton that we take the advance which we did through dense timber and bushes, where we could see nothing. It was hot, the shell over head and the bullets like hail, and soon a line of rebs seemed to rise in front of us, give us a volley and run. This staggered my Company and one or more companies to our right. As the men started to the rear I jumped ahead of them and started them forward again. I passed my former 1st Sergeant now <u>Lieutenant</u> <u>Guthrie</u> mortally wounded. I took his hand a moment, and this is the only time I ever remember of feeling bad in battle.[48]

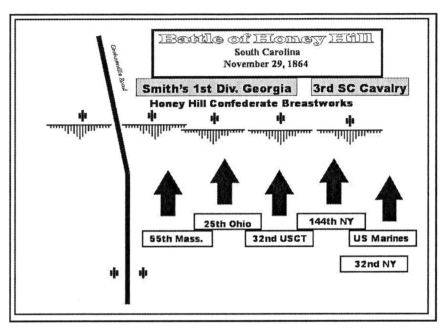

Troop Dispositions, The Battle of Honey Hill,
SC, November 29, 1864

The 54th Massachusetts Colored Regiment was at our left my company being on the left of our regiment. The rebs had artillery (some seven pieces we have since learned) in a redout in our front, with breast-works for their Infantry, but owing to the timber we could see nothing. We had driven a line of battle which they had in front of, and below the fort or redout, back, some of my men being so close that the powder marks were about their wounds. The right of our regiment seemed to reach beyond their line, while still to our right was a full colored regiment—a lot of raw niggers, who would not advance, though scarcely under fire except artillery shot, mostly over head, and to the right of them were several hundred marines, who did not lose a man. The 54th Massachusetts on our left extended to the road or center of our line, but did not advance as far as we did by about eight rods. We halted and held this line nearer the enemy than any other troops. Getting short of ammunition I ran back to the flank of the colored regiment and got a thousand rounds box and distributed among my boys, and some twenty minutes later a colored soldier brought us another box, and we held our own, but it was an awful hot place. We used all the ammunition as by rapid firing we kept the rebs down and as our fire slackened theirs increased. The Colonel then ordered us to fall back a few rods to a little cross road we had passed, which we did bringing the wounded. The day was hot, and I sat down with my back to a pine tree some six inches in diameter when a shell cut the tree off some twenty feet where I sat. The boys said I could jump farther and quicker from a sitting posture, than any other man. We lay in this position perhaps a half hour and then the whole force fell back, marching clear back to the landing. There were about two-thousand rebs sent out from Savannah, by General Hardee, and about eight-thousand of us, under command of General Hatch. The loss in my company was five men killed or wounded and twenty man wounded, a loss of fifty per cent of the men engaged. Loss of our regiment 126, killed or wounded, including Major and Adjutant killed. This was about one third of the entire loss on our side. Many of our troops were "white glove soldiers" who had done garrison duty only, and did not like the smell of powder. The 156th New York in the left wing lost heavily and did good fighting. Our troops were badly handled, no generalship, strategy or tactics. As a diversion in Sherman's favor the fight may have amounted to a little, but nothing to what it would have if we had brushed the rebs away and cut the Savannah and Charleston Rail Road, as we could have done under an efficient commander. When I saw the awful loss in my company, the useless sacrifice of noble men it seemed too bad. Lieutenant E. A. Guthrie, Sergeant Moses D. Grandy, Sergeant Henry Benson, that model soldier and others, gone forever.—Battle of Honey Hill, S.C. November 30th, 1864.

We lay at the landing a day or two. I was somewhat disabled. A ball, at Honey Hill, having torn away my boot just below my ankle, bruised my foot so as to lame it. An expedition was started up the river; being unable to walk, I was left in charge of the camp, but some ugly rumors coming back, I took the first boat and joined my company before night, about the time, Marsh of my company was killed by a cannon shot, the only loss in the company that day. Our position the at Deveaux Neck was near and within sight of the Rail Road and near enough to the rebs to have some fighting every day. Our regiment cut a swath through a strip of timber to give our artillery a better chance and had some brisk fighting on December 6th and 7th. We heard from Sherman's army here, and soon the rebs evacuated their strong position along the Rail Road including a couple strong forts, and we moved up to Pocataligo, where I heard from and saw some members of my old regiment, the 55th Ohio then with Sherman's army.

About February 1st, 1865 we started toward Charleston and had plenty of fighting, marching and skirmishing. Our regiment the 25th Ohio, was one of the best, in fact <u>the best</u> fighting regiment in the "Coast Division," and actually did most of the real fighting, making some very bad marches, often wading streams or bayou's waist deep........[49]

*   *   *   *

Editor's Note: On file in the archives of the Ohio Historical Society is the Wildman collection of original letters written by a father and his son who both served in the Civil War in different regiments. Son Corporal Samuel Wildman served as one of Capt. Mesnard's non-commissioned officers in Company B of the 25th Ohio Volunteer Infantry. A transcript of Corporal Wildman's letter written following the Battle of Honey Hill adds a fascinating additional view from the front lines of Capt. Mesnard's battle line.

*   *   *   *

Cpl. Samuel Wildman, Company B, 25th OVI
(letter to his father)
Boyds Landing, Near Pocataligo Bridge, S. Co.
Monday, Dec. 5, 1864

At last my <u>real</u> soldier life has commenced. I have "smelt gunpowder." Seen the smoke of battle, heard the crash of artillery and musketry, done my duties as well as I could in the front of battle al day long and come out unscathed.

A week ago to-day, the 25th Regiment left camp at Fort Howell and marched to Hilton Head, where we embarked immediately on the "Cosmopolitan," a large steamer, generally used as a hospital boat, but appropriated to transporting troops on occasions.

The harbor was full of transports loaded with soldiers, to the number of six or eight thousand, bound, none of us knew whither.

About three o'clock Tuesday morning, the expedition started. At first fortune seemed impropietous, for the whole fleet got into the wrong channel and at daylight we had no impropietous, for the whole fleet got into the wrong channel and at daylight we had not passed Seabrook Landing.

The fleet turned back to get the channel, and about half way between Seabrook and the Head. The "Cosmopolitan" ran aground on a sand bar and was passed by the rest of the squadron. After several attempts to get off the bar, during which we were assisted by the "Enoch Dean," the troops were taken aboard other steamers. Two or three companies of the 25th, among them Co. "B," took the "Nemalia" General Fosters flag ship and arrived at our place of debarkation about three or four o'clock, P.M., having passed two or three of the other steamers on our way.[50]

We were now at Boyd's landing where we disembarked, finding many troops already ashore. Long before this time we had surmised as our ultimate destination the Pocataligo Bridge, on the Charleston and Savannah RR. Several attempts have been made during the war to force a passage to this bridge and burn it, but all have failed thus far. I believe our troops had never until now effected a landing so near the bridge as this point.

We halted perhaps an hour and there started inland, the 127th New York taking the lead, followed by the 25th Ohio. We were divided into two brigades, under the command of Gens. Potter and Hatch. The 25th was in that of Gen. Potter. Union pickets had been stationed along the road to a considerable distance from the landing. I will not detail all the incidents of our march, which lasted till one or two o'clock Wednesday morning. We missed our way twice and were traveling much of the night on the wrong road. At the time mentioned, we halted at a church, stationed at cross roads only about four miles from the Landing.

Just at daylight we were awakened by the firing of our pickets. It proved to be a false alarm, but we did not again lie down.

About seven o'clock, I think, in the morning of Wednesday, November 30th, we again commenced our advance, and soon found the enemy. A battery of their artillery was posted on the road in front and shelled us as we advanced. As soon as we ere near enough for their shells to begin to take effect, we formed in line of battle, the right wing of the 25th on the right of the road and the left wing on the left, in fields covered with tall, dry grass and weeds.

We continued to advance along these fields when the left wing found its onward course opposed by a dense wood. I cannot describe these South Carolina forests. They must be much like the chapparel of Mexico which I have read of, full of a thick under-growth of thorny vines, so dense that the eye can penetrate but a few rods into them, and seeming like an impassable obstruction in the way of a marching column. Even our skirmish line did not try to advance, but the whole line of battle halted a few minutes and then moved by the right flank to the road and crossed. I am describing, you understand, the movements of the left wing, only of the 25th, we having lost sight of the companies on the right of the regiment where we first separated from them.

Now we found ourselves on the right of the road, and again steadily advance, the shells of the enemy's battery bursting overhead, in front and in rear of us, but fortunately without effect. We soon found another obstacle to our passage, more invincible than the first. The high grass of the field had been set on fire between us and the rebels, perhaps purposely, perhaps accidentally, by the fire of the artillery. The wind was blowing in our faces, and the broad sheet of flame swept rapidly toward us, roaring and crackling in its onward course. Major Randall who was in command of the left wing of the 25th moved us by the flank to the other side of the road again, when we advanced in spite of thorny bush and rebel shell and shot. We relieved the skirmish line, which had been composed of the 127th New York, if I remember correctly, and pushed on.[51]

A battery of our own artillery unlimbered in the road on our right and we halted to await the effect of their fire. They opened on the enemy on a few well directed shots silenced the latter and removed the principal obstacle to our progress. The rebel battery fell back, we returned to the road and again moved forward by the flanks. The right wing of the 25th joined up and we were glad to learn that they had lost only one man thus far wounded.

Onward we still pushed undeterred by the occasional skirmishing in front, which became more frequent until, finally, there was an almost continual rattle of small arms. I hardly know how it commenced, but before I expected it, we were formed in line of battle, the 154th New York and 32d USCT on our right, and the 55 Massachusetts Colored Reg't on our left. The line extended, I know not now much further in both directions, but the regiments named are the only ones whose positions I knew. A tremendous roar of musketry had commenced along the line, but we steadily advanced, right into the tangled wall of vines and briers, which clung to us as we tore our way through them.

I was on the left of the 25th Regiment which had become badly mixed with the 55th Massachusetts, and, it is not surprising that I found myself among black faces instead of white, and totally at a loss to find the whereabouts of my comrades. I soon saw white men on my left and pushing through to them found that they were the right of the 144th New York Regiment. By this time I had been joined by two of our boys who had been separated from the 25th in the same manner as myself and were on the point of falling in with the 144th, when some on gave us a clue to the position of our regiment which we soon after found. All this time I think we had lost no men in our company, but we were not long to remain unscathed.

We advanced perhaps half a mile in the woods, which I think were somewhat more open than they had been before we reached the road, when at last our onward progress was stopped by a more determined resistance than we had yet met. We were before an entrenchment of some kind although the density of the woods prevented our seeing it at the time, and the rebels poured a murderous fire into our ranks. ~ Sergeant Grandy was shot down close to me, mortally wounded, and Lowell Reece fell nearer the right of the company, a bullet passing through his wrist, and wounding him in the face, as his hand was raised in the act of loading. Corporal Williams was wounded and carried to the rear and also William Benson and Orderly/Sergeant McGuckin, nearly at the same time. I think all within the first few minutes after our onward progress had been stopped, in front of the rebel fortification.

I saw upwards of an hour we loaded and fired, not in unbroken ranks, for we were fighting (loading and firing) every man for himself and on his own hook, standing, kneeling, or lying, according as the nature of the ground offered opportunities of "shelter."[52]

I saw Ira Sturges loading and firing a little way to my left, and joined him. He was standing behind a tree close to which Watros of Co. "B" and a man of another company lay Wounded. It was the hottest place I saw all day, the bullets cutting the grass, striking the trees, and whistling all around us. I examined Watros' wound and finding that he could walk with a little assistance, helped him a few rods to the rear and bound up his wound, a bad one.

Editor's Note: End of Part I

Part II

At length I find trying to continue my letter which was almost illegible from having been carried so long in a knapsack. (ed. Note: a few pages of the letter are heavily stained)

FRIENDS AND DESCENDANTS
OF
JOHNSON'S ISLAND

★

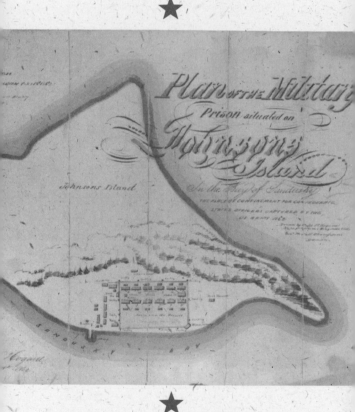

★

A non-profit organization dedicated to the
preservation and maintenance of the
Johnson's Island Prisoner of War Depot,
a Civil War prison recognized as a
National Historic Landmark.

MEMBERSHIP

Financial contributions help to preserve and maintain Johnson's Island for future generations. The following membership categories offer a way to become involved with the Friends and Descendants of Johnson's Island but gifts of any amount are always welcome.

Individual Member $25

Supporting Member $50

Contributing Member $100
    Gould Print (1864 map)

Charter Member $500
    Name on bronze plaque

Benefactor $1,000
    Name on bronze plaque,
    "Our Mess" numbered print

For more information about the
Friends and Descendants of Johnson's Island
or to make a donation, contact the following:

Friends and Descendants
of Johnson's Island
3646 Confederate Drive
Johnson's Island, OH 43440

E-mail: dbush@heidelberg.edu
Phone: 419-448-2327
Fax: 419-448-2236
www.johnsonsisland.com

I will continue where I left off in my description of the Battle of "Honey Hill."

Watros was wounded in the neck. I helped him a little way to the rear and made him as easy as I could. Returned to the tree where I had left Ira Sturges and commenced loading and firing as before. Sergeant Henry Benson joined us and talked a few minutes with me, telling he had just assisted John Perdue (badly wounded) off the field. While we still stood loading and firing another "messenger of death" struck Benson down in his tracks. He fell on his face without a word or groan. I turned him on his back, with his head on his knapsack and removed his waist belt, unbuttoned his vest, shirt, & c. He was shot through the lungs.

For some time this contest went on when our ammunition gave out and the battle line fell back in good order to the road, by the side of which there was a ditch and bank which served as an intrenchment.

Soon after dark, we retreated under cover of our artillery which shelled the rebel works far into the night. We moved silently back, past the church and cross roads and bivouacked at the Landing.

It had been a desperate fight for the numbers engaged. The 25th lost in killed and wounded and missing 162. Company "B" loss was three killed and nineteen wounded or a total of 22 our of 52 engaged—nearly half the company.

We shot away about 100 rounds of ammunition to a man.

~   ~   ~   ~

Thursday, Dec. 1st our regiment did nothing of importance. Went to the front ~ about two miles from the landing during the forenoon but returned without doing anything. Friday morning Gen'l Foster took the 25th aboard the "Nemaha" his flagship with the intentions of attempting the capture of a rebel shore battery some distance up the river, near Port Royal Ferry. There was so dense a fog that the expedition was given up and we returned to Boyd's....54

*   *   *   *

Early on the morning of December 3d, the Regiment received orders to prepare for an expedition and was embarked at 5 P.M. on board the steamers Nemaha and Plato, and proceeded across the Broad River and some distance up the Coosaw, but a heavy fog coming on the steamer was ordered back to Boyd's Neck.

On the next morning the Regiment took the same steamers, and after going some miles up the Coosaw disembarked on the mainland at a place since known as Blair's Landing, and marched towards the interior. After some little skirmishing, the Regiment succeeded in gaining the Beaufort road, in rear of the enemy, who abandoned their works, leaving two twenty-four pound howitzers and caissons. There being no transportation, Co. Haughton ordered one of the guns spiked and caisson destroyed. The other gun and caisson were hauled by hand to Port Royal Ferry.

On the morning of December 6th General Potter's brigade, of the Coast Division, was embarked on steamers, and proceeding up Broad River effected a landing on Deveaux's Neck, some ten miles above Boyd's Neck. The enemy's pickets retreated and our troops pushed forward rapidly, soon encountering the rebels in force, posted advantageously on the opposite side of a marsh which extended the whole length of their line.[55]

✷   ✷   ✷   ✷

Editor's Note: Corporal Samuel Wildman's letter to his father continued to relate the son's close encounter with enemy fire at Gregory's Landing.

Corporal Samuel Wildman, Company B, 25th OVI:

About noon of Friday, Capt. Mesnard, who was actg' as provost Marshall at the landing sent me to Hilton Head in charge of three rebel prisoners and two guards. Sunday morning, about daylight, the 25th was embarked on one or two transports and again started up the river to take the rebel battery before mentioned.

Landed about 11 o'clock, made a quick march and took the Jonnies in the rear. There were only about 40 of them and they got out of sight speedily. We took two twenty-four pounders and brought off one of them with us. Destroyed the other, together with a large amount of ammunition, a wall tent and c.

Made a rapid march without rest several miles to Port Royal Ferry and embarked on our transport which had come to the ferry to meet us. We had marched some seventeen miles during the day, and it was now about dark ~ steamer back to Boyds.[56]

Tuesday morning we, with several regiments of infantry, artillery, and marines took transports and about 9 o'clock A.M. arrived at Gregory's Landing three or four miles from our present location. We landed and immediately marched inland. Skirmishing soon commenced and a heavy musketry fire followed. A line of battle was formed, the 25th on the left.

Five or six of us on the left of Co. "B," deployed as skirmishers in the woods on a slight rise of ground, and halted, expecting an attack at that point. The attack was made, but on the right, instead of left and we skirmishers did not get closely engaged. The fire continued for some time when the rebel line fell back.

While I was in these woods I had one pretty close call. A German whose name I do not know, advanced a little way in front of the skirmish line to the lower ground, and I soon after followed him. We were moving along rather carelessly, when a shot was fired from a thicket a short distance in front, and my companion turned round with a cry of pain and rain back. He was shot through the shoulder. I saw that I was getting into pretty hot (close) quarters and turned back also. Another shot was fired and a bullet whistled near me. I turned round and saw a puff of smoke just rising from the thicket. I blazed away at it and then "skedaddled" back to the skirmish line.

We did not get with the rest of the company again for some time, as the line of battle advanced and the skirmishers on the left flank remained in the rear. When we joined the boys, they were lying in a field by the side of a road, the line having halted. The 25th was in two ranks, its left toward the enemy. I fell in, in my usual place.

The rebels commenced shell at us and some of them fell rather disagreeably close. Hardine D. Marsh of our company had his leg broken by a piece of one of them. He was the only man wounded in Co. "B" during the day.

We moved our position, so as to get out of range of the rebel fire and bivouached for the night.

Wednesday morning Dec. 7th, we fell back to the front of the slope on which the battle of Tuesday had been fought and intrenched. There was some skirmishing during the forenoon, but we were not engaged.

Last night the news was announced to us that General Sherman had invested Savannah and had already taken Fort McAllister by storm. We had quite a celebration over the news, guns firing, men cheering, bands playing, & c.[57]

*   *   *   *

The 127th New York and 25th Ohio were ordered to charge the enemy, and did so under heavy and well-directed fire. The 127th wavered some, but seeing the 25th moving steadily it rallied easily, and both regiments going in with a rush carried the rebel works in gallant style. The rebels retreated from their first line in disorder, but made a stubborn rally at their second line, on the west line of the Savannah and Charleston pike. Col. Haughton, seeing the advantage of immediate action, without waiting for support, charged the second line, and the enemy retreated, leaving all their killed and wounded on the battlefield. Some more skirmishing took place but, night coming on, the troops went into camp on the battlefield.

This action was called the battle of Gregory Landing. The Regiment sustained the following loss:

KILLED—Richard D. Faucett and George Volk (A), Hardin D. Marsh (B).

WOUNDED—Co. A—Lieut. Elisha Biggerstaff; Sergeant Geo. W. Iden; Privates Wm. Bodi and Harvey Wood. Co. C—Lieut. O. W. Williams, acting adjutant. Co. D—Capt. W. W. King; Privates Hiram Clapper and Josiah Kimball. Co. E—Privates Nathan Jump, Samuel Heminger. Co. G—Lieut. Samuel T. Hutchinson. Co. I—Privates Hiram Kiff, Ed. Whitford, and Martin Schmidt. Co. K—Lewis Pettel.

Lieuts. O.W. Williams and Samuel T. Hutchinson were wounded at Honey Hill a few days before, but would not report at the hospital after having wounds dressed, and neither were fit to enter this engagement. They came as volunteers. Lieut. Williams was shot through the bowels, and considered mortally wounded. He partially recovered, however, and is now (1883) living at Norwalk, Ohio, serving as treasurer of Huron County. Lieut. Huchinson was shot through the body, but finally recovered, and is now (1883) living in Ohio. Capt. King was severely wounded, and while being taken to Ohio, and near his home, met with a railroad accident, and was severely injured. He recovered, but never rejoined his regiment as the war was over before he recovered from his wounds.

On the morning of the 18th of December, 1864, a reconnaissance was made by General Potter and the enemy found strongly entrenched on the Charleston & Savannah Railroad and, supported by good works, mounting guns of heavy calibre.

General Hatch commanding the division, determined to cut a road through the woods to the railroad, and the next morning the 25th Ohio was selected for that purpose. Indeed, it is difficult to remember any special work in the department for which this Regiment was not selected.

A heavy skirmish line was thrown forward, supported by several regiments, and the 25th followed, felling trees in good backwoodsman style. A road had been cleared through a dense forest for over a mile when the skirmishers became actively engaged, and the 144th New York, after a few minutes firing, fell back. Col. Haughton immediately formed his Regiment, the men willingly giving up axes for muskets, and took the place of the New York regiment. Seeing nothing to shoot at, he ordered the men to kneel down; the grass was very high, and the Regiment was easily concealed. Supposing the federal forces had fallen back, the rebels came forward in heavy force, with the usual rebel yell. When within thirty yards of the 25th, Col. Haughton gave the command to fire, and a terribly destructive volley was poured into the dense ranks of the enemy, which sent them to their works in disorder. They opened a heavy fire through the thicket, and it became general along the whole line. Darkness put an end to the firing, and the troops were shortly afterwards withdrawn, going into a strongly-entrenched camp about two miles east of the railroad.

The skirmishing and battle of the day are called under the general name of the battle of Deveaux's Neck. During the day the Regiment suffered the following casualties:

KILLED—Co. D—Private James Barnett. Co. I—Hollis Hutchins. Co. K—John Hilt.

WOUNDED—Co. A—Privates W. D. Clark, John Behr. Co. B—Corporal Dennis H. Odell; Private George M. Plummer. Co. C—Privates William Prouty, George W. Morgan, John Masters. Co. D—Sergts. D. H. Connell, D. M. Hammond; Privates S. M. Burkhart, James Combs, John Ralston, John Koonse,

Levi Stump, E. Eckelberry. Co. E—Sergts. A. F. Stump, William Stump; Corporal Volney Dubel;; Privates James Harrington, Edwin Sharp, Edward Hinds, Conrad Leasch, Franklin Wright, Levi Shroyer, James Zimmerman, Christian Fosh, Aaron Alvord. Co. F—Sergt. Harvey D. Moore; Corporal Thomas Evans; Private James Hilt, Addison Lalcy. Co. G—Privates Eli F. Beard, Malcomb McFall, Lucius Moore, Jacob Lips, Amos D. Armstead, Lewsi Livensparger. Co. H—Privates Leroy Craig, Samuel W. Robinson, William Gillespie. Co. I—Private Lewis Engle. Co. K—Corporals Joseph Moore, George S. Frazier; privates HarveyJ. Williams, R. O. Burdo, John Pettis, Nathan Vold, C. Tieterman, Charles Ripkie, Philip Haszensahl.

*   *   *   *

Editor's Note: 2ⁿᵈ Lt. Hugh Ballantyne provides another view of the intense role played by the 25ᵗʰ Ohio in the Battle of Honey Hill in his letter and article published by the The National Tribune in 1919.

2ⁿᵈ Lt. Hugh Ballantyne, Company C, 25th Ohio:
(Letter to Editor, The National Tribune, August 1, 1919)[58]

Editor, National Tribune: A few words about Honey Hill and my recollection of it. In the first place, General Hatch was no good. We marched all night, Nov. 25, 1864 until 2 p.m. and that brought us back to a church, where we should have stopped early in the morning. We stacked arms, lay down behind a hedge fence and the next morning I knew our bugles sounded "Attention, Battalion! Get up and fall in; and when you get tired you can rest again," (you know what that means). We made coffee and had hardtack and sow belly then fell in. The next order was "Sling your knapsacks." So we piled them up and left a over them, and that was the last we saw of them. The next order was "Right about face, guard forward by the file left." Through an opening in that hedge fence across a road into that field of broom straw about neck high until we halted 200 yards from a church with a road between us leading straight to the guns of the 3ʳᵈ N.Y Battery, and took the road and it was about 40 feet wide. The left wing of our regiment, the 25ᵗʰ Ohio, left of the road and the right wing the right of the road. Co. A was thrown out as skirmishers on the right of the road, Co. B on the left. By this time it was 6:30 a.m., and the command "Forward March," was given. Of course, Co. A was a hundred yards in advance. We did not march more than 100 yards when the skirmishers were into it hot with the 12ᵗʰ Georgia. Laying in that broom grass we were kind of glad to see them. Co.

A captured three of them and sent them back, and that's how I know they were the 12th. We had met them before at Gettysburg July 1, 1863.

Say those Georgia boys were great fighters but they could not stand the bayonet. We charged them 3 times that day. But it was no good. You see we never stopped until we had those Georgia boys in behind Charleston and Savannah Railroad. We were in thick underbrush on the opposite side, and I don't know how far we were from the railroad, but it could not have been far. The underbrush was so thick you couldn't see 15 feet. And we stayed right there all day. Every time they raised that Rebel yell, Col. Houghton gave the command "Fix bayonets; lay down." We never said anything or fired a shot until they were within 20 feet of us, then we yelled, "Come on 25th, we are going to the railroad." Well, old 25th went right on to the railroad, but they couldn't hold it. Some were captured and hung right along the railroad. Gen. Hatch was taken out of that station about that time and Gen. Potter was our next commander. That man was alright. Fight anything to the finish and he called the 25th "Houghton's Walrus." He went from Georgetown to Camden, S.C. I don't see how any of us have lived so long.[59]

*   *   *   *

Chapter 12

Coast Division Campaign—Capture of Charleston

The first of January, 1865, found the 25th Ohio still an integral part of the Coast Division, and in the entrenched camp on Deveaux's Neck.

The Regiment had suffered severely since leaving Hilton Head, losing 208 officers and enlisted men killed or severely wounded. Over a hundred men had been slightly wounded who remained with the Regiment, and that number is not included in the above figures (Not a man had been captured, or left upon the field wounded), which would be swelled by the addition of over 300.

Some of the wounded officers were among the best in the Regiment, and would never return to it. Without exception, those officers killed had all earned reputations for bravery and efficiency. The death of Major Randall caused the promotion of Capt. E. C. Culp, of Company A, the senior captain in the Regiment.

The position of the Regiment at the Neck was anything but a safe one. The enemy encircled it on three sides, and the daily hissing of shell over the camp, and the constant picket firing, showed no intention on the part of the rebels to leave their strong position on the Charleston & Savannah Railroad. The trains ran regularly over the road in spite of our artillery which, only in a few instances, did any damage.

It was useless to get the camp and garrison equipment from Hilton Head, as at any moment we might be compelled to march inland, or retreat. The suffering among the troops was severe, as the only shelter was branches, leaves and dirt. But the light sand could not withstand the heavy rains. In these miserable hovels the men burrowed like foxes.

National Archives and Records Administration
Major E.C. Culp is takes command of the 25th Ohio
and seeks permission to acquire current regiment muster roll
at the Headquarters, Dept. of the South

On the morning of January 15th, the Regiment marched to the railroad, only encountering a few of the enemy. The works on the Coosahatchie and Tillifinney rivers had been evacuated the night previous. The railroad was destroyed by the regiment, for several miles, and at night we went into camp in the rebel fort on the Tillifinney. The 16th and 17th were fully occupied in burning ties and twisting rails. The right wing of Sherman's army was encamped but a few miles distant, and the 25th boys interchanged visits with their friends in several Ohio regiments. Two of the old divisions in the eleventh corps formed a part of the twentieth corps, and we met several of our old comrades.

The Regiment remained in the vicinity of Fort Tillifinny until morning of the 20th of January, when it marched toward Pocataligo, and encamped on the Salkahatchie.

On the morning of the 20th, a reconnaissance was made by the Regiment on the Savannah and Charleston Railroad, and the enemy found strongly entrenched on the opposite side of the Salkehatchie, having burned the railroad bridge in their front. Considerable firing took place, but resulted in no damage, and the Regiment returned to camp late in the evening.

The next morning the left wing of the Regiment, under Major Culp, returned to the position occupied by the Regiment the day before, and remained there until relieved by the 127th New York, when it rejoined the Regiment in the entrenchments at Pocataligo. The Coast Division was to occupy all the approaches to Charleston from the south, and press the enemy as much as possible, in order to keep a large force of the enemy in its front, and thus weaken the force in front of Sherman.

The Regiment remained at Pocataligo until the evening of February 3d, when it marched to Gardner's Corner, reaching that place at midnight. For a shore march, the men never experienced a more severe one.

On the morning of the 4th, the march was resumed to Combahee Ferry where it was intended to cross the Regiment and secure a position on the opposite side. A crossing was effected under a severe artillery fire. Rice fields extended for several miles up and down the river, and about one mile in width. On the verge of the fields the rebels had erected several earth works, which commanded all the approaches, which consisted principally of dykes.

*　　　　*　　　　*　　　　*

Editor's Note: Captain. Mesnard relates rather strong, unpleasant memories of the regiment's march to Charleston, noting his first real encounter with personal fear and the challenge it held for his position of leadership.

Captain Luther Mesnard, commanding Company B, 25th OVI:

About February 1st, 1865 we started toward Charleston and had plenty of fighting, marching and skirmishing. Our regiment, the 25th Ohio, was one of the best, in fact the best fighting regiment in the "Coast Division," and actually did most of the real fighting, making some very bad marches, often wading streams or baoyus waist deep. I remember one day my company, as usual, was on the skirmish line and had driven the enemy some miles, finally at "Indian Hill" they made a stand, laying down a rail fence and lying down behind the rails and earth thrown up. We fired at them a while and I sent a squad to the left to flank them and was about to charge up the hill as I know we could drive them, a rear guard only, and yet four to ten times the number in my company, but somehow I was nervous, was afraid, that's the word. I never was more so in my whole army experience. I did not let any one know how scared I was, not alone on my own account, but I knew that if we started up that hill some of us would fall.....[60]

∗   ∗   ∗   ∗

After the crossing was made, we attempted to turn the enemy's flank, but without success, and General Hatch ordered the place abandoned, and the Regiment to march to the assistance of the division, near the Salkehatchie. Three men were killed outright, and one dying in a few hours. There were: Robert A. Petrie and Rudolph Nihies (K), and William Compton (G).

The next day the general deemed it advisable to gain possession of some crossroads, three miles in advance, and the 25th was ordered to that duty, supported by two or three other regiments. The crossroads were gained, the enemy using their artillery freely, but without effect. They retired a short distance over a branch of the Salkehatchie, taking a strong position, after partially destroying the bridge.

During the night Col. Haughton advanced his pickets to the bank of the river, and Lieut. Kehn, with sixteen men selected from Companies I and C, all good rifle shots, were ordered to charge over the bridge, just at daylight, and get positions as sharpshooters, to protect the crossing of the balance of the Regiment.

Lieut. Kehn and his men made a gallant charge, but when in the center of the bridge they discovered, for the first time, that the bridge was destroyed for several rods on the rebel side. Lieut. Kehn took in the situation and ordered a retreat. Three men were severely wounded, but the charging party had nearly all secured cover before the rebels recovered from their astonishment sufficiently to fire. The wounded were: John S. Rhodes and Arthur Wharton (I), and Henry Schofield (A).

A considerable force was left here to keep the enemy occupied and, on the 9th the 25th, with a section of artillery, was ordered to march and, accompanied by Generals Hatch and Potter, once more crossed the railroad and penetrated some distance in the enemy's country among the rich rice plantations. Upon returning, the railroad was destroyed for a considerable distance, the enemy making their defense as usual with artillery, which did little damage.

On the 11th, Major Culp was ordered to take the left wing of the Regiment and return to the place occupied on the 8th. An attack was threatened at that point, which was only guarded by the 127th New York. Constant skirmishing was had with the enemy until late in the evening when the balance of the regiment came up and the entire command (25th Ohio) made a flank movement to Combahee Ferry, where a crossing was effected without loss, the demonstration farther up the river having caused the enemy to evacuate this point.

*　　　　*　　　　*　　　　*

Editor's Note: Captain Mesnard continues his recollections of the long, disputed march along the Cambahee River:

At the Cambahee River we marched twenty five miles down the river; did some brilliant fighting; marched back to the main army. General Hatch thought the rebs had evacuated the breast-works at other or north end of Causeway crossing marsh and river, and detailed the 25th Ohio to find out. Companies B and I were sent ahead under my command supported by the regiment. These two companies dashed into the road and along the Causeway to the bridge which had been entirely cut away. This was not more than a hundred yards—probably not over 50 yards from the breast-works which proved to be occupied by a thousan men or more, and they fired as fast as possible. We got back and out of the road with the loss of but two men, a great wonder to me always.[61]

*　　　　*　　　　*　　　　*

The Regiment encamped on the plantation of Mr. Lowdes. One more important crossing had been wrested from the enemy and now only the Edisto and Ashapoo rivers remained between the Coast Division and Charleston.

The next morning the Regiment left Lowdes' Plantation, and marched several miles to the Ashapoo without molestation. The rebels had destroyed both bridges and were in small force on the opposite side. General Hatch, who still accompanied the 25th, wished to obtain a footing on the rebel side before it was re-enforced, and Col. Haughton, with a few men, crossed the river in a small boat some distance up the river and drove the rebels from their position. The Regiment crossed that evening.

The next morning one or two other regiments came up, and the 25th was again sent forward on a reconnaissance to the forks of the Jacksonboro and Parker's Ferry roads, where it was ordered to halt.

The Regiment remained there until the next day, the 16th. Scouts were sent out for several miles without encountering any large body of the enemy, and the negros who came in reported that the rebels were evacuating Charleston. These reports were sent back to the general and permission asked to move on. It was not granted, however, and the same day the Regiment was ordered back to Ashapoo, where it remained until the morning of the 19th when it was once more ordered to take the advance, and marched to the South Edisto. A few scouting parties of rebel cavalry were met, but they did not impede the march.

On the 20th the Regiment marched several miles down the Edisto and finally crossed in flat-boats, without opposition. The 21st was spent chiefly in foraging; several abandoned rebel fortifications were discovered, mounting heavy guns. The march was resumed the next day to the North Edisto.

From this date the movements of the Regiments were of an eccentric character, until it was demonstrated to the most obtuse mind that the rebels no longer occupied the Palmetto city. For miles south of the Ashley river the country was covered with fortifications and hundreds of pieces of artillery fell into our hands—one of the results of Sherman's grand march.

On the morning of the 26th of February, the Regiment crossed the Ashley River, and marched through Charleston to the South Carolina Railroad depot where it went into quarters.

✶   ✶   ✶   ✶

Editor's note: Lt. Col. Culp's account of the 25th's entry and brief stay in Charleston does not touch on one significant event, restoring the United States flag at Fort Sumter. Capt. David R. Hunt, Quartermaster for the regiment, relates the symbolic raising of the flag by Major Robert Anderson in February 1865, in his 1903 article in the Ohio Commandry, Military Order of the Loyal Legion of the United States.

Capt. David R. Hunt, Quartermaster and Co's. E & F, 25th OVI
"Restoring the Flag at Fort Sumter," Ohio MOLLUS, February, 1865

"Major General Q. A. Gilmore was in command of the Department of the South, consisting of North and South Carolina, Georgia and Florida, with headquarters at Hilton Head. Major Genereal Cahs. Devins was in command of the District of South Carolina, with headquarters at Charleston. Brigadier General John P. Hatch was in command of the post of Charleston. I was Depot Quartermaster, in charge of Land and Marine Transportation; Disbursing and Purchasing Quartermaster of the Department, with headquarters at Charleston....[62]

We had been in possession of Charleston but a short time. About February 26th, 1865, the rebels evacuated and our troops entered the city. We had scarcely commenced our work upn the necessary repairs and rebuilding of the streets, depots, railroads an wharves. The city was in a dilapidated condition. Streets had been torn up, paving material had been used to construct batteries and works upon the bay fronts; trenches and earthworks surrounded the city, crossing the approaches and along the Cooper and Ashley Rivers; railroads had been torn up and destroyed; the depots, car-houses, locomotives and all rail-road machine shops had been blown up and destroyed by the Confederates as they evacuated the city. The streets were beds of sand. The portion of the city burned by the shells from the "Swamp Angel" during the bombardment was just as we had found it' so that the visitors would see this stricken city in its deplorable devastation, with few changes, as left by the Confederates when they evacuated Charleston.

My orders were to prepare for the reception, and care for the visitors, and to furnish quarters, land and marine transportation, and arrange for their enter-tainment.....The writer was selected as a member of a General Committee, which position, in connection with his duties as Quartermaster, placed him in close relation with all that occurred on that occasion...

.I might with propriety here remark that from the entry of our army to the months afterward many distinguished army and navy officials of our own and representatives of foreign governments, also citizens of the North and foreign lands, came to Charleston to examine the great defenses and wonderful engi-neering of the Confederate Government, made by General Beauregard at Charleston and upon the islands...."[63]

Harper's Weekly engraving, April 29, 1865
Original Fort Sumter flag raised again at Charleston

*   *   *   *

Editor's Note: Following the ceremonial April 14, 1865 raising of the original flag by Bvt. Brig. General Robert Anderson, a feature article appeared on the event in Harper's Weekly, *noting the significance of the occasion and participation by Henry Ward Beecher and General Anderson.*

"The old flag floats again on Sumter! Four years ago it was the hope, the prayer, the vow of the American people. To-day the vow is fulfilled. The hand of him who defended it against the assault of treason, of him who saluted it sadly as he marched his little band away, now, with all the strength of an aroused and regenerated nation supporting him, raises it once more to it place, and the stars that have still shone are undimmed in our hearts now shine tranquilly in triumph, and salute the earth and sky with the benediction of peace.

To be called the orator of a nation upon such a day was an honor which might have oppressed any man. It will not be questioned that Mr. Beecher did so. His oration is of the noblest spirit and the loftiest eloquence. It is in the highest degree picturesque and powerful. Certainly it was particularly fit that a man, fully inspired by the eternal truth that has achieved the victory, the opening of an era which is to secure it.

Even amidst the wall of our sorrow its voice will be heard and its tone will satisfy. Even in our hearts' grief we can feel the solemn thrill that the flag which in weakness is raised in glory and power."[64]

*   *   *   *

"We had a limited supply of flags and bunting. I used all I had in my department; we had borrowed all not in use from the navy, and we purchased all the red, white and blue material we could find in the stores—a very limited quantity—and with it made quite a show, with decorations more prominent at the several headquarters.

There was an anxious excitement prevailing in the army and navy. The re-raising of the original flag that had floated over Fort Sumter, by the officer who so gallantly defended it, and who did not surrender troop nor flag, was an incident calculated to inspire extraordinary interest. Especially so, since the striking down of this flag and the fall of Fort Sumter formed the overt acts that fired the hearts of the loyal North and compelled the opening of the war. That this same flag was soon to float over Fort Sumter after four years' struggle, was, as I say, calculated to animate and excite every one who was to participate in the restoration. The festivities and rejoicings are beyond my power to describe.

At this time the war was not over; at least we had not learned that Lee had surrendered; but we were imbued with an idea and belief that this was to be one of the closing scenes of the great tragedy—that the war was soon to be over!

In my department I issued an order that every vehicle in Charleston must be placed at the disposal of the visitors. I had every ambulance and army wagon, mule and horse team detailed for service; also mules and horses under saddles; and such a make-up it was! It was a strange, conglomerate combination of two wheels, four wheels and what-not transportation.[65]

About 9 o'clock of April 14, 1865, the military and naval escort was in line. The small steamers commenced to arrive and disembark the visitors, who were placed in the vehicles, without much reference to distinction. The military band furnished marching music and the parade started. Regardless of conditions, our visitors were full of patriotism, and gave hearty cheers as we passed

Harper's Weekly engraving, April 29, 1865
Bvt. Brig. General Robert Anderson Raises the Stars & Stripes once again over Fort Sumter.

the many places of interest—East and South Batteries, old St. Michael, the Citadel Arsenal, Dry-docks, Official Headquarters, the race course, and the burned portion of the city, which had been destroyed by the "Swamp Angel."

This portion of the route was of universal interest. The last place of interest visited was the old Slave Market, building and pen, where all left the vehicles. The auction block, or dias, was just the same as it appeared when the last human being was sold. Mr. Wm. Lloyd Garrison stepped upon it and made a speech, or prayer, I forget now which, followed by Henry Ward Beecher and others. After a short walk from the place we re-embarked and went to Fort Sumter.

…About 12 o'clock noon the services commenced with prayer by Rev. Martin Harris, Chaplain United States Army; reading of Scriptures by Rev. R.S. Storrs, followed by an address by Henry Ward Beecher; a poem, and other speeches; the doxology by the audience, and closing with a prayer and benediction by Rev. R. S. Storrs.

Major Anderson had been very sick, and was then far from strong or well. He read the General Order of the War Department, and making a very feeling, but brief speech, presented the original flag that had been hauled down Sunday, April 14, 1861. Seamen soon bent it to the halyards, and, too feeble to raise it himself, he held fast to the rope until the assistants had raised it to the masthead. An anthem, cheers, music by the band, and thundering guns from Forts Moultrie, Sumter, Wagner, Sullivan, Morris, Folly, James, Johnson and other island batteries, and from the land batteries in and around Charleston, saluted the flag. And Old glory was to wave again and forever, supported and protected alike by North and South, a reunited country under one flag. Major Anderson was carried to the steamer exhausted and in collapse."[66]

Chapter 13

Goose Creek—Potter's Raid—The War Over

Our stay in Charleston was of short duration. General Potter had already marched into the country, and the 25th and the 107th Ohio regiments, and the 56th New York, were ordered to re-enforce him. The 25th left Charleston on the last day of February, going by cars on the Northeast Railroad to Goose Creek, twenty miles distant.

Three regiments, under the command of Col. C. H, Vanwyck, of the 56th New York, marched without interruption to the Santee River, and, returning, came up with Gen. Potter's column at Biggins' Church. The whole division returned to the coast, marching down the north side of the Cooper River, and crossing the bay to Charleston on the evening of March 10th. The 25th took its old quarters in the depot, where it remained until the 12th, when it recrossed Charleston Bay, and went into a very pleasant camp on Mount Pleasant.

Col. Haughton went to Hilton Head, returning with all the regiment books, papers and baggage, and the reports, which had been delayed since November, were rapidly made out.

We remained in camp at Mount Pleasant until the 2d of April, upon the after-noon of which day we were embarked on the steamer W.W. Coit and on the morning of the 3d left for Georgetown, arriving there in the evening.

Several regiments had preceded us and on the morning of April 5th, the entire force under command of Gen. E. E. Potter marched from Georgetown towards the interior. The expedition was ordered by General Sherman for the purpose of destroying all railroad communications and rolling stock in east-ern South Carolina. We marched on the Kinston road. The first brigade, composed of the 25th and 107th Ohio, and the 157th New York, commanded by Col. P.P. Brown, of the latter regiment, had the advance. After a march of eighteen miles, without meeting the enemy, the division encamped in a dense pine forest. Our march had been through an almost unbroken wilderness of pines and the country did not have a promising outlook for forage.

The march was resumed next morning at 7 o'clock, the colored brigade, composed of the 54th Mass., and 32d and 102d U.S.C.T., having the advance. The country gradually improved in appearance, and foraging parties were sent out, generally under charge of the brigade quartermasters. Some skirmishing took place with small parties of the enemy's cavalry and a few prisoners were taken; but without any particular interruption we marched twenty-one miles, and encamped for the night six miles from Kingstree.

That night our foragers brought in large quantities of hams and sweet potatoes, and plenty of transportation for the whole command. The next morning we marched at 7 o'clock, the 25th having the advance; as the enemy had burned the bridge over Black River, Kingstree was left to our right. About 10 o'clock we reached the Northeastern Railroad which was thoroughly destroyed for several miles.

The country over which we were now marching was very good, and furnished plenty of subsistence for man and beast. All gin mill and cotton in the dwellings were burned. We marched eighteen miles that day, skirmishing some with the enemy. Again our foragers came in heavily laden with ham, eggs and sweet potatoes, and we were indeed living upon the fat of the land.

The next morning, April 8th, we marched at the usual hour, 7 o'clock the enemy hovering in front and on our flanks, but making no serious resistance and, after a march of twenty miles, we reached Manning. Our small detachment of cavalry had a skirmish in the edge of town, and lost one man killed, said to have been treacherously shot by a rebel who had surrendered to him.

Manning was a very pretty place, and contained some handsome public buildings. The leading paper of the town was called the "Manning (sic., Clarendon) Banner," and recommended the assassination of General Potter. One side of the paper had been printed and the other side was ready for the press. Major Culp took possession of the office and with the assistance of Col. Cooper, of the 107th, and some printers in the 25th, got out during the night a revised edition of the Banner, changing the name to the *"Banner of Freedom."* Before leaving Manning the printing office was destroyed.

Courtesy of Clarendon County Archives and History Center
Clarendon Banner, September 11, 1860, shows the newspaper's masthead as
it likely appeared prior to the arrival of Union soldiers.

*   *   *   *

Editor's Note:, "Clarendon Banner-of Freedom," The Illustrated Recollections of
Potter's Raid, April 5-21, 1865. Union soldier-printers took possession of the
Manning newspaper office and added war propaganda to the original articles
intended for publication. The following is an excerpt from the "edited" Manning
newspaper.

Courtesy of the Charleston Library Society
First issue of the "The Clarendon Banner—Of Freedom"

"The Clarendon Banner of Freedom," Salutatory
(typed transcript of exerpt)

"It *may* be expected of us to appear very humble in invading this *sanctum*; whence has issued so many articles of the straightest Secession orthodox, but for our part we "can't see it." We respect venerable institutions, but when they become also damnable, we bow our knee no more.

An extract or two from this sheet shows sufficiently what the *animus* of its former editor *was* when we tell our readers that the same individual implored our protection for his press and other printing materials tonight, they will understand what his present position is, and when we assure then that this is probably the last paper that will ever be issued from this office, and that by the morning ashes will mark where it stood, they will know *our* position.

We understand that our General does not intend to burn the town, but if we have our way, this office shall no more poison the political atmosphere of the country with its foul odors. The newspapers of the South have done more towards bring about this Rebellion than aught else, and they should not be spared.[67]

*　　　*　　　*　　　*

"The Clarendon Banner—Of Freedom," full page view

✻   ✻   ✻   ✻

Editor's Note: This military propaganda piece was produced by printers of the 25th Ohio Volunteer Infantry and 107th Ohio Volunteer Infantry after they had taken over the Manning, South Carolina newspaper office, reset the type for the proposed next edition of the "Clarendon Banner" and changed the name of the paper to the "Banner of Freedom."

*   *   *   *

On the morning of the 9th we marched from Manning, intending to reach Sumter, twenty miles distant, that evening. It was ascertained that the rebels had concentrated their forces, and, with three pieces of artillery, were strongly posted at Dingles' Mills, four miles from Sumter. Skirmishing was kept up constantly without materially impeding the march, and we finally reached a pleasant place five miles from Sumter and one mile from Dingles' Mills. A halt for dinner and rest was ordered, preparatory to the expected engagement, for it was evident the rebels intended to make considerable resistance.

At 2 o'clock we advanced towards the enemy's position. The country was open with the exception of a swamp in our front, in which the rebels were concealed. The enemy's artillery opening, the 25th filed to the right, and the 107th Ohio to the left, in line of battle, while the cooks and contrabands changed base rapidly to the rear.

Our skirmishers advanced to the edge of the swamp. And found the bridge burning and the enemy behind good earthworks on the opposite side of the swamp. The 25th Ohio moved to a natural embankment just at the edge of the swamp, which offered good protection, and with it left wing resting on the road, and near the burning bridge, awaited the orders to charge.

The 157th New York, under Lieut. Col. Carmichael, was sent to the left to wade the swamp and turn the enemy's right, while the 107th Ohio and Company B, of the 25th, kept up a strong and effective fire from their position, After waiting some time, word came to Col. Haughton that Col. Carmichael had got through the swamps, and cheers from his regiment informed us he was charging the enemy's right. This being the signal agreed upon, the 25th Ohio charged across the burning bridge, capturing the rebel artillery. The rebels retreated, leaving their dead and wounded on the field.

*   *   *   *

Editor's Note: Lt. Edmund C. Clark, commanding Battery F, Third New York Light Artillery, reports turning infantrymen of the 25th Ohio into "artillerymen."

His report of operations for April 2-25 describes how Lt. Clark Converted the captured Confederate artillery into a make-shift Union battery.

Lt. Edmund C. Clark, commanding 3rd N.Y. Artillery, Battery F:

...We were first engaged on the 9th at Dingles's Mill, where....On April 10, command of one section of 12-pound howitzers and one 6-pound iron gun with caisson. One sergeant, two corporals, twenty-five privates of the Twenty-fifth Regiment were detailed to work the three guns captured at Dingle's Mill. At 12:00 a.m. fired a salute of fifteen guns from the captured howitzers in honor the victory gained at Richmond, Petersburg, Va., Mobile and Selma, Ala...April 12, the iron gun under Sergeant Troxel was sent to report to Colonel Carmichael, commanding One hundred and fifty-seventy New York Volunteers, then on the Statesburg road...April 15, the iron gun went forward on the Statesburg road with the twenty-fifth Ohio Volunteers, fired five rounds... Three miles from Singleton's plantation I posted the Napoleons on the left of the road and fired twenty-five rounds. At 6 p.m. one howitzer reported to Colonel Haughton, Twenty-fifth Ohio Volunteers, as rear guards, the iron gun taking its place in the column.[68]

Tom J. Edwards' collection
Sgt. Isaac Troxel's ship pass, 1865, New York to Hilton Head

*   *   *   *

We pushed rapidly forward, formed line of battle, and pushed our skirmishers into the next piece of woods, and there awaited the arrival of the other regiments. The 107th Ohio soon came up at double quick, and forming on the right of the road, we once more moved forward.

In going over fences, the 25th Ohio had moved by the "right of companies to the front," and for convenience were still marching in that order. A thicket appeared in our front, and behind a strong fence, which skirted it, the rebels made another stand.

Our skirmishers had sought shelter, and those present will never forget the rapid commands given by Co. Haughton, who prided himself upon having the same command over the Regiment in battle that he did on dress-parade. His wonderful voice could be heard over a mile, as it rang out, *"By company into line, march!"* *"Fix bayonets!"* *"Double-quick, march!"* *"Charge Bayonets!"* The militia evidently were unaccustomed to such a string of orders so promptly executed, and fled in dismay.

The 107th Ohio had done the work well on its side of the road, and without further opposition we marched into Sumter, both regiments singing "Rally 'Round the Flag." Not a man in the Regiment was killed, or more than slightly wounded, during the entire day, which was somewhat remarkable.

Sumter was a beautiful little city, with a wealth of shade, many elegant residences, and two female seminaries in full blast. This was the first visitation of Yankee troops, and the inhabitants used much common sense in their intercourse with the soldiers. The "Sumter Watchman" was nearly ready for the press, and our corps of printers were soon at work getting out another number of the "Banner of Freedom." Which had quite a circulation after we left.

*　　　*　　　*　　　*

Editor's Note: In the summer of 1998, my research uncovered a copies of "The Sumter Watchman" and "The Banner of Freedom" by the printers of the 25th Ohio Volunteer Infantry, in the archives of the South Caroliniana Library, the University of South Carolina, Columbia, SC. It was the second printing of "The Banner of Freedom," this time in Sumter following the Battle of Dingle's Mill.

The "Sumter Watchman" as it may have appeared before the "printers of the 25th Ohio Volunteer Infantry printed their second edition of "The Banner of Freedom" and destroyed the printing office.

On the morning of April 10, 1865, the "Sumter Watchman" takes on a new appearance and becomes "The Banner of Freedom," a war propaganda tool to be distributed throughout the local area.

A curious coincidence was in the false dispatches we got up from the "Seat of War in Virginia," announcing the surrender of Lee to Grant. The dispatches were dated upon the day of the surrender, although we knew nothing of the surrender for several days after.

Upon our march to Sumter, and while in that town, the negros had flocked to us by the thousands, and of all sizes and colors. It became a serious problem how to dispose of them. Our wagon train had also increased in size, and was now a sight to behold. Vehicles of all descriptions: wagons, buggies, carriages, coaches, and in fact, everything imaginable that was ever placed on wheels—a most absurd procession, and lengthening for miles on the road. We had destroyed millions of dollars worth of cotton, commissary stores, locomotives and cars, and the North-eastern Railroad for many miles. The The Wilmington & Manchester Railroad still remained entire, and on the Camden branch was the bulk of the rolling stock from several railroads.

The head of our column marched from Sumter at six o'clock in the morning of April 11th, moving west on the Manchester road. The 25th was to cover the rear, and did not march until much later, as it took some hours to get all the contrabands cared for. We marched eighteen miles that day, and encamped in the afternoon on the Singleton plantation, in a beautiful grove of live oaks, on of the fairest portions of South Carolina. The Singleton mansion was a fine residence, and the outhouses, negro quarters, etc., neat and convenient. The mansion was used by Gen. Potter for his headquarters. The family had fled upon our approach. We remained in camp on the plantation on the 12th, and sent the contrabands to the river, twenty miles distant. Col. Carmichael, with the 157th New York, went to Stateburg, thirteen miles, and destroyed some Confederate stores.

The next day the 25th was ordered to take some by-roads, and come in rear of the rebels on the Stateburg road. The day was hot, but the Regiment marched rapidly, and reached the main road without encountering other than small detachments of rebel cavalry. The country over which we marched was exceedingly beautiful, with numerous elegant residences, admirably located. The inhabitants had never seen Yankee soldiers before, and were terribly frightened. No property was destroyed, to their great relief and joy.

On the morning of the 15th, four days after Lee had surrendered at Appomattox, and of which we knew nothing, the 25th received orders to proceed to Stateburg, and there await the balance of the division. We met the enemy a mile from camp, and commenced a lively skirmish, driving them back about a mile to Red Hill, where they had erected works, and were prepared to make a good resistance. Companies A and B were on the skirmish line, and the Regiment in the road, marching by the flank, advanced from the center.

*   *   *   *

Editor's Note: Private Jacob Welch made brief entries in his diary of the 25th's next seven days march from a posture of fighting to one of peace.

Private Jacob Welch, Co.G, 25th OVI:
(excerpt from personal diary, April, 1865)

15th marched and met the rebs and drove them til
2 o'clock next morning
16th marched towards Camden. Met the rebs and drive them.
Went on picket.
17th went to Camden and fought and drove the rebs.
18th started for Statesburg. Met the rebs noon, drove them til night. Rained.
Went on picket.
19th marched to Stateburg and captured 15 Rebs. Fought them all day and
camped on Singletons Plantation.
20th Captured 145 cars and 15 locomotives and burned them.
21st march. Stopped for dinner. Cessation of hostilities order came
22nd marched in piece…..[69]

*   *   *   *

Our skirmishers fell back, and Col. Haughton gave the command, *"By wing into line, march!"* *"Fix bayonet!"* *"Charge Bayonet!"* The rebels were driven from their works, although they retired sullenly and in better order than usual. Col. Haughton deemed it unadvisable to pursue the enemy with his small Regiment, and asked for reinforcements. In short time, Gen.Potter came up with the balance of the division. Six companies, under command of Major E. C. Culp, of the 25th, were advanced as skirmishers, and with the 107th Ohio struck the enemy's right. They were driven from their second position, and we moved forward, skirmishing continually.

Meanwhile General Potter had learned that the rebels had made arrangements to meet us on that road in strong force, and concluded to flank them. The 25th Ohio was left to follow out the original intention, apparently, of marching on Stateburg, in order to cover the new movement, and withdraw quietly after dark, and then follow the column. The plan succeeded admirably, and with six companies of skirmishers we drove the rebels to their main works on the hills in front of Stateburg. It was then very dark and raining hard. Major Culp sent back company after company until he was left with two men, and after replenishing the picket fires, they joined their command. In the charge at Red Hill the Regiment sustained the following loss:

Dennis Keesee Collection
Captain William P. Scott, Co. A,
wounded, Statesburg engagement

KILLED—Private Samuel Baker (K)

WOUNDED—Capt. Wm. P. Scott (A), Private Isaiah Eagy (D), Frank Dreere and Samuel Potter (E), Thomas J. Meyers (G), Charles Shrupp (I), Sherman B. Hinds, Stephen Shirley and Charles W. Smith (K).

At 3 o'clock in the morning the command halted, made coffee, and rested until daylight, when it moved forward toward Camden. The colored brigade was in front, and met the enemy fifteen miles from Camden, and after skirmishing for about two miles, we halted for the night, camping at Spring Hill. The country was quite mountainous, and looked some like western Virginia. The land was poor, and the inhabitants mainly "white trash"— not quite as intelligent as the negros.

The next morning, April 17th, the 25th Ohio had the advance, and skirmishing commenced as soon as we broke camp. No halt was made, however, until we reached the last swamp between us and Camden, where the rebels had made quite extensive works, and were in considerable force. Major Culp, with Companies E, K, G and B waded the swamp some distance to the left, and struck the enemy on the flank, Col. Haughton at the same time charging the enemy in front with the balance of the Regiment; they broke and fled in disorder, and at 3 o'clock p.m. we marched into Camden.

The inhabitants were pretty thoroughly subjugated, and in favor of peace on any terms. They were not particularly in love with Sherman's army, and some pretty hard stories to tell, which were, most of them, true enough.

As before mentioned, the object of the expedition was to destroy the rolling stock and railroads in eastern and central South Carolina. The greater portion of the rolling stock belonging to several roads was now on the Camden branch of the Manchester & Wilmington Railroad. We destroyed the railroad at

Manchester, and now had the cars between us and that point, and expected considerable fighting before getting to them.

At 7 o'clock on the morning after entering Camden, our main force marched on the pike towards Stateburg, while the 107th Ohio marched down the railroad. We met with no serious opposition until reaching Swift Creek, five miles from Camden, Here the enemy were in strong force and behind good works, extending through the swamp where the nature of the ground would permit, and upon the hills on the opposite side of the river.

Our skirmishers were advanced to the edge of the swamp, but found the water too deep to wade. The 107th Ohio, 54th Massachusetts and 102 U.S.C.T. were sent to the right some distance, with a colored man, a native of that country, to pilot them through the swamps. The 25th Ohio was moved to the edge of the swamp, and gained possession of some rebel works constructed in anticipation of our march to Camden by that road. The right of the Regiment rested on the railroad, and we were to charge across the trestle work as soon as our flanking regiments made their attack. We lay in this position several hours, and then came the cheers from the other regiments, when we charged in front, the rebels retreating in disorder. After marching several miles through a drenching rain, we encamped for the night.

On the morning of the 19th, we marched early, expecting to meet the enemy in force at Rafting Creek; but we were barely out of camp when we struck open fields, and found the rebels posted back of rail breastworks with one piece of artillery. The 157th New York took the left of the road and the 25th Ohio the right. We advanced in line of battle, driving the rebels before us, until they reached higher ground, where, supported by several pieces of artillery, they intended to make a stand. The 25th advanced steadily under a galling artillery fire until within one hundred yards of the enemy's position, when Col. Haughton ordered a charge, and the rebels retreated across Rafting Creek.

Our usual flanking expedient was again resorted to, and with the usual success, the rebels being driven from their position with considerable loss. The enemy made another stand at the swamp near Stateburg, but was easily driven back. In fact, it became hard work to keep up with them. Without much more opposition we reached Singleton's plantation, having marched twenty-five miles in seven hours, and almost constantly under fire. Only three men were wounded during the day.

There was never better marching or skirmishing, and for our reward we had the rebel rolling stock safely penned. The next morning, April 20th, the 25th Ohio wa sent to the railroad, where for two miles the road was crowded with cars, including sixteen locomotives. The cars were loaded with clothing, ammunition, provision, and in fact, everything imaginable. The Regiment was bivouacked some distance from the railroad, and men detailed to fire the train. Several cars were loaded entirely with powder, and in other cars were thousands of loaded shells. The explosions were terrific, and for several hours it seemed as if a battle was being fought. After completely destroying the train the Regiment returned to camp at Singleton's. The rebel cavalry still hovered about, and fired into camp continually, but without much damage.

On the 21st we marched from Singleton's plantation towards the Santee River, the 25th Ohio as rear guard. While on Governor Manning's plantation, and within sight of his mansion, the rebel cavalry made an attack on the two companies acting as rear guard, but were easily repulsed with some loss to them. A swamp being in our front, Gen. Potter ordered a halt. While resting, a rebel officer, Col. Rhett, came to our rear guard under a white flag, and desired to see Gen. Pottter, saying that he was bearing dispatches to that general from General Beauregard, announcing that Generals Lee and Johnston had surrendered, and the war was over.

The joy that filled our hearts was supreme. It was one hundred miles from there to Georgetown, and we marched it in three days and a half, the last two days each man having issued to him two ears of corn.

On the 28th of April, 1865, we were placed on the steamer W. W. Coit, and taken to Charleston, from whence we went into our old camp at Mount Pleasant.

Chapter 14

Building Railroads—Garrison Duty— Muster-out

On the 6th of May the Regiment was taken to Charleston, and on the 7th, marched sixteen miles towards Summerville, and the next day went into that place, and encamped near the depot.

On the 12th we went on the cars to Ridgefield, ten miles from Summerville, repaired the railroad in several places, and on the 17th went to Branchville. Co. Haughton's instructions were to go on to Orangeburg unless he received orders to the contrary. While remaining at Branchville he heard that orders were on the way detaining him at that place, while a colored regiment would be sent to Orangebug. In order to go on the latter place it was necessary to repair the railroad in several places. Captain L. B. Mesnard was sent with Companies B and G to do the work, and in three hours laid 120 ties, spiked down rails, built a bridge twenty-five feet long, and broke and fitted rails in four places. That night the Regiment went on to Orangeburg, and secured their camp at that pleasant town.

*　　　*　　　*　　　*

Editor's Note:. It is interesting to note that a number of officers came back from their furloughs with wives at their sides, perhaps a sign that fear of hostilities had greatly subsided. This is evidenced in Captain Mesnard's diary through the description of his efforts in helping the local Carolina citizenry rebuild its economy.

Captain Luther Mesnard, commanding, Co. B, 25th OVI:

After our return to Charleston we learned of Lincoln's assassination. It was awful news, lamented by friend and foe. Our regiment was soon sent out to Summerville, and from there to Orangeburg. I tried to resign from the army and come home, but instead was granted a furlough. When I returned to the regiment it was at Columbia, South Carolina. We were the only troops there for many months, doing provost duty in that part of the state....I was Post Commissary and Quartermaster...We issued many rations to destitute citizens. This was the reconstruction period. I attended sessions of the state legislature and was present at the time when the act of secession was rescinded....I was appointed District Provost Marshall.....December 6th, 1865 I was married near Syracuse, New York, my wife returning to South Carolina with me. Major E. E. Culp, myself and our wives boarded at Dr. Lynch's...My duties ad Provost Marshall brought me in contact with citizens a good deal, especially with the colored people and their trouble with the whites. During this service after the close of the war I had a fine opportunity to study the South, her ways and her people. I saw and conversed with many ex-confederate soldiers. Many who had been in the same battles I had. Had many long talks with Mr. Milton, who had been General Lee's Adjutant General.[70]

∗   ∗   ∗   ∗

On the 23d of May, the 25th Ohio broke camp at Orangeburg and marched forty-five miles to Columbia, reaching the latter city on the 25th, and encamping in the college campus.

∗   ∗   ∗   ∗

Editor's Note: The archives of the Caroliniana Library at the University of South Carolina contain records of the 25th Ohio's encampment on the college campus. One document, identified as "S.C. College, Columbia, Dec. 5th/865" provides an inventory of buildings and rooms assigned to Col. Haughton to be "occupied by Military." Also on file is what appears to be a draft letter (editing marks throughout the letter) to the Commander of the South Carolina District, Bvt. Brig. General Aldelbert Ames, dated January 16th, 1866. General Ames had commanded the 25th Ohio's Second Brigade of General Barlow's 1st Division (11th Corps) at the Battle of Gettysburg. The Trustees' request asked General Ames to remove the military from the college grounds and facilities since classes had resumed and they wished to regain full control of the college buildings and property. The South Carolina College which had closed during the war, was rechartered as the University of South Carolina in 1865.

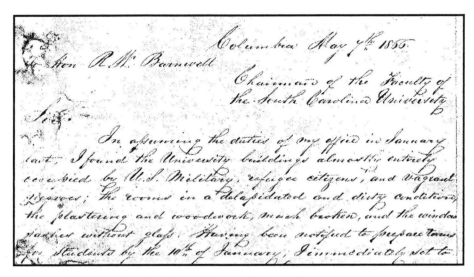

Courtesy of the University of South Carolina, Caroliniana Library
USC Marshall William H. Oechard's May 7, 1866 report on condition of university campus following military occupation.

*   *   *   *

It was the earnest wish of the officers and men of the Regiment to be immediately mustered out of the service. The long service of the Regiment, the alacrity with which it answered the call of the Government for veteran reenlistment, justified the relief that we would soon be at home with our friends. Such, however, was not to be the case, and our companies were scattered over the State of South Carolina upon odious garrison duty.

Capt. McConnaugh, in charge of Companies D and G, was sent to Winnsboro, June 8th. Following that assignment, Capt. Ferguson with Companies F and K, was sent to Camden, and upon June 25th, Capt. Murray was sent to Newberry.

During the month of July, 1865, these garrisons were withdrawn, and Colonel Haughton was assigned to command the fourth sub-district of the Military District of Charleston, with headquarters in Columbia.

Upon September 6th, Companies D, F, I and K were ordered to Orangeburg, but returned to Columbia on the 27th.

Upon September 11th, the first sub-district, Department of Western South Carolina, was created, comprising the judicial districts of Fairfield, Newberry, Edgefield, Lexington and Richland, with Col. Haughton as district commander.

Col. William P. Richardson, who had been severely wounded at Chancellorsville, had, after partial recovery, been placed in command at Camp Chase, Ohio, where he remained during the balance of the war. He returned to the Regiment at Columbia, during the month of September, 1865 and succeeded Col. Haughton, who was immediately afterwards assigned to the command of the second sub-district, with headquarters at Chester, and Companies B and E went to garrisons in that city.

During the month of October, Company F relieved Company G, at Winnsboro, and the latter company marched to Chester.

Upon November 7th, the companies returned to Columbia from Chester, and the next day Colonel Haughton assumed command of the first sub-district, relieving Col. Richardson, who was assigned to another command.

Col. Richardson did not return to the Regiment, and shortly afterwards resigned, having been breveted brigadier general for long and faithful service.

*   *   *   *

Editor's Note: Few officers commanded more respect and admiration than Col. William Pitt Richardson. A serious shoulder wound suffered at the Battle of Chancellorsville would have sent many a soldier back home away from the front. However, Col. Richardson's dedication caused him to remain in his country's service through the final muster out of the 25th Ohio in June, 1866. His commendable service did not go unnoticed. On December 7, 1864, he was awarded a Brevet commission as Brigadier General. Born in Washington County, Pennsylvania May 25, 1824, Col. Richardson subsequently completed studies at Washington College which led him to a career in teaching in Steubenville, Ohio, not far distant from his Pennsylvania home. Col. Richardson married a Virginia girl, Sarah Smith, in 1848. He enlisted in a volunteer company of the 3d Ohio Regiment and served under General Taylor in the Mexican War, participating in the march from Matamoras to Buena Vista. Following the war, he moved to Harrison County, Ohio and took up the study of law with Allen C. Turner, while still teaching school. He was admitted to the bar in 1852 and moved to Woodsfield, Ohio in

1853 where he served as Principal of Woodsfield Seminary and later entered into the practice of law. He served two terms as Monroe County's Prosecuting Attorney and continued his military interests, holding the rank of Brigadier General in the Ohio militia until the outbreak of the war of the rebellion. William Richardson was offered a Major's commission by the State of Ohio and succeeded in raising two companies of men immediately after the attack on Fort Sumter; subsequently designated companies B and C of the 25th Ohio Volunteer Infantry. He was quickly promoted to a Lt. Colonelcy as the regiment moved to the field. He was subsequently promoted to the Colonelcy of his regiment in May, 1862, succeeding Col. James A. Jones who had to resign his commission due to ill health. Col. Richardson was age 37 at the time of his appointment He continued to direct the activities of the 25th Ohio until May, 1963 at which time he was forced to take a temporary command assignment at Camp Chase, Ohio until his disabling battle injury healed and he was fit for field duty. Interestingly, he was elected as the Attorney-General of the state of Ohio during his service at Camp Chase and these duties delayed his return to the regiment. In September 1865, he joined the Coastal Division in South Carolina and was initially placed over a subdistrict headquartered in Columbia. His assignment was then changed to assume command of the District of East South Carolina, headquartered in Darlington. After being mustered out of the service in June 1866, he was appointed Collector of Internal Revenue for the Fifteenth Congressional District. About four years later he began a law practice in Marietta, Ohio. Col. Richardson also served as a director of the Marietta, Pittsburg, & Cleveland Railroad. He died in 1886 at the age of 62 and is buried in Marietta, Ohio. As a commander, Col. Richardson possessed the confidence and esteem of his men.

*   *   *   *

Lieut. Col. Haughton was promoted to full colonel, a rank to which he had long been entitled, having been regimental commander for nearly three years, and having done more to bring the Regiment into a state of perfect drill and discipline than all the other field officers combined. He was a man of remarkable courage and perfect self-possession under fire, handling the Regiment in battle as easily as upon dress parade. He was breveted brigadier general for meritorious conduct in several engagements, and long and efficient service.

*   *   *   *

Editor's Note: Evidence of the provost duties conducted in South Carolina in 1865—1866 by the 25th Ohio is found in the published writings of Grace Elmore.

(*A Heritage of Woe: The Civil War Diary of Grace Brown Elmore,1861-1868,* *1997*). *Headquartered on the campus of South Carolina College (now the University of South Carolina, Columbia, SC), the regiment remained long after the war's end to act as an occupational police force. Grace Elmore whose plantation was in the Columbia area, makes mention of the contracts of freedom which Union forces were instructed to enforce.*

HEADQUARTERS, DISTRICT OF WESTERN SOUTH CAROLINA,
FOURTH SEPARATE BRIGADE,
Columbia, S. C., January 13 1866.

SPECIAL ORDER
No. 11

Major E. C. Culp 25th Ohio
Vet. Vol. Left is hereby detailed as

The National Archives and Records Administration

Headquartered in Columbia, 25th OVI commander E.C. Culp was also detailed to serve on a Court Marshal Board and as Assistant Inspector General of the District of Port Royal.

Grace Elmore, private citizen, Columbia, South Carolina:

...our life for four years has been the "baseless fabric of vision," and we can deal with the hard realities of the present. We have truly said goodbye to being ladies of leisure, my time is fully occupied, often not having time to sleep. Rise at 5 o'clock, dress, come down to see after breakfast, then a multitude of small cares: among them reading to Jack his contract, which he ought to know by heart. For every day he make some demand and some I decline, he says, "but, Miss Grace, ain't it in de contract?" Whereupon I take him gravely to the library and read the document signed by the parties in the presence of Yankee Colonel Haughton, and which I told Jack was binding....[71]

*   *   *   *

Major E. C. Culp was promoted to Lieut. Col., vice Haughton, promoted, and also received the brevets of lieutenant colonel and colonel. Major Culp had been detailed from the Regiment since the 1st of May, doing duty upon Gen.

Gilmore's staff as an inspector general of the department. At his earliest request, he was relieved from duty and returned to the Regiment at Columbia during the month of December, 1865.

Capt. D. R. Hunt, who served the Regiment as Quartermaster very successfully, had also been detailed from the Regiment early in April, and until the muster-out of the Regiment served as depot and department quartermaster, receiving the brevet rank of Lieut. Colonel for excellent service in that department.

During the winter of 1865-6, and spring of 1866, garrisons were maintained at various other stations, those not mentioned being Lieut. Livinsparger at Winnsboro, Lieut. Biggerstaff at Edgefield and Hamburg, and Lieut. O. P. Hershey at Lexington. When the spring of 1866 opened, and a year had passed since the close of the war, the dissatisfaction assumed the form of desertion and many of the oldest and best soldiers of the Regiment, many of them carrying marks of rebel bullets, took French leave.

These men are today borne upon the rolls as deserters, and cannot obtain back pay, pensions, or use soldier's filings for securing public lands.

When we reflect that those who fought against the Government for four years, many of them deserters from the Federal army, navy, or halls of Congress, have been fully and freely pardoned, restored to full citizenship, and a number of them this day, (March 20, 1885) Cabinet officers, United States Senators, members of Congress, Governors of States, eminent judges, and high department officers, is it not time that those few solders of a gallant Regiment, who fought for the government four long years, and then deserted a year after the war closed, should be restored to honorable positions?

*   *   *   *

Editor's Note: State troops were eventually replaced by United States troops which continued martial law and occupation of Columbia, South Carolina. In 1873 James S. Pike, a journalist and former part-owner of the New York "Tribune," came to the Palmetto State to report on the progress of reconstruction there. He observed, "Among the significant peculiarities to be observed in Columbia is the presence of United States troops. They occupy barracks on the outskirts of town, in a pleasant quarter, where they drill daily, where the flag always floats, and where military music is heard at sunset....Near by the parade grounds are the college buildings of the University of South Carolina. Before the war, their walls sheltered some two hundred students. Their young blood was fired by the first tap of the drum, and they all rushed to the field. They have not come back. What was to be a pastime proved a stern reality. The buildings look worn and desolate, and only a handful of scholars and a few poorly-paid professors remain."[72]

Upon the 30th of April, 1866, the Regiment marched to Summerville, near Charleston, and garrisoned the surrounding country. Lieut. Col. E. C. Culp was sent with two companies of the Regiment, and a portion of the 126th U.S. colored troops, to the Sea Island District, with headquarters upon Edisto Island.

*   *   *   *

Editor's Note: The war years were long and even the most dedicated among the veterans was eager to return home to family and friends. It was much to ask of war weary "volunteers" to remain on duty beyond the summer after the Confederate surrender at Appomattox. Yet, while other regiments were being mustered out of the service, the 25th Ohio was called upon to remain on provost duty as an occupational force in South Carolina; a requirement that was difficult for even the most dedicated soldier to understand. But stay they did, for over one year after the war had officially ended.

Family and friends on the homefront could not understand the delay in returning loved ones home. On February 12, 1866, Mrs. Benjamin Scott wrote to Governor Cox, appealing to him humanity to muster out the 25th Ohio. She wrote"…soon as Jeff Davis was caught our brave boys wrote to us they would soon be home when the order came that they were to be retained (.) many a brave man that had faced the cannons mouth on the field of deadly strife now wept like children. How do you think we feel deprived of our loved ones for the benefit of that hot bed of treason S.C.(?) where is the united States Regulars…..."[73]

The last commander of the 25th Ohio, Lt. Col. Edward C. Culp (author of this book), made a strong petition in the Spring of 1866 to Ohio Governor J.D. Cox, asking for relief from a burden of service that had now extended five years.

The following is a copy of Col. Culp's appeal:

Lt. Col. Edward C. Culp, commanding, 25th OVI:

Headquarters 25th Regt O.V.I Infty

Columbia S. C. April 4, 1866

His Excellency,
J.D. Cox, Governor of Ohio

Sir: ~ I have the honor to acknowledge the receipt of you letter of the 28th inst. and to thank you for the interest manifested in our welfare.

In reply I have to state that no prospect now exists for the muster-out of this Regiment. Several petitions have been forwarded by the officers and enlisted men to the Secretary of War and the universal answer has been that the order for muster-out be issued as soon as practicable. Yet during the intervening time and since these answers have been returned, several Regiments have gone home from this state. The injustice shown this Regiment by the mustering-out of junior Regiments is too palpable. The men are becoming restive and many desertions have taken place. The Regiment is now being paid up to the 1st of March and it is an understood thing among the enlistment men that if no orders are received this month for the muster-out they will desert in masse_____ It is utter folly to say that this state of affairs could have been prevented by the officers.

The veterans who enlisted with the express understanding that they were to be discharged at the close of the War, whether in a political view that time has arrived, is no matter to them. Hostilities were suspended nine months ago and the war has been declared at an end officially in some of the States.[74]

The men have waited patiently for the order of muster-out, though feeling that the Government has no right to retain them in service. They now say that they are tired of waiting for honorable discharge and while they will commit no malicious act, they intend to go to their homes and the government may keep the money due them. Lt. Col. Haughton now commanding this Sub Dist. has been to Charleston and Conversed with Gen. Sickles but received no satisfactory answer and now we have not hopes of getting mustered-out unless through the action of our state authorities.

I feel deeply in this matter and earnestly hope that after nearly five years of honorable service we may go home with untarnished honor: but it cannot be if the regiment is retained in the service two months longer. I have already given you a statement of time in service, losses & c. and will now only repeat that the Regiment was organized from three months companies in June 1866.[75]

I have the honor to be very respectfully Your Obt Servt
    EC Culp
    Major Comdg Regt

$*$ $*$ $*$ $*$

Upon the 6th of June, 1866, the long-looked-for orders for muster-out were received, upon the 7^{th,} the Regiment left Charleston harbor on the steamer Flamveau, arrived after a pleasant passage, in New York June 10th, and in Tod Barracks, Columbus, Ohio, June 12th, was mustered out of the service, June 16th, 1866, after over five years of service, but faintly outlined in the preceding pages.

Epilogue

"Quaeque ipse vidi et quorum pars fui"
"That which I have seen….and, of this, I am a part."

Referring to Col. Culp's Latin phrase, *"Quaeque ipse vidi…et quorum pars fui,"* it is hoped that the reader, who has now traveled the pages of this book, portraying the life and times of the 25th Ohio Volunteer Infantry soldier (*that which I have seen*), will now feel a part (*and of this, I am a part*) of this rich history and will have a renewed appreciation for the United States of America for which so many fought and died.

Whether reading, researching, or writing the history of the 25th Ohio Volunteer Infantry, one cannot help but be drawn into the events, victories, tragedies, and human drama as told in the words of the veterans themselves. Their writings bring this historic period in our country's history to life in such a manner that the reader can almost feel a presence, or spirit, of these brave soldiers sharing their experiences. As a researcher handling several thousand handwritten documents and regimental orders on file in the National Archives repository, I somehow felt transported back in time and sensed a kind of kinship with these citizens turned soldiers.

The centerpiece for this book has been Col. Edward C. Culp's 1885 book, <u>The 25th Ohio Volunteer Infantry in the War for the Union</u>. Full credit must be given to him for his inspired, articulate narrative of this regiment's five years of service, 1861-1866. Incorporating the writings and observations of other 25th Ohio officers and enlisted men in this rare book, it is hoped that these shared perspectives add further creditability to Col. Culp's own writings and insightful, exciting accounts of the role played by this regiment during the war between the states. The addition of photographs, drawings, and maps related to the 25th Ohio was intended to enhance the vividness of this composite narrative. Like the pieces of a puzzle coming together to form a beautiful picture, published and unpublished archival materials from public and private collections were assembled into a more complete story of dedication, patriotism, and bravery of boys who became men through the experience of war.

As indicated in Col. Culp's original preface, it was his intent to publish a second edition for the purpose of correcting mistakes and coordinating his recollections with those of other 25th OVI veterans. This did not, however, take place as Col. Culp's personal priorities became otherwise directed in the later part of his life following the war. It is my sincere hope that the publication of this edited version of Culp's rare book, in some measure, contributes to his wish.

It seems appropriate that a few words about the remainder of Edward Clinton Culp's life be shared with the reader. In 1866, Col. Culp returned to civilian life in Norwalk, Ohio where he entered a partnership with a fellow veteran, Charles P. Wickham, in the hardware business of Preston, Culp and Wickham. Colonel Culp and Major Wickham (55th OVI) had served together on staff duty in the war. In his pension disposition, Wickham, a member of the US Congress from the 14th District of the State of Ohio, stated that he "was intimately associated with said Edward C. Culp on staff duty and found him ever ready for duty and attentive to orders." Col. Culp was a newlywed, having just married Lucy E. Preston the previous November while on leave. In addition to his business pursuits, Col. Culp was elected as Sheriff of Huron County (Ohio), serving 1869 to 1873. One duty, however, would not set well with Sheriff Culp. Having faced five arduous years of conflict during the Civil War, Sheriff Culp was no stranger to death. But one death in Huron County would prove difficult for him to handle. He was charged with the execution of Bennet Scop, convicted of the murder of a local peddler, Jacob Goodman; the last such execution in Huron County. In spite of Scop's conviction, Edward Culp was not convinced of his guilt. A final appeal to then Ohio Governor Rutherford B. Hayes (later U.S. President) was unsuccessful, and Sheriff Culp reluctantly carried out the sentence in August, 1870.

Between 1870 and 1880, interest in westward expansion was building up among a number of local Norwalk residents. The 1862 Homestead Act had been signed into law by President Abraham Lincoln to encourage settlement of

270 million acres of public domain land in the western United States. Each homesteader had to be at least 21 years of age and the head of a household to claim a 160 acre parcel of land. Col. Culp, his wife, Lucy, his three children (John, Charles, and Frank), and his brother Charles joined the movement to Kansas territory, becoming among the early homestead settlers of Salina in 1879. Edward Culp launched a career in real estate, investments, and insurance; and became active in civic and political affairs. He worked for Massachusetts Life for several years, subsequently organizing Kansas Mutual Life and the Hamilton Investment Company. It was in Salina that he and wife had their third child, Mary, in 1881.

Col. Culp served as a delegate to the National Republican Conventions in 1884 and 1900. His strong faith in God, perhaps kindled during his war years, led him in 1887 to found and organize the Isis Temple Mystic Shrine (Masonic Lodge) in Salina. Culp, a thirty-three degree Mason, served as its first Potentate; a position he held for four consecutive years. When the Spanish American War broke out, Col. Culp submitted his name for consideration to appointment as a brigadier general from the State of Kansas, however another distinguished Kansan was selected. Col. Culp also served as secretary for the Committee on Ceremonies at the 1892 Chicago World's Fair and later served in the same capacity for the 1904 World's Fair in St. Louis, Missouri. It was while carrying out these latter duties that he became ill and retreated to his brother Charles' home in Kansas City where he died a short time later on May 16, 1904, at age 61. He left his wife and four children: John P., Dr. Charles W., Frank G. (Taxco, Mexico), and Mary Culp.

Isis Temple, Salina, Kansas
Edward C. Culp
First Potentate, Isis Temple

His obituary was prominently displayed on the front page of the daily and weekly Salina newspapers. Reference in the articles was made to his distinguished military service during the war of the rebellion as the 23 year old commander of the 25th Ohio Volunteer Infantry. Oddly, no mention was made of his 1885 published regimental history. One of the writers noted that his passing, as with other early Kansas settlers, was "One by one, like the leaves they are falling." The May 18, 1904, Salina Evening Journal obituary stated that Col. Culp's funeral would not have been complete without the handsome American flag draped over his casket. "The old flag, he who rested beneath it's folds had followed [it] in his boyhood...the same flag that...bore in the strength of his young manhood at Gettysburg..." With the muster-out of the 25th Ohio in June, 1866, more than 2,000 25th Ohio young men had given a measure of their lives to preserve the Union, abolish slavery, and to defend the Banner of Freedom. It is hoped that the reader has enjoyed this collective story of patriotism and dedication and that it is a lasting tribute to the memory of this fine regiment.

Thomas J. Edwards,
Lakeside, Ohio
2003

Bibliography

Books and Articles

Institutional Publications

Crumb, Herb S., Editor, <u>The Eleventh Corps Artillery At Gettysburg,</u> The Papers of Major Thomas Ward Osborn, Edmonston Publishing, Inc., New York: Hamilton, 1991.

Dyer, Frederick H.; <u>A Compendium of the War of the Rebellion,</u> Vol. 2, Dayton, Ohio: Morningside Press, 1979.

<u>Biographical Encyclopedia of Ohio of the Nineteenth Century,</u> Cincinnati and Philadelphia, 1876.

Hunt, David R., *Restoring the Flag at Fort Sumter* <u>Sketches of War History,</u> Vol. 5 (MOLLUS) Cincinnati, Ohio, 1903.

Hunt, Roger D., <u>Brevet Brigadier Generals in Blue</u>, Olde Soldier Books, Incorporated, 1990.

Isis Temple, "75th Anniversary 1887 Diamond Jubilee Ceremonial, 1962."

Monfort, E.R., "From Grafton to McDowell Through Gart's Valley," <u>Sketches of War History, 1861-1865, Ohio Comandery, MOLLUS,</u> Wilmington, NC: Broadfoot Publishing Company, 1991.

National Park Civil War Series, "The Battle of Chancellorsville," Eastern National Park and Monument Association, 1995.

National Park Civil War Series, "The Battle of Gettysburg," Eastern National Park and Monument Association, 1994.

National Park Civil War Series, "The Second Battle of Manassas," Eastern National Park and Monument Association, 1995.

Report of the Ohio, Gettysburg Memorial Committee; Columbus, Ohio: Nitschke Brothers, 1887.

Roster Commission; Official Roster of the Soldiers of the State of Ohio in the War of the Rebellion, Vol. 3, Cincinnati, Ohio: Ohio Valley Publishing and Manufacturing Company, 1886.

U.S. War Department. *The War of the Rebellion: A Compilation of the Official Records of the Union and Confederate Armies*, 128 volumes, Washington D.C., U.S. Government Printing Office, 1880-1901.

Works by Named Authors

Archer, John, M.; The Hour was One of Horror: East Cemetery Hill at Gettysburg, Gettysburg: Thomas Publications, 1997.

Baumgartner, Richard A., Buckeye Blood: Ohio at Gettysburg, Huntington, W.Va.: Blue Acorn Press, 2003.

Brown, Grace Elmore, edited by Marli F. Weiner, A Heritage of Woe: The Civil War Diary of Grace Brown Elmore,1861-1868, (Southern Voices from the Past), University of Georgia Press, 1997.

Culp, Edward C.; The 25th Ohio Veteran Volunteer Infantry in the War for the Union; Topeka Kansas: George W. Crane & Company, 1885; original on file with the Ohio Historical Society, Columbus, Ohio; microfilm reprints (1973) available from University Microfilms, Ann Arbor Michigan.

Edgar, Walter, South Carolina, A History, Columbia, SC: University of South Carolina Press, 1998.

Fox, William F.; Regimental Losses in the American Civil War, 1861-1865; Albany, New York : Albany Publishing Company, 1889.

Samuel H. Hurst, Journal - History of the Seventy-third Ohio Volunteer Infantry, Chillicothe, Ohio, 1866.

Hamblen, Charles P., Connecticut Yankees at Gettysburg, Kent, Ohio: Kent State University Press, 1993.
Hartwig, D. Scott, "The 11th Army Corps on July 1, 1863," The Gettysburg Magazine, January 1990.

Hennessy, John J., Return to Bull Run: The Campaign and Battle of Second Manassas, Norman, Oklahoma: The University of Oklahoma Press, 1999.

Hunt, Roger D. and Brown, Jack R., Brevet Brigadier Generals in Blue, Gaithersburg, Md.: Olde Soldier Books, Inc., 1997.

Johnson, Robert U. and Buel, Clarence C., editors, Battles and Leaders of the Civil War, 3 vols., New York: The Century Company, 1888.

Jones, Terry L., "Going Back Into the Union At Last, A Louisiana Tiger's account of the Gettysburg Campaign," Civil War Times Illustrated, January/February, 1991.

Martin, David G. Martin; Gettysburg, July 1; Conshohocken, PA.: Combined Books, Inc., 1996.

Mesnard, Luther B.; "the Rise and Survival of Private Mesnard," Civil War Times, Illustrated; Part I (January, 1986); and Part II (February, 1986).

Moore, John Hammond, Southern Homefront, 1861-1865, Columbia, SC: Saummerhouse Press, 1998.

Pfanz, Harry W.; Culp's Hill & Cemetery Hill; The University of North Carolina Press, Chapel Hill, 1993.

Pfanz, Harry W.; Gettysburg, The Second Day; The University of North Carolina Press, Chapel Hill, 1987.

Pike, James S., The Prostrate State: South Carolina Under Negro Government(October, 1873), introduction by Henry Steele Commanger, New York: Loring & Mussey, 1935.

Reid, Whitelaw; Ohio in the War: Her Statesmen, Her Generals & Soldiers, Vol. 2, Cincinatti, The Robert Clark Company, 1895.

Sears, Stephen W. Sears, Chancellorsville, New York: Houghton Mifflin Company, 1996.

Smith, Jacob, Camps and Campaigns: of the 107th Regiment Ohio Volunteer Infantry, from August 1862 to July 1865, 1919; and reprint, Navarre, Ohio: Indian River Graphics, 2000.

Thigpen, Allan D., the Illustrated Recollections of Potter's Raid, April 5-21, 1865, Gamecock City Printing, Inc., Sumter, SC, 1998.

Time-Life Books, The Civil War, Gettysburg, by Chamnp Clark, Alexandria, Virginia, 1987.

Time-Life Books, Voices of the Civil War, Shenandoah 1862, Alexandria, Virginia, 1997.

Time-Life Books, Voices of the Civil War, Gettysburg, Alexandria, Virginia, 1997.

Newspapers and Periodicals

Army Correspondence, 1861-1866; Microfilm, The Spirit of (Woodsfield, Ohio), The Ohio Historical Society.

Baird, Col. William, The National Tribune, "The 32d Regiment, U.S.C.T. At The Battle of Honey Hill," 1919.

Ballentyne, Hugh (Co. C), The National Tribune,"Letter to the Editor, Honey Hill," 25th Ohio, August 1, 1919.

Bragg, William Harris; "The Fight at Honey Hill," Civil War Times Illustrated, January, 1984.

"Col. Nat Haugton Dead," *The Toledo Blade (Toledo, Ohio)*, January 31, 1899.

Culp, Edward C., *The National Tribune*, "Gettysburg: Reminiscences of the Great Fight by a Participant," March 19, 1895.

 Jones, James A., *The Norwalk Daily Reflector*, " The Gallant Hero of Two Wars," May 22, 1893.

"Masonic Funeral Over the Remains of the Late Colonel E. E. Culp," *Salina Evening Journal*, May 18, 1904.

"Remains of Colonel Culp Escorted by Comrades," *Salina Evening Journal*, May 17, 1904.

The Palmetto Herald, December, 1864, S. W. Mason & Company.

Manuscripts, Diaries, and Papers

Descriptive Books, Companies A - E, 25th Ohio Infantry; filed with muster rolls, RG 84, Stack Area 8W3, Row 7, Compartment 10, Shelf C; National Archives and Records Administration.

Document, Hollis Correspondence (Lt. Joseph H. Hollis), Indiana Magazine of History, Vol. XXXVI, The Department of History of Indiana University, Bloomington, Indiana, 1940.

Emanuel L. Riley, 25th Ohio Volunteer Infantry, "Letter to Mr. John Ward," June 19, 1861,

Sgt. Thomas Evans Diary, (transcript), The Ohio Historical Society.

Miscellaneous Regimental Papers (Boxes 3646, 3647 and 3648), 25th Ohio Infantry; filed with muster rolls, RG 84, Stack Area 8W3, Row 7, Compartment 10, Shelf C; National Archives and Records Administration.

Descriptive Books, Companies F - K, 25th Ohio Infantry; filed with muster rolls, RG 84, Stack Area 8W3, Row 7, Compartment 10, Shelf C; National Archives and Records Administration

Gettysburg Sketch, the Robert L. .Brake Collection (sketch of unit service at Gettysburg, United States Army Military History Institute; Carlisle Barracks, Pa. 17013-5008 Civil War Miscellaneous Files.

Lamkin, Alfred Avery; Diaries, 1853-1872, Western Historical Manuscript Collection, University of Missouri.

James D. McMunn, 25th Ohio Volunteer Infantry, "Letter to his brother, C. McMunn;" in possession of Dona Dunn.

Capt. Luther B. Mesnard Reminiscence (typed transcript), United States Army Military History Institute, Carlisle Barracks, Pa. 17013-5008 Civil War Miscellaneous Files, May 6, 1901.

Morning Reports, Cos. A, B, C and D, 25th Ohio Infantry; filed with muster rolls, RG 84, Stack Area 8W3, Row 7, Compartment 10, Shelf C; National Archives and Records Administration.

Morning Reports, Cos. E, F and G, 25th Ohio Infantry; filed with muster rolls, RG 84, Stack Area 8W3, Row 7, Compartment 10, Shelf C; National Archives and Records Administration.

Morning Reports, Cos. H, I and K, 25th Ohio Infantry; filed with muster rolls, RG 84, Stack Area 8W3, Row 7, Compartment 10, Shelf C; National Archives and Records Administration

James D. McMunn, 25th Ohio Volunteer Infantry, "letter to his brother, C. McMunn," in possession of Donna Dunn.

Joseph A. Palmer, "Copy of a letter to Mr. Burt C. Wilder, July 20, 1913," Private collection, Dan Rivera.

Emanuel L. Riley, 25th Ohio Volunteer Infantry, "letter to Mr. John Ward," June 19, 1861.

Samuel G. Shirk, 25th Ohio Volunteer Infantry, "letter to Mr. Morrie Danford," March 14, 1864, in possession of Mr. Tom J. Edwards.

Regimental Descriptive Book, 25th Ohio Infantry; filed with muster rolls, RG 84, Stack Area 8W3, Row 7, Compartment 10, Shelf C; National Archives and Records Administration.

Regimental Endorsement Book, 25th Ohio Infantry; filed with muster rolls, RG 84, Stack Area 8W3, Row 7, Compartment 10, Shelf C; National Archives and Records Administration.

Regimental Order Book, 25th Ohio Infantry; filed with muster rolls, RG 84, Stack Area 8W3, Row 7, Compartment 10, Shelf C; National Archives and Records Administration.

"Sketch of the 25th Ohio at Gettysburg," Brake Collection, Box 11, U. S. Army Military History Institute, Archives Branch, Carlisle, Pennsylvania.

The Clarendon Banner - Of Freedom, the Charleston Library Society, Charleston, SC.

The Banner of Freedom, Caroliniana Library, University of South Carolina.

Jacob Welch, "Diary, 1864 - 1865," 25th Ohio Volunteer Infantry, in possession of Richard W. Welch.

Wildman, Samuel; Wildman Family Papers (Cpl. Wildman, 1864-1866), gift of   Mrs. Ellen Fenner Lilie (1973) ; Ohio Historical Society, Columbus. Ohio.

John Turner Wood, United States Army Military History Institute, enlisted man's letter to his mother, Sept. 17, 1862 to March 31, 1863 & March 2-31, 1865.

John T. Wood, Civil War Miscellaneous Collection, "letters to his mother, 1862 - 1863, and March 1865," U. S. Army Military History Institute, Archives Branch, Carlisle, Pennsylvania.

CHAPTER 1

[1] "Departure of our Volunteers," Army Correspondence, The Spirit of Democracy, June 12, 1861, Ohio Historical Society microfilm collection.

CHAPTER 2

[2] Reid, Whitelaw; Ohio in the War: Her Statesmen, Her Generals & Soldiers, Vol. 2, pp. 176-181; Bergman Books (ISBN #0963603612); Cincinnati: The Robert Clarke Company, 1895.

[3] Joseph A. Palmer, "copy of a letter to Mr. Burt C. Wildere, July 20, 1913," private collection, Dan Rivera.

CHAPTER 3

[4] *The War of the Rebellion: A Compilation of the Official Records of the Union and Confederate Armies*, Washington, DC, 1884, Series I, Vol. XIV, pt., *p. 497.*

[5] Ibid

[7] *The War of the Rebellion: A Compilation of the Official Records of the Union and Confederate Armies*, Washington, DC, 1884, Series I, Vol. XIV, pt., *p. 497.*

CHAPTER 4

[8] U.S. War Department, *The War of the Rebellion: A Compilation of the Official Records of the Union and Confederate Armies*, Vol. XII, Chapter XXIV, Washington, D.C., U.S. Government Printing Office, 1880-1901, pp. 466-467.

[9] Ibid.

[10] U.S. War Department, *The War of the Rebellion: A Compilation of the Official Records of the Union and Confederate Armies*, Vol. XII, Chapter XXIV, Washington, D.C., U.S. Government Printing Office, 1880-1901, pp. 463-464.

[11] Ibid.

[12] Monfort, E. R., "From Grafton to McDowell Through Gart's Valley," *Sketches of War History, 1861-1865, Ohio Commandery, MOLLUS,* Broadfoot Publishing Company,

185

Wilmington, N.C., 1888; courtesy U.S. Military History Institute, Archives Branch, Carlisle, Pennsylvania.

[13] U.S. War Department, _The War of the Rebellion: A Compilation of the Official Records of the Union and Confederate Armies,_ Vol. XII, Chapter XXIV, Washington, D.C., U.S. Government Printing Office, 1880-1901, Report of Colonel Nathaniel C. McLean, Seventy-fifth Ohio Infantry, pp. 468.

[14] VFM 2506, Thomas J. Evans' Papers, Diary, Ohio Historical Society.

CHAPTER 5

[15] MccMunn, James D.,"Letter to brother, August 17, 1862, Rapidan Station, Virginia," private collection of Lt. Col. Don Dunn, Waldorf, Maryland.

[16] Journal—History of the Seventy-third Ohio Volunteer Infantry, by Samuel B. Hurst, late commander of the Regiment, Chillicothe, Ohio, 1866.

CHAPTER 6

[17] Miscellaneous Regimental Papers (Boxes 3646, 3647 and 3648), 25th Ohio Infantry; filed with muster rolls, RG 84, Stack Area 8W3, Row 7, Compartment 10, Shelf C; National Archives and Records Administration.

[18] Ibid.

[19] Ibid.

[20] Ibid.

[21] Ibid.

[22] Series I, Volume XXXVII, No. 244, The War of the Rebellion: A Compilation of the Official Records of the Union and Confederate Armies, Washington, DC, Government Printing Office, 1889-1901, pp. 637-638.

[23] Series I, Volume XXXVII, No. 244, The War of the Rebellion: A Compilation of the Official Records of the Union and Confederate Armies, Washington, DC, Government Printing Office, 1889-1901, pp. 640-641.

[24] Ibid.

[25] Series I, Volume XXXVII, No. 244, The War of the Rebellion: A Compilation of the Official Records of the Union and Confederate Armies, Washington, DC, Government Printing Office, 1889-1901, pp. 642-643.

[26] Ibid.

[27] Sergeant Thomas J. Evans' Diary, transcript submitted by Lawrence T. Evans, May, 1953, The Ohio Historical Society, Columbus, Ohio

[28] Ibid.

[29] "The Indiana Magazine of History," Vol. XXXVI, 1940, Documents, Hollis Correspondence, pp. 275-294, Indiana State Library.

CHAPTER 7

[30] Lamkin, Alfred Avery; Diaries, 1853-1872, Western Historical Manuscript Collection, University of Missouri.

CHAPTER 8

[31] Edward C. Culp, National Tribune, March 19, 1885.

[32] Ibid.

[33] Ibid.

[34] Ibid.

[35] Series I, Volume XXXIX, No. 248, The War of the Rebellion: A Compilation of the Official Records of the Union and Confederate Armies, Washington, DC, Government Printing Office, 1889-1901, p. 720.

[36] The Eleventh Corps Artillery At Gettysburg, The Papers of Major Thomas Ward Osborn, Edited by Herb S. Crumb, Edmonston Publishing, Inc., Hamilton, New York, 1991, pp. 10—13.

[37] Edward C. Culp, National Tribune, March 19, 1885.

[38] Culp's Hill & Cemetery Hill, by Harry W. Pfanz, Chapel Hill: University of North Carolina Press, 1993, p. 257.

[38] Buckeye Blood: Ohio at Gettysburg, by Richard A. Baumgartner, Huntington, W. Va: Blue Acorn Press, 2003, p. 200; and The Spirit of Democracy, August 19, 1863.

[39] Series I, Volume XXXIX, No. 246, The War of the Rebellion: A Compilation of the Official Records of the Union and Confederate Armies, Washington, DC, Government Printing Office, 1889-1901, p. 716.

[40] Buckeye Blood: Ohio at Gettysburg, by Richard A. Baumgartner, Huntington, W. Va: Blue Acorn Press, 2003, p. 168; and the Norwalk Reflector, July 21, 1863.

[41] The 25th Ohio Regiment," The Spirit of Democracy, Woodsfield, Ohio, July 15, 1863, Ohio Historical Society, Ohio Historical Center, Archives/Library Division.

[42] Ibid.

CHAPTER 9 (no endnotes)

CHAPTER 10

[43] Letter to Mr. Morrie Danford, written by Sergeant Samuel Shirk, Company I, 25th Ohio Volunteer Infantry, March 14, 1864, camp near Washington, DC, Tom J. Edwards' collection.

[44] John T. Wood, Civil War Miscellaneous Collection, "letters to his mother, September 17, 1862 to March 31, 1863, and March 1865," U. S. Army Military History Institute, Archives Branch, Carlisle, Pennsylvania.

CHAPTER 11

[45] U.S. War Department. The War of the Rebellion: A Compilation of the Official Records of the Union and Confederate Armies, Series I, Vol.XII, Chapter XLIV Washington D.C., U.S. Government Printing Office, 1880-1901, Report of Colonel Nathaniel C. McLean, Seventy-fifth Ohio, p. 429.

[46] Diary, Capt. Luther B. Mesnard Reminiscence (typed transcript), United States Army Military History Institute, Carlisle Barracks, Pa. 17013-5008 Civil War Miscellaneous Files, pp. 49-60, May 6, 1901.

[47] Ibid.

[48] Ibid.

[49] Ibid.

[50] Wildman, Samuel; Wildman Family Papers (Cpl. Wildman, 1864-1866), gift of Mrs. Ellen Fenner Lilie (1973) ; Ohio Historical Society, Columbus. Ohio.

[51] Ibid.

[52] Ibid.

[54] Ibid.

[55] Ibid.

[56] Ibid.

[57] Ibid.

[58] *The National Tribune,*"Letter to the Editor, Honey Hill," Hugh Ballentyne, Co. C, 25th Ohio, August 1, 1919.

[59] Ibid.

CHAPTER 12

[60] Diary, Capt. Luther B. Mesnard (typed transcript), United States Army Military History Institute, Carlisle Barracks, Pa. 17013-5008 Civil War Miscellaneous Files, pp. 49-60, May 6, 1901.

[61] Ibid.

[62] Hunt, David R., *Restoring the Flag at Fort Sumter,* "*Sketches of War History, 1861— 1865,*" *(MOLLUS), 1903;* United States Army Military History Institute, Carlisle Barracks, Pa., pp. 522—530.

[63] Ibid

[64] Harper's Weekly, April 29, 1865.

[65] Hunt, David R., *Restoring the Flag at Fort Sumter,* "*Sketches of War History, 1861— 1865,*" *(MOLLUS), 1903;* United States Army Military History Institute, Carlisle Barracks, Pa., pp. 522—530.

[66] Ibid

CHAPTER 13

[67] April 9, 1865 issue of <u>The Clarendon Banner—Freedom.</u>, transcript taken from original copy, courtesy of the Charleston Library Society, Charleston, South Carolina.

[68] <u>The Illustrated Recollections of Potter's Raid, April 5—21, 1865</u>, by Allan D. Thigpen, Gamecock City Printing, Inc., Sumter, SC, 1998, p. 635; and <u>The War of the Rebellion: A Compilation of the Official Records of the Union and Confederate Armies</u>, Series 2, Vol. 47, Part 2.

[69] Jacob Welch, "Diary, 1864—1865," 25th Ohio Volunteer Infantry, in possession of Richard W. Welch.

CHAPTER 14

[70] Diary, Capt. Luther B. Mesnard (typed transcript), United States Army Military History Institute, Carlisle Barracks, Pa. 17013-5008 Civil War Miscellaneous Files, pp. 49-60, May 6, 1901.

[71] <u>A Heritage of Woe: The Civil War Diary of Grace Brown Elmore,1861-1868,</u> University of Georgia, Marli F. Weiner (ed.), 1997; and <u>Southern Homefront</u>, John Hammond Moore, Summerhouse Press, Columbia, South Carolina, p. 42.

[72] <u>The Prostrate State: South Carolina Under Negro Government</u> (October, 1873), James S. Pike, introduction by Henry Steele Commanger, New York: Loring & Mussye, 1935, v—xx and 79—84.

[73] "Letter from Mrs. Benjamin Scott to Governor J.D. Cos," Perrysburg, February 12, 1866, Correspondence to the Governor and Adjutant General of Ohio, 1861—1866, Sereies 147, Ohio Historical Society.

[74] Miscellaneous Regimental Papers, 25th Ohio Volunteer Infantry; filed with muster rolls, RG94 Misc. Regimental Papers, Boxes 3646—3648, AGO Adjutant General's Office, national Archives and Records Administration.

[75] Ibid

Appendix

Regimental Roster
(alphabetized)

The 25th Ohio Volunteer Infantry, 1861-1866

Editor's Note: The reader's indulgence is requested, for the probability of error exists when transcribing the names and records of nearly 2,000 veterans. It is highly recommended that those persons wishing more detailed and accurate military service and pension records contact the National Archives and Records Administration in Washington, D.C. (http://www.nara.gov). For a nominal fee and a reasonable waiting period, valuable and informative historical and genealogical information can be secured.

Source: **Official Roster of the Soldiers of the State of Ohio in the War of the Rebellion**, Volume 3, Cincinatti, Ohio: Ohio Valley Pub. & Mfg Co, 1886, pp. 166-226.

First Company Muster:

> Company A (St. Clairsville) June 5, 1861, Camp Jackson, Ohio
> Company B (Woodsfield) June 5, 1861, Camp Jackson, Ohio
> Company C (Woodsfield) June 10, 1861, Camp Jackson, Ohio
> Company D (Richland, Huron & Fayette Counties) June 8, 1861, Camp Jackson, Ohio; transferred to 12th Ohio Battery Light Artillery, 03-12-62.
> Company E (Fremont) June 12, 1861, Camp Jackson, Ohio
> Company F (Steubenville) June 13, 1861, Camp Jackson, Ohio
> Company G (Seneca Muskingum & Jefferson Counties) June 18, 1861, Camp Jackson, Ohio.

Company H (McConnelsville) June 26, 1861, Camp Jackson, Ohio
Company I (Summerfield) June 26, 1861, Camp Jackson, Ohio
Company K (Toledo) June 24, 1861, Columbus, Ohio

Name	Rank	Age	Enlistment Date	Remarks

Field and Staff:

James A. Jones, Colonel, age 48, entered service for period of 3 years, June 24, 1861. Resigned May 16, 1862

William P. Richardson, Colonel, age 37, entered service for period of 3 years, June 22, 1861.
Promoted from Lieut. Colonel May 16, 1862; wounded May 3, 1863 in battle of Chancellorsville, Va.; brevetted Brig. General Dec. 7, 1864; discharged May 9, 1866, by order of War Department.

George Webster, Lt. Col, age 36, entered service for period of 3 years, June 28, 1861.
Promoted from Major May 16, 1862; resigned July 30, 1862 to accept commission as Colonel of 98th O.V.I..

James F. Charlesworth, Lt. Col., age 36, entered service for period of 3 years, June 5, 1861.
Promoted to Major from Captain Co. A May 16, 1862; Lt. Col. July 30, 1862; discharged May 13, 1863 for wounds received June 8, 1862 in battle of Cross Keys, Va..

Jeremiah Williams, Lt. Col., age 29, entered service for period of 3 years, June 10, 1861.
Promoted to Major from Captain Co. C July 30, 1862; Lt. Col. May 3, 1863; wounded and captured July 1, 1863 at battle of Gettysburg, Pa.; prisoner of war in Libby Rebel Prison at Richmond, Va. eleven months; discharged June 21, 1864 by order of War Department.

Nathaniel Haughton, Lt. Col., age 31, entered service for period of 3 years, June 24, 1861.
Promoted to Major from Captain Co. A Aug. 4, 1863; wounded July 1, 1863 at battle of Gettysburg, Pa.; Lt. Col. July 13, 1864; brevetted Brig. General March 13, 1865; Col. May 25, 1866, but not mustered; mustered out with regiment June 18, 1866.

John W. Bowlus, Major, age 21, entered service for period of 3 years, June 4, 1861.
Promoted from Captain Co. C May 13, 1863; discharged Aug. 5, 1863 by order of the War Department.

Carrington E. Randall, Major, age 23, entered service for period of 3 years, June 12, 1861.
Promoted from Captain Co. G Aug. 11, 1864; died Dec. 16, 1864 or wounds received Nov. 30, 1864 in battle of Honey Hill, SC.

Edward C. Culp, Major, age 18, entered service for period of 3 years, June 8, 1861.
Promoted to Sergt. Major from Sergeant Co. D Nov. 1, 1861; 2d Lieutenant Co. C May 6, 1862; taken prisoner at Mt. Jackson June 14, 1862 and exchanged Sept 16, 1862; Major from Capt. Co. A Jan. 6, 1865; Lieut. Col. May 25, 1866, but not mustered; mustered out with regiment June 18, 1866; breveted Lt. Col. and Col. June 22, 1867.

Louis G. Meyers, Surgeon, age 37, entered service for period of 3 years, July 26, 1861. Mustered out July 16, 1864, on expiration of term of service.

William Walton, Surgeon, age..., entered service for period of 3 years, Oct. 7, 1862.. Promoted from Asst. Surgeon Aug. 8, 1864; mustered out with regiment June 18, 1866.

George R. Weeks, Asst. Surgeon, age 35, entered service for period of 3 years, July 2, 1861. Promoted to Surgeon 24th O.V.I. July 23, 1861.

Lawrence G. Andrews, Asst. Surgeon, age 32, entered service for period of 3 years, July 26, 1861. Resigned May 21, 1863.

William F. Dean, Asst. Surgeon, age..., entered service for period of 3 years, July 13, 1862. Died Sept. 23, 1862 at Georgetown, D.C.

Eli M. Wilson, Asst. Surgeon, age..., entered service for period of 3 years, Aug. 8, 1864. Mustered out with regiment June 18, 1866.

William J. Hoyt, Adjutant, age 25, entered service for period of 3 years, July 1, 1861.. Resigned January 23, 1863.

George G. Edgerton, Adjutant, age 28, entered service for period of 3 years, June 12, 1861.
Promoted from private Co. E May 6, 1863; discharged Nov. 20, 1863 by order of the War Department.

John O. Archbold, Adjutant, age 21, entered service for period of 3 years, June 10, 1861.
Promoted from 2d Lieutenant Co. C May 25, 1864; died Dec. 1, 1864 of wounds received Nov. 30, 1864 in battle of Honey Hill, S.C..

Andrew J. Hale, R.Q.M. (Regimental Quarter Master), age 33, entered service for period of 3 years, June 4, 1861.Promoted from 2d Lieutenant Co. E June 20, 1861; resigned Feb. 21, 1863.

David R. Hunt, R.Q.M., age 21, entered service for period of 3 years, June 12, 1861.

Promoted to Com. (commissary) Sergeant fron private Co. E Nov. 1, 1861; Regt. Quartermaster Jan. 23, 1863; Captain Co. F March 15, 1864.

George N. Holcomb, R.Q.M., age25, entered service for period of 3 years, June 12, 1861.

Appointed from 1st Lieutenant Co. G April 1, 1864; promoted to Captain Co. H Aug. 11, 1864.

Phineas Gano, R.Q.M., age 23, entered service for period of 3 years, June 10, 1861.

Promoted to Q.M. Sergeant from private Co. B Oct. 8, 1863; Regt. Quartermaster Aug. 11, 1864; discharged July 18, 1865, by order of War Department, veteran.

William J. Kyle, R.Q.M., age 18, entered service for period of 3 years, June 18, 1861.

Appointed from 1st Lieutenant Co. I Sept. 28, 1865; mustered out with regiment June 18, 1866.

Zachariah Ragan, Chaplain, age 57, entered service for period of 3 years, June 12, 1861.

Transferred as Hospital Chaplain Dec. 9, 1862 at Memphis, Tenn..

Robert F. Jackson, Serg. Major, age 21, entered service for period of 3 years, June 8, 1861.

Promoted from 1st Sergeant Co. D July 26, 1861; to 1st Lieutenant and Adjutant 32d O.V.I. Aug. 31, 1861.

Hezekiah Thomas, Serg. Major, age 24, entered service for period of 3 years, June 5, 1861.

Promoted from Sergeant Co. A Sept. 1, 1862; to 1st Lieutenant Co. E Aug. 11, 1864; veteran.

John Walton, Serg. Major, age 20, entered service for period of 3 years, June 10, 1861.

Promoted from private Co. C Oct. 112, 1864; to 2d Lieutenant Co. B Feb. 10, 1865.

John M. Rhodes, Serg. Major, age 22, entered service for period of 3 years, June 26, 1861.

Promoted from Sergeant Co. I Sept. 1, 1865; mustered out with regiment June 18, 1866.

Abner J. Phelps, Q.M.S, age 42, entered service for period of 3 years, June 17, 1861.

Promoted from private Co. D June 20, 1861; discharged March 23, 1863, on Surgeon's certificate of disability.

William Herring, Q.M.S., age 22, entered service for period of 3 years, June 121, 1861.

Promoted from private Co. E April 1, 1863; discharged Oct 8, 1863 on Surgeon's certificate of disability.

Daniel J. Crooks, Q.M.S., age 26, entered service for period of 3 years, June 18, 1861.

Promoted from private Co. A Nov. 5, 1864; to 2d Lieutenant Co. A Sept. 4, 1865; veteran.

Zachariah Dailey, Q.M.S., age 21, entered service for period of 3 years, June 26, 1861.

Promoted from Sergeant Co. I Oct. 1, 1865; mustered out with regiment June 18, 1866.

Samuel P. Houston, Com Serg., age 22, entered service for period of 3 years, June 13, 1861.

Promoted from Corporal Co. F July 21, 1861; reduced to ranks Co. F Nov. 1, 1861.

Joseph C. Coulter, Com Serg., age 19, entered service for period of 3 years, July 23, 1861.

Promoted from private Co. F March 1, 1863; discharged and re-enlisted Co. F Jan. 1, 1864. veteran.

Austin Haughton, Com Serg., age 19, entered service for period of 3 years, June 24, 1861.

Promoted from private Co. K March 16, 1864; to 2d Lieutenant Co. H Oct. 12, 1864.

B. Volney Howard, Com Serg., age 30, entered service for period of 3 years, Feb. 13, 1864.

Promoted from Sergeant Co. B Nov. 5, 1864; to 2d Lieutenant Co. C Sept. 4, 1865.

James B. Henthorn, Com Serg., age 18, entered service for period of 3 years, June 10, 1861.

Promoted from Sergeant Co. C Oct. 1, 1865; mustered out with regiment June 18, 1866.

Edward Ellis, Hos. St'd (Hospital Steward), age 40, entered service for period of 3 years, June 20, 1861. Promoted from 1st Sergeant Co. I July 18, 1861; died Oct 30, 1861.

Oliver W. Williams, Hos. St'd, age 19, entered service for period of 3 years, June 18, 1861.

Promoted from private Co. G Nov. 1, 1861; to 2d Lieutenant Co. C May 25, 1864; veteran.

Thomas H. Ferrel, Hos. St'd, age 21, entered service for period of 3 years, June 5, 1861.

Promoted from Sergeant Co A June 12, 1864; to 2d Lieutenant Co. I Nov. 18, 1864.

John Weyer, Hos. St'd, age 23, entered service for period of 3 years, June 5, 1861.

Promoted from Sergeant Co. A March 19, 1865; mustered out with regiment June 18, 1866.

Adoniram J. Hess, Prin, Mus. (Principal Musician), age 18, entered service for period of 3 years, June 10, 1861.Promoted from Musician Co. C June 28, 1861; reduced to ranks Co. C Aug. 31, 1861.

Thomas Stevenson, Prin. Mus., age 22, entered service for period of 3 years, July 3, 1861.

Promoted from Musician Co. I Sept, 1, 1861; reduced to ranks Co. I Sept. 1, 1862.

William Shaner, Prin. Mus., age 18, entered service for period of 3 years, June 10, 1861.

Promoted from Musican Co. B May 1, 1863; reduced to ranks Co. B Jan 1, 1864.

Benjamin S. Gilmore, Prin. Mus., age 35, entered service for period of 3 years, June 12, 1861.

Promoted from Musician Co. E Sept, 1, 1863; discharged and re-enlisted Co. E Jan 1, 1864; veteran.

James H. McBride, Prin. Mus., age 18, entered service for period of 3 years, June 18, 1861.

Promoted from Musician Co. I April 1, 1864; reduced to ranks Co. I July 19, 1864.

Benjamin F. Crabil, Prin. Mus., age 18, entered service for period of 3 years, June 13, 1861.

Promoted from Musician Co. F. June 20, 1864; reduced to ranks Co. F July 1, 1865.

George McBride, Prin Mus., age 21, entered service for period of 3 years, June 5, 1861.

Promoted from Musician Co. A July 1, 1865; mustered out with regiment June 18, 1866; veteran.

Albert J. Cavenaugh, Prin. Mus., age 20, entered service for period of 3 years, June 10, 1861.

Promoted from private Co. C Jan. 1, 1866; mustered out with regiment June 18, 1866; veteran.

A

Lewis Ackerman, Private, age 38, entered service for period of 3 years, Oct. 6, 1864.
Company I: Discharged July 15, 1865, by Order of the War Department.

Joseph Acres, Sergeant, age 19, entered service for period of 3 years, June 5, 1861.
Company A: Wounded June 8, 1862 in battle of Cross Keys, Va. and May 3, 1863 at Chancellorsville, Va.; appointed Corporal Aug. 1, 1864; Sergeant.....; mustered out with company June 18, 1866; veteran.

Frank B. Adams, Private, age 20, entered service for period of 1 year, Oct. 12, 1864.
Company G: Discharged...on Surgeon's certificate of disability.

George W. Adams, Private, age 18, entered service for period of 3 years, July 9, 1861.
Company H: Transferred to Co. C 75th O.VI. Jan. 16, 1864; from Co. C 75th O.V.I. June 12, 1864; mustered out July 16, 1864 at Columbus, Ohio on expiration of term of service.

William J. Akers, Private, age 20, entered service for period of 3 years, June 10, 1861.
Company C: Reduced from Sergeant...; transferred to Co. C 75th O.V.I. Jan 16, 1864; from Co. C 75th O.V.I. May 6, 1864; mustered out July 16, 1864 at Camp Chase, Ohio on expiration of term of service.

Daniel H. Alden, Sergeant, age 18, entered service for period of 3 years, Aug. 7, 1862.
Company E: Appointed Corporal Dec. 29, 1862; Sergeant May 3, 1864; discharged July 15, 1865 by order of War Department.

George Alfred, Private, age 22, entered service for period of 3 years, June 18, 1861.
Company G: On muster-in roll, but no further record found.

George F. Alfred, Corporal, age 25, entered service for period of 3 years, June 12, 1861.
Company E: Appointed Corporal April 3, 1863; killed May 2, 1863 in battle of Chancellorsville, Va..

Stephen Alge, Private, age 35, entered service for period of 3 years, Oct. 9, 1862.
Company B: Transferred from Co....107th O.V.I. July 13, 1865; mustered out Oct. 9, 1865 at Charleston, S.C. on expiration of term of service.

George W. Algyer, Private, age 20, entered service for period of 3 years, June 12, 1861.

Company E: Wounded May 8, 1862 in battle of McDowell, Va.; discharged July 12, 1862 on Surgeon's certificate of disability.

Aaron M. Alvord, Private, age 23, entered service for period of 1 year, Oct. 15, 1864.

Company E: Wounded Dec. 6, 1864 in battle of Deveaux Neck, S.C.; mustered Oct. 16, 1865 on expiration of term of service.

George P. Allen, Private, age 45, entered service for period of 1 year, Sept. 12, 1864.

Company A: Discharged July 15, 1865 by order of the War Department.

William A. Allen, Sergeant, age 25, entered service for period of 3 years, June 26, 1861.

Company I: Discharged Aug. 8, 1862 on Surgeon's certificate of disability.

George W. Alltop, Private, age 22, entered service for period of 3 years, June 26, 1861.

Company I: Transferred to Co. C 75th O.V.I. Jan. 16, 1864; from Co. C 75th O.V.I. June 12, 1864; mustered out July 16, 1864 on expiration of term of service.

William Alum, Private, age 44, entered service for period of 3 years, June 18, 1861.

Company A: Discharged Sept. 1, 1862, on Surgeon's certificate of disability.

Charles Alwin, Private, age 24, entered service for period of 3 years, June 8, 1861.

Company D: Transferred to 12th Battery O.L.A. March 121, 1862.

Andrew J. Ames, Corporal, age 22, entered service for period of 3 years, June 18, 1861.

Company G: appointed Corporal…; wounded May 2, 1863 in battle of Chancellorsville, Va.; mustered out July 16, 1864 on expiration of term of service.

Henry Amway, Private, age 28, entered service for period of 3 years, June 10, 1861.

Company C; Mustered out July 16, 1864 at Camp Chase, Ohio on expiration of term of service.

Ezekiel Anderson, Private, age 22, entered service for period of 3 years, June 13, 1861.

Company F: Mustered out July 16, 1864 on expiration of term of service.

John Anderson, Private, age 18, entered service for period of 1 year, Oct. 5, 1864.

Company F: no record given.

William F. Anderson, Private, age 22, entered service for period of 3 years, July 14, 1862.

Company A: Died Sept. 8, 1862 at Philadelphia Pa.

Israel Andrew, Private, age 43, entered service for period of 1 year, Oct. 7, 1864.

Company A: Mustered out Oct. 7, 1865 on expiration of term of service.

Charles Andrews, Private, age 18, entered service for period of 3 years, Feb. 29, 1864.

Company B: Mustered out with company June 18, 1866.

Lawrence G. Andrews, Asst. Surgeon, age 32, entered service for period of 3 years, July 26, 1861. Resigned May 21, 1863.

Darwin W. Angel, Private, age 35, entered service for period of 3 years, Feb. 26, 1864.

Company B: Discharged June 8, 1865 at Camp Dennison, Ohio by order of the War Department.

Abraham W. Angel, Private, age 44, entered service for period of 3 years, Feb. 29, 1864.

Company K: Discharged July 15, 1865 by Order of War Department.

George Angel, Private, age 43, entered service for period of 3 years, Feb. 29, 1864.

Company K: no record given.

Samuel Angus, Private, age 35, entered service for period of 1 year, Sept. 29, 1864.

Company A: Mustered out Oct. 8, 1865, on expiration of term of service.

Fred R. Angus, Private, age 39, entered service for period of 1 year, Sept. 28, 1864.

Company A: Discharged July 15, 1865 by order of the War Department.

Henry Ankney, Private, age 37, entered service for period of 1 year, Aug. 31, 1864.

Company E: Discharged July 15, 1865 by order of War Department.

Alston C. Archibald, 1st Sergeant, age 25, entered service for period of 3 years, June 10, 1861.

Company B: Promoted to 2d Lieutenant Co. C Oct. 16, 1861, but not mustered; discharged March 11, 1862 by order of the War Department.

John O. Archibold, Adjutant, age 21, entered service for period of 3 years, June 10, 1861.

Promoted from 2d Lieutenant Co. C May 25, 1864; died Dec. 1, 1864 of wounds received Nov. 30, 1864 in battle of Honey Hill, S.C..Company B: Appointed Corporal....; wounded May 3, 1863 in battle of Chancellorsville, Va.; promoted to 2d Lieutenant Co. C July 30, 1862.

Company C: Promoted from Corporal Co. B July 30, 1862; to 1st Lieutenant and Adjutant May 25, 1864.

Wilson L. Archbald, Private, age 22, entered service for period of nine months, Oct. 7, 1862.

Company H: Drafted; mustered out July 19, 1863 on expiration of term of service.

Michael Archer, Private, age 19, entered service for period of 3 years, June 10, 1861.

Company B: Mustered out July 16, 1864 on expiration of term of service.

Francis Armstrong, Private, age 19, entered service for period of 3 years, June 10, 1861.

Company C; Wounded May 2, 1863 in battle of Chancellorsville, Va.; transferred to Co. B 75th O.V.I. Jan. 16, 1864; from Co. B 75th O.V.I. May 6, 1864; mustered out July 16, 1864 at Camp Chase, Ohio on expiration of term of service.

George Armstrong, Private, age 21, entered service for period of 3 years, June 8, 1861.

Company D: Transferred to 12th Battery O.L.A. March 121, 1862.

John Armstrong, Private, age25, entered service for period of 3 years, June 13, 1861.

Company F: discharged Nov. 19, 1861 on Surgeon's certificate of disability.

Florence Arriman, Corporal, age 24, entered service for period of 3 years, June 20, 1861.

Company F: Appointed Corporal Jan. 1, 1864; mustered out with company June 18, 1866; veteran.

John M. Ashfield. Private, age 26, entered service for period of 3 years, June 26, 1861.

Company I: Discharged April 15, 1862 on Surgeon's certificate of disability.

William Askew, 1st Lieutenant, age 36, entered service for period of 3 years, June 4, 1861.

Company A: Promoted to Captain Co. I Sept. 5, 1861.Company I: Captain. Promoted from 1st Lieutenant Co. A Sept. 5, 1861; resigned May 14, 1863.

Howard F. Atherton, Private, age 20, entered service for period of 3 years, June 26, 1861.

Company I: Mustered out July 16, 1864 on expiration of term of service.

George C. Aubert, Corporal, age 34, entered service for period of 3 years, June 20, 1861.

Company F: Discharged Dec. 11, 1862 on Surgeon's certificate of disability.

Henry Aufdergarden, Private, age 19, entered service for period of 3 years, Feb. 29, 1864.

Company K: no record given.

Augustus Augert, Private, age 33, entered service for period of 3 years, Jan. 3, 1864.

Company F: no record given.

Amos D. Augstad, Private, age 19, entered service for period of 1 year, Oct. 6, 1864.

Company G: Mustered out Oct. 6, 1865 at Charleston, S.C. on expiration of term of service.

George M. Aulter, Private, age 34, entered service for period of 3 years, June 20, 1861.

Company F; Wounded Dec. 13, 1861 in battle of Camp Alleghany, W. Va.; discharged April 5, 1865 on surgeon's certificate of disability.

Gustave A. Augsperger. Private, age 22, entered service for period of 3 years, Sept. 30, 1862.

Company B: Transferred by Co....107th O.V.I. July 13, 1865; mustered out Oct. 8, 1865 at Charleston, S.C. on expiration of term of service.

B

Jacob W. Bach, Private, age 22, entered service for period of 3 years, Oct. 11, 1862.

Company A: Transferred from 107th O.V.I. July 13, 1865; mustered out Oct. 16, 1865 on expiration of term of service.

James Bacon, Private, age 22, entered service for period of 3 years, June 12, 1861.

Company E: Wounded May 2, 1863 in battle of Chancellorsville, Va. and July 1, 1863 in battle of Gettysburg, Pa.; mustered out with company June 18, 1866; veteran.

David Baer, Private, age 18, entered service for period of 1 year, Oct. 6, 1864.

Company G; Discharged July 15, 1865 by order of War Department.

Elias Baile, Private, age 28, entered service for period of 3 years, June 5, 1861.

Company A: Mustered out July 16, 1864 on expiration of term of service.

Charles H. Bailey, Private, age 36, entered service for period of 3 years, Feb. 27, 1864.

Company B: Discharged March 14, 1866 by order of the War Department.

Jacob H. Bailey, Private, age 20, entered service for period of 3 years, June 10, 1861.

Company C; Wounded May 8, 1862 in battle of McDowell, Va. and Aug. 30, 1862 in battle of bull Run, Va. and May 2, 1863 in battle of Chancellorsville, Va.; prisoner of war...; discharged Dec. 23, 1863, to re-enlist in Co. H.

Jacob H. Bailey, Private, age 27, entered service for period of 3 years, June 26, 1861.

Company K: Transferred to Co. K 75th O.V.I. Jan, 16, 1864; from Co. C 75th O.V.I. June 12, 1864; mustered out with company June 18, 1866; veteran.

Nelson Bailey, Private, age 18, entered service for period of 1 year, Feb. 20, 1865.
Company C: Mustered out Feb. 24, 1866 on expiration of term of service.
Charles A. Baker, Private, age 20, entered service for period of 3 years, Feb. 21, 1862.
Company I: Mustered out with company June 18, 1866; veteran
Charles O. Baker, Private, age 24, entered service for period of 3 years, June 24, 1861.
Company K: Reduced from Corporal Sept. 9, 1861; discharged…at Columbus, Ohio on Surgeon's certificate of disability.
James M. Baker, Private, age 19, entered service for period of 3 years, June 10, 1861.
Company C: Transferred to Co. C 75th O.V.I. Jan. 16, 1864; from Co. C 75th O.V.I. May 6, 1864; mustered out July 16, 1864 at Camp Chase, Ohio on expiration of term of service.
John Baker, Sergeant, age 19, entered service for period of 3 years, June 24, 1861.
Company K: Mustered as private; appointed Sergeant April 1, 1864; veteran.
Samuel Baker, Private, age 21, entered service for period of 1 year, Sept. 27, 1864.
Company D; Mustered out July 15, 1865 by order of War Department.
Wesley Baker, Private, age 18, entered service for period of 1 year, Oct. 4, 1864.
Company D: Mustered out with company Oct. 20, 1865.
Theodore Baldinger, Private, age 26, entered service for period of 3 years, March 26, 1864.
Company I: Transferred from Co…107th O.V.I. July 13, 1865; discharged Aug. 1, 1865 on Surgeon's certificate of disability.
Rush P. Baldwin, Private, age 19, entered service for period of 3 years, June 18, 1861.
Company G; Discharged Nov. 21, 1861 at Cheat Mountain, Va. on Surgeon's certificate of disability.
Joseph L. Ball, 2d Lieutenant, age 29, entered service for period of 3 years, June 26, 1861.
Company I: Discharged Oct. 6, 1862 by order of War Department.
Hugh Ballentine, Private, age 18, entered service for period of 3 years, Feb. 28, 1864.
Company C: Mustered out with company June 18, 1866.
David Bandy, Private, age 43, entered service for period of 1 year, Oct. 4, 1864.
Company D: Killed Nov. 30, 1864 in battle of Honey Hill, South Carolina.

William D. Banks, Private, age 18, entered service for period of 3 years, June 8, 1861.

Company D: Transferred to 12th Battery O.L.A. March 12, 1862.

William W. Banning, Corporal, age 21, entered service for period of 3 years, June 8, 1861.

Company D: Transferred to 12th Battery O.L.A. March 12, 1862.

Joseph Barger, Private, age 20, entered service for period of 3 years, Feb. 23, 1864.

Company K: no record given.

Thomas J. Barklay, Sergeant, age 22, entered service for period of 3 years, June 26, 1861.

Company H: Appointed Corporal July 12, 1862; Sergeant Aug. 19, 1863; reduced from Sergeant Jan. 21, 1864; wounded Nov. 30, 1864 in battle of Honey Hill, S. C.; appointed Sergeant from private June 1, 1866; mustered out with company June 18, 1866; veteran.

Benjamin Barlow, Corporal, age 19, entered service for period of 3 years, June 26, 1861.

Company I: Appointed Corporal April 1, 1864; died July 23, 1865 at Beaufort, S.C.; veteran.

William C. Barlow, Corporal, age 21, entered service for period of 3 years, June 26, 1861.

Company I: Appointed Corporal Nov. 1, 1861; discharged June 6, 1862 on Surgeon's certificate of disability.

William C. Barlow, Private, age 23, entered service for period of 3 years, June 26, 1861.

Company I: Wounded Dec. 13, 1861 in battle of Camp Alleghany, W. Va.; mustered out with company June 18, 1866; veteran.

James W. Barnes, Private age 32, entered service for period of 3 years, June 12, 1861.

Company E: Wounded Aug. 30, 1862 in battle of Bull Run, Va.; discharged Dec. 3, 1863 on Surgeon's certificate of disability.

Martin V. Barnes, Private, age 21, entered service for period of 3 years, June 10, 1861.

Company C; Killed July 1, 1863 in battle of Gettysburg, Pa..

Thomas Barnes, Private, age 25, entered service for period of 3 years, June 26, 1861.

Company I: Killed Dec. 1, 1861 at Grafton, Va..

William T. Barnes, Private, age 40, entered service for period of 3 years, Feb. 26, 1864.

Company I: Discharged Dec. 12, 1865 on Surgeon's certificate of disability.

Jacob L. Barnette, Sergeant, age 25, entered service for period of 3 years, June 26, 1861.
Company I: Wounded July 1, 1863 in battle of Gettysburg, Pa.; appointed Corporal Sept. 30, 1863; mustered out July 18, 1864 on expiration of term of service.
James W. Barnhart, Private, age 18, entered service for period of 1 year, Oct. 4, 1864.
Company D: Killed Dec. 9, 1864 in battle of Deveaux Neck, South Carolina.
Henry Barnup, Sergeant, age 19, entered service for period of 3 years, June 12, 1861.
Company E: Appointed Corporal April 1, 1864; Sergeant Nov. 17, 1865; mustered out with company June 18, 1866; veteran.
William H. Barr, Private, age 20, entered service for period of 3 years, July 23, 1861.
Company F: discharged Nov. 19, 1861 on Surgeon's certificate of disability.
John Barrack, Private, age 44, entered service for period of 1 year, Sept. 24, 1864.
Company F: Discharged July 15, 1865 by order of War Department.
Cornelius S. Barrell, Corporal, age 22, entered service for period of 3 years, June 26, 1861.
Company H: Appointed Corporal Nov. 7, 1861; died Jan. 26, 1862 at Washington, D.C..
John Barrell, Private, age 40, entered service for period of 3 years, June 26, 1861.
Company H: Transferred to Veteran Reserve Corps Oct. 2, 1863 by order of War Department.
Alexander Barrette, Private, age 27, entered service for period of 3 years, June 5, 1861.
Company A: Mustered out with company June 18, 1866; veteran.
William Barrell, Sergeant, age 38, entered service for period of 3 years, June 26, 1861.
Company H: Reduced from Corporal...3, 1862; appointed Corporal Jan, 1, 1866; mustered out with company June 18, 1866; veteran.
William A. Barrell, Private, age 19, entered service for period of 3 years, Feb. 11, 1864.
Company H: Wounded Nov. 30, 1864 in battle of Honey Hill, S.C.; discharged May 30, 1865 at Columbus Ohio by order of War Department.
Edward Barrette, Private, age 33, entered service for period of 3 years, Aug. 16, 1862.

Company F: Wounded July 1, 1863 in battle of Gettysburg, Pa.; reduced June 1, 1865; discharged July 15, 1865 by order of War Department.

John Barrette, Private, age 21, entered service for period of 3 years, June 13, 1861.

Company E: Discharged Aug. 1, 1861 on Surgeon's certificate of disability.

Benjamin Bartlett, Private, age 18, entered service for period of 3 years, July 9, 1861.

Company H: Died Nov. 22, 1861 at Beverly, W. Va..

James C. Bassford, Private, age 19, entered service for period of 3 years, June 26, 1861.

Company I: Transferred to Co. C 75th O.V.I. Jan. 16, 1864; from Co. C 75th O.V.I. June

12, 1864; mustered out July 16, 1864 on expiration of term of service.

Quimby Batdorff, Musician, age 16, entered service for period of 3 years, February 29, 1864.

Company B; Mustered out with company June 18, 1866.

Daniel Bates, Private, age 18, entered service for period of 3 years, Feb. 29, 1864.

Company I: Mustered out with company June 18, 1866.

Thomas Battin, Corporal, age 19, entered service for period of 3 years, June 10, 1866.

Company C: Appointed Corporal April 1, 1862; wounded Aug. 29, 1862 in battle of Bull Run, Va. and May 2, 1863 in battle of Chancellorsville, Va.; mustered out July 16, 1864 at Camp Chase, Ohio on Surgeon's certificate of disability; veteran.

William Battin, Private, age 21, entered service for period of 3 years, June 10, 1861.

Company C: transferred to Co. C 75th O.V.I. Jan. 16, 1864; from Co. C 75th O.V.I. May 6, 1864; mustered out July 16, 1864 at Camp Chase, Ohio on expiration of term of service.

William H. Battin, Corporal, age 19, entered service for period of 3 years, June 10, 1861.

Company C: Appointed Corporal Nov. 5, 1864; discharged May 8, 1864 at Charleston, S.C. on Surgeon's certificate of disability; veteran.

George W. Baty, Private, age 20, entered service for period of 1 year, Sept. 21, 1864.

Company D: Mustered out July 15, 1865 by order of War Department.

William Baugher, Private, age 39, entered service for period of 3 years, June 13, 1861.

Company F: Reduced from Corporal June 15, 1862; discharged Sept. 20, on Surgeon's certificate of disability.

Christian Baughman, Private, age 21, entered service for period of 3 years, June 24, 1861.

Company K: Wounded May 2, 1863 in batle of Chancellorsville, Va.; transferred to Veteran Reserve Corps Nov. 30, 1863 by order of War Department.

Samuel Baughman, Corporal, age 22, entered service for period of 3 years, June 18, 1861.

Company G: discharged Aug. 30, 1862 at Columbus, Ohio by order of War Department.

E. I. Baughner, Private 22, entered service for period of 3 years, June 10, 1861.

Company B: Discharged Dec. 31, 1861 at Beverly, W. Va. on Surgeon's certificate of disability.

George W. Bayless, Private, age 22, entered service for period of 3 years, June 16, 1861.

Company A; Discharged March 26, 1863 on Surgeon's certificate of disability.

George C. Beach, Private, age 20, entered service for period of 3 years, June 10, 1861.

Company C; Wounded May 2, 1863 in battle of Chancellorsville, Va.; transferred to Veteran Reserve Corps Sept. 1, 1863 by order of War Department.

William Beach, Private, age 19, entered service for period of 3 years, July 9, 1861.

Company H: Transferred to Co. C 75th O.V.I. Jan. 16, 1864; from Co. C 75th O.V.I. June 12, 1864; mustered out July 16, 1864 at Columbus, Ohio on expiration of term of service.

Frederick T. Beagle, Private, age 18, entered service for period of 3 years, June 12, 1861.

Company E: Wounded May 2, 1863 in battle of Chancellorsville, Va.; transferred to Veteran Reserve Corps March 15, 1864 by order of War Department.

John W. Beall, private, age 22, entered service for period of 3 years, June 26, 1861.

Company I: Transferred to Co. C 75th O.V.I. Jan. 16, 1864; from Co. C 75th O.V.I. June 12, 1864; mustered out July 16, 1864 on expiration of term of service.

Leander J. Beall, Sergeant, age 19, entered service for period of 3 years, June 5, 1861.

Company A: Appointed Corporal Feb. 1, 1865; Sergeant May 1, 1866; mustered out with company June 18, 1866; veteran.

Samuel Beall, Private, age 33, entered service for period of 3 years, June 5, 1861.

Company A: Discharged Sept. 12, 1862 for wounds received May 8, 1862 in battle of McDowell, Va.

Eli F. Beard, Corporal, age 20, entered service for period of 3 years, June 18, 1861.

Company G: Appointed Corporal...; wounded June 8, 1862 in battle of Cross Keys, Va.; discharged March 22, 1865 at Beaufort, S.C. on Surgeon's certificate of disability; veteran.

John L. Beard, Private, age 23, entered service for period of 1 year, Sept. 6, 1864.

Company E: Discharged July 15, 1865 by order of War Department.

Wallen M. Beatty, Corporal, age 18, entered service for period of 3 years, Oct. 8, 1864.

Company D: Appointed Corporal Aug. 1, 1865; mustered out with company Oct. 20, 1865..

Isaac Beaver, Private, 26, entered service for period of 3 years, June 10, 1861.

Company B: Transferred to Co. C March 20, 1864; veteran.

Company C: Transferred from Co. B March 20, 1864; discharged March 29, 1866 at Columbus, Ohio on Surgeon's certificate of disability; veteran.

Elijah Beckette, Private, age 22, entered service for period of 3 years, June 10, 1861.

Company C: Died Jan. 29, 1862 at Beverly, W. Va. of wound received Dec. 13, 1861 in battle of Camp Alleghany, W. Va..

Charles Beck, Private, age 25, entered service for period of 3 years, June 10, 1861.

Company B: Wounded Dec. 12, 1861 in battle of Camp Alleghany, W. Va. discharged Oct. 2, 1862 on Surgeon's certificate of disability.

Frederick J. Beck, Private, age 21, entered service for period of 3 years, June 10, 1861.

Company B: Wounded July 1, 1863 in battle of Gettysburg, Pa.; transferred to Co. B 75 O.V.I. March 20, 1864.

Company C: Transferred from Co. B March 20, 1864; mustered out July 16, 1864 at Columbus, Ohio on expiration of term of service.

John M. Beelman, Private, age 18, entered service for period of 3 years, June 8, 1861.

Company D: Transferred to 12th Battery O.L.A. March 12, 1862.

John Behr, Private, age 18, entered service for period of 1 year, Oct. 8, 1864.

Company A: Wounded Dec. 6, 1864 in battle of Deveaux Neck, S.C.; mustered out Oct. 8, 1865 on expiration of term of service.

George Beir, Corporal, age 23, entered service for period of 3 years, June 18, 1861.

Company G: Appointed Corporal June 1, 1866; mustered out with company June 18, 1866; veteran.

Daniel Bell, Private, age 30, entered service for period of 3 years, Aug. 20, 1862.
Company F: discharged July 13, 1865 by order of War Department.

Maurice S. Bell, 1st Lieutenant, age 30, entered service for period of 1 year, Oct. 18, 1864.
Company D: Wounded Nov. 30, 1864 in battle of Honey Hill, S.C.; mustered out with company Oct. 20, 1865.

William Bell, Private, age 25, entered service for period of 3 years, June 27, 1864.
Company C: Transferred from Co. F 107th O.V.I. July 13, 1865; mustered out with company June 18, 1866.

William Bellville, Corporal, age 40, entered service for period of 3 years, March 7, 1864.
Company K: Appointed Corporal April 1, 1866; mustered out with company June 18, 1866.

Henry Bemard, Private, age 28, entered service for period of 3 years, Dec. 19, 1863.
Company K: Transferred from Co....107th O.V.I. July 13, 1865.

Reuben Bemis, Private, age 39, entered service for period of 3 years, Feb. 29, 1864.
Company B; Discharged May 19, 1865 on Surgeon's certificate of disability.

Martin Bender, Private, age 27, entered service for period of 3 years, June 24, 1861.
Company K: Wounded May 3, 1863 in battle of Chancellorsville, Va.; mustered out July 16, 1864 on expiration of term of service.

Platt S. Benjamin, Private, age..., entered service for period of...years,...18....
Company I: Discharged Dec. 26, 1865 by order of War Department.

John Benney, Private, age 25, entered service for period of 3 years, June 18, 1861.
Company G: Killed Aug. 30, 1862 in battle of Bull Run, Va..

Isaac Bennington, Private, age 32, entered service for period of 3 years, Oct. 17, 1862.
Company A: Mustered out Oct. 17, 1865 on expiration of term of service.

Martin Bennington, Private, age 19, entered service for period of 3 years, Nov. 15, 1862.
Company A: Mustered out Nov. 23, 1865 on expiration of term of service.

Benoi Bennette Private, age 24, entered service for period of 3 years, June 10, 1864.

Company C; Absent sick...; in U.S. General Hospital at Hilton's Head, S.C.; mustered out June 18, 1866 by order of War Department; veteran.

Charles R. Benson, Corporal, age 30, entered service for period of 3 years, Feb. 22, 1864.

Company B: Appointed Corporal June 25, 1866; mustered out with company June 18, 1866.

Benjamin Benson, Private, age 30, entered service for period of 3 years, Feb. 18, 1864.

Company B: no record given.

George Benson, Private, age 37, entered service for period of 3 years, Feb. 27, 1864.

Company B: Died Sept. 6, 1864 in General Hospital at Hilton Head, S.C..

Henry Benson, Sergeant, age 23 entered service for period of 3 years, Feb. 19,1864.

Company B: Appointed Corporal March 16, 1864; Sergeant Nov. 5, 1864; killed Nov. 30, 1864 in battle of Honey Hill, S.C..

William Benson, Private, age 26, entered service for period of 3 years, Feb. 22, 1864.

Company B: Wounded Nov. 30, 1864 in battle of Honey Hill, S.C.; mustered out with company June 18, 1866.

James Benway, Private, age 19, entered service for period of 3 years, June 24, 1861.

Company K: Transferred to 75th O.V.I. Jan. 1, 1864.

Erwin M. Bergstreser, Private, age 22, entered service for period of 3 years, June 18, 1861.

Company G: Discharged April 16, 1863 at Columbus, Ohio by order of War Department.

Daniel Berry, Private, age 23, entered service for period of 3 years, June 10, 1861.

Company B: Wounded Aug. 29, 1862 in battle of Bull Run, Va.; discharged Oct. 31, 1862 at Washington, D.C. on Surgeon's certificate of disability.

William H. Beymer, Sergeant, age 21, entered service for period of 3 years, Feb. 17, 1862.

Company I: Appointed Corporal Nov. 5, 1864; Sergeant Jan. 1, 1866; mustered out with company June 18, 1866; veteran.

James C. Bickford, Private, age 24, entered service for period of 9 months, Oct. 7, 1862.

Company I: Drafter; wounded July 1, 1863 in battle of Gettysburg, Pa; mustered out July 7, 1863 on expiration of term of service.

John Bidgley, Private, age 21, entered service for period of 3 years, June 12, 1861.

Company E: no record given.

Obediah Bidgley, Private, age 18, entered service for period of 3 years, Feb. 22, 1864.

Company E: Mustered out with company June 18, 1866.

John Bier, Private, age 29, entered service for period of 3 years, Feb. 22, 1864.

Company K: Mustered out with company June 18, 1866.

Elisha Biggerstaff, 1st Lieutenant, age 23, entered service for period of 3 years, June 12, 1861.

Company A: Promoted for 2d Lieutenant Co. E May 25, 1864; wounded Dec. 6, 1864 in battle of Deveaux Neck, S.C.; mustered out with company June 18, 1866.; veteran.

Company E: Wounded Aug. 30, 1862 in battle of Bull Run, Va.; promoted from 1st Sergeant April 13, 1864; to 1st Lieutenant Co. A May 25, 1864; veteran.

Sewell C. Biggs, Corporal, age 33, entered service for period of 3 years, Feb. 19, 1864.

Company B: Appointed Corporal Aug. 1, 1865; mustered out with company June 18, 1866.

Henry Billings, Private, age 24, entered service for period of 1 year, Sept. 2, 1864.

Company C: Discharged July 15, 1865 by order of War Department.

Frederick C. Bingel, Private, age 21, entered service for period of 3 years, Aug. 6, 1862.

Company F: Transferred to 4th U.S. Cavalry Oct. 31, 1862 by order of War Department.

Thaddeus S. Birch, Private, age 44, entered service for period of 3 years, Feb. 20, 1864.

Company K: Discharged Aug. 11, 1865 on Surgeon's certificate of disability.

Frank Bisel, Private, age 18, entered service for period of 3 years, June 8, 1861.

Company D: Transferred to 12th Battery O.L.A. March 12, 1862.

Benjamin F. Bixby, Private, age 18, entered service for period of 3 years, Sept. 30, 1864.

Company D: Mustered out July 15, 1865 by order of the War Department.

John Bixler, Private, age 21, entered service for period of 1 year, Sept. 29, 1864.

Company D: Mustered out on July 15, 1865 by order of War Department.

William Bixler, Private, age 18, entered service for period of 1 year, Sept. 29, 1864.

Company D: Mustered out on July 15, 1865 by order of War Department.

Henry Bixler, Corporal, age 18, entered service for period of 1 year, Oct. 3, 1864.

Company D: Appointed Corporal July 1, 1865; mustered out with company Oct. 20, 1865.

Samuel Black, Private, age 24, entered service for period of 3 years, Feb. 19, 1864.

Company E: no record given.

Benjamin W. Blandy, 2d Lieutenant, age 22, entered service for period of 3 years, June 4, 1861.Company G: Promoted to 1st Lieutenant May 2, 1862, but not mustered; resigned Sept. 19, 1862 at Washington, D.C..

Theodore Blocher, Private, age 18, entered service for period of 3 years, Oct. 11, 1862.

Company A: Transferred from 107th O.V.I. July 15, 1865; mustered Oct. 11, 1865 on expiration of term of service.

William F. Bloor, 1st Lieutenant, age 28, entered service for period of 3 years, June 14, 1861

Company A: Promoted from private June 1, 1863; to 1st Lieutenant Co. C March 15, 1864.

Company B: Promoted from 2d Lieutenant Co. A March 15, 1864; mustered out July 16, 1864 at Camp Chase, Ohio on expiration of term of service.

Anderson Blue, Private, age 23, entered service for period of 3 years, June 8, 1861.

Company D: Transferred to 12th Battery O.L.A. March 12, 1862.

Lewis C. Boegehold, Private, age 18, entered service for period of 3 years, June 24, 1861.

Company K: Transferred from Co....107th O.V.I. July 13, 1864; mustered out July 15, 1864 on expiration of term of service.

Gustave Boeham, Private, age19, entered service for period of 3 years, Sept. 26, 1863.

Company K: Transferred from Co....107th O.V.I. July 13, 1865.

Cicero H. Boden, Private, age 18, entered service for period of 3 years, June 8, 1861.

Company D: Transferred to 12th Battery O.L.A. March 12, 1862.

William Bodi, Private, age 22, entered service for period of 1 year, Oct. 4, 1864.

Company A: Wounded Dec. 6, 1864 in battle of Devaux Neck, S.C.; mustered out Oct. 4, 1865 on expiration of term of service.

Smith Bodkins, Private, age 21, entered service for period of 3 years, June 10, 1861

Company C: no record given.

George W. Bogart, Private, age 25, entered service for period of 1 year, Oct. 3, 1863.

Company D: Mustered out with company Oct. 20, 1865.

Lewis C. Boegehold, Private, age 18, entered service for period of 3 years, June 24, 1861.

Company K: Transferred to Co....107th O.V.I. July 13, 1864; mustered out July 15, 1864 on expiration of term of service.

Joseph Boggs, Private, age 24, entered service for period of 3 years, June 5, 1861.

Company A: Discharged March 30, 1862 on Surgeon's certificate of disability.

Frederick Bogle, Private, age 40, entered service for period of 3 years, Sept. 9, 1863.

Company I: no record given

James C.Bolen, Private, age 20, entered service for period of 3 years, June 5, 1861.

Company A: Wounded Dec. 12, 1861 in battle of Camp Alleghany, W.Va. and May 3, 1863 in battle of Chancellorsville, Va.; mustered out July 16, 1864 on expiration of term of service.

John H. Bolesmayer, Private, age 29, entered service for period of 3 years, June 24, 1861.

Company K: Transferred to Co. C 75th O.V.I. Jan. 16, 1864; from Co. C 75th O.V.I. June 13, 1864; mustered out July 16, 1864 on expiration of term of service.

Henry Booth, Private, age 22, entered service for period of 1 year, Oct. 5, 1864.

Company F: no record given.

Walter Booth, Private, age 32, entered service for period of 3 years, Feb. 22, 1862.

Company F: Transferred to 4th U.S. Cavalry Oct. 31, 1862 by order of War Department.

Joseph Borat, Private, age 18, entered service for period of 3 years, March 12, 1864.

Company B; Mustered out with company June 18, 1866.

William Boroway, Private, age 17, entered service for period of 3 years, Oct. 7, 1862.

Company A: Transferred from 107th O.V.I. July 15, 1865; mustered out Oct. 16, 1865 on expiration of term of service.

Leander Boston, Private, age 20, entered service for period of 3 years, June 10, 1861.

Company C; Died March 18, 1863 at Brook's Station, Va..

Dempsey Boswell, Wagoner, age 27, entered service for period of 3 years, June 26, 1861.

Company H: Appointed Wagoner Oct. 1, 1861; mustered out July 16, 1865 on expiration of term of service.

Isaac S. Bowers, Private, age 42, entered service for period of 1 year, Sept. 25, 1864.

Company F; Discharged July 15, 1865 by order of War Department.

John Bowers, Private, age 21, entered service for period of 3 years, Feb. 27, 1864.

Company B; Wounded Nov. 3, 1864 in battle fo Honey Hill, S.C.; discharged May 30, 1865 at Camp Dennison, Ohio on Surgeon's certificate of disability.

John Bowers, Private, age 18, entered service for period of 1 year, Sept. 6, 1864.

Company K: Killed Nov. 30, 1864 in battle of Honey Hill, S.C..

John W. Bowlus, Major, age 21, entered service for period of 3 years, June 4, 1861.

Promoted from Captain Co. C May 13, 1863; discharged Aug. 5, 1863 by order of the War Department

Company C: Promoted from 1st Lieutenant Co. E May 16, 1862; to Major May 13, 1863.

Company E: Promoted to Captain Co. C May 16, 1862.

Lewis H. Bowlus, Sergeant, age 22, entered service for period of 3 years, June 12, 1861.

Company E: Appointed Sergeant from Corporal Aug. 1, 1861; discharged May 16, 1862 on Surgeon's certificate of disability.

James N. Bowman, Private, age 21, entered service for period of 3 years, June 10, 1861.

Company B: Discharged May 7, 1862 on Surgeon's certificate of disability.

William R. Bowman, Private, age 22, entered service for period of 3 years, June 10, 1861.

Company C; Transferred from Co. B March 20, 1864; mustered out July 16, 1864 at Columbus, Ohio on expiration of term of service.

Blydon H. Boyce, Sergeant, age 26, entered service for period of 3 years, June 18, 1861.

Company G: Mustered as private; appointed Sergeant...; wounded May 2, 1863 in battle of Chancellorsville, Va.; mustered out July 16, 1864 at Hilton Head, S.C. on expiration of term of service.

Henry Boyce, Private, age 33, entered service for period of 1 year, Sept. 3, 1864.

Company C; Discharged July 15, 1865 by order of War Department.

George Bracy, Private, age 19, entered service for period of 3 years, June 8, 1861.

Company D: Transferred to 12th Battery O.L.A. March 12, 1862.

Albert Bradley, Private, age 18, entered service for period of 3 years, June 8, 1861.

Company D: Transferred to 12th Battery O.L.A. March 12, 1862.

William H. Branson, Corporal, age 22, entered service for period of 3 years, July 23, 1861.

Company F; appointed Corporal Sept. 1, 1863; transferred to Co. C 75th O.V.I. Jan 16, 1864; from Co. C 75th O.V.I. June 12, 1864; mustered out July 16, 1864 on expiration of term of service.

James Breach, Private, age 20, entered service for period of 3 years, June 26, 1861.

Company I: Wounded Dec. 13, 1861 in battle of Camp Alleghany, W. Va.; discharged Oct. 1, 1862 on Surgeon's certificate of disability.

Lewis H. Brent, Musician, age 16, entered service for period of 3 years, June 26, 1861.

Company H: Transferred to Co. C 75th O.V.I. Jan. 16, 1864; from Co. C. 75th O.V.I. June 12, 1864; mustered out July 16, 1864 at Columbus, Ohio on expiration of term of service.

James E. Bridge, Private, age 32, entered service for period of 3 years, June 24, 1861.

Company K: no record given.

Joseph Briggle, Private, age 18, entered service for period of 3 years, Feb. 23, 1864.

Company K: Transferred from Co....107th O.V.I. July 13, 1865; mustered out with company June 18, 1866.

Sewell C. Briggs, Corporal, age 33, entered service for period of 3 years, Feb. 19, 1864.

Company B: Appointed Corporal Sept, 28, 1865; mustered out with company June 18, 1866.

Newton A. Briggs, Private, age 19, entered service for period of 3 years, June 8, 1861.

Company D: Transferred to 12th Battery O.L.A. March 12, 1862.

John Britigam, Private, age 31, entered service for period of 1 year, Oct. 1, 1864.

Company F: Mustered out with company June 15, 1865 on expiration of term of service.

Slater B. Brock, Sergeant, age 23, entered service for period of 3 years, June 10, 1861.

Company B: Wounded May 8, 1862 in battle of McDowell, Va.; transferred to Co. C March 1, 1864.

Company C: Transferred from Co. B as Sergeant March 20, 1864; mustered out July 16, 1864 at Camp Chase, Ohio on expiration of term of service.

Jesse I. Brooks, Private, age 18, entered service for period of 1 year, Oct. 6, 1864.

Company F: Died Oct. 13, 1865 at Barnwell C.H., S.C..

Samuel J. Brooks, 2d Lieutenant, age 23, entered service for period of 3 years, June 20, 1861.

Company F: Promoted from 1st Sergeant Co. I Feb. 10, 1865; to 1st Lieutenant Sept. 4, 1865, but not mustered; mustered out with company June 18, 1866.

Samuel J. Brooks, 1st Sergeant, age 18, entered service for period of 3 years, June 26, 1861.

Company I: Wounded May 8, 1862 in battle of McDowell, a. and July 1, 1863 in battle of Gettysburg, Pa.; appointed from Sergeant Aug. 2, 1864; promoted to 2d Lieutenant Co. F Feb. 10, 1865; veteran.

Abraham Brown, Private, age 35, entered service for period of 1 year, Oct. 6, 1864.

Company A: Mustered out Oct.. 6, 1865 on expiration of term of service.

Benjamin F. Brown, Corporal, age 20, entered service for period of 3 years, Feb. 26, 1864.

Company I: Wounded Nov. 30, 1864 in battle of Honey Hill, S.C.; appointed Corporal Oct. 1, 1865; mustered out with company June 18, 1866.

Elijah Brown, Private, age 22, entered service for period of 3 years, June 10, 1861.

Company B: Transferred to Co. H June 13, 1864.

Company H: Transferred from Co. B June 13, 1864; mustered out July 16, 1864 at Columbus, Ohio on expiration of term of service.

Francis Brown, Corporal, age 19, entered service for period of 3 years, Feb. 29, 1864.

Company B: Appointed Corporal Feb. 1,1866; mustered out with company June 18, 1866.

George Brown, Private, age 28, entered service for period of 3 years, June 24, 1861.

Company K: Wounded May 2, 1863 in battle of Chancellorsville, Va.; transferred to Veteran Reserve Corps Nov. 30, 1863 by order of War Department.

Israel Brown, Corporal, age 21, entered service for period of 3 years, June 20, 1861.

Company F: Appointed Corporal June 1, 1866; mustered out with company June 18, 1866; veteran.

John Brown, Private, age 33, entered service for period of 3 years, Jan. 27, 1864.
Company A: no record given.

John Brown, Private, age 24, entered service for period of 3 years, June 10, 1861.

Company B; Transferred to Co. H June 13, 1864.

Company H: Transferred from Company B June 13, 1864; mustered out July 16, 1864 at Columbus, Ohio on expiration of term of service.

John Brown, Private, age 21, entered service for period of 3 years, Dec. 10, 1863.

Company F: no record given.

Jonathan Brown, Captain, age 34, entered service for period of 3 years, June 4, 1861.

Company K: Resigned March 20, 1863.

Joseph W. Brown, Private, age 24, entered service for period of 3 years, June 10, 1861.

Company B: Wounded May 3, 1863 in battle of Chancellorsville, Va.; transferred to Co. C March 20, 1864.

Company C: Transferred from Co. B March 20, 1864; mustered out July 16, 1864 at Columbus, Ohio on expiration of term of service.

Mark Brown, Private, 19, entered service for period of 3 years, June 10, 1861.

Company B: Died June 8, 1862 in hospital at Huttonsville, West Virginia.

Martin Brown, Private, age 18, entered service for period of 3 years, Feb. 22, 1864.

Company B: Mustered out with company June 18, 1866.

Theodore Brown, Private, age 18, entered service for period of 3 years, June 8, 1861.

Company D: Transferred to 12th Battery O.L.A. March 12, 1862.

William Brown, Private, age 23, entered service for period of 3 years, Dec. 12, 1863.

Company F: no record given.

William H. Brown, Private, age 20, entered service for period of 3 years, June 8, 1861.

Company D: Wounded Dec. 12, 1861 in battle of Camp Alleghany, W. Va.; transferred to 12th Battery O.L.A. March 12, 1862.

William H. Brown, Corporal, age 21, entered service for period of 1 year, Oct. 1, 1864.

Company F: Appointed Corporal Aug. 1, 1865; mustered out Oct. 1, 1865 on expiration of term of service.

William H. Brown, Private, age 20, entered service for period of 3 years, June 26, 1861.

Company I: Wounded May 8, 1862 in battle of McDowell, Va.; discharged Sept. 16, 1862 on Surgeon's certificate of disability.

William J. Brown, Private, age 21, entered service for period of 3 years, June 26, 1861.

Company I: Mustered out July 16, 1864 on expiration of term of service.

Andrew Brownell, Private, age 18, entered service for period of 3 years, Oct. 14, 1862.

Company A: Transferred from 107th O.V.I. July 15, 1865; mustered out Oct...., 1865 on expiration of term of service.

Daniel Brownlee, Private, age 23, entered service for period of 3 years, Aug. 9,1862.

Company F; Discharged July 13, 1865 by order of War Department.

John Brownlee, Private, age 18, entered service for period of 3 years, June 13, 1861.

Company F: Mustered out with company June 18, 1866; veteran.

John H. W. Brugeman, Private, age 24, entered service for period of 3 years, July 16, 1864.

Company B; Transferred from Co. B 107th O.V.I. July 13, 1865.

Christian Bruner, Private, age 33, entered service for period of 1 year, Oct. 8, 1864.

Company H: Mustered out Oct. 7, 1865 on expiration of term of service.

Harmon Buckleman, Private, age 22, entered service for period of 3 years, June 10, 1861.

Company C: Discharged Jan 20, 1863 at Philadelphia, Pa. on Surgeon's certificate of disability.

John Buckley, Private, age 35, entered service for period of 3 years, Feb. 27, 1864.

Company K: no record given.

Edwin V. Buckner, Corporal, age 31, entered service for period of 3 years, June 24, 1861.

Company K: Discharged Jan. 18, 1862 at Stafford C.H., Va. on Surgeon's certificate of disability.

William H. Bundy, Private, age 20, entered service for period of 3 years, June 26, 1861.

Company H: Reduced from Corporal Sept. 4, 1861; discharged Aug. 20, 1862 on Surgeon's certificate of disability.

John W. Bunting, Corporal, age 21, entered service for period of 3 years, June 26, 1861.

Company I: Appointed Corporal Feb. 1, 1863; mustered out with company June 18, 1866; veteran.

Thomas H. Bunting, Private, age 19, entered service for period of 3 years, June 26, 1861.

Company I: Veteran.

Thomas Burchfield, Private, age 20, entered service for period of 3 years, Aug. 15, 1862.

Company F: Transferred to Co. C 75th O.V.I. Jan. 16, 1864; from Co. C 75th O.V. I. June 12, 1864; discharged July 15, 1865 by order of War Department.

James H. Burdo, Private, age 26, entered service for period of 3 years, Feb. 29, 1864.

Company K: Discharged Aug. 25, 1865 by Order of War Department.

R. D. Burdo, Private, age 18, entered service for period of 3 years, Feb. 19, 1864.

Company K: Wounded Dec. 6, 1864 in battle of Gregory's Landing, S.C.; mustered out with company June 18, 1866.

William Burgess, Corporal, age 23, entered service for period of 3 years, June 18, 1861.

Company G: Appointed Corporal Sept. 1, 1865; mustered out with company June 18, 1866.

George Burk, Corporal, age 20, entered service for period of 3 years, Feb. 29, 1864.

Company B: Appointed Corporal Feb. 1, 1865.

Patrick Burk, Private, age 21, entered service for period of 3 years, June 13, 1861.

Company F: Wounded June 8, 1862 in battle of Cross Keys, Virginia.

Magnus Burkhart, Private, age 20, entered service for period of 1 year, Sept. 30, 1864.

Company D: Mustered out July 15, 1865 by order of War Department.

Isaac Burkheimer, Private, age 19, entered service for period of 1 year, Oct. 5, 1864.

Company F: Died Dec. 15, 1864 in U.S. General Hospital at Hilton Head, S.C. of wounds received Nov. 30, 1864 in battle of Honey Hill, S.C.

Joshua Burkhead, Private, age 22, entered service for period of 3 years, June 5, 1861.

Company A: Mustered out with company June 18, 1866; veteran.

Alonzo N. Burlingame, Private, age 21, entered service for period of 3 years, June 26, 1861.

Company H: Killed Aug. 30, 1862 in battle of Bull Run, Va..

James E. Burns, Private, age23, entered service for period of 1 year, Sept. 20, 1864.

Company F: no record given.

John Burns, Private, age 23, entered service for period of 1 year, Oct. 7, 1864.

Company D: no record given..

Lawrence Burns, Private, age 19, entered service for period of 3 years, June 24, 1861.
Company K: Died May 24, 1863 at Division Hospital Brook's Station, Va. of wounds received May 2, 1863 in battle of Chancellorsville, Va..
James A. Burson, Private, age 19, entered service for period of 3 years, March 15, 1862.
Company A: Discharged Sept. 12, 1862 for wounds received May 8, 1862 in battle of McDowell, Va.
Joseph Bush, Private, age 45, entered service for period of 3 years, June 18, 1861.
Company G: Discharged April 25, 1862 at Brook's Station, Va. by order of War Department.
Griffith Butler, Private, age 20, entered service for period of 3 years, June 26, 1861,
Company H: transferred to Co. C 75th O.V.I. Jan. 16, 1864; from Co. C 75th O.V.I. June 12, 1864; mustered out July 16, 1864 at Columbus, Ohio on expiration of term of service.
Levi Butler, Private, age 27, entered service for period of 3 years, June 5, 1861.
Company A: Killed May 3, 1863 in battle of Chancellorsville, Va.
Thomas Butler, Private, age 28, entered service for period of 3 years, Oct. 14, 1862.
Company A: Transferred from 107th O.V.I. July 13, 1865; mustered out Oct. 16, 1865 on expiration of term of service.
Thomas Butler, Private, age 35, entered service for period of 1 year, Oct 15, 1864.
Company K: Drafted; mustered out Oct. 15, 1865 on expiration of term of service.
Andrew Byers, Private, age 18, entered service for period of 1 year, Sept. 16, 1864.
Company K: Discharged July 15, 1865 by order of War Department.
Otho W. Byroad, Private, age 19, entered service for period of 3 years, June 8, 1861.
Company D: Transferred to 12th Battery O.L.A. March 12, 1862.

C

John Cahill, Private, age 18, entered service for period of 3 years, July 23, 1861.
Company F: Transferred to 4th U.S. Cavalry Nov. 15, 1862.
Thomas Cain, Private, age 22, entered service for period of 3 years, June 10, 1861.
Company B; Transferred to Co. C March 20, 1864; veteran.

Company C: Transferred from Co. B March 20, 1864; mustered out with company June 18, 1866; veteran.

William H. Cait, Private, age18, entered service for period of 3 years, Feb. 27, 1864.

Company B: Died Nov. 2, 1864 at DeCamp General Hospital, New York.

Patrick Calahan, Private, age 35, entered service for period of 3 years, March 17, 1864.

Company B: Transferred from Co....107th O.V.I. July 13, 1865; mustered out with company June 18, 1866.

Samuel T. Calland, Private, age 19, entered service for period of 3 years, June 26, 1861.

Company I: Reduced from Corporal...; wounded June 8, 1862 in battle of Cross Keys, Va. and July 1, 1863 in battle of Gettysburg, Pa.; discharged July 13, 1865 on Surgeon's certificate of disability.

John Cale, Private, age 21, entered service for period of 3 years, June 18, 1861. Company G; Discharged...at Fort McHenry, Md. on Surgeon's certificate of disability.

James W. Calvert, Sergeant, age 18, entered service for period of 3 years, June 26, 1861.

Company I: Appointed Corporal April 1, 1864; Sergeant Oct. 1, 1865; mustered out with company June 18, 1866; veteran.

William Camden, Private, age 31, entered service for period of 3 years, June 26, 1861.

Company H: no record given.

Neil Cameron, Private, age 37, entered service for period of 3 years, June 24, 1861.

Company K: Killed May 8, 1862 in battle of McDowell, Va..

James C. Campbell, Private, age 37, entered service for period of 3 years, Oct. 3, 1862.

Company A: Transferred to Veteran Reserve Corps Aug. 1, 1863 by order of War Department.

Jesse Campbell, Private, age 18, entered service for period of 3 years, June 10, 1861.

Company C: Wounded July 1, 1863 in battle of Gettysburg, Pa.; mustered out July 16, 1864 at Camp Chase, Ohio on expiration of term of service.

Frederick Cannell, Private, age 19, entered service for period of 3 years, June 12, 1861.

Company E: Discharged Nov. 22, 1861 on Surgeon's certificate of disability.

Michael Cantwell, Private, age 21, entered service for period of 3 years, June 13, 1861.

Company F: Transferred to Company C, 75th O.V.I. Jan. 16, 1864; from Co. C 75th O.V.I. June 12, 1864; mustered out July 15, 1864 on expiration of term of service.

George Capper, Private, age 36, entered service for period of 3 years, Sept. 20, 1864.

Company C: Discharged July 15, 1865 by order of War Department.

Howard Carman, Private, age 21, entered service for period of 3 years, June 12, 1861.

Company E: Wounded Nov. 30, 1864 in battle of Honey Hill, S. C.; discharged July 15, 1865 by order of War Department.

Calvin A. Carpenter, Private, age 20, entered service for period of 3 years, June 24, 1861.

Company K: transferred to Co. C 75th O.V.I. Jan. 16, 1864; from Co. C 75th O.V.I. June 13, 1864; mustered out July 16, 1864 on expiration of term of service.

Bryan Carrigan, Musician, age 17, entered service for period of 3 years, Feb. 15, 1864.

Company E: Mustered out with company June 18, 1866.

John Carrigan, Private, age 29, entered service for period of 1 year, Oct. 6, 1864.

Company D: Mustered out with company Oct. 20, 1865.

James H. Carrol, Private, age 32, entered service for period of 1 year, Oct. 4, 1864.

Company A: Mustered out Oct. 4, 1865 on expiration of term of service.

Vincent Carrol, Sergeant, age 19, entered service for period of 3 years, July 27, 1861.

Company E: Appointed Sergeant from private June 1, 1863; wounded July 1, 1863 in battle of Gettysburg, Pa.; transferred to Veteran Reserve Corps Dec. 1, 1863 by order of War Department.

William Carrol, Private, age 24, entered service for period of 3 years, June 24, 1861.

Company K: Discharged June 18, 1862 at Mt. Jackson, Va. on Surgeon's certificate of disability.

James I. Carrothers, Sergeant, age 23, entered service for period of 3 years, June 10, 1861.

Company B: Promoted to 2d Lieutenant Co. K 78th O.V.I. Jan. 11, 1862.

John Carruthers, Private, age 18, entered service for period of 1 year, Sept. 28, 1864.

Company D: Mustered out July 15, 1865 by order of War Department.

Theodore Carter, Private, age 27, entered service for period of 3 years, March 15, 1862.
Company A: Mustered out with company June 18, 1866; veteran.
Irvin F. Carvin, Private, age 24, entered service for period of 3 years, June 24, 1861.
Company K: Reduced from Sergeant May 1, 1863; mustered out July 16, 1864 on expiration of term of service.
Frederick Cashdollar, Private, age 36, entered service for period of 1 year, Sept. 25, 1864.
Company F: Discharged July 15, 1865 by order of War Department.
Charles M. Cass, Private, age 21, entered service for period of 3 years, July 10, 1861.
Company K: Discharged Aug. 25, 1862 at Columbus, Ohio for wounds received June 2, 1862 in battle of Cross Keys, Va..
George Cass, Private, age 26, entered service for period of 3 years, June 5, 1861.
Company A: Wounded Aug. 29, 1862 in battle of bull Run, Va.; discharged Feb..., 1863 at Fort Schuyler, N.Y. on Surgeon's certificate of disability.
David Casteel, Private, age 37, entered service for period of 3 years, June 20, 1861.
Company F: Mustered out July 16, 1864 on expiration of term of service.
James Castor, Private, age 25, entered service for period of 3 years, June 26, 1861.
Company H: no record given.
Alpheus A. W. Catlette, Private, age 28, entered service for period of 3 years, Dec. 8, 1863.
Company C: Discharged Aug. 2, 1865 at Columbus, Ohio on Surgeon's certificate of disability.
Victor Catlin, Private, age 24, entered service for period of 3 years, Feb. 23, 1864.
Company B; Discharged July 6, 1866 by order of the War Department.
Charles Caul, Corporal, age 41, entered service for period of 3 years, June 12, 1861.
Company E: Appointed Corporal April 1, 1862; transferred to Veteran Reserve Corps Jan. 29, 1864 by order of War Department.
Albert J. Cavenaugh, Private, age 20, entered service for period of 3 years, June 10, 1861.
Company C; Promoted to Principal musician Jan. 1, 1866; veteran.
William Caw, Private, age 27, entered service for period of 1 year, Oct. 15, 1864.Company F; Discharged July 15, 1865 by order of War Department.

William Chadwick, Private, age 19, entered service for period of 3 years, June 26, 1861.
Company H: Transferred to Co. C 75th O.V.I. Jan. 16, 1864; from Co. C 75th O.V.I. June 12, 864; mustered out July 16, 1864 at Columbus, Ohio on expiration of term of service.
Charles Chalett, Private, age 18, entered service for period of 3 years, June 24, 1865.
Company K: Wounded July 1, 1863 in battle of Gettysburg, Pa.; mustered out July 16, 1864 on expiration of term of service.
Abraham W. Chamberlain, age 19, entered service for period of 1 year, Oct. 7, 1864.
Company G: Mustered out Oct. 7, 1865 at Charleston, S.C. on expiration of term of service.
Wesley Chamberlin, 1st. Lieutenant, age 37, entered service for period of 3 years, June 4, 1861.
Company G: Resigned April 28, 1862 at McDowell, Va..
William W. Chamberlin, Private, age 37, entered service for period of 3 years, June 18, 1861.
Company G: Discharged Nov. 16, 1863 at Strafford C.H., Va. on Surgeon's certificate of disability.
Jesse Chance, Private, age 19, entered service for period of 3 years, Aug. 7, 1862.
Company E: Discharged March 2, 1865 to accept promotion as 2d Lieutenant 104 U.S. Colored Troops.
Thomas Chaney, Private, age 27, entered service for period of 3 years, Oct. 15, 1862.
Company K: Mustered out Oct. 15, 1865 on expiration of term of service.
James F. Charlesworth, Capt., Co. A, age 36, entered service for period of 3 years, June 5 1861.
Company A: Promoted to Major from Captain Co. A, May 16, 1862; Lt. Col. May 3, 1863; wounded and captured July 1, 1863 at battle of Gettysburg, Pa; prisoner of War in Libby Rebel Prison at Richmond, Va. eleven months; discharged June 21, 1864, by order of War Department.
Charles F. Chase, Private, age 18, entered service for period of 3 years, June 10, 1861.
Company B: Discharged July 16, 1864 on Surgeon's certificate of disability.
Byron Cherry, Private, age 18, entered service for period of 1 year, Aug. 31, 1864.
Company E: Discharged July 15, 1865 by order of War Department.

Charles Cherry, Private, age 44, entered service for period of 1 year, Aug. 31, 1864.

Company E: Discharged July 15, 1865 by order of War Department.

Clark O. Childs, Private, age 21, entered service for period of 3 years, June 8, 1861.

Company D: Transferred to 12th Battery O.L.A. March 12, 1862

George M. Chumasero, Private, age 44, entered service for period of 3 years, Feb. 25, 1864.

Company G: Discharged…1864 at Hilton Head, S.C. on Surgeon's certificate of disability.

William M. Chumasero, Private, age 18, entered service for period of 3 years, Feb. 25, 1864.

Company G: Discharged June 8, 1865 at Alexandria, Va. on Surgeon's certificate of disability.

John A. Church, Private, age 19, entered service for period of 3 years, June 24, 1861.

Company K: Transferred to Co. C 75th O.V.I. Jan. 16, 1864; from Co. C 75th O.V.I. June 13, 1864; mustered out July 16, 1864 on expiration of term of service.

Charles Cimmerer, Private, age 22, entered service for period of 3 years, June 12, 1861.

Company E: no record given.

Hiram Clapper, Private, age 18, entered service for period of 1 year, Sept. 30, 1864.

Company D: Mustered out July 15, 1865 by order of War Department.

Albert V. H. Clark, Private, age 20, entered service for period of 3 years, June 20, 1861.

Company F: Discharged June 21, 1862 on Surgeon's certificate of disability.

George Clark, Private, age 18, entered service for period of 3 years, Feb. 22, 1864.

Company I: Mustered out with company June 18, 1866.

James Clark, Corporal, age 21, entered service for period of 3 years, June 12, 1861.

Company E: Discharged Dec. 6, 1862 on Surgeon's certificate of disability.

Joseph L Clark, Private, age 21, entered service for period of 3 years, June 8, 1861.

Company D: Transferred to 12th Battery O.L.A. March 12, 1862.

Uriah B. Clark, Wagoner, age 35, entered service for period of 3 years, June 13, 1861.

Company F: discharged Jan. 1, 1864 on Surgeon's certificate of disability.

William D. Clark, Private, age 21, entered service for period of 3 years, Dec. 4 1863.
Company A: Wounded Dec. 6, 1864 in battle of Deveaux, S.C.; discharged July 16, 1865 on Surgeon's certificate of disability.
David Clearly, Private, age 39, entered service for period of 3 years, Feb. 27, 1864.
Company I: Died Aug. 8, 1864 at Hilton Head, S.C..
Samuel Cleary, Private, age 30, entered service for period of 3 years, June 26, 1861.
Company I: Discharged March 1, 1863 on Surgeon's certificate of disability.
George W. Cleland, Private, age 25, entered service for period of 3 years, June 12, 1861.
Company E: Discharged Aug. 9, 1862 on Surgeon's certificate of disability.
George S. Clements, Sergeant, age 22, entered service for period of 3 years, June 26, 1861.
Company H; Appointed Corporal Sept. 1, 1863; wounded Nov. 30, 1864 in battle of Honey Hill, S.C.; appointed Sergeant April 1, 1864; discharged July 26, 1864 at New York by order of War Department; veteran.
William W. Cleveland, Private, age 28, entered service for period of 3 years, Feb. 23, 1864.
Company B; Discharged Feb. 13, 1865 at Cleveland, Ohio on Surgeon's certificate of disability.
James E. Clifford, Private, age 19, entered service for period of 3 years, June 5, 1861.
Company A: Killed July 1, 1863 in battle of Gettysburg, Pa..
John K. Cline, Private, age 32, entered service for period of 3 years, March 24, 1862.
Company G: no record given.
William Clinger, Private, age 35, entered service for period of 1 year, Sept. 6, 1864.
Company E: Discharged July 15, 1865 by order of the War Department.
George H. Clock, Private, age 27, entered service for period of 3 years, June 8, 1861.
Company D: Transferred to 12th Battery O.L.A. March 12, 1862.
Alban Cluff, Private, age 44, entered service for period of 1 year, Oct. 6, 1864.
Company D: Absent, sick May 5, 1865, in Hilton Head Hospital, S.C.; mustered out with company Oct. 20, 1865.
William A. Cluff, Private, age 18, entered service for period of 1 year, Oct. 6, 1864.
Company D: Mustered out with company Oct. 20, 1865.

Thomas C. Coalwell, Sergeant, age 21, entered service for period of 3 years, June 12, 1861.

Company E: Appointed Corporal Aug. 1, 1861; Sergeant Nov. 1, 1861; died May 29, 1862 of wounds received May 8, 1862 in battle of McDowell, Virginia.

Daniel S. Coe, Corporal, age 21, entered service for period of 3 years, June 8, 1861.

Company D: Wounded Dec. 12, 1861 in battle of Camp Alleghany, W. Va.; transferred to 12th Battery O.L.A. March 12, 1862.

James M. Coffee, Private, age 24, entered service for period of nine months, Oct. 7, 1862.

Company H: Drafted; mustered out July 19, 1863, on expiration of term of service.

James D. Coffman, Private, age 22, entered service for period of 3 years, June 10, 1861.

Company B: Mustered out July 18, 1864 on expiration of service.

Wilson S. Colby, Private, age 29, entered service for period of 3 years, Nov. 12, 1861.

Company A: Mustered out of service Nov. 12, 1864 on expiration of term of service.

Vernon Coleman, Private, age 32, entered service for period of 3 years, Jan. 9, 1864.

Company F: no record given.

Andrew Collins, Private, age 30, entered service for period of 3 years, June 20, 1861.

Company I: Reduced from Corporal....

Charles I. Collins, Private, age 40, entered service for period of 3 years, June 20, 1861.

Company F: Died Nov. 23, 1861 in hospital at Huttonsville, West Virginia.

James Collins, Private, age 39, entered service for period of 3 years, June 13, 1861.

Company F; Discharged Jan. 20, 1862 on Surgeon's certificate of disability.

John A. Collins, Private, age 30, entered service for period of 3 years, July 17, 1861.

Company F: Discharged Feb. 4, 1862 on Surgeon's certificate of disability.

Joseph Collins, Private, age 22, entered service for period of 3 years, Dec. 11, 1863.

Company C: Discharged June 15, 1865 at Camp Chase, Ohio by order of War Department.

Warren Collins, Private, age 19, entered service for period of 3 years, June 8, 1861.

Company D: Transferred to 12th Battery O.L.A. March 121, 1862.

Joseph R. Collims, Private, age 43, entered service for period of 1 year, Sept. 13, 1864.

Company F; Discharged July 15, 1865 by order of War Department.

James A. Combs, Musician, age 18, entered service for period of 1 year, Oct. 7, 1864.

Company D: Mustered out with company Oct. 20, 1865.

John W. Compton, Private, age 19, entered service for period of 1 year, Oct. 5, 1864.

Company G: Discharged Aug. 11, 1865 at Hilton Head, S.C. on Surgeon's certificate of disability.

William Compton, Private, age 18, entered service for period of 1 year, Oct. 5, 1864.

Company G: Discharged May 16, 1865 at Camp Dennison, Ohio on Surgeon's certificate of disability.

Elbridge Comstock, Private, age 21 entered service for period of 3 years, June 12, 1861.

Company E: Wounded Aug. 30, 1862 in battle of Bull Run, Va.; discharged Dec. 6, 1862 on Surgeon's certificate of disability.

Charles H. Conger, Private, age 18, entered service for period of 3 years, June 24, 1861.

Company K: Wounded July 1, 1863 in battle of Gettysburg, Pa.; transferred to Co. C 75th O.V.I. Jan. 16, 1864; from Co. C 75th O.V.I. June 13, 1864; mustered out July 16, 1864 on expiration of term of service.

Stephen J. Conger, Private, age 28, entered service for period of 3 years, June 10, 1861.

Company B: Died April 10, 1862 in hospital at Beverly, West Virginia.

Jesse Conley, Private, age 23, entered service for period of 3 years, Feb. 18, 1864.

Company C: Discharged June 26, 1865 at Camp Dennison, Ohio on Surgeon's certificate of disability.

William A. Connally, Private, age 20, entered service for period of year, Oct. 8, 1864.

Company F; Mustered out Oct. 8, 1865 on expiration of term of service.

Amos J. Connell, Private, age 18, entered service for period of 1 year, Oct. 12, 1864.

Company D: Sick March 6, 1865, in hospital at Hilton Head, S.C.; discharged Aug. 31, 1865 at DeCamp Hospital, New York on Surgeon's certificate of disability.

David H. Connel, 1st Sergeant, age 26, entered service for period of 3 years, Oct. 8, 1864.

Company D: Mustered as private; appointed 1st Sergeant....; discharged March 12, 1865 to accept promotion as 2d Lieutenant Co. K 34th U.S. Colored Troops March 13, 1865.

Frederick Conrad, Private, age 24, entered service for period of 3 years, Feb. 28, 1864.

Company K: Wounded Nov. 30, 1864 in battle of Honey Hill, S.C.; discharged May 6, 1865 on Surgeon's certificate of disability.

James Conroy, Private, age 24, entered service for period of 3 years, June 20, 1861.

Company F; Wounded July 1, 1863 in battle of Gettysburg, Pa.; mustered out with company June 18, 1866 at Columbus, Ohio; veteran.

Edward Consodine, Private, age 22, entered service for period of 3 years, Feb. 20, 1864.

Company G: Mustered out with company June 18, 1866.

Michael Consodine, Private, age 38, entered service for period of 1 year, Sept. 29, 1864.

Company I: Wounded Nov. 30, 1864 in battle of Honey Hill, S.C.; discharged July 15, 1865 by order of War Department.

John Conway, Private, age 18, entered service for period of 3 years, June 4, 1861.

Company A: Discharged Aug. 23, 1865 on Surgeon's certificate of disability; veteran.

Michael Cook, Private, age 18, entered service for period of 1 year, Feb. 18, 1866.

Company A: Mustered out Feb. 18, 1865 on expiration of term of service.

Walter G. Cook, Private, age 28, entered service for period of 1 year, Sept. 28, 1864.

Company K: Discharged Oct. 6, 1865 by order of War Department.

William Cook, Private, age 32, entered service for period of 1 year, Oct. 3, 1864.
Company D: Mustered out with company Oct. 20,1 865.

Wallace H. Cooley, Private, age 19, entered service for period of 3 years, June 26, 1861.

Company I: Mustered out July 16, 1864 on expiration of term of service.

George W. Cooper, Corporal, age 30, entered service for period of 3 years, July 23, 1861.

Company F: Appointed Corporal July 1, 1865; discharged May 21, 1866 by order of War Department.

John Cooper, Private, age 35, entered service for period of 3 years, Jan. 9, 1864.
Company F: no record given.

Stephen W. Cooper, Private, age 31, entered service for period of 1 year, Jan. 5, 1865.
Company E: Mustered out Jan. 11, 1866 on expiration of term of service.

Thomas J. Cooper, Private, age 19, entered service for period of 3 years, June 26, 1861.
Company H: Transferred to Co. C 75th O.V.I. Jan. 16, 1864; from Co. C 75th O.V.I. June 12, 1864; mustered out July 16, 1864 on expiration of term of service.

Wesley H. Cooper, Sergeant, age 19, entered service for period of 1 year, Sept. 14, 1864.
Company I: Appointed from private April 1, 1865; discharged Oct. 1, 1865 by order of War Department.

Wesley H. Cooper, Private, age 18, entered service for period of 3 years, June 24, 1864.
Company K: Wounded June 8, 1862 in battle of Cross Keys, Va.; transferred to Co. C 75th O.V.I. Jan. 16, 1864; from Co. C 75th O.V.I. June 12, 1864; mustered out July 16, 1864 on expiration of term of service.

William L. Cooper, Corporal, age 43, entered service for period of 3 years, June 13, 1861.
Company F; Appointed Corporal Nov. 27, 1861; discharged Aug. 15, 1862 on surgeon's certificate of disability.

George S. Copeland, Private, age 34, entered service for period of 3 years, July 10, 1861.
Company K: no record given.

Samuel Coppersmith, Private, age 22, entered service for period of 3 years, June 10, 1861.
Company C; Discharged Nov. 14, 1862 at Hopewell Gap, Va. on Surgeon's certificate of disability.

Frederick Corbin, Private, age 29, entered service for period of 1 year, Oct. 7, 1864.
Company D: no record given.

Alfred G. Cornelius, 2d Lieutenant, age 35, entered service for period of 3 years, June 26, 1861.
Company E: Promoted from private Co. H Sept. 11, 1862 resigned April 1, 1863 at Brook's Station, Va.
Company H: Promoted to 2d Lieutenant Co. E Sept. 11, 1862.

William Cornwell, Sergeant, age 26, entered service for period of 1 year, Oct. 7, 1864.

Company D: Mustered as private; appointed Sergeant July 1, 1865; mustered out with company Oct. 20, 1865.

Oscar Cotant, Private, age 17, entered service for period of 1 year, Sept. 5, 1864.
Company E: Wounded Nov. 30, 1864 in battle of Honey Hill, S.C.; discharged July 15, 1865 by order of War Department.

Joseph C. Coulter, Private, age 19, entered service for period of 3 years, July 23, 1861.
Company F: Promoted to Com. Sergeant March 1, 1863; reduced to ranks Jan. 1, 1864; mustered out with company June 18, 1866; veteran.

Gailord Cowles, Private, age 40, entered service for period of 3 years, Feb. 27, 1864.
Company B: Mustered out with company June 18, 1866.

John L. Cox, Sergeant, age 23, entered service for period of 3 years, June 26, 1861.
Company H: Discharged Dec. 3, 1862 at Washington, D.C. on Surgeon's certificate of disability.

Charles Coy, Corporal, age 18, entered service for period of 1 year, Oct. 3, 1864.
Company D: Appointed Corporal July 1, 1865; mustered out with company Oct. 20, 1865.

Benjamin F. Crabill, Musician, age 18, entered service for period of 3 years, June 20, 1861.
Company F: Promoted to Principal Musician July 20, 1864; reduced to ranks July 1, 1865; mustered out with company June 18, 1866; veteran.

Jacob A. Crabill, Musician, age 30, entered service for period of 3 years, June 20, 1861.
Company F: Died April 24, 1862 at McDowell, Va..

David Craig, 1st Sergeant, age 21, entered service for period of 3 years, June 26, 1861.
Company H: Wounded Dec. 12, 1861 in battle of Camp Alleghany, W. Va.; May 3, 1863 in battle of Chancellorsville, Va.; and July 2, 1863 in battle of Gettysburg, Pa.; appointed Corporal April 11, 1864; Sergeant May 1, 1865; 1st Sergeant Mar. 21, 1866; mustered out with company June 18, 1866; veteran.

John S. Craig, Private, age 36, entered service for period of 1 year, Sept. 22, 1864.
Company F: Discharged July 15, 1865 by order of War Department.

Josua B. Craig, Private, age 37, entered service for period of 3 years, Feb. 25, 1864.
Company I: Mustered out with company June 18, 1866.

Leroy S. Craig, Private, age 31, entered service for period of 1 year, Oct. 13, 1864.
Company H: Wounded Dec. 6, 1864 in battle of Gregory's Landing, S.C.; discharged May 23, 1865 by order of War Department.

William Craig, Private, age 23, entered service for period of 3 years, June 10, 1861.
Company C: Wounded May 2, 1863 in battle of Chancellorsville, Va.: transferred to 75th O.V.I. Jan. 16, 1864; from 75th O.V.I. May 20, 1864; mustered out July 16, 1864 at Camp Chase, Ohio on expiration of term of service.

Moses Cram, Private, age 44, entered service for period of 3 years, June 18, 1861.
Company G: Discharged Nov. 21, 1861 at Cheat Mountain, Va. on Surgeon's certificate of disability.

James M. Cranker, Musician, age 18, **Feb. 29, 1864.**
Company K: Mustered out with company June 18, 1866.

George Crawford, Private, age 18, entered service for period of 3 years, June 8, 1861.
Company D: Transferred to 12th Battery O.L.A. March 12, 1862.

John Crawford, Private, age 20, entered service for period of 3 years, June 8, 1861.
Company D: Transferred to 12th Battery O.L.A. March 12, 1862.

Reginald Crawford, Private, age 19, entered service for period of 3 years, June 24, 1861.
Company K: Wounded June 8, 1862 in battle of Cross Keys, Va.; mustered out july 16, 1864 on expiration of term of service.

Samuel Crawford, Private, age 20, entered service for period of 3 years, June 13, 1861.
Company F: Veteran.

Thomas S. Crawford, Private, age 31, entered service for period of 1 year, Oct. 4, 1864.
Company D: Mustered out with company Oct. 20, 1865.

John Creene, Corporal, age 25, entered service for period of 3 years, Jan. 5, 1864.
Company I: Transferred from Co. E 107th O.V.I. July 13, 1865; appointed Corporal Oct. 1, 1865; absent, sick Jan. 1, 1866; mustered out June 18, 1866 by order of War Department.

Noah Crestlieb, Private, age 32, entered service for period of 3 years, Feb. 25, 1864.
Company B: Discharged March 17, 1866 at Columbia, S.C. by order of the War Department.

Robert Creighton, Private, age 22, entered service for period of 3 years, June 5, 1861.

Company A: Wounded Aug. 29, 1862 in battle of Bull Run, Va. and July 1, 1863 in battle of Gettysburg, Pa.; discharged Dec. 31 at Columbus Ohio by order of War Department.

William H. Criswell, 1st Sergeant, age 20, entered service for period of 3 years, June 5, 1861.

Company A: Wounded Aug. 29, 1862 in battle of Bull Run, Va.; appointed Sergeant from private April 1, 1864; 1st Sergeant June 7, 1865; discharged January 18, 1866, by order of War Department; veteran.

Daniel J. Crooks, 2d Lieutenant, age 26, entered service for period of 3 years, June 18, 1861.

Company A: Wounded Dec. 12, 1861 in battle of Camp Allegheny, W. Va.; promoted to Q.M. Sergeant from Corporal Nov. 5, 1864; 2d Lieutenant Sept. 4, 1865; mustered out with company June 18, 1866; veteran.

Andrew J. Crossley, Private, age 24, entered service for period of 3 years, June 18, 1861.

Company G; Discharged Nov. 21, 1861 at Cheat Mountain, Va. on Surgeon's certificate of disability.

Jacob Crossley, Sergeant, age 21, entered service for period of 3 years, March 16, 1864.

Company G: Appointed Corporal Sept. 1, 1865; Sergeant June 1, 1866; mustered out with company June 18, 1866.

John A. Crossley, Private, age 22, entered service for period of 3 years, Feb. 20, 1864.

Company G: Mustered out with company June 18, 1866.

John T. Crow, Private, age 23, entered service for period of 3 years, June 5, 1861.

Company A: Mustered out July 16, 1864 on expiration of term of service.

Robert Crow, Private, age 18, entered service for period of 3 years, Feb. 22, 1864.

Company I: Mustered out with company June 18, 1866.

Moses H. Crowell, Captain, age 35, entered service for period of 3 years, June 4, 1861.

Company E: Resigned June 1, 1863 at Brook's Station, Va..

Robert H. Culley, Musician, age 18, entered service for period of 3 years, June 12, 1861.

Company E: Transferred to Co. C 75th O.V.I. June 12, 1864; mustered out July 16, 1864 at Columbus, Ohio on expiration of term of service.

Charles C. Culp, Private, age18, entered service for period of 1 year, Oct. 12, 1864.

Company A: Mustered out Oct. 12, 1865 on expiration of term of service.

Edward C. Culp, Major, age 18, entered service for period of 3 years, June 8, 1861.

Promoted to Sergt. Major from Sergeant Co. D Nov. 1, 1861; 2d Lieutenant Co. C May 6, 1862; taken prisoner at Mt. Jackson June 14, 1862 and exchanged Sept 16, 1862; Major from Capt. Co. A Jan. 6, 1865; Lieut. Col. May 25, 1866, but not mustered; mustered out with regiment June 18, 1866; breveted Lt. Col. and Col. June 22, 1867.

Company A: Promoted from 1st Lieutenant Co. F March 15, 1864; to Major January 6, 1865.

Company C: Promoted from Sergeant Major May 6, 1862; to 1st Lieutenant Co. F Sept. 11, 1862.

Company D: Promoted to Sergt. Major Nov. 1, 1861.

Company F: Promoted from 2d Lieutenant Co. C Sept. 11, 1862; to Capt. Co. G Aug. 11, 1864.

John J. Cummings, Private, age 36, entered service for period of 3 years, June 18, 1861.

Company G: Reduced from Corporal…; transferred to 75th O.V.I. Jan. 6, 1864; from 75th O.V.I. June 12, 1864; mustered out July 16, 1864 on expiration of term of service.

Wesley B. Cummings, Private, age 18, entered service for period of 3 years, June 8, 1861.

Company D: Transferred to 12th Battery O.L.A. March 12, 1862.

Robert B. Cumpton, Private, age 22, entered service for period of 3 years, June 8, 1861.

Company D: Wounded Dec. 12, 1861 in battle of Camp Alleghany, W. Va.; transferred to 12th Battery O.L.A. March 12, 1862.

David Cunningham, Private, age 18, entered service for period of 3 years, Feb. 29, 1864.

Company B: Mustered out with company June 18, 1866.

James W. Cunningham, Private, age 28, entered service for period of 3 years, June 10, 1861.

Company C: Reduced from Corporal June 1, 1862; discharged Nov. 14, 1862 at Hopewell Gap, Va. on Surgeon's certificate of disability.

John J. Cunningham, Private, age 36, entered service for period of 3 years, June 18, 1861.

Company G: Reduced from Corporal…; transferred to 75th O.V.I. Jan. 6, 1864; from 75th O.V.I. June 12, 1864; mustered out July 16, 1864 on expiration of term of service.

John T. Cunningham, Private, age 19, entered service for period of 3 years, June 10, 1861.

Company C: Transferred to Co. C 75th O.V.I. March 20, 1864; from Co. C 75th O.V.I. May 6, 1864; mustered out July 16, 1864 at Columbus, Ohio on expiration of term of service.

Joseph W. Cunningham, Corporal, age 21, entered service for period of 3 years, June 26, 1861.

Company I: Died July 28, 1863 of wounds received July 1, 1863 in battle of Gettysburg, Pa..

Josiah O. Curl, Corporal, age 29, entered service for period of 3 years, June 20, 1861.

Company F: Appointed Corporal Oct. 16, 1862; transferred to Co. C 75th O.V.I. Jan. 16, 1864; from Co. C 75th O.V.I. June 12, 1864; mustered out July 16, 1864 on expiration of term of service.

Lafayette Curtis, Corporal, age 18, entered service for period of 3 years, Feb. 22, 1864.

Company B: Appointed Corporal Sept. 6, 1865.

Thomas Cuthbertson, Corporal, age 21, entered service for period of 3 years, June 18, 1861.

Company G: Appointed Corporal...; wounded July 1, 1863, in battle of Gettysburg, Pa.; mustered out July 16, 1864 at Hilton Head, S.C. on expiration of term of service.

William Cutshaw, Private, age 18, entered service for period of 3 years, Feb. 2, 1863.

Company A: Transferred to Veteran Reserve Corps Aug, 1, 1863 by order of the War Department.

D

Hamilton Dailey, Private, age 18, entered service for period of 3 years, Feb. 29, 1864.

Company C; Mustered out with company June 18, 1865.

Peter Dailey, Private, age 23, entered service for period of 3 years, June 10, 1861.

Company B: no record given.

Company C: Transferred to Co. C 75th O.V.I. Jan. 16, 1864; from Co. C 75th O.V.I. May 6, 1864; mustered out July 16, 1864 at Camp Chase, Ohio on expiration of term of service

Zachariah Dailey, Sergeant, age 21, entered service for period of 3 years, June 26, 1861.

Company I: Appointed Corporal Feb. 20, 1863; wounded July 1, 1863 in battle of Gettysburg, Pa.; appointed Sergeant April 1, 1865; promoted to Q.M. Sergeant Oct. 1, 1865; veteran.

Samuel Dale, Private, age 27, entered service for period of 1 year, Sept. 27, 1864.

Company I: Discharged July 15, 1865 by order of War Department.

Michael F. Danford, Private, age 32, entered service for period of 3 years, June 26, 1861.

Company H: Reduced from Sergeant…; wounded May 3, 1863 in battle of Chancellorsville, Va. and July 2, 1863 in battle of Gettysburg, Pa.; mustered out July 16, 1864 on expiration of term of service.

Clayton P. Danforth, Corporal, 18, entered service for period of 3 years, Feb. 27, 1864.

Company B: Appointed Corporal Feb. 1, 1865; discharged Sept. 6, 1865 at DeCamp Hospital, New York on Surgeon's certificate of disability.

Samuel J. Daniel, Private, age 25, entered service for period of 3 years, June 26, 1861.

Company I: Transferred from (to)Co. C 75th O.V.I. Jan. 16, 1864; from Co. C 75th O.V.I. June 12, 1864; mustered out July 16, 1864 on expiration of term of service.

John Darnell, Private, age 19, entered service for period of 3 years, June 26, 1861.

Company H: no record given.

Albert Darval, Private, age 42, entered service for period of 3 years, Feb. 23, 1864.

Company K: nor record given.

Conrad Daum, Private, age 18, entered service for period of 3 years, June 24, 1861.

Company K: died July 1, 1862 at Winchester, Va. of wounds received June 8, 1862 in battle of Cross Keys, Va..

Andrew J. Davis, Private, age 23, entered service for period of 3 years, June 12, 1861.

Company E: Mustered out July 16, 1864 on expiration of term of service.

Edmund C. Davis, Corporal, age 18, entered service for period of 3 years, Feb. 29, 1864.

Company B: Appointed Corporal June 1, 1866; mustered out with company June 18, 1866.

Ezra L. Davis, Private, age 22, entered service for period of nine months, Oct. 7, 1862.

Company H: Drafted: mustered out July 19, 1863 on expiration of term of service.

Frances A. Davis, 1st Lieutenant, age 27, entered service for period of 3 years, June 4, 1861.

Company H: discharged Sept. 11, 1862 at Washington D.C. on Surgeon's certificate of disability.

Jesse M. Davis, Private, age 19, entered service for period of 3 years, June 26, 1861.

Company H: Veteran.

John W. Davis, Private, age 19, entered service for period of 3 years, June 26, 1861.

Company H: no record given.

Kinsey Davis, Private, age 22, entered service for period of 3 years, June 26, 1861.

Company I: Reduced from Corporal Feb. 2, 1864 at his own request; mustered out with company June 18, 1866; veteran.

Nathaniel Davis, Private, age 25, entered service for period of 3 years, June 8, 1861.

Company D; Transferred to 12th Battery O.L.A. March 12, 1862.

William Davis, Private, age 40, entered service for period of 3 years, July 9, 1861.

Company H: Transferred to Co. C 75th O.V.I. Jan. 16, 1864; from Co. C 75th O.V.I. June 12, 864; mustered out July 16, 1864 at Columbus, Ohio on expiration of term of service.

William H. Davis, 2d Lieutenant, age 30, entered service for period of 3 years, June 26, 1861.

Company H: Appointed 1st Sergeant from Corporal April 1, 1862; promoted to 2d Lieutenant Sept. 11, 1862.

William L. Davis, Musician, age 16, entered service for period of 3 years, June 26, 1861.

Company H: Mustered out with company June 18, 1866; veteran.

Zeno F. Davis, Private, age 18, entered service for period of 3 years, June 26, 1861.

Company H: Wounded May 2, 1863 in battle of Chancellorsville, Va.; transferred to Co. c 75th O.V.I. Jan. 16, 1864; from Co. C 75th O.V.I. June 12, 1864; mustered out July 16, 1864 at Columbus, Ohio on expiration of term of service.

Benjamin Dawson, Private, age 18, entered service for period of 3 years, June 26, 1861.

Company H: Died June 24, 1862 at Winchester, Va..

Calvin A. Day, Private, age 18, entered service for period of 3 years, June 8, 1861.
Company D: Transferred to 12th Battery O.L.A. March 12, 1862.

John B. Day, Private, age 18, entered service for period of 3 years, Jan. 28, 1863.
Company A: Mustered out Feb. 5, 1866 at Charleston, SC on expiration of term of service.

Maynard H. Dean, Private, age 21, entered service for period of 3 years, June 24, 1861.
Company K: Transferred to Veteran Reserve Corps Nov. 30, 1863 by order of War Department.

William F. Dean, Asst. Surgeon, age..., entered service for period of 3 years, July 13, 1862. Died Sept. 23, 1862 at Georgetown, D.C.

Charles A. Debolt, Private, age 19, entered service for period of 3 years, June 24, 1861.
Company K: Wounded May 8, 1862 in battle of McDowell, Va.; veteran.

Jacob Decker, Private, age 37, entered service for period of 1 year, Oct. 2, 1864.
Company A: Mustered out Oct. 2, 1865 on expiration of term of service.

Marcus L. Decker, Corporal, age 25, entered service for period of 3 years, June 24, 1861.
Company K: Killed Dec. 31, 1861 in battle of Baldwin Camp, Virginia.

Franklin Deer, Private, age 20, entered service for period of 3 years, Feb. 20, 1864.
Company E: Wounded April 15, 1865 in battle of Red Hill, S.C.; mustered out with company June 18, 1866.

Levi Delancy, Private, age 44, entered service for period of 9 months, March 7, 1862.
Company K: Drafter: mustered out Dec. 7, 1862 on expiration of term of service.

Thomas Delvin, Private, age 18, entered service for period of 3 years, June 24, 1861.
Company K: Died Dec. 21, 1861 at Huttonsville, W. Va..

Emanuel Denoon, Corporal, age 21, entered service for period of 3 years, June 26, 1861.
Company I: Appointed Corporal Nov. 1, 1861; discharged June 6, 1862 on Surgeon's certificate of disability.

James Depew, Private, age 21, entered service for period of 3 years, July 27, 1861.
Company H: discharged July 18, 1862 at Camp Chase, Ohio on Surgeon's certificate of disability.

Levi H. Derby, Private, age 18, entered service for period of 3 years, Feb. 22, 1864.

Company B; : Mustered out with company June 18, 1866.

Lorenzo Dero, Private, age 19, entered service for period of 3 years, Feb. 22, 1864.

Company C; Transferred from Co. F 107th O.V.I. July 13, 1865.

Samuel H. Deselms, Private, age 27, entered service for period of 3 years, June 12, 1861.

Company E: Wounded July 1, 1863 in battle of Gettysburg, Pa.; veteran.

Andrew Dick, Private, age 43, entered service for period of 3 years, Aug. 14, 1862.

Company F: Discharged April 22, 1863 by order of War Department.

John N. Dickie, Private, age 18, entered service for period of 3 years, July 13, 1861.

Company G: Transferred to Co. C 75th O.V.I. Jan. 16, 1864; from Co. C 75th O.V.I. June 12, 1864; mustered out July 16, 1864 on expiration of term of service.

Edward Diems, Private, age 32, entered service for period of 3 years, June 13, 1861.

Company F: Discharged March 1, 1863 on Surgeon's certificate of disability.

Kilan Dienst, Private, age 39, entered service for period of 1 year, Jan. 13, 1865.

Company C; Mustered out Jan. 13, 1866 at Charleston, S.C..

Robert Dietgold, Private, age 20, entered service for period of 3 years, Oct. 20, 1862.

Company K: Transferred from Co....107th O.V.I. July 13, 1865; mustered out Oct. 20, 1865 on expiration of term of service.

John Dillon, Private, age 28, entered service for period of 1 year, Sept. 28, 1864.

Company F: Mustered out Oct. 1, 1865 on expiration of term of service.

Patrick Dillon, Private, age 18, entered service for period of 3 years, Nov. 13, 1863.

Company B; Transferred from Co. B 107th O.V.I. July 13, 1865; discharged Feb. 24, 1866 at Columbia, S.C. by order of War Department.

Darius Dirlam, 1st Lieutenant, age 32, entered service for period of 3 years, June 4, 1861.

Company D: Wounded Dec. 12, 1861 in battle of Camp Alleghany, W. Va.; transferred to 12th Battery O.L.A. March 12, 1862.

John Dirrest, Private, age 19, entered service for period of 3 years, Dec. 31, 1863.

Company F: no record given.

Joseph Dixon, Private, age 22, entered service for period of 3 years, June 10, 1861.

Company C: Wounded July 1, 1863 in battle of Gettysburg, Pa.; mustered on July 16, 1864 at Camp Chase, Ohio on expiration of term of service.

George W. Dobbins, Private, age 21, entered service for period of 3 years, June 26, 1861.
Company I: Died Aug. 14, 1864 at Hilton, Head, S.C.; veteran.
John W. Doherty, Private, age 18, entered service for period of 3 years, June 10, 1861.
Company B; Wounded Aug. 29, 1862 in battle of Bull Run, Va.; discharged March 11, 1863 at Baltimore, Md. On Surgeon's certificate of disability.
Maurice Donahue, Private, age 19, entered service for period of 3 years, July 9, 1861.
Company H: Transferred to Co. C 75th O.V.I. Jan. 16, 1864; from Co. C 75th O.V.I. June 12, 1864; mustered out July 16, 1864 on expiration of term of service.
Hugh Donely, Private, age 27, entered service for period of 3 years, June 5, 1861.
Company A: Discharged Sept. 2, 1862 at Camp Chase, Ohio on Surgeon's certificate of disability.
Reuben Donley, Private, age 21, entered service for period of 3 years, June 5, 1861.
Company A: Died Oct. 2, 1862 at Alexandria, Va. of wounds received in battle of Bull Run, Va.
Zachariah Donley, Private, age 18, entered service for period of 3 years, June 26, 1861.
Company I: Died April 8, 1864 at Hilton Head, S. C..
Frances Dorand, Private age31, entered service for period of 3 years, Feb. 11, 1864.
Company F: Mustered out with company June 18, 1866.
Emanuel P. Dotson, Private, age 22, entered service for period of 3 years, June 20, 1861.
Company F: discharged May 4, 1862 on Surgeon's certificate of disability.
Isaiah Downs, Private, age 29, entered service for period of 3 years, June 18, 1861.
Company G; Discharged...at Baltimore, Md. On Surgeon's certificate of disability.
Henry Drago, Private, age 27, entered service for period of 3 years, Dec. 26, 1863.
Company K: no record given.
John Drake, Private, age 25, entered service for period of 3 years, March 7, 1864.
Company B: no record given.
James A. Driggs, Sergeant, age 22, entered service for period of 3 years, June 10, 1861.

Company B: Wounded Aug. 29, 1862 in 2d Battle of Bull Run, Va.; appointed Corporal June 13, 1861; appointed Sergeant May 21, 1862; promoted to 1st Lieutenant Co. C March 20, 1864; veteran.

Company C: Transferred from Co. B as Sergeant Jan. 1, 1864; promoted to 2d Lieutenant March 15, 1864; discharged April 13, 1864; veteran.

John B. Driggs, Private, age 19, entered service for period of 3 years, June 10, 1861.

Company B: Transferred to Co. H June 13, 1864.

Company H: Transferred from Co. B June 13, 1864; mustered out July 16, 1864 at Columbus, Ohio on expiration of term of service.

William D. Driggs, Private, age 20, entered service for period of 3 years, June 10, 1861.

Company B: Killed May 8, 1862 in battle of McDowell, Va..

Reuben Drippard, Corporal, age 32, entered service for period of 3 years, June 24, 1861.

Company K: Appointed Corporal May 28, 1863; wounded July 1, 1863 in battle of Gettysburg, Pa.; discharged April 13, 1864 on Surgeon's certificate of disability.

John H. Driscol, Private, age 23, entered service for period of 3 years, June 24, 1861.

Company K: Killed Dec. 31, 1861 in battle of Baldwin's Camp, Va..

Alexander Drum, Private, age 23, entered service for period of 3 years, June 10, 1861.

Company C; Wounded May 2, 1863 in battle of Chancellorsville, Va.; transferred to Co. C 75th O.V.I. Jan. 16, 1864; from Co. C 75th O.V.I. May 6, 1864; mustered out July 16, 1864 at Camp Chase, Ohio on expiration of term of service.

William R. Drum, Private, age 32, entered service for period of 3 years, June 10, 1861.

Company C; Transferred to Co. C 75th O.V.I. Jan. 16, 1864; from Co. C 75th O.V.I. May 6, 1864; mustered out July 16, 1864 at Camp Chase, Ohio on expiration of term of service.

Fredoline Dryer, Private, age 43, entered service for period of 1 year, Oct. 1, 1864.

Company K: Discharged July 15, 1865 by order of War Department.

Vorey Duble, Sergeant, age 19, entered service for period of 3 years, July 17, 1862.

Company E: Appointed corporal Aug. 1, 1864; wounded Dec. 6, 1864 in battle of Deveaux Neck, S.C.; appointed Sergeant April 1, 1865; discharged July 15, 1865 by order of War Department.

John C. Duff, Private, age 22, entered service for period of 3 years, June 10, 1861.
Company B: Wounded May 3, 1862 in battle of Chancellorsville, Va.; transferred to Co. C March 20, 1864; veteran.
Company C: Transferred from Co. B March 20, 1864; mustered out with company June 18, 1866; veteran.
William Duff, Private, age 21, entered service for period of 3 years, June 8, 1861.
Company D: Transferred to 12th Battery O.L.A. March 12, 1862.
Patrick Duffy, Private, age 34, entered service for period of 3 years, Feb. 22, 1864.
Company E: Discharged July 21, 1865 by order of War Department.
George Dugan, Private, age 223, entered service for period of 3 years, June 12, 1861.
Company E: Wounded May 2, 1863 in battle of Chancellorsville, Va.; transferred to Veteran Reserve Corps Nov. 11, 1863 by order of War Department.
John C. Duff, Private, age 22, entered service for period of 3 years, June 10, 1861.
Company B: Wounded May 3, 1863 in battle of Chancellorsville, Va.; transferred to Co. C March 20, 1864; veteran.
George Dunks, Wagoner, age 20, entered service for period of 3 years, June 8, 1861.
Company B: Transferred to 12th Battery O.L.A. March 12, 1862.
Elisha Dunn, Private, age 25, entered service for period of 3 years, June 26, 1861.
Company I: Died April 8, 1864 at Hilton Head, S.C.; veteran.
John A. Dunn, Private, age 18, entered service for period of 1 year, Oct. 14, 1864.
Company A: Mustered out Oct. 14, 1866 at Charleston, S.C. on expiration of term of service.
John S. Dunn, 1st Sergeant, age 19, entered service for period of 3 years, June 26, 1861.
Company H: Appointed Corporal Dec. 3, 1862; Sergeant Feb. 11, 1864; 1st Sergeant Nov. 8, 1864; promoted to 2d Lieutenant Co.. I Sept. 4, 1865; veteran.
Company I: 2d Lieutenant. Promoted from 1st Sergeant Co. H Sept. 4, 1865; mustered out with company June 18, 1866; veteran.
Jonathan Dunn, Private, age 26, entered service for period of 3 years, June 10, 1861.

Company C: Wounded Dec. 12, 1861 in battle of Camp Alleghany, W. Va.; discharged April 14, 1863 at Brook's Station, Va. on Surgeon's certificate of disability.

Oscar J. Dunn, Private, age 21, entered service for period of 1 year, Oct. 6, 1864.

Company H: Killed Nov. 30, 1864 in battle of Honey Hill, South Carolina.

Oscar J. Dunn. Private, age 18, entered service for period of 3 years, June 26, 1861.

Company H: Transferred to Co. C 75th O.V.I. Jan 16, 1864; from Co. C 75th O.V.I. June 12, 1864; mustered out July 16, 1864 at Columbus, Ohio at expiration of term of service.

Thomas Dunn, Corporal, age 23, entered service for period of 3 years, June 24, 1861.

Company K: Killed July 1, 1863 in battle of Gettysburg, Pa..

William F. Dunn, Corporal, age 21, entered service for period of 3 years, June 26, 1861.

Company H: Discharged Sept. 30, 1861 in West Virginia on Surgeon's certificate of disability.

James M. Dunnington, Private, age 21, entered service for period of 3 years, July 9, 1861.

Company H: Transferred to Co. C 75th O.V.I. Jan. 16, 1864; from Co. C 75th O.V.I. June 12, 864; mustered out July 16, 1864 at Columbus, Ohio on expiration of term of service.

Company H: Transferred to Co. C 75th O.V.I. Jan, 16, 1864; from Co. C 75th O.V.I. June 12, 1864; mustered out July 16, 1864 at Columbus, Ohio on expiration of term of service.

William R. Durfee, Private, age 21, entered service for period of 1 year, Sept. 20, 1864.

Company I: Discharged July 15, 1865 by order of War Department.

Joseph Dyarrman, Sergeant, age 20, entered service for period of 3 years, July 12, 1861.

Company G: Mustered as private; appointed Sergeant...; wounded July 1, 1863 in battle of Gettysburg, Pa. and Nov. 30, 1864 at Honey Hill, S.C.; veteran.

E

George W. Eager, Private, age 25, entered service for period of 1 year, Oct. 8, 1864.

Company H: Mustered out Oct. 7, 1865 on expiration of term of service.

Isaiah Eagy, Private, age 18, entered service for period of 1 year, Sept. 26, 1864.

Company D: Mustered out July 15, 1865 by order of War Department.

James A. Easterman, Private, age 18, entered service for period of 3 years, Sept.21, 1864.Company C: Died Jan. 19, 1865 at Hilton Head, S.C. of wounds received in battle of Honey Hill, S.C..

John J. Easthorn, Private, age 20, entered service for period of 1 year, June 10, 1861.
Company B; Killed June 8, 1862 in battle of Cross Keys, Va..

Oscar Easterbrook, Private, age 19, entered service for period of 3 years, Feb. 29, 1864.
Company B: Killed July 1, 1863 in battle of Gettysburg, Pa.

Isaiah Eastlick, Private, age 26, entered service for period of 3 years, June 12, 1861.
Company E: Discharged Dec. 16, 1861 on Surgeon's certificate of disability.

Amander Eaton, Private, age 44, entered service for period of 3 years, June 18, 1861.
Company G: Discharged Nov. 21, 1861 at Cheat Mountain, W. Va. on Surgeon's certificate of disability.

Barzilla M. Eaveland, Private, age 35, entered service for period of 3 years, June 26, 1861.
Company H: Killed May 8, 1862 in battle of McDowell, Va..

Frederick E. Eberhart, Private, age 30, entered service for period of 3 years, June 13, 1861.
Company F: Discharged Nov. 19, 1861 on Surgeon's certificate of disability.

Solomon Ebersole, 1st Sergeant, age 21, entered service for period of 3 years, June 13, 1861.
Company F: Appointed Corporal April 16, 1863; Sergeant Oct. 14, 1863; 1st Sergeant Jan. 1, 1864; died Sept. 9, 1864 in hospital at Hilton Head, S.C.; veteran.

Phillip Eckert, Private, age 19, entered service for period of 1 year, Oct. 4, 1864.
Company E; Mustered out Oct. 4, 1865 on expiration of term of service.

Jacob Eddy, Private, age 38, entered service for period of 1 year, Oct. 4, 1864.
Company D: Mustered out with company Oct. 20, 1865.

Samuel Edgar, Private, age 19, entered service for period of 3 years, June 12, 1861.
Company E; Wounded July 1, 1863 in battle of Gettysburg, Pa.; transferred to Co. C 75th O.V.I. Jan. 16, 1864; mustered out July 16, 1864 at Columbus, Ohio on expiration of term of service.

George Edge, Private, age 24, entered service for period of 1 year, Feb. 20, 1864.
Company C: discharged....; at Columbus, Ohio.

George G. Edgerton, Adjutant, age 28, entered service for period of 3 years, June 12, 1861.

Promoted from private Co. E May 6, 1863; discharged Nov. 20, 1863 by order of the War Department.

Company E: Promotion to 1st Lieutenant and Adjutant May 6, 1863.

John C. Edwards, Private, age 19, entered service for period of 3 years, June 26, 1861.

Company H: Discharged July 16, 1861 at Columbus, Ohio by civil authority.

Elijah Ekleberry, Private, age 19, entered service for period of 3 years, Feb. 11, 1862.

Company F: Died Oct. 6, 1862 in hospital in Alexandria, Va..

Ezekiel Ekelberry, Private, age 32, entered service for period of 1 year, Oct. 31, 1864.

Company D: Mustered out with company Oct. 20, 1865.

William Elliger, Private, age 20, entered service for period of 3 years, June 10, 1861.

Company B: Killed July 1, 1863 in battle of Gettysburg, Pa.

Emory R. Elliott, Private, age 18. entered service for period of 1 year, Oct. 5, 1864.

Company G: Discharged June 15, 1865 at Hilton Head, S.C. on Surgeon's certificate of disability.

John H. Elliott, Private, age 21, entered service for period of 3 years, Feb. 8, 1864.

Company A: No record given

Reuben Elliott, Private, age 24, entered service for period of 3 years, Jan. 1, 1864.

Company C: Transferred from Co. C 107th O.V.I. July 13, 1865.

Edward Ellis, 1st Sergeant, age 40, entered service for period of 3 years, June 26, 1861.

Company I: Promoted to Hospital Steward July 18, 1861.

George Elsworth, Private, age 25, entered service for period of 3 years, Jan. 5, 1864.

Company I: Transferred from Co. E 107th O.V.I. July 13, 1865; mustered our with company July 18, 1866.

Lewis Emery, Private, age 21, entered service for period of 3 years, June 24, 1864.

Company K: Died March 13, 1862 at Beverly, W.Va..

Jacob Emig, Private, age 21, entered service for period of 3 years, Oct. 3, 1864.

Company C: Transferred from Co. C 107th O.V.I....; discharged Aug. 26, 1865 at New York by order of War Department.

Lewis Engle, Private, age 27, entered service for period of 1 year, Sept. 30, 1864.

Company I: Wounded Dec. 6, 1864 in battle of Deveaux Neck, S.C.; discharged July 15, 1865 by order of War Department.

W.H. Ephraim, Private, age 19, entered service for period of 3 years, June 18, 1861.
Company G: no record given.

Christian E. Evans, Private, age 18, entered service for period of 3 years, June 24, 1861.
Company K: Wounded May 8, 1862 in battle of McDowell, Va. and July 1, 1863 in battle of Gettysburg, Pa.; transferred to Co. C 75th O.V.I. Jan. 16, 1864; from Co. C 75th O.V.I. June 1, 1864; mustered out July 16, 1864 on expiration of term of service.

John Evans, Private, age 23, entered service for period of 1 year, Oct. 4, 1864.
Company D: no record given.

Thomas J. Evans, Sergeant, age 21, entered service for period of 3 years, Feb. 17, 1864.
Company F: Appointed Corporal Nov. 5, 1864; Sergeant July 1, 1865; mustered out with company June 18, 1866.

Thomas Evans, Private, age…., entered service for period of 3 years, Feb. 11, 1862.
Company F: Captured at Battle of Chancellorsville, May 2, 1863.

Thomas Evans, Private, age 30, entered service for period of 1 year, Nov. 12, 1864.
Company K: Mustered out Nov. 12, 1865 on expiration of term of service.

John Evingham, Private, age 20, entered service for period of 3 years, June 12, 1861.
Company E; Wounded May 8, 1862 in battle of McDowell, Va.; discharged Oct. 13, 1862 on Surgeon's certificate of disability.

John Ewalt, Private, age 21, entered service for period of 3 years, June 18, 1861.
Company G: Transferred to Co. C 75th O.V.I. Jan. 16, 1864; from Co. C 75th O.V.I. June 12, 864; mustered out July 16, 1864 on expiration of term of service.

F

George Fagan, Private, age 23, entered service for period of 1 year, Oct. 4, 1864.
Company D: no record given.

Ammi B. Fairbanks, Sergeant, age 23, entered service for period of 3 years, June 8, 1861.
Company D: Transferred to 12th Battery O.L.A. March 12, 1862.

William W. Fallon, Private, age 20, entered service for period of 3 years, June 10, 1861.

Company C: Mustered out with company June 18, 1866.

Martin L. Fallwell, Private, age 24, entered service for period of 3 years, June 10, 1861.

Company C: Mustered out with company June 18, 1861; veteran.

Nathan Falk, Corporal, age 33, entered service for period of 3 years, Feb. 25, 1864.

Company K: Wounded Dec. 6, 1864 in battle of Gregory's Landing, S.C.; appointed Corporal Feb. 1, 1865; discharged April 25, 1866 by order of War Department.

Richard Farmer, Corporal, age 43, entered service for period of 3 years, Feb 12, 1863.

Company G: Appointed Corporal Nov. 1, 1865; mustered out with company June 18, 1866.

John Farrell, Private, age 20 entered service for period of 3 years, June 12, 1861.

Company E: Killed Aug. 30, 1862 in battle of bull Run, Va..

Josiah Faught, Private, age 23, entered service for period of 3 years, June 12, 1861.

Company E: Killed May 8, 1862 in battle of McDowell, Va..

Joseph Faulk, Private, age 26, entered service for period of 1 year, Oct. 5, 1864.

Company D: Mustered out with company July 15, 1865.

Ira Faust, Private, age 26, entered service for period of 1 year, Sept. 30, 1864.

Company F: Mustered out Oct. 1, 1864 on expiration of term of service.

William Faylon, Private, age 18, entered service for period of 3 years, Aug. 4, 1862.

Company E: Discharged Aug. 12, 1864 on Surgeon's certificate of disability.

Richard D. Fawcette, Private, age 18, entered service for period of 3 years, Mar. 15, 1862.

Company A: Killed Dec. 6, 1864 in battle of Deveaux Neck, S.C..

Sumner B. Felt, Sergeant, age 18, entered service for period of 3 years, Feb. 17, 1862.

Company K: Wounded May 3, 1863 in battle of Chancellorsville, Va.; appointed Corporal April 1, 1864; Sergeant April 1, 1866; mustered out with company June 18, 1866; veteran.

John Fenton, Sergeant, age 38, entered service for period of 3 years, June 18, 1861.

Company G: Transferred to Co. C 75th O.V.I. Jan. 16, 1864; from Co. C 75th O.V.I June 12, 1864; mustered out July 16, 1864 at Columbia, S. C. on expiration of term of service.

William H. Fenton, Private, age 41, entered service for period of 3 years, June 24, 1861.

Company K: Reduced from Corporal July 19, 1861; discharged Nov. 6, 1862 at Baltimore, Md. on Surgeon's certificate of disability.

Charles W. Ferguson, 1st Lieutenant, age 36, entered service for period of 3 years, March 16, 1864.

Company B: Promoted to Captain Co. K Aug. 11, 1864.

Joseph Ferguson, Private, age 18, entered service for period of 3 years, June 8, 1861.

Company D: Transferred to 12th Battery O.L.A. March 12, 1862.

Lewis Fermenn, Private, age 18, entered service for period of 3 years, June 8, 1861.

Company D: Transferred to 12th Battery O.L.A. March 12, 1862.

Thomas H. Ferrel, Sergeant, age 21, entered service for period of 3 years, June 5, 1861.

Company A: Appointed from Corporal…..; promoted to Hospital Steward June 12, 1864; veteran.

Company I: 2d Lieutenant. Promoted from Hospital Steward Nov. 18, 1864; Captain 104th U.S. Colored Troops June 15, 1865.

Henry Fight, Private, age 18, entered service for period of 3 years, Dec. 31, 1863.

Company B; Transferred from Co.….107th O.V.I. July 13, 1865; mustered out with company June 18, 1866.

Maurice Fillize, Private, age 23, entered service for period of 3 years, Oct. 10, 1862.

Company I: Transferred from 107th O.V. I. July 13, 1865; mustered out Oct. 9, 1865 on expiration of term of service.

Thomas M. Finley, Private, age 18, entered service for period of 3 years, Feb. 18, 1864.

Company C: no record given.

Augustus Fisher, Private, age 28, entered service for period of 3 years, June 10, 1861.

Company C: Killed May 2, 1863 in battle of Chancellorsville, Va..

John D. Fisher, Private, age 21, entered service for period of 3 years, June 18, 1861.

Company G: Mustered out July 16, 1864 on expiration of term of service.

John W. Fisher, Corporal, age 21, entered service for period of 3 years, June 10, 1861.

Company C: Appointed Corporal Jan. 1, 1862; discharged Dec. 5, 1862 at Alexandria, Va. on Surgeon's certificate of disability.

Sanford Fisher, Private, age 18, entered service for period of 1 year, Sept. 27, 1864.

Company D: Mustered out July 15, 1865 by order of War Department.

William F. Fisher, Private, age 22, entered service for period of 3 years, June 8, 1861.

Company D: Transferred to 12th Battery O.L.A. March 12, 1862.

Henry Fight, Private, age 18, entered service for period of 3 years, Dec. 21, 1863.

Company B: Transferred from Co....107th O.V.I. July 13, 1865; mustered out with company June 18, 1866.

Luther Flagg, Corporal, age 22, entered service for period of 3 years, June 26, 1861.

Company H: Died July 1, 1862 at Winchester, Va..

Samuel Fleck, Private, age 21, entered service for period of 3 years, June 8, 1861.

Company D: Transferred to 12th Battery O.L.A. march 12, 1862.

William B. Flemming, Sergeant, age 22, entered service for period of 3 years, June 8, 1861.

Company D: Transferred to 12th Battery O.L.A. March 12, 1862.

David Flower, Private, age 32, entered service for period of 1 year, Oct. 4, 1864.

Company D: Wounded Nov. 30, 1864 in battle of Honey Hill, S.C.; discharged June 27, 1865 at Camp Dennison Hospital, Ohio on Surgeon's certificate of disability.

Maurice T. Floyd, Private, age 21, entered service for period of 3 years, June 26, 1861.

Company I: Died May 24, 1862 at Staunton, Va..

John H. Flynn, Private, age 21, entered service for period of 3 years, June 24, 1861.

Company K: Discharged Nov. 2, 1862 at Cheat Mountain, W. Va. on Surgeon's certificate of disability.

Abraham Foae, Private, age 43, entered service for period of 1 year, Sept. 5, 1864.

Company E: Discharged July 15, 1865 by order of War Department.

Samuel Foae, Private, age 18, entered service for period of 1 year, Sept. 5, 1864.

Company E: Discharged July 15, 1865 by order of War Department.

William W. Fogle, Private, age entered service for period of 3 years, June 26, 1861.

Company H: Mustered out with company June 18, 1866; veteran.

John W. Forbes, Private, age 23, entered service for period of 3 years, June 24, 1861.

Company K: Appointed Corporal Sept. 9, 1861; reduced July 10, 1862; discharged Nov. 6, 1862 at Alexandria, Va. on Surgeon's certificate of disability.

Henry H. Ford, Private, age 24, entered service for period of 3 years, June 10, 1861.

Company B: Killed May 2, 1863 in battle of Chancellorsville, Va.

Jasper N. Ford, Private, age 29, entered service for period of 1 year, Sept. 25, 1864.

Company F: Discharged July 15, 1865 by order of War Department.

Edwin O. Forrester, Private, age 20, entered service for period of 3 years, June 13, 1861.

Company F: Discharged Aug. 31, 1862 on Surgeon's certificate of disability.

Samuel M. Forrester, Musician, age 27, entered service for period of 3 years, June 13, 1861.

Company F: Appointed Musician...; died June 20, 1864 at Seabro, S.C.; veteran.

Gabriel Fortig, Private, age 35, entered service for period of 3 years, Oct. 8, 1862.

Company I: Transferred from 107th O.V.I. July 13, 1865; mustered out Oct. 8, 1865 on expiration of term of service.

Robert Foster, Private, age 21, entered service for period of 1 year, Aug. 31, 1864.

Company E: Discharged July 15, 1865 by order of War Department.

Thomas Foster, Private, age 23, entered service for period of 3 years, June 26, 1861.

Company H: no record given.

John Foughty, Private, age 20, entered service for period of 3 years, Feb. 29, 1864.

Company B; Transferred from Co...107th O.V.I. July 13, 1865; mustered out with company June 18, 1866.

William L. Fouts, 1st Lieutenant, age 20, entered service for period of 3 years, June 25, 1861.

Company F: Promoted from 1st Sergeant Co. H Oct. 17, 1864; to 1st Lieutenant Co. K Feb. 10, 1865.

Company H: Appointed Corporal Dec. 30, 1861; Sergeant Dec. 3, 1862; 1st Sergeant April 1, 1864; promoted to 2d Lieutenant Co. F Oct. 17, 1864; veteran.

Company K: Promoted from 2d Lieutenant Co. F Feb. 10, 1865; mustered out with company June 18, 1866.

Jefferson Foutz, Corporal, age 18, entered service for period of 3 years, June 26, 1861.

Company H: Wounded May 3, 1863 in battle of Chancellorsville, Va.; appointed Corporal June 1, 1866; mustered out with company June 18, 1866; veteran.

Martin L. Fowell, Private, age 24, entered service for period of 3 years, June 10, 1861.
Company H: Transferred from Co. B June 13, 1864; mustered out July 16, 1864 at Columbus, Ohio on expiration of term of service.
Robert A. Fowler, Private, age 21, entered service for period of 3 years, June 5, 1861.
Company A: Wounded Aug. 30, 1862 in battle of Bull Run, Va.; died Feb. 27, 1862 at Philadelphia, Pa.
Thomas W. Fowler, Corporal, age 36, entered service for period of 3 years, June 5, 1861.
Company A: Wounded July 1, 1863 in battle of Gettysburg, Pa.; mustered out with company June 18, 1866; veteran.
Daniel Fox, Sergeant, age 38, entered service for period of 1 year, Oct. 3, 1864.
Company D: Mustered as private; appointed Sergeant Aug 1, 1865; mustered out with company Oct. 20, 1865.
George S. Frazier, Sergeant, age 21, entered service for period of 3 years, June 24, 1861.
Company K: Appointed Corporal April 1, 1864; wounded Dec. 6, 1864 in battle of Gregory's Landing, S.C.; appointed Sergeant Feb. 1, 1865; veteran.
Christian Frankhouser, Private, age 33, entered service for period of 3 years, June 10, 1861.
Company C: Discharged Jan. 20, 1863 at Stafford C.H., Va. on Surgeon's certificate of disability.
Samuel Frannitz, Private, age 42, entered service for period of 3 years, June 12, 1861.
Company E: Mustered out July 16, 1864 on expiration of term of service.
Stephen Frazar, Private, age 18, entered service for period of 1 year, Sept. 23, 1864.
Company A: Mustered out Sept. 23, 1865 on expiration of term of service.
August Freeh, Private, age 18, entered service for period of 3 years, June 12, 1864.
Company E: Wounded Dec. 13,1861 in battle of Camp Alleghany, W. Va. and May 2, 1863 in battle of Chancellorsville, Va.; transferred to Co. C 75th O.V.I. Jan. 16, 1864; from Co. C 75th O.V.I. June 12, 1864; mustered out July 10, 1864 at Columbus, Ohio on expiration of term of service.
George Frick, Private, age 18, entered service for period of 3 years, June 10, 1861.
Company C: Wounded May 2, 1863 in battle of Chancellorsville, Va.; transferred to Co. C 75th O.V.I. Jan. 16, 1864; from Co. C 75th O.V.I. May 6, 1864; mustered out on expiration of term of service.

Jacob Fritchy, Private, age 43, entered service for period of 3 years, Dec. 17, 1863.
Company C: Transferred from Co. F 107th O.V.I. July 13, 1865; mustered out with company June 18, 1866.
David M. Fry, Private, age 22, entered service for period of 3 years, June 10, 1861.
Company C: Discharged Jan. 1, 1863 at Washington, D.C. on Surgeon's certificate of disability.
John Fry, Corporal, age 31, entered service for period of 3 years, June 10, 1861.
Company C: Appointed Corporal Nov. 1, 1862; killed July 3, 1863 in battle of Gettysburg, Pa..
John Fryman, Corporal, age 20, entered service for period of 1 year, Oct. 12, 1864.
Company F: Appointed Corporal Aug. 1, 1865; mustered out Oct. 12, 1865 on expiration of term of service.
Jonathan C. Fuller, Private, age 23, entered service for period of 3 years, June 20, 1861.
Company F: Discharged Oct. 18, 1862 on Surgeon's certificate of disability.
Oliver Fuller, Private, age 20, entered service for period of 1 year, Feb. 24, 1865.
Company C: Transferred from Co. F 107th O.V.I. July 13, 1865; mustered out on Feb. 24, 1866 at Charleston, S.C. on expiration of term of service.
Andrew Fulton, Sergeant, 23, entered service for period of 3 years, June 28, 1861.
Company Appointed Corporal June 1, 1865; Sergeant May 18, 1866; mustered out with company June 18, 1866; veteran.
Robert M. Fulton, 1st Sergeant, age 21, entered service for period of 3 years, June 5, 1861.
Company A: Wounded May 2, 1863 in battle of Chancellorsville, Va.; appointed Corporal April 1, 1864; Sergeant April 1, 1865; 1st Sergeant May 18, 1866; mustered out with company June 18, 1866; veteran.
Charles Furenback, Private, age 26, entered service for period of 3 years, June 24, 1861.
Company K: Killed Sept. 12, 1861 in battle of Cheat Mountain, W. Va..
George Furney, Private, age 24, entered service for period of 3 years, Feb. 13, 1864.
Company K: Died...in Port Hospital at Columbia, S.C.

G

Phillip Gable, Private, age 24, entered service for period of 3 years, June 5, 1861.

Company A: Transferred from 75th O.V.I. June 13, 1864; mustered out July 16, 1864 on expiration of term of service.

Leonard W. Gaddis, Sergeant, age 19, entered service for period of 3 years, June 18, 1861.

Company G: Appointed Corporal June 1, 1865; Sergeant Oct. 1, 1865; mustered out with Company June 18, 1866; veteran.

Benjamin Gallaher, Private, age 33, entered service for period of 3 years, Oct. 8, 1862.

Company A: Transferred to Veteran Reserve Corps Aug. 1, 1863, by order of War Department.

John Galligher, Private, age 30, entered service for period of 3 years, June 27, 1861.

Company G: no record given.

Joseph Gallaher, Private, age 22, entered service for period of 3 years, June 5, 1861.

Company A: Transferred to 75th O.V.I. Jan. 15, 1864; from 75th O.V.I. June 13, 1864; mustered out July 16, 1864 on expiration of term of service.

William Gallaher, Private, age 34, entered service for period of 3 years, Oct. 7, 1862.

Company A: Transferred to Veteran Reserve Corps Aug. 1, 1863, by order of War Department.

Thomas Gallaher, Private, age 25, entered service for period of 3 years, Oct. 13, 1862.

Company A: Transferred to Veteran Reserve Corps Aug. 1, 1863, by order of War Department.

Joseph S. Gannill, Private, age 21, entered service for period of 1 year, Oct. 7, 1864.

Company G: Mustered out Oct. 7, 1865 at Charleston, S.C. on expiration of term of service.

Phineas Gano, Private, age 23, entered service for period of 3 years, June 10, 1861.

Company B: Promoted to Q.M. Sergeant Oct. 8, 1863.

Wilson H. Gano, Private, age 29, entered service for period of 3 years, Aug. 7, 1863.

Company E: Discharged July 15, 1865 by order of War Department.

Reuben E. Gant, Private, age 21, entered service for period of 3 years, June 26, 1861.
Company I: Veteran.
William Gant, Private, age 22, entered service for period of 3 years, June 26, 1861.
Company I: Wounded July 1, 1863 in battle of Gettysburg, Pa.; transferred to Co. C 75th O.V.I. Jan. 16, 1864; from Co. C 75th O.V.I. June 12, 1864; mustered out July 16, 1864 on expiration of term of service.
Andrew Ganter, Private, age 22, entered service for period of 3 years, Aug. 1, 1864.
Company B: Transferred from Co....107th O.V.I. July 13, 1865; mustered out with company June 18, 1866.
Alfred K. Garner, Private, age 18, entered service for period of 3 years, March 1, 1864.
Company I: Transferred from Co. H 107th O.V.I. July 13, 1865; mustered out with company June 18, 1866.
Joseph G. Garrette, Private, age 18, entered service for period of 3 years, Feb. 20, 1864.
Company I: Mustered out with company June 18, 1866.
John A. Garrisane, Private, age 22, entered service for period of 3 years, June 13, 1861.
Company F: Mustered out July 16, 1864 on expiration of term of service.
John Garung, Private, age 18, entered service for period of 3 years, Feb. 23, 1864.
Company K: no record given.
John Garvin, Private, age 18, entered service for period of 3 years, Feb. 23, 1864.
Company K: no record given.
David K. Gauff, Private, age 29, entered service for period of 3 years, Feb. 22, 1864.
Company B; Mustered out with company June 18, 1866.
William Gazaway, Corporal, age 23, entered service for period of 3 years, June 13, 1861.
Company F: Discharged Nov. 5, 1862 on Surgeon's certificate of disability.
Miles Geary, Private, age 21, entered service for period of 1 year, Sept. 19, 1864.
Company H: Discharged July 15, 1865 at Charleston, S.C. by order of War Department.

Christian Gerber, Private, age 19, entered service for period of 3 years, Oct. 11, 1862.
Company A: Transferred from 107th O.V.I. July 13, 1865; mustered out Oct. 11, 1865 on expiration of term of service.
Samuel Gerr, Private, age 32, entered service for period of 1 year, Oct. 12, 1864.
Company F: Mustered out Oct. 12, 1865 on expiration of term of service.
Wilhelm Giehrke, Private, age 23, entered service for period of 3 years, Dec. 28, 1863.
Company I: Transferred from 107th O.V.I. July 13, 1865.
William Gift, Private, age 21, entered service for period of 3 years, July 9, 1861.
Company H: no record given.
Frank H. Gill, Private, age 19, entered service for period of 1 year, Sept. 9, 1864.
Company I: Discharged July 15, 1865 by order of War Department.
John Gillispie, Corporal, age 29, entered service for period of 3 years, July 3, 1861.
Company H: Wounded May 3, 1863 in battle of Chancellorsville, Va. and July 2, 1863 in battle of Gettysburg, Pa.; appointed Corporal April 1, 1864; killed Nov. 30, 1864 in battle of Honey Hill, S. C.; veteran.
Samuel M. Gillespie, Private, age 18, entered service for period of 3 years, Feb. 29, 1864.
Company H: Wounded Nov. 30, 1864 in battle of Honey Hill, S.C.; discharged June 8, 1865 by order of War Department.
William Gillispie, Corporal, age 21, entered service for period of 3 years, June 26, 1861.
Company H: Wounded Dec. 6, 1864 in battle of Gregory's Landing, S.C.; appointed Corporal June 1, 1866; mustered out with company June 18, 1866; veteran.
Benjamin S. Gilmore, Private, age 35, entered service for period of 3 years, June 12, 1861.
Company E: Promoted to Principal Musician Sept 1, 1863; discharged and re-enlisted as private Jan. 1, 1864; mustered out with company June 18, 1866; veteran.
Frederick Gilyer, Corporal, age 22, entered service for period of 3 years, June 12, 1861.
Company E: Wounded May 8, 1862 in battle of McDowell, Va. and Nov. 30, 1864 in battle of Honey Hill, S.C.; appointed Corporal May 16, 1866; mustered out with company June 18, 1866; veteran.

Peter Glass, Private, age 25, entered service for period of 3 years, March 2, 1864.

Company A: Transferred from 107th O.V.I. July 12, 1865; mustered out with company June 18, 1866.

Samuel Glasgow, Private, age 24, entered service for period of 3 years, June 5, 1861.

Company A: Mustered out July 16, 1864, on expiration of term of service.

John W. Goady, Private, age 32, entered service for period of 1 year, Aug. 16, 1864.

Company F: Discharged July 15, 1864 by order of War Department.

Levi Golden, Private, age 18, entered service for period of 3 years, June 26, 1861.

Company H: no record given.

Andrew J. Gordell, Private, age 31, entered service for period of 3 years, Feb. 25, 1864.

Company B: Mustered out with company June 18, 1866.

Samuel M. Gordon, private, age 21, entered service for period of 3 years, June 26, 1861.

Company H: Transferred to Battery G, 5th U.S. Artillery, Nov. 15, 1863.

William Gore, Private, age 18, entered service for period of 1 year, Oct. 10, 1864.

Company A: Mustered out Oct. 10, 1865 on expiration of term of service.

James Gowdey, Private, age 18, entered service for period of 3 years, Nov. 23, 1863.

Company B; Transferred from Co...107th O.V.I. June 13, 1865; mustered out with company June 18, 1866.

James D. Graff, Private, age 23, entered service for period of 3 years, June 24, 1861.

Company K: Mustered out July 16, 1864 on expiration of term of service.

Enoch Grandon, Private, age 18, entered service for period of 3 years, Feb. 25, 1864.

Company I: Mustered out with company June 18, 1866.

Moses D. Grandy, Sergeant, age 21, entered service for period of 3 years, Feb. 26, 1864.

Company B: Appointed from private March 16, 1864; killed Nov. 30, 1864 in battle of Honey Hill, S.C..

John F. Granger, Private, age 20, entered service for period of 3 years, June 20, 1861.

Company F: Died Aug. 17, 1862 at Delphos, Ohio.

Jeremiah Grant, Private, age 18, entered service for period of 3 years, Feb. 17, 1864.

Company E: Died Dec. 4, 1864 of wounds received Nov. 30, 1864 in battle of Honey Hill, S.C..

Reuben E. Grant, Private, age 21, entered service for period of 3 years, June 26, 1861.

Company I: Veteran.

Robert F. Grant, Private, age 25, entered service for period of 3 years, June 26, 1861.

Company I: Died June 12, 1862 of wounds received June 8, 1862 in battle of Cross Keys.

William Grau, Private, age 39, entered service for period of 3 years, Jan. 1, 1864.

Company C: Transferred from Co. C 107th O.V.I. July 13, 1865.

Orlando Gray, Private, age 25, entered service for period of 3 years, June 24, 1861.

Company K: no record given.

William Gray, Private, age 32, entered service for period of 1 year, Sept. 3, 1864.

Company E: Discharged July 15, 1865 by order of War Department.

William R. Gray, Private, age 25, entered service for period of 3 years, March 8, 1862.

Company G: Transferred to Co. C 75th O.V.I. Jan 16, 1864; from Co. C 75th O.V.I. June 12, 1864; mustered out July 16, 1864 on expiration of term of service.

George W. Greeling, Sergeant, age 22, entered service for period of 3 years, June 18, 1861.

Company G: Mustered as private; appointed Sergeant...; veteran.

Lewis R. Green, Captain, age 21, June 4, 1861.

Company H: Died Sept. 5, 1862 at Washington, D.C.

John Greene, Private, age 18, entered service for period of 3 years, Mar. 7, 1864.
Company B; no record given.

John Greene, Corporal, age 25, entered service for period of 3 years, Jan. 5, 1864.

Company I: Transferred from Co. E 107th O.V.I. July 13, 1865; appointed Corporal Oct. 1, 1865;absent, sick Jan. 1, 1866; mustered out June 18, 1866 by order of War Department.

Martin W. Greene, Private, age 19, entered service for period of 1 year, Oct. 7, 1864.

Company A: Mustered out Oct. 7, 1865 on expiration of term of service.

William M. Greene, Private, age 19, entered service for period of 3 years, June 10, 1861.
Company B: no record given.
Henry Greer, private, age 19, entered service for period of 3 years, June 13, 1861.
Company F: Transferred to Co. C 75th O.V.I. Jan.16, 1864; from Co. C 75th O.V.I. June 12, 1864; mustered out July 16, 1864 on expiration of term of service.
James Greer, Private, age 23, entered service for period of 1 year, Sept. 19, 1864.
Company C: Discharged July 15, 1865 by order of the War Department.
Alphonso E. Gregory, Private, age 18, entered service for period of 3 years, June 8, 1861.
Company D: Transferred to 12th Battery O.L.A. March 12, 1862.
George Gress, Corporal, age 20, entered service for period of 3 years, Dec. 30, 1863.
Company A: Appointed Corporal May 1, 1866; mustered out with company June 18, 1866.
John W. Grier, Private, age 18, entered service for period of 3 years, June 26, 1861.
Company H: Wounded Nov. 30, 1864 in battle of Honey Hill, S. C.; veteran.
Chauncey Griffith. Private, age 22, entered service for period of 3 years, June 24, 1861.
Company K: Discharged June 25, 1862 at Columbus, Ohio on Surgeon's certificate of disability.
Joseph S. Grim, Corporal, age 35, entered service for period of 3 years, Feb. 18, 1864.
Company K: Died in general hospital at Hilton Head, S.C. of wounds received in battle of Honey Hill, S,C.
Thomas Grimes, Private, age 22, entered service for period of 3 years, June 8, 1861.
Company D: Transferred to 12th Battery O.L.A. March 12, 1862.
Thomas S. Grissel, Private, age 20, entered service for period of 3 years, June 10, 1861.
Company C: Killed June 8, 1862 in battle of Cross Keyes, Va..
Daniel D. Grover, Private, age 26, entered service for period of 3 years, July 16, 1861.
Company K: no record given.
William H. Gulick, Private, age 21, entered service for period of 3 years, June 18, 1861. Company G: Killed July 1, 1862 in battle of Gettysburg, Pa..

Ethan W. Guthrie, 1st Sergeant, age 23, entered service for period of 3 years, February 20, 1864.

Company B: Mustered as private; appointed 1st Sergeant....; promoted to 2d Lieutenant Co. G October 12, 1864.

Company G: Promoted from 1st Sergeant Co. B Oct. 121, 1864; died April 8, 1865 of wounds received Nov. 30, 1864 in battle of Honey Hill, S.C..

Leander A. Guyette, Musician, age 17, entered service for period of 3 years, Feb. 29, 1864.

Company I: Mustered out with company June 18, 1866.

H

William Hadnet, Private, age 19, entered service for period of 3 years, June 24, 1861.

Company K: Reduced from Corporal...; mustered out July 16, 1864 on expiration of term of service.

William C. Hagerman, Private, age 21, entered service for period of 1 year, Aug. 29, 1864.

Company G: Discharged...by order of War Department.

John H. Hague, Private, age 36, entered service for period of 1 year, Oct. 4, 1864.

Company D: Died Aug. 20, 1865 in Port Hospital, Columbia, S.C..

Hiram S. Hahn, Private, age 23, entered service for period of 3 years, June 5, 1861.

Company A: Wounded May 8, 1862 in battle of McDowell, Va.; transferred to 75th O.V.I. Jan. 15, 1864; from 75th O.V.I. June 3, 1864; mustered out July 16, 1864 on expiration of term of service.

Frederick Halderman, Corporal, age 20, entered service for period of 3 years, June 12, 1861.

Company E: Appointed Corporal June 1, 1866; mustered out with company June 18, 1866; veteran.

Andrew J. Hale, 2d, Lieutenant, age 33, entered service for period of 3 years, June 4, 1861.

Company E: Promoted to Regt. Quartermaster July 11, 1861.

Lorenzo S. Haley, Sergeant, age 20, entered service for period of 3 years, Feb. 26, 1864.

Company B: Appointed Corporal March 16, 1864; Sergeant May 9, 1864; promoted to 2d Lieutenant 104th Colored Troops, U.S. June 14, 1865.

Harvey M. Hall, Private, age 20, entered service for period of 3 years, June 12, 1861.
Company E: Wounded Nov. 30, 1864 in battle of Honey Hill, S.C.; veteran.
James W. Hall, Corporal, age 18, entered service for period of 3 years, June 24, 1861.
Company K: Appointed Corporal April 1, 1864; mustered out with company June 18, 1866; veteran.
John Hall, Sergeant, age 24, entered service for period of 3 years, July 10, 1861.
Company C: Appointed Corporal March 1, 1864; Sergeant Nov. 1, 1865; mustered out with company June 18, 1861; veteran.
John Hall, Private, age 21, entered service for period of 3 years, June 10, 1861.
Company C: Mustered out with company June 18, 1866; veteran.
Howard Hallette, Sergeant, age 19, entered service for period of 3 years, June 26, 1861.
Company I: Appointed from private Jan. 1, 1862; wounded May 8, 1862 in battle of McDowell, Va.; mustered out July 16, 1864 on expiration of term of service.
Mathias Hamberling, Private, age 36, entered service for period of 3 years, July 26, 1864.
Company I: Transferred from Co. H 107th O.V.I. July 13, 1865; absent sick...; in hospital at Cleveland, Ohio; mustered out June 18, 1866 by order of War Department.
George Hamey, Private, age 22, entered service for period of 3 years, June 18, 1861.
Company G; Discharged Nov. 10, 1862 at Portsmouth, Va. by order of War Department.
James W. Hamilton, Private, age 20, entered service for period of 3 years, Feb. 26, 1864.
Company I: Mustered out with company June 18, 1866.
Patrick L. Hamilton, Wagoner, age 21, entered service for period of 3 years, June 10, 1861.
Company B: Transferred to Co. C. March 20, 1864.; veteran.
Company C: Transferred from Co. B March 20, 1864; mustered out with company June 18, 1866; veteran.
William Hamilton, Private, age 29, entered service for period of 3 years, June 10, 1861.
Company C: Transferred to Co. C 75th O.V.I. Jan. 16, 1864; from Co. C 75th O.V.I. May 2, 1864; mustered out July 16, 1864 at Camp Chase, Ohio on expiration of term of service.

David Hammond, Sergeant, age 26, entered service for period of 1 year, April 6, 1864.

Company D: Mustered as private; appointed Sergeant...; discharged March 1, 1865 to accept promotion as 2d Lieutenant 34th U.S. Colored Troops.

James P. Hammond, Private age 21, entered service for period of 1 year, Oct. 19, 1864.

Company H; Mustered out Oct. 7, 1865 on expiration of term of service.

John T. Hancock, Private, age 27, entered service for period of 3 years, June 13, 1861.

Company F: Transferred to Co. C 75th O.V.I. Jan. 16, 1864; from 75th O.V.I. June 12, 1864; mustered out July 16, 1864 on expiration of term of service.

Joseph J. Hapton, Private, age 29, entered service for period of 3 years, June 10, 1861.

Company B: Wounded Dec. 12, 1861 in battle of Camp Alleghany, Va.; transferred to Co. H June 13, 1864.

Company H: Transferred from Co. B June 13, 1864 at Columbus, Ohio on expiration of term of service.

George Hardinger, Private, age 27, entered service for period of 1 year, Oct. 8, 1864.

Company D: Mustered out with company Oct. 20, 1865.

Andrew J. Harkins, Private, age 31, entered service for period of 3 years, Feb. 28, 1864.

Company K: Mustered out with company June 18, 1866.

Joseph Harkins, Private, age 22, entered service for period of 3 years, June 26, 1861.

Company H: Discharged Dec, 22, 1862 at Baltimore, Md. on Surgeon's certificate of disability.

John Harlem, Private, age 35, entered service for period of 3 years, June 26, 1861.

Company I: Reduced from Corporal...; transferred to Co. C 75th O.V.I. Jan. 16, 1864; from Co. C 75th O.V.I. June 12, 1864; mustered out July 16, 1864 on expiration of term of service.

Israel Harley, Corporal, age 25, entered service for period of 1 year, Oct. 12, 1864.

Company D: Appointed Corporal July 1, 1965; mustered out with company Oct. 20, 1865.

Samuel Harley, Private, age 24, entered service for period of 1 year, Oct. 12, 1864.

Company D: Mustered out with company Oct. 20, 1865.

Carmon Harmon, Private, age 19, entered service for period of 9 months, Oct. 7, 1862.

Company K: Drafted; mustered out July 7, 1863 on expiration of term of service.

Cyrus Harmon, Private, age 32, entered service for period of 3 years, June 26, 1861.

Company H: no record given.

Nathan Harmon, Private, age 37, entered service for period of 9 months, Oct. 7, 1862.

Company K: Drafted; mustered out July 7, 1863 on expiration of term of service.

George Harman, Private age 19, entered service for period of 3 years, June 13, 1861.

Company F: Wounded May 2, 1863 in battle of Chancellorsville, Va.; mustered out July 16, 1864 on expiration of term of service.

August Harp, Private, age 37, entered service for period of 3 years, Dec. 14, 1863.

Company C: Transferred from Co. C 107th O.V.I. July 13, 1865.

Isaac Harper, Private, age 25, entered service for period of 3 years, June 26, 1861.

Company I: Wounded July 1, 1863 in battle of Gettysburg, Pa.; transferred to Co. C 75th O.V.I. June 16, 1864; from Company C 75th O.V.I. June 12, 1864; mustered out July 16, 1864 on expiration of term of service.

Michael Harris, Private, age 20, entered service for period of 3 years, June 27, 1861.

Company G: Discharged April 24, 1862 at Brook's Station, Va. on Surgeon's certificate of disability.

James Harrington, Private, age 34, entered service for period of 1 year, Sept. 5, 1864.

Company E: Died Jan. 16, 1865 of wounds received Dec. 9, 1864 in battle of Deveaux Neck, S.C.

John Harrington, Private, age 23, entered service for period of 1 year, Sept. 12, 1864.

Company K: Discharged July 15, 1865 by order of War Department.

Benjamin Harrison, Musician, age 18, entered service for period of 3 years, June 8, 1861.

Company D: Transferred to 12th Battery O.L.A. March 12, 1862.

Charles H. Harrison, Private, age 21, entered service for period of 3 years, June 18, 1861.

Company G: Killed July 1, 1863, in battle of Gettysburg, Pa..

John W. Harrison, Private, age 23, entered service for period of 3 years, June 10, 1861.

Company C: Killed May 2, 1863 in battle of Chancellorsville, Va..

William Harrison, Private, age 41, entered service for period of 3 years, June 5, 1861.

Company A: Wounded June 8, 1862 in battle of Cross Keys, Va.; transferred to 75th O.V.I. Jan. 15, 1865 by order of the War Department.

Zachariah Harrison, Private, age 43, entered service for period of 1 year, Sept. 21, 1864.

Company D: no record given.

David S. Harsh, Private, age 18, entered service for period of 1 year, Sept. 27, 1864.

Company D: Mustered out July 15, 1865 by order of War Department.

Benjamin Harson, Private, age 44, entered service for period of 1 year, Sept. 16, 1864.

Company C: Discharged July 15, 1865 by order of War Department.

Albert Hartley, Private, age 37, entered service for period of 1 year, Nov. 1, 1864.

Company K: Drafted; mustered out Nov. 1, 1865 on expiration of term of service.

David Hartley, Private, age 19, entered service for period of 3 years, June 26, 1861.

Company H: Wounded Aug. 29, 1862 in battle of Bull Run, Va.; discharged Feb. 18, 1863 at Camp Chase, Ohio on Surgeon's certificate of disability.

Gustave Hartman, Private, age 41, entered service for period of 3 years, Dec. 27, 1863.

Company K: Transferred from Co..... 107th O.V.I. July 13, 1865; discharged Dec. 15, 1865 on Surgeon's certificate of disability.

Philip Hasenzahl, Corporal, age 33, entered service for period of 3 years, Dec. 21, 1863.

Company K: Transferred to Co. C 75th O.V.I. Jan, 16, 1864; from Co. C 75th O.V.I. June 12, 1864; appointed Corporal July 1, 1865; discharged June 2, 1866 by order of the War Department.

Charles H. Hastings, Sergeant, age 25, entered service for period of 3 years, Feb. 27, 1864.

Company B; Appointed Corporal March 16, 1864; Sergeant Feb. 1, 1866; mustered out with company June 18, 1866.

George Hasteings, Private, age 22, entered service for period of 3 years, Feb. 27, 1864.

Company B: no record given.

Peter Hasty, Private, age 18, entered service for period of 3 years, Dec. 23, 1863. Company G: Transferred from Co. F 107th O.V.I. July 13, 1865; discharged...1866 by order of War Department.

Jacob W. Hatton, Private, age 18, entered service for period of 3 years, June 26, 1861. Company H: Transferred to Co. C 75th O.V.I. Jan. 16, 1864;from Co. C 75th O.V.I. June 12, 1864; mustered out July 16, 1864 at Columbus, Ohio on expiration of term of service.

Henry I. Haudwalt, Private, age 18, entered service for period of 1 year, Oct. 18, 1864. Company G; Mustered out Oct. 18, 1865 at Charleston, S.C. on expiration of term of service.

Austin Haughton, 2d Lieutenant, age 19, entered service for period of 3 years, June 24, 1861. Company H: Promoted from Com. Sergeant Oct. 12, 1864; died Dec. 7, 1864 of wounds received in action.

Austin Haughton, Private, age 19, entered service for period of 3 years, June 24, 1861. Company K: Promoted to Com. Sergeant March 16, 1864; veteran. (duplicate?)

Bristol Haughton, Wagoner, age 21, entered service for period of 3 years, Feb. 27, 1864. Company B: Mustered out with company June 18, 1866.

David Haughton, Private, age 25, entered service for period of 3 years, June 8, 1861. Company D: transferred to 12th Battery O.L.A. March 12, 1862.

Nathaniel Haughton, Lt. Col., age 31, entered service for period of 3 years, June 24, 1861. Promoted to Major from Captain Co. A Aug. 4, 1863; wounded July 1, 1863 at battle of Gettysburg, Pa.; Lt. Col. July 13, 1864; brevetted Brig. General March 13, 1865; Col. May 25, 1866, but not mustered; mustered out with regiment June 18, 1866. Company A: Promoted from 1st Lieutenant Co. K July 30, 1862; wounded July 1, 1863 in the battle of Gettysburg, Pa.; promoted to Major Aug. 4, 1863. Company K: Promoted to Captain Co A July 30, 1862.

Solon Haughton, Sergeant, age 19, entered service for period of 3 years, Nov. 14, 1861. Company K: Appointed from private Nov. 16, 1862; discharged Aug. 6, 1862 at Columbus, Ohio on Surgeon's certificate of disability.

Eli Hawker, Private, age 22, entered service for period of 3 years, June 5, 1861. Company A: Discharged March 16, 1863 on Surgeons certificate of disability.

Benjamin F. Hawkes, 2d Lieutenant, age..., entered service for period of 3 years, July 12, 1861.

Company E: Promoted to Lieut. Colonel 78th O.V.I. Feb. 6, 1862.

George W. Hawkins, Private, age 18, entered service for period of 1 year, Sept. 12, 1864.

Company K: Died Dec. 21, 1864 at Beaufort, S.C..

Barclay B. Haycock, Private, age 20, entered service for period of 1 year, Sept. 24, 1864.

Company D: Mustered out July 15, 1865 by order of War Department.

Oliver V. Haycock, Private, age 21, entered service for period of 1 year, Sept. 24, 1864.

Company D: Mustered out July 15, 1865 by order of War Department.

Abraham Hayden, Private, age 43, entered service for period of 3 years, June 10, 1861.

Company B: Transferred to Co. H June 13, 1864.

Company H: Transferred from Co. B June 13, 1864; mustered out July 16, 1864 at Columbus Ohio on expiration of term of service.

Jonathan Hayden, Private, age 35, entered service for period of 3 years, June 26, 1861.

Company I: Killed Dec. 13, 1861 in battle of Camp Alleghany, W.Va..

Barton S. Hays, Private, age 27, entered service for period of 3 years, June 24, 1861.

Company K: Discharged Nov. 27, 1861 at Cheat Mountain, W. Va. on surgeon's certificate of disability.

Abraham Head, Sergeant, age 24, entered service for period of 3 years, June 5, 1861.

Company A: Wounded May 3, 1863 in battle of Chancellorsville, Va.; appointed Sergeant from Corporal.....: transferred to Co....., 75th O.V.I....; from Co..... 75th O.V.I.,. June 13, 1864; mustered out July 18, 1864, on expiration of term of service.

Isaac M. Headley, Private, age 21, entered service for period of 3 years, June 10, 1861.

Company C: Killed May 2, 1863 in battle of Chancellorsville, Va..

David H. Heath, Private, age 21, entered service for period of 1 year, Sept. 28, 1864.

Company I: Discharged July 15, 1864 by order of War Department.

Monta Heath, Private, age 19, entered service for period of 3 years, June 12, 1861.

Company E: no record given.

John R. Hedge, Private, age 21, entered service for period of 3 years, June 5, 1861.
Company A: Discharged Nov. 8, 1862 at Columbus, Ohio on Surgeons certificate of disability.
Edward H. Heibert, Private, age 32, entered service for period of 3 years, Jan. 4, 1864.
Company A: Transferred from 107th O.V.I. July 13, 1865; in hospital May 18, 1865 at Charleston, S.C.; mustered out June 18, 1866 by order of War Department.
John Helt, Private, 40, entered service for period of 1 year, Feb. 24, 1865.
Company C: transferred from Co. F 107th O.V.I. July 13, 1865; mustered out Feb. 24, 1866 on expiration of term of service.
Flavius Heller, Corporal, age 25, entered service for period of 3 years, June 8, 1861.
Company D: Transferred to 12th Battery O.L.A. March 12, 1862.
Samuel Hemminger, Private, age 24, entered service for period of 3 years, Feb. 23, 1864.
Company E: Wounded Dec. 6, 1864 in battle of Gregory's Landing, S.C.; discharged Aug. 15, 1865 on Surgeon's certificate of disability.
Thomas C. Hemminger, Private, age 21, entered service for period of 3 years, June 12, 1861.
Company E; Died April 4, 1862.
Beverley Henderson, Cook, age 18, entered service for period of 3 years, Oct. 31, 1863.
Company K: Colored under cook; transferred from Co....107th O.V.I. July 13, 1865; mustered out with company June 18, 1866.
David Henderson, Private, age 20, entered service for period of 1 year, Oct. 4, 1864.
Company D: Mustered out with company Oct. 20, 1865.
George W. Henderson, Private, age 25, entered service for period of 3 years, June 10, 1861.
Company C: Mustered out with company June 18, 1866; veteran.
John Henderson, Private, age 29, entered service for period of 3 years, Feb. 10, 1864.
Company C: discharged May 9, 1865 at Hart's Island, New York on Surgeon's certificate of disability.
George Hendrickson, Private, age 18, entered service for period of 1 year, Oct. 1, 1864.
Company I: Mustered out Oct. 1, 1865 on expiration of term of service.

David S. Henry, Private, age 31, entered service for period of 1 year, Oct. 15, 1864.

Company E: Mustered out Oct. 15, 1865 on expiration of term of service.

Perley B. Henry, Corporal, age 19, entered service for period of 3 years, Dec. 14, 1863.

Company H: Appointed Corporal March 21, 1866; mustered out with company June 18, 1866.

Samuel Henry, Private, age 44, entered service for period of 3 years, June 5, 1861.

Company A: Wounded Dec. 12, 1861 in battle of Camp Alleghany, W. Va.; discharged Dec. 5, 1863 at Wheeling, W. Va. on Surgeon's certificate of disability.

Alonzo P. Henthorn, Sergeant, age 19, entered service for period of 3 years, June 10, 1861.

Company C: appointed Corporal Feb 1, 1862; Sergeant April 1, 1862; wounded June 8, 1862 in battle of Cross Keys, Va.; discharged Sept. 16, 1862 at Camp Chase, Ohio on Surgeon's certificate of disability.

James B. Henthorn, Sergeant, age 18, entered service for period of 3 years, June 10, 1861.

Company C: Mustered as private; appointed as Sergeant...; promoted to Com Sergeant Oct. 1, 1865; veteran.

James M. Henthorn, Private, age 18, entered service for period of 3 years, March 7, 1864.

Company C: Killed Nov. 30, 1864 in battle of Honey Hill, South Carolina.

Lafayette Henthorn, Private, age 18, entered service for period of 3 years, June 10, 1861.

Company C: Killed May 2, 1863 in battle of Chancellorsville, Va..

William Herring, Quartermaster Sergeant, entered service for period of 3 years, June 12, 1861.

Company E: Field and Staff, promoted from private Co. E April 1, 1863; discharged Oct. 8, 1863 on Surgeon's certificate of disability.

William Henthorn, Sergeant, age 38, entered service for period of 3 years, June 10, 1861.

Company C: Appointed from Corporal Oct. 1, 1861; died Dec. 18, 1861 at Huttonsville, W.Va. of wounds received Dec. 13, 1861 in battle of Camp Alleghany, W. Va..

William J. Henthorn, Private, age 21, entered service for period of 3 years, June 10, 1861.

Company C: Wounded Dec. 12, 1861 in battle of Camp Alleghany, W. Va.; transferred to Co. C 75th O.V.I. Jan. 16, 1864; from Co. C 75th O.V.I. May 6,

1864; mustered out July 16, 1864 at Camp Chase, Ohio on expiration of term of service.

Company K: Killed May 2, 1863 in battle of Chancellorsville, Va..

William Herring, Private, age 22, entered service for period of 3 years, June 12, 1861.

Company E: Reduced from Corporal Feb. 28, 1862 at his own request; promoted to Q.M. Sergeant April 1, 1861

Smith Herrington, Private, age 38, entered service for period of 1 year, Sept. 2, 1864.

Company C: Discharged May 9, 1865 at Hilton Head, S.C. on Surgeon's certificate of disability.

Oliver P. Hershey, 2d Lieutenant, age 22, entered service for period of 3 years, June 12, 1861.

Company E: Wounded Jan. 2, 1862 in battle of Huntsville, W. Va.; appointed Corporal March 1, 1862; Sergeant Aug. 1, 1863; 1st Sergeant May 4, 1864; promoted to 2d Lieutenant Oct. 17, 1864; 1st Lieutenant Co. H May 18, 1865; veteran.

Company H: Promoted from 2d Lieutenant Co. E May 18, 1865; resigned March 26, 1866.

Adoniram J. Hess, Private, age 18, entered service for period of 3 years, June 10, 1861.

Company C: Transferred to Co. C 75th O.V.I. Jan. 16, 1864; from Co. C 75th O.V.I. May 6, 1864; mustered out on July 16, 1864 at Camp Chase, Ohio on expiration of term of service.

Joseph Hess, Wagoner, age 22, entered service for period of 3 years, June 12, 1861.

Company E: Mustered out with company June 18, 1866.

Jeremiah Hicks, Private, age 37, entered service for period of 3 years, June 10, 1861.

Company C: Mustered out with company June 18, 1866; veteran.

Edward H. Hiebert, Private, age 32, entered service for period of 3 years, January 4, 1864.

Company A: Transferred from 107th O.V.I. July 13, 1865; in hospital May 18, 1865 at Charleston, S.C.; mustered out June 18, 1866 by order of War Department.

John Hiet, Private, age 42, entered service for period of 3 years, Feb. 20, 1864.

Company K: Killed Dec. 6, 1864 in battle of Gregory's Landing, S.C..

George Hifner, Private, age18, entered service for period of 3 years, Feb. 26, 1864.

Company K: died Dec. 3, 1865 in Lexington District Hospital, S.C..

Arthur Higgins, Captain, age 40, entered service for period of 3 years, June 5, 1861.

Company A: Promoted from 2d Lieutenant Oct. 16, 1861; wounded May 8, 1862 in battle of McDowell, Va.; promoted to Captain Co. H Oct 20, 1862.

Company H: Promoted from 1st Lieutenant Co. A Cot. 20, 1862; resigned May 16, 1863.

David Highman, Private, age 19, entered service for period of 3 years, March 19, 1862.

Company E: Killed July 3, 1863 in battle of Gettysburg, Pennsylvania.

Duncan Highman, Private, age 19, entered service for period of 3 years, June 10, 1861.

Company B: Wounded July 1, 1863 in battle of Gettysbrug, Pa.; transferred to Co. C March 20, 1864.

Company C: Transferred from Co. B March 20, 1864; mustered out July 16, 1864 at Camp Chase, Ohio on expiration of term of service.

Isaac S. Hill, Private, age 24, entered service for period of 3 years, June 18, 1861.

Company G: Transferred to Co. C 75th O.V.I. Jan. 16, 1864; from Co. C 75th O.V.I. May 16, 1864; mustered out July 16, 1864 on expiration of term of service.

John E. Hill, Corporal, age 21, entered service for period of 3 years, June 10, 1861.

Company B: Discharged April 15, 1863 Brooks Station, Va. by order of the War Department.

John R. Hill, Private, age 50, entered service for period of 3 years, June 18, 1861.

Company G: Mustered out with company June 18, 1866; veteran.

Lorenzo D. Hill, Private, age 32, entered service for period of 3 years, June 26, 1861.

Company I: Wounded July 1, 1863 in battle of Gettysburg, Pa.; transferred to Co. C 75th O.V.I. June 16, 1864; from Co. C 75th O.V.I. June 12, 1864; mustered out July 16, 1864 on expiration of term of service.

Samuel F. Hill, Private, age 25, entered service for period of 1 year, Sept. 2, 1864.

Company G: Discharged Oct. 1, 1865 by order of War Department.

Alton Hiluck, Private, age 28, entered service for period of 3 years, Nov. 21, 1863.

Company G: Transferred from 107th O.V.I. July 13, 1865; discharged...by order of War Department.

Frederick Hinck, Private, age 25, entered service for period of 3 years, June 8, 1861.
Company D: Transferred to 12th Battery O.L.A. March 12, 1862.
Edwin Hinds, Private, age 23, entered service for period of 1 year, Sept. 1, 1864.
Company E; Wounded Dec. 6, 1864 in battle of Gregory's Landing, S.C.; discharged July 15, 1865 by order of War Department.
George Hinds, Private, age 18, entered service for period of 1 year, Aug. 31, 1864.
Company E: Discharged July 15, 1865 by order of War Department.
John M. Hinds, Private, age 19, entered service for period of 3 years, June 10, 1861.
Company B; Wounded May 3, 1863 in battle of Chancellorsville, Va.; transferred to Co. C
March 20, 1864; veteran.
Company C: Transferred from Co. B March 20, 1864; mustered out with company June 18,
1866; veteran.
Maxwell Hinds, Private, age 18, entered service for period of 3 years, Dec. 8, 1863.
Company C: Mustered out with company June 18, 1866.
Sherman Hinds, Private, age 19, entered service for period of 3 years, Feb. 20, 1864.
Company K: Wounded April 15, 1865 in battle of Red Hill, S.C.; discharged June 17, 1865
order of War Department.
Joseph Hoag, Private, age 18, entered service for period of 3 years, Dec. 21, 1863.
Company B: Transferred from Co. B 107th O.V.I. July 13, 1865.
John H. Hoarst, Private, age 25, entered service for period of 3 years, Oct. 4, 1862.
Company G: Transferred from 107th O.V.I. July 13, 1865; discharged...by order of War Department.
Samuel Hoffman, Sergeant, age 20, entered service for period of 3 years, Feb. 22, 1864.
Company E: Appointed Corporal July 1, 1865; Sergeant May 19, 1866; mustered out with company June 18, 1866.
George M. Holcomb, Captain, age 25, entered service for period of 3 years, June 12, 1861.
Company C: Promoted from Regt. Quartermaster Aug. 11, 1864; mustered out with company June 18, 1866.

Company E: Appointed 1st Sergeant from Sergeant March 7, 1862; promoted to 2d Lieutenant April 1, 1863; 1st Lieutenant Co. G March 15, 1864.

Company G: Promoted from 2d Lieutenant Co. E March 15, 1864; appointed Regt. Quartermaster April 1, 1864.

George Holderman, Private, age 22, entered service for period of 1 year, Feb. 11, 1865.

Company E: no record given.

Alexander E. Holland, Private, age 19, entered service for period of 3 years, June 10, 1861.

Company C: Transferred to Co. C 75th O.V.I. Jan. 16, 1864; from Co. C 75th O.V.I. May 6, 1864; mustered out July 16, 1864 at Camp Chase, Ohio on expiration of term of service.

John W. Holland, Private, age 21, entered service for period of 3 years, June 5, 1861.

Company A: Wounded Dec. 12, 1861 in battle of Camp Alleghany, W. Va.; transferred to 75th O.V.I. Jan. 15, 1865.

Joshua S. Holland, Private, age 19, entered service for period of 3 years, Feb. 27, 1864.

Company A: Mustered out with company June 18, 1866.

D. A. Hollingsworth, Private, age…, entered service for period of 3 years, June 10. 1861

Company B: Discharged March 4, 1863 at Cumberland, Md. On Surgeon's certificate of disability.

Joseph H. Hollis, 2d Lieutenant, age25, entered service for period of 3 years, June 13, 1864.

Company F: Promoted from 1st Sergeant Sept. 11, 1862; mustered out July 16, 1864 on expiration of term of service.

Lewis Hollister, Private, age 18, entered service for period of 1 year, Sept. 19, 1864.

Company K: discharged July 15, 1865 by order of War Department.

Alvin W. Holloway, Private, age 21, entered service for period of 1 year, Sept. 28, 1864.

Company I: Discharged July 15, 1865 by order of War Department.

William S. Holloway, Private, age 26, entered service for period of 3 years, June 24, 1861.

Company K: Mustered out July 16, 1864 on expiration of term of service.

William Holman, Corporal, age 31, entered service for period of 3 years, Feb. 23, 1864.

Company B: Wounded Nov. 30, 1864 in battle of Honey Hill, S.C.; appointed Corporal July 21, 1865; mustered out with company June 18, 1866.

John Holschew, Private, age 18, entered service for period of 3 years, Feb. 15, 1864.
Company C; Died Oct. 12, 1864 at Hilton Head, S.C..

Charles Hoober, Private, age 25, entered service for period of 3 years, June 5, 1861.
Company A: Veteran.

Charles C. Hook, Private, age 18, entered service for period of 3 years, Dec. 31, 1863.
Company H: Died April 8, 1865 at Beaufort S.C..

Jacob Hoover, Private, age 18, Private, age 20, entered service for period of 1 year, Sept. 26, 1864.
Company D: Mustered out July 15, 1865 by order of War Department.

Richard Hopkins, Private, age 18, entered service for period of 1 year, Oct. 12, 1864.
Company G: Mustered on Oct. 12, 1865 at Charleston, S.C. on expiration of term of service.

Silas M. Hopkins, Private, age 41, entered service for period of 1 year, Oct. 5, 1864.
Company G: Mustered out Oct. 5, 1865 at Charleston, S.C. on expiration of term of service.

James L. Hopper, Private, age 25, entered service for period of 3 years, June 10, 1861.
Company C: Killed June 8, 1862 in battle of Cross Keyes, Va..

Augustine Horner, Private, age 21, entered service for period of 3 years, June 13, 1861.
Company F: Discharged Aug. 17, 1862 on Surgeon's certificate of disability.

George W. Horner, Private, age 21, entered service for period of 3 years, June 13, 1861.
Company F: Discharged Aug. 17, 1862 on Surgeon's certificate of disability.

John W. Horseman, Private, age 41, entered service for period of 3 years, June 26, 1861.
Company H: Transferred to Co. C 75th O.V.I. Jan. 16, 1864; from Co. C 75th O.V,I. June 12, 1861; mustered out July 16, 1864 at Columbus, Ohio on expiration of term of service.

George W. Horton, Private, age 32, entered service for period of 1 year, Sept. 22, 1864.
Company C: Discharged July 15, 1865 by order of War Department.

John W. Hoskins, Private, age 20, entered service for period of 3 years, June 10, 1861.

Company C: Wounded Aug. 29, 1862 in battle of bull Run, Va.; transferred to Veteran Reserve Corps Aug. 1, 1863 by order of War Department.

Arthur Hotchkiss, Private, age 30, entered service for period of 1 year, Sept. 13, 1864.

Company K: Discharged July 15, 1865 by order of War Department.

James House, Private, age 18, entered service for period of 3 years, Feb. 28, 1864.

Company C: Died July 14, 1864 at Hilton Head, S.C..

Reason House, Private, age 28, entered service for period of 3 years, June 10, 1861.

Company B: Drowned Sept. 29, 1861 at Fetterman, Va..

James C. Houston, Private, age 43, entered service for period of 3 years, June 30, 1861.

Company G: Wounded Aug. 29, 1862 in battle of Bull Run, Va.; discharged…at Alexandria, Va. on Surgeon's certificate of disability.

John W. Houston, 2d Lieutenant, age 21, entered service for period of 3 years, June 26, 1861.

Company I: Appointed Corporal Jan. 1, 1862; reduced…; wounded June 8, 1862 in battle of McDowell, Va.; promoted to 2d Lieutenant from private June 3, 1863; mustered out July 16, 1864 on expiration of term of service.

John W. Houston, Private, age 18, entered service for period of 3 years, June 26, 1861.

Company I: Transferred to 75th O.V.I. July 13, 1863; from 75th O.V.I. June 12, 1864; mustered out July 16, 1864 on expiration of term of service.

Joseph Houston, Private, age 23, entered service for period of 3 years, June 24, 1861.

Company K: Appointed corporal Jan. 26, 1862; Sergeant Sept. 1, 1862; reduced to ranks…; transferred to Co. C 75th O.V.I. Jan. 16, 1864; from Co. C 75th O.V.I. June 1, 1864; mustered out July 16, 1864 on expiration f term of service.

Samuel P. Houston, 2d Lieutenant, age 22, entered service for period of 3 years, June 13, 1861.

Company F: Promoted to Com Sergeant from Corporal July 26, 1861;transferred from Field and Staff as private Nov. 1, 1861; promoted to 2d Lieutenant April 17, 1862; resigned March 6, 1863.

George Hoverland, Private, age 20, entered service for period of 3 years, Oct. 11, 1862.

Company A: Transferred from 107th O.V.I. July 15, 1865; mustered out Oct. 11, 1865 on expiration of term of service.

B. Volney Howard, Sergeant, age 30, entered service for period of 3 years, Feb. 13, 1864.

Company B: Appointed from private March 16, 1864; killed Nov. 30, 1864 in battle of Honey Hill, S.C..

Company C: Promoted from Com Sergeant Sept. 4, 1865; to 1st Lieutenant June 15, 1866, but not mustered; mustered out with company June 18, 1866.

William Howard, Private, age 41, entered service for period of 3 years, Feb. 29, 1864.

Company B: Discharged May 30, 1865 at Camp Dennison, Ohio on Surgeon's certificate of disability.

Thomas Howell, Sergeant, age 19, entered service for period of 3 years, June 12, 1861.

Company E: Wounded July 1, 1863 in battle of Gettysburg, Pa.; appointed Corporal Jan. 1, 1864; Sergeant Nov. 1, 1864; died Jan. 1, 1865 of wound received Nov. 30, 1864 in battle of Honey Hill, S.C.; veteran.

William J. Hoyt, Adjutant, age 25, entered service for period of 3 years, July 1, 1861.. Resigned January 23, 1863.

Edward D. Hubbell, Private, age 18, entered service for period of 3 years, June 8, 1861.

Company D: Transferred to 12th Battery O.L.A. March 12, 1862.

Daniel Hubbie, Corporal, age 41, entered service for period of 3 years, June 12, 1861.

Company E: Discharged Dec. 3, 1862 on Surgeon's certificate of disability.

Hiram Hughes, Private, age 22, entered service for period of 3 years, June 26, 1861.

Company H: Killed July 2, 1863 in battle of Gettysburg, Pa..

Joel Hudley, Private, age18, entered service for period of 3 years, Feb. 25, 1864.

Company B: Mustered out with company June 18, 1866.

Thomas B. Hudson, Private, age 24, entered service for period of 3 years, June 10, 1861.

Company C: no record given.

Elias Huffman. Corporal, age 23, entered service for period of 3 years, June 10, 1861.

Company B: Company B: Discharged Feb. 4, 1862 at Huttonsville, W. Va. on Surgeon's certificate of disability.

John A. Huffman, Musician, age 23, entered service for period of 3 years, June 10, 1861.

Company B: Transferred to Co. D 14th Regt. Veteran Reserve Corps July..., 1863; mustered out June 11, 1864 at Washington, D.C..

John C. Huffman, Private, age 40, entered service for period of 1 year, Oct. 12, 1864.

Company F: Mustered out Oct. 12, 1865 on expiration of term of service.

Michael Huffman, Private, age 24, entered service for period of 1 year, Oct. 5, 1864.

Company F: Died May 7, 1865 in DeCamp Hospital at David's Island, New York

Christopher Hughes, Private, age 19, entered service for period of 3 years, Nov. 22, 1862.

Company A: discharged May 4, 1865 by order of War Department.

Hiram Hughes, Private, age 22, entered service for period of 3 years, June 26, 1861.

Company H: Killed July 2, 1863 in battle of Gettysburg, Pa..

William S. Hughes, Private, age 20, entered service for period of 3 years, Oct. 9, 1862.

Company A: Wounded Nov. 30, 1864 in battle of Honey Hill, S.C.; mustered out Oct. 9, 1865 on expiration of term of service.

David R. Hunt, Private, age 21, entered service for period of 3 years, June 12, 1861.

Company E: Reduced from Sergeant Aug. 1, 1861; promoted to Com. Sergeant Nov. 1, 1861.

David R. Hunt, Captain, age 21, entered service for period of 3 years, June 12, 1861.

Company F: Promoted from 1st Lieutenant and Regt. Quartermaster March 15, 1864; detached as Act. Regt. Quartermaster March 22, 1865 at Charleston, S.C.; mustered out with company June 18, 1866.

Jacob Hunt, Private, age 44, entered service for period of 3 years, Feb. 25, 1864.

Company B: Discharged April 15, 1866 Columbia, S.C. by order of the War Department.

Michael Huntsman, Private, age…, entered service for period of 3 years, Dec. 13, 1862.

Company A: No record of service given.

Samuel B. Hurd, Private, age 22, entered service for period of 3 years, June 10, 1861.

Company B: Wounded July 1, 1863 in battle of Gettysburg, Pa.; transferred to Co. H June 13, 1864.

Company H: Transferred from Co. B June 13, 1864; mustered out July 16, 1864 at Columbus, Ohio on expiration of term of service.

Emile A. Husson, Private, age 38, entered service for period of 3 years, June 20, 1861.
Company F: Reduced from Corporal April 1, 1863; killed Aug. 1, 1863 in the mountains of Virginia while scouting.
Andrew J. Hutchins, Private, age 27, entered service for period of 3 years, June 24, 18671.
Company K: Wounded Dec. 13, 1861 in battle of Camp Alleghany, W. Va. and May 3, 1863 in battle of Chancellorsville, Va.; discharged May 12, 1864 on surgeon's certificate of disability.
Byron Hutchins, Corporal, age 18, entered service for period of 3 years, Feb. 23, 1864.
Company E: Appointed Corporal June 1, 1866; mustered out with company June 18, 1866.
Hollis Hutchins, Jr., Private, age 19, entered service for period of 3 years, June 26, 1861.
Company I: Died Dec. 27, 1864 of wounds received Dec. 9, 1864 in battle of Judson Hill, S.C.; veteran.
John Q. Hutchins, Private, age 20, entered service for period of 3 years, June 12, 1861.
Company E: Transferred to Co. C 75th O.V.I. Jan. 16, 1864; mustered out July 16, 1864 at Columbus, Ohio on expiration of term of service.
Shubal Hutchins, Private, age 31, entered service for period of 9 months, Oct. 7, 1862.
Company K: Wounded May 3, 1863 in battle of Chancellorsville, Va.; mustered out July 7, 1893 on expiration of term of service.
Isaac F. Hutchison, Private, age 18, entered service for period of 3 years, June 10, 1861.
Company C: Wounded May 2, 1863 in battle of Chancellorsville, Va.; died May 29, 1863 at Brooks Station, Va..
John R. Hutchison, Private, age 30, entered service for period of 1 year, Oct. 14, 1864.
Company F: Discharged June 29, 1865 on Surgeon's certificate of disability.
Samuel F. Hutchison, 1st Sergeant, age 20, entered service for period of 3 years, June 10, 1861.
Company C: Appointed Corporal Dec. 31, 1861; wounded May 8, 1862 in battle of McDowell, Va.; appointed Sergeant July 1, 1862; 1st Sergeant Sept 19, 1865; promoted to 1st Lieutenant Co. G. Oct. 121, 1864; veteran.
Company G: Promoted from 1st Sergeant Co. C Oct 12, 1864; discharged April 4, 1865 for wounds received Dec. 9, 1864 in battle of Deveaux Neck, South Carolina.

William S. Hutto, Private, age 19, entered service for period of 3 years, June 12, 1861.
Company E: Discharged Nov. 18, 1861 on Surgeon's certificate of disability.
George Huyrall, Private, age 27, entered service for period of 3 years, April 6, 1864.
Company I: Transferred from Co....107th O.V.I. July 13, 1865; discharged July 26, 1865 on Surgeon's certificate of disability.
Andrew Hyatt, Private, age 25, entered service for period of 1 year, Sept. 24 1864.
Company G: Discharged...by order of War Department.
John Hyatt, Private, age 25, entered service for period of 3 years, June 26, 1861.
Company H: Mustered out with company June 18, 1866; veteran.
George A. Hyke, Private, age 23, entered service for period of 3 years, June 24, 1861.
Company K: Died Sept. 6, 1862 at Washington, D.C. of wound received Aug. 30, 1862 in battle of Bull Run, Va..
John W. Hyke, Private, age 19, entered service for period of 3 years, Feb. 17, 1862.
Company G: Discharged July 10, 1862 at Columbus, Ohio by order of War Department.
James Hyler, Sergeant, age 19, entered service for period of 3 years, July 9, 1861.
Company H: Appointed Corporal June 18, 1862; Sergeant Oct., 1862; wounded May 3, 1863 in battle of Chancellorsville, Va. and July 2, 1863 in battle of Gettysburg, Pa.; mustered out July 16, 1864 on expiration of term of service.

I

George W. Iden, 2d Lieutenant, age 23, entered service for period of 3 years, June 18, 1861.
Company A: Wounded May 8, 1862 in battle of McDowell, Va.; appointed Sergeant from Corporal April 1, 1864; 1st Sergeant Nov. 5, 1864; wounded Dec. 6, 1864 in battle of Deveaux Neck, S.C.; promoted to 2d Lieutenant Co. E May 18, 1865; veteran.
Company E: Promoted from 1st Sergeant Co. A May 25, 1864; mustered out July 16, 1864 on expiration of term of service.
David C. Ingler, Private, age 20, entered service for period of 3 years, June 13, 1861.
Company F: Reduced from Corporal Sept. 1, 1861; killed May 2, 1863 in battle of Chancellorsville, Va..

William H. Irwin, Corporal, age 39, entered service for period of 3 years, June 13, 1861.

Company F: Appointed Corporal Sept. 1, 1863; transferred to Co. C 75th O.V.I. Jan. 16., 1864; from Co. C 75th O.V.I. June 112, 1864; mustered out July 16, 1864 on expiration of term of service.

Drewer C. Iverson, Private, age 42, entered service for period of 3 years, June 5, 1861.

Company A: discharged Oct. 1, 1862 at Georgetown, D.C. for wound received May 8, 1862 in battle of McDowell, Va. and Aug. 29, 1862 at Bull Run, Va.

J

Fish Jackson, 1st Sergeant, age 20, entered service for period of 1 year, Oct. 1, 1864.

Company D: Mustered as private; appointed 1st Sergeant July 1, 1865; mustered out with company Oct. 20, 1865.

Manning H. Jackson, Private, age 22, entered service for period of 3 years, Aug. 7, 1862.

Company E: Discharged July 15, 1865 by order of War Department.

Robert F. Jackson, 1st Sergeant, age 21, entered service for period of 1 year, Oct. 18, 1864.

Company D: Transferred to 112th Battery O.L.A. March 12, 1862.

William Jackson, Private, age 25, entered service for period of 3 years, June 18, 1861.

Company G: no record given.

Virgil Jacobs, Private, age 38, entered service for period of 3 years, June 12, 1861.

Company E: Transferred to Veteran Reserve Corps July 1, 1863 by order of War Department.

Jacob James, Corporal, age 18, entered service for period of 3 years, Dec. 31, 1863.

Company A: Appointed Corporal May 1, 1866; mustered out with company June 18, 1866.

John E. Jamison, Private, age 21, entered service for period of 3 years, June 8, 1861.

Company D: Transferred to 12th Battery O.L.A. March 12, 1862.

Thomas J. Janney, 1st Lieutenant, age 19, entered service for period of 3 years, Jan. 8, 1862.

Company I: Promoted from 2d Lieutenant Co. K Sept. 19, 1862; resigned July 28, 1863.

Company K: Promoted to 1st Lieutenant Co. I Sept. 19, 1862.

Ralph T. Jeffery, Private, age 18, entered service for period of 3 years, June 10, 1861.

Company B: Transferred to Co. C March 20, 1864; veteran.

Company C: Transferred from Co. B March 20, 1864; appointed Corporal Aug. 1, 1864; died Oct. 30, 1864 at Hilton Head, S.C..

Andrew M. Jeffres, Private, age 18, entered service for period of 3 years, June 5, 1861.

Company A: Absent July 4, 1862 in Strasburg Hospital, Va.; mustered out July 16, 1864 by order of the War Department.

Harvey Jeffreys, Private, age 19, entered service for period of 3 years, June 10, 1861.

Company C: Died June 10, 1862 at Mt. Jackson, Va..

John Jell, Private, age 29, entered service for period of 3 years, June 12, 1861.

Company E: Discharged Aug. 7, 1862 on Surgeon's certificate of disability.

Anthony Jeremy, Private, age 39, entered service for period of 3 years, June 24, 1861.

Company K: Transferred to Co. C 75th O.V.I. Jan. 16, 1864; from Co. C 75th O.V.I. June 12, 1864; mustered out July 16, 1864 on expiration of term of service.

Josephus Jewell, Private, age 36, entered service for period of 3 years, Mar. 4, 1864.

Company A: Discharged Mar. 14, 1865 at Camp Dennison, Ohio on Surgeon's certificate of disability.

Aaron C. Johnson, Captain, age 39 entered service for period of 3 years, June 4, 1861.

Company D: Transferred to 12th Battery O.L.A. March 12, 1862.

Benjamin R. Johnson, Private, age 27, entered service for period of 3 years, June 5, 1861.

Company A: Mustered out July 16, 1864 on expiration of term of service.

Edward Johnson, Private, age 20, entered service for period of 3 years, Dec. 9, 1863.

Company G: Transferred from Co. F 107th O.V.I. July 13, 1865; mustered out with company June 18, 1866.

Henry Johnson, Sergeant, age 29, entered service for period of 3 years, June 5, 1861.

Company A: no record given

Isaac Johnson, Private, age 21, entered service for period of 3 years, June 10, 1861.

Company C: Discharged June 15, 1865 at Columbus, Ohio by order of the War Department; veteran.

James Johnston, Private, age 18, entered service for period of 1 year, Oct. 6, 1864.

Company G: Mustered out Oct. 6, 1865 at Charleston, S.C. on expiration of term of service.

James W. Johnston, Private, age 30, entered service for period of 1 year, Oct. 5, 1864.

Company F; Mustered out Oct. 5, 1865 on expiration of term of service.

John H. Johnston, Sergeant, age 25, entered service for period of 3 years, June 26, 1861.

Company I: Appointed Corporal Jan. 31, 1862; Sergeant Jan. 31, 1863; wounded July 1, 1863 in battle of Gettysburg, Pa.; mustered out July 16, 1864 on expiration of term of service.

William A. Johnston, Private, age 21, entered service for period of 3 years, June 26, 1861.

Company I: Transferred to Co. C 75th O.V.I. Jan. 16, 1864; from Co. C 75th O.V.I. June 12, 1864; mustered out July 16, 1864 on expiration of term of service.

John W. Jonen, Musician, age 18, entered service for period of 3 years, March 22, 1864.

Company B: Transferred from Co....107th O.V.I. July 13, 1865; mustered out with company June 18, 1866.

Benjamin F. Jones, Private, age 22, entered service for period of 3 years, June 8, 1861.

Company D: Wounded Dec. 12, 1861 in battle of Camp Alleghany, W. Va.; transferred to 12th Battery O.L.A. March 12, 1862.

Charles B. Jones, Captain, age 30, entered service for period of 3 years, June 4, 1861.

Company B: Promoted from 1st Lieutenant July 7, 1862; resigned March 24, 1863.

Charles L. Jones, Private, age 18, entered service for period of 3 years, June 29, 1864.

Company I: Transferred from Co. E 107th O.V.I. July 13, 1865; mustered out with company June 18, 1866.

Cornelius L. Jones, Private, age 44, entered service for period of 3 years, June 10, 1861.

Company B: Discharged July 28, 1862 at Cumberland, Md. on Surgeon's certificate of disability.

Gideon M. Jones, Private, age 40, entered service for period of 3 years, Feb. 27, 1864.

Company B: Wounded Nov. 30, 1864 in battle of Honey Hill, S.C.; died Jan. 14, 1865 in hospital at Hilton Head, S.C..

Henry Jones, Private, age 21, entered service for period of 3 years, June 10, 1861.

Company B: Wounded May 3, 1863 in battle of Chancellorsville, Va.; transferred to Co. C March 20, 1864; veteran.

James Jones, Private, age 21, entered service for period of 3 years, June 24, 1861.

Company K: Wounded June 8, 1862 in battle of Cross Keys, Va..

James A. Jones, Colonel, age 48, entered service for period of 3 years, June 24, 1861. Resigned May 16, 1862

James M. Jones, Corporal, age 29, entered service for period of 3 years, June 20, 1861.

Company F: Reduced from Sergeant April 14, 1863; mustered out July 16, 1864 on expiration of term of service.

John N. Jones, Private, age 19, entered service for period of 3 years, Feb. 20, 1862.

Company E: Mustered out March 13, 1865 on expiration of term of service.

Job Jones, Private, age 30, entered service for period of 3 years, Aug. 13, 1862.

Company F: Discharged July 26, 1863 on Surgeon's certificate of disability.

Phillip M. Jones, Private, age 19, entered service for period of 3 years, June 26, 1861.

Company I" Discharged Feb. 28, 1863 on Surgeon's certificate of Disability.

Thomas Jones, Private, age 19, entered service for period of 3 years, July 19, 1861.

Company F: Discharged..., for wounds received Dec. 13, 1861 in battle of Camp Alleghany, Va..

William H. Jones, Private, age 18, entered service for period of 1 year, Oct. 3, 1864.

Company D: Transferred to 12th Battery O.L.A. March 12, 1862.

Christian Joseph, Sergeant, age 22, entered service for period of 3 years, Feb. 22, 1864.

Company E: Appointed Corporal Aug. 1, 1865; Sergeant June 1, 1866; mustered out with company June 18, 1866.

Nathan Jump, Private, age 24, entered service for period of 1 year, Aug. 31, 1864.

Company E: Wounded Dec. 6, 1864 in battle of Gregory's Landing, S.C.; discharged July 15, 1865 by order of War Department.

Charles Jurson, Private, age 18, entered service for period of 3 years, June 8, 1861.
Company D: Mustered out July 15, 1865 by order of War Department.
James Justus, Sergeant, age 23, entered service for period of 3 years, June 5, 1861.
Company A: Appointed Corporal April 1, 1864; Sergeant Nov. 5, 1864; discharged May 9, 1865, by order of War Department; veteran.

K

Simon I. Kahn, Private, age 18, entered service for period of 3 years, July 12, 1861.
Company G: Wounded June 8, 1862 in battle of Cross Keys, Va.; mustered out July 16, 1864 at Hilton Head, S.C. on expiration of term of service.
Enos Kameron, Private, age 23, entered service for period of 3 years, June 24, 1861.
Company K: Wounded May 2, 1873 in battle of Chancellorsville, Va.; transferred to Co. C 75th O.V.I. Jan. 16, 1864; from Co. C 75th O.V.I. June 12, 1864; mustered out July 15, 1864 on expiration of term of service.
Patrick Kane, Private, age 29, entered service for period of 3 years, June 5, 1861.
Company A: no record given.
Elijah S. Karns, Sergeant, age 19, entered service for period of 3 years, June 18, 1861.
Company G: Wounded May 2, 1863 in battle of Chancellorsville, Va.; appointed Corporal Nov. 5, 1864; Sergeant Aug. 1, 1865; mustered out with company June 18, 1861; veteran.
Hughey S. Karnes, Private, age 29, entered service for period of 1 year, Oct. 14, 1864.
Company G: Discharged Oct. 14, 1865 at Charleston, S.C. by order of War Department.
William H. Kast, Sergeant, age 26, entered service for period of 3 years, June 10, 1861.
Company C: Appointed from Corporal May 20, 1862; wounded May 2, 1863 in battle of Chancellorsville, Va.; mustered out July 16, 1864 at Camp Chase, Ohio on expiration of term of service.
Jonas R. Kawbel, Private, age 22, entered service for period of 1 year, Oct. 5, 1864.
Company D: Mustered out with company Oct. 20, 1865.

Levi Keadle, Private, age 18, entered service for period of 3 years, June 10, 1861.

Company B; Died Feb. 25, 1862 at Huttonsville, W. Va..

Isaac P. M. Kean, Private, age 18, entered service for period of 3 years, June 26, 1861.

Company H: no record given.

Simon Keck, Private, age 19, entered service for period of 1 year, Sept. 30, 1864.

Company G: Discharged Oct. 30, 1865 at Charleston, S.C. by order of War Department.

Benjamin F. Keen, Private, age 22, entered service for period of 3 years, June 10, 1861.

Company B; Transferred to Co. H June 13, 1864.

Company H: Transferred from Co. B June 13, 1864; mustered out July 16, 1864 at Columbus, Ohio on expiration of service.

William J. Keen, Private, age 21, entered service for period of 3 years, July 9, 1861.

Company H: Transferred to Co. C 75th O.V.I. Jan. 16, 1864; from Co. C 75th O.V.I. June 12, 1864; mustered out July 16, 1864 at Columbus, Ohio on expiration of term of service.

John H. Kehn, 1st Lieutenant, age 30, entered service for period of 3 years, June 23, 1861.

Company I: Promoted to 2d Lieutenant from Sergeant Co. K Nov. 23, 1863; 1st Lieutenant May 25, 1864; resigned July 8, 1865.

Company K: Appointed Corporal July 19, 1862; Sergeant Sept. 1, 1862; promoted to 2d Lieutenant Co. I Nov. 23, 1863; veteran.

Samuel Keifer, Private, age 21, entered service for period of 3 years, June 8, 1861.

Company D: Transferred to 12th Battery O.L.A. march 12, 1862.

Absalom Keller, Private, age 24, entered service for period of 3 years, Aug. 7, 1862.

Company E: Died Nov. 9, 1863.

Alpheus Keller, Private, age 32, entered service for period of 1 year, Oct. 7, 1864.

Company D: Mustered out with company Oct. 20, 1865.

Isaac N. Keller, Private, age 21, entered service for period of 1 year, Oct. 9, 1864.

Company G: Discharged Oct. 9, 1865 at Charleston, S.C. by order of War Department.

Lewis H. Keller, Private, age 29, entered service for period of 3 years, Aug. 7, 1862.

Company E: Discharged July 15, 1865 by order of War Department.

Clark Kelley, Sergeant, age 24, entered service for period of 3 years, June 24, 1861.

Company K: Appointed Corporal April 1, 1864; Sergeant Aug. 1, 1864; mustered out with company June 18, 1866; veteran.

Edward Kelley, Corporal, age 18, entered service for period of 3 years, Feb. 27, 1864.

Company B: Appointed Corporal May 19, 1866; mustered out with company June 18, 1866.

James Kelley, Private, age 22, entered service for period of 3 years, June 5, 1861.

Company A: no record given.

William J. Kelley, Private, age 19, entered service for period of 3 years, June 10, 1861.

Company C: Died Dec. 29, 1861 at Huttonsville, W. Va.

Gideon Kellog, Private, age 18, entered service for period of 3 years, Feb. 29, 1864.

Company B: Mustered out with company June 18, 1866.

James L. Kemper, Sergeant, age 33, entered service for period of 1 year, Oct. 8, 1864.

Company D: Mustered as private; appointed Sergeant Aug. 1, 1865; mustered out with company Oct. 20, 1865.

George F. Kemps, Private, age 22, entered service for period of 3 years, Nov. 10, 1863.

Company K: Mustered out with company June 18, 1866.

Robert Kennedy, Corporal, age 28, entered service for period of 3 years, June 5, 1861.

Company A: Discharged Dec. 10, 1863 at David's Island, New York Harbor, on Surgeon's certificate of disability.

Richard Kenney, Corporal, age 25, entered service for period of 3 years, Feb. 18, 1864.

Company E: Appointed Corporal June 1, 1866; mustered out with company June 18, 1866.

Noah Kensor, Private, age 20, entered service for period of 3 years, June 18, 1861.

Company G: Mustered out July 16, 1864 on expiration of term of service.

John W. Kent, Corporal, age 19, entered service for period of 3 years, June 5, 1861.

Appointed Corporal June 1, 1865; mustered out with company June 18, 1866; veteran.

Frederick Kentz, Private, age 18, entered service for period of 1 year, Oct. 11, 1864.

Company G: Discharged Oct. 11, 1865 at Charleston, S.C. by order of War Department.

K

John M. Kerr, Private, age 19, entered service for period of 3 years, Aug. 11, 1862.

Company F: Transferred to 75th O.V.I. Jan. 16, 1864; from 75th O.V.I. June 12, 1864; discharged July 15, 1865 by order of War Department.

Matthias Kessler, Private, age 22, entered service for period of 1 year, Feb. 27, 1865.

Company C: Transferred from Co. F 107th O.V.I. July 13, 1865; mustered out Feb. 27, 1866 at Charleston, S.C. on expiration of term of service.

George Kessler, Private, age 44, entered service for period of 3 years, June 12, 1861.

Company E: Discharged Aug. 12, 1862 on surgeon's certificate of disability.

George Kester, Private, age 28, entered service for period of 3 years, June 8, 1861.

Company D: Transferred to 12th Battery O.L.A. March 12, 1862.

William P. Ketchum, Corporal, age 20, entered service for period of 3 years, June 24, 1861.

Company K: Transferred to Veteran Reserve Corps Oct. 30, 1863 by order of War Department.

John Ketner, Private, age 24, entered service for period of 1 year, Sept. 30, 1864.
Company I: Discharged July 15, 1865 by order of War Department.

Aaron Ketrow, Private, age 19, entered service for period of year, Sept. 10, 1864.

Company C: Discharged July 15, 1865 by order of War Department.

Gottlieb Kettler, Private, age 32, entered service for period of 3 years, Oct. 9, 1862.

Company C: Transferred from Co. C 107th O.V.I. July 13, 1865; mustered out Oct. 12, 1865 at Charleston, S.C. on expiration of term of service.

John B. Keyser, Sergeant, age 31, entered service for period of 1 year, Oct. 7, 1864.

Company D: Mustered as private; appointed Sergeant July 1, 1865; mustered out with company July 20, 1865.

Franklin Kieth, Private, age 18, entered service for period of 3 years, Feb. 22, 1864.
Company B: no record given.
Hiram Kiff, Private, age 37, entered service for period of 1 year, Sept. 26, 1864.
Company I: Wounded Dec. 6, 1864 in battle of Gregory's Landing, S.C.; discharged July 15, 1865 by order of War Department.
Jared Kimball, Private, age 19, entered service for period of 1 year, Sept. 20, 1864.
Company I: Discharged July 15, 1865 by order of War Department.
Blair Kincaid, Private, age 18, entered service for period of 3 years, June 26, 1861.
Company H: Appointed Corporal Sept. 1, 1863; reduced Jan. 1, 1865; veteran.
McArthur Kincaid, Private, age 18, entered service for period of 3 years, Feb. 11, 1864.
Company H: no record given.
Andrew D. King, Corporal, age 21, entered service for period of 3 years, July 14, 1862.
Company A: Appointed Corporal Feb, 1, 1865; discharged July 15, 1865 by order of War Department.
Charles H. King, Corporal, age 19, entered service for period of 3 years, June 5, 1861.
Company A: Wounded Dec. 12, 1861 in battle of Camp Alleghany, W. Va.; appointed Corporal Jan. 6, 1862; promoted to 2d Lieutenant Co. G. Jan. 24, 1863.
Company G: Promoted from Corporal Co. A Jan. 24, 1863; wounded July 1, 1863 in battle of Gettysburg, Pa.; promoted to 1st Lieutenant Co. K March 15, 1864.
Company K: Promoted from 2d Lieutenant Co. G March 15, 1864; discharged March 1, 1865 on Surgeon's certificate of disability.
Lyman King, Private, age 18, entered service for period of 3 years, Nov. 1, 1863.
Company C; Discharged April 18, 1866, by order of War Department.
William W. King, Captain, age 23, entered service for period of 1 year, Oct. 18, 1864.
Company D: Discharged April 25, 1865 at Annapolis, Md. for wounds received Dec. 9, 1864 in Battle of Deveaux Neck, S.C..
Dewitt Kinney. Private, age 22, entered service for period of 3 years, Mar. 9, 1864.
Company B: Discharged May 14, 1865 at Philadelphia, Pa. by order of War Department.

Dewitt C. Kinney, Private, age 26, entered service for period of 3 years, June 5, 1861.

Company A: Mustered out July 16, 1864 on expiration of term of service.

Josephus S. Kinney, Sergeant, age 30, entered service for period of 3 years, June 5, 1861.

Company A: Wounded June 8, 1862 in battle of Cross Keys, Va.; appointed Corporal April 1, 1864; Sergeant June 1, 1865; mustered out with company June 18, 1866; veteran.

Isaac M. Kirk, 2d Lieutenant, age 23, entered service for period of 3 years, June 26, 1861.

Company B: Promoted from Corporal Co. I June 30, 1862; to 1st Lieutenant Co. I March 20, 1863.

Company I: 1st Lieutenant. Appointed Corporal Jan. 1, 1862; Sergeant June 20, 1862; promoted to 2d Lieutenant Co. B June 30, 1862; 1st Lieutenant March 20, 1863.

Edward A. Kitchens, Private, age 19, entered service for period of 1 year, Sept. 27, 1864.

Company I: Discharged July 15, 1864.

Samuel Klafinger, Private, age 18, entered service for period of 3 years, Dec. 29, 1863.

Company C; Transferred from Co. F 107th O.V.I. July 13. 1865; killed Dec. 27, 1865 at Newberry, S.C. in Rebel riot.

Charles Kline, Private, age 17, entered service for period of 1 year, Oct. 11, 1864.

Company A: Wounded Nov. 30, 1864 in battle of Honey Hill, S.C.; mustered out Oct. 11, 1865 on expiration of term of service.

John Kliuck, Corporal, age 19, entered service for period of 3 years, July 10, 1861.

Company K: Wounded May 2, 1863 in battle of Chancellorsville, Va.; transferred to Veteran Reserve Corps Nov. 10, 1863 by order of War Department.

August Knaack, Sergeant, age 29, entered service for period of 3 years, June 24, 1861.

Company K: Killed Nov. 30, 1864 in battle of Honey Hill, S.C.; veteran.

Fred Knechenmeister, Private, age 28, entered service for period of 1 year, Sept. 12, 1864.

Company K: Discharged July 15, 1865 by order of War Department.

Porter Knight, Private, age 18, entered service for period of 3 years, Mar. 9, 1864.

Company B: Discharged May 19, 1865 on Surgeon's certificate of disability.

Daniel Knisely, Private, age 18, entered service for period of 3 years, Feb. 23, 1864.
Company E: Wounded Nov. 30, 1864 in battle of Honey Hill, S.C.; mustered out with company June 18, 1866.
Cemrens I. Kohr, Corporal, age19, entered service for period of 3 years, Feb. 23, 1864.
Company K: Appointed Corporal April 1, 1866; mustered out with company June 18, 1866.
Gustave Kolby, Corporal, age 27, entered service for period of 3 years, June 20, 1861.
Company F: Appointed Corporal...; transferred to Co. C 75th O.V.I. Jan. 16, 1864; from Co. C 75th O.V.I. June 12, 1864; mustered out July 16, 1864 on expiration of term of service.
John Koontz, Private, age 18, entered service for period of 1 year, Oct. 4, 1864.
Company D: Mustered out with company Oct. 20, 1865.
John D. Kountz, 1st Sergeant, age 23, entered service for period of 3 years, June 5, 1861.
Died January 5, 1862 at Barnesville, Ohio.
Daniel Kramer, Corporal, age 44 entered service for period of 1 year, Oct. 3, 1864.
Company D: Appointed Corporal Aug. 1, 1865; mustered out with company Oct. 20, 1865.
John Krappenberger, Private, age 34, entered service for period of 3 years, June 12, 1861.
Company E: no record given.
Joseph A. Kulenbaugh, Private, age 44, entered service for period of 3 years, June 18, 1861.
Company G: Discharged June 1, 1864 at Washington, D.C. by order of War Department.
John C. Kuly, Private, age 27, entered service for period of 3 years, June 27, 1861.
Company G: Discharged July 27, 1862 at Clarksville, Md. on Surgeon's certificate of disability.
Isaac Kurfman, Private, age 18, entered service for period of 3 years, Aug. 11, 1862.
Company F: Discharged July 15, 1865 by order of War Department.
Samuel P. Kyle, Corporal, age 18, entered service for period of 3 years, Feb. 25, 1864.
Company G: Appointed Corporal Aug. 1, 1865; mustered out with company June 18, 1866.

William J. Kyle, 2d Lieutenant, 18, entered service for period of 3 years, June 18, 1861.

Company C: Promoted from 1st Sergeant Co. G Nov. 18, 1864; to 1st Lieutenant Co. I Sept. 4, 1865.

Company G: Mustered as private; appointed 1st Sergeant...; wounded June 8, 1862 in battle of Cross Keys, Va.; promoted to 2d Lieutenant Co. C Nov. 18, 1864; veteran.

Company I: (listed as James. W. Kyle) 1st Lieutenant. Promoted from 2d Lieutenant Co. C Sept. 4, 1865; appointed Regt. Quartermaster Sept. 28, 1865.

L

Anderson Lacy, Private, age 31, entered service for period of 1 year, Oct. 1, 1864.

Company F: Discharged May 2, 1865 on Surgeon's certificate of disability.

Garwood P. Lacy, 1st Sergeant, age 18, entered service for period of 3 years, June 10, 1861.

Company B: Appointed Corporal...; transferred to Co. C March 1, 1864; veteran.

Company C: Transferred from Co. B as Corporal March 20, 1864; appointed Sergeant March 20, 1864; 1st Sergeant Nov. 1, 1864; mustered out with company June 18, 1866; veteran.

Charles Ladd, Sergeant, age 24, entered service for period of 3 years, June 12, 1861.

Company E: Wounded Aug. 30, 1862 in battle of Bull Run, Va.; died July 6, 1863 of wounds received July 1, 1863 in battle of Gettysburg, Va..

Charles Ladd, Private, age 24, entered service for period of 3 years, June 18, 1861.

Company G; On muster-in roll, but no further record found.

Andrew J. Lake, Musician, age 18, entered service for period of 3 years, Feb. 19, 1864.

Company E: Mustered out with company June 18, 1866.

Henry Lambert, Artificer, age 23, entered service for period of 3 years, June 5, 1861.

Company A: Wounded May 8, 1862 in battle of McDowell, Va.; mustered with company June 18, 1866; veteran.

Alfred A. Lamkin, 2d Lieutenant, age 25, entered service for period of 3 years, June 8, 1861.

Company C: Transferred from Co. F April 9, 1863; resigned Nov. 8, 1863.

Company F; Promoted from Sergeant Co. G Jan. 23, 1863; transferred to Co. C April 9, 1863.

Company G: Mustered as private; appointed Sergeant...; wounded June 8, 1862 in battle of Cross Keys, Va.; promoted to 2d Lieutenant Co. F Jan. 23, 1863.

Frederick M. Lang, Private, age 35, entered service for period of 3 years, June 24, 1861.

Company K: Discharged Dec. 27, 1863 at Huttonsville, W. Va. on Surgeon's certificate of disability.

James Langan, Private, age 37, entered service for period of 1 year, Oct. 6, 1864.

Company D: Mustered out with company Oct. 20, 1864.

Henry Lape, Private, age 37, entered service for period of 1 year, Sept. 23, 1864.

Company G; Discharged Oct. 1, 1865 at Washington, D.C. by order of War Department.

Ernest Lapham, Sergeant, age 18, entered service for period of 3 years, Feb. 25, 1864.

Company G: Appointed Corporal Aug. 1, 1865; Sergeant Jan. 1, 1866; mustered out with company June 18, 1866.

John Larkin, Private, age 22, entered service for period of 3 years, June 13, 1861.

Company F: no record given.

Thomas Latz, Private, age 43, entered service for period of 3 years, June 18, 1861.

Company G: Discharged Nov. 1, 1862 at Hopewell Gap, Va. on Surgeon's certificate of disability.

William Lauchly, Private, age 20, entered service for period of 3 years, Dec. 13, 1863.

Company G: Transferred from Co. B 107th O.V.I. June 13, 1865; mustered out with company June 18, 1866.

John Laughlin, Private, age 18, entered service for period of 3 years, Feb. 29, 1864.

Company K: Died Nov. 2m 1865 at Port Hospital, Columbia, South Carolina.

Julius H. Laughlin, Private, age 18, entered service for period of 1 year, Oct. 12, 1864.

Company D: Mustered out with company Oct. 20, 1865.

Mark Lawrence, Private, age 21, entered service for period of 3 years, June 10, 1861.

Company B; Wounded May 2, 1863 in battle of Chancellorsville, Va.; transferred to Co. H June 13, 1864.

Company H: Transferred from Co. B June 13, 1864; mustered out July 16, 1864 at Columbus, Ohio on expiration of term of service.

John Leary, Corporal, age 18, entered service for period of 3 years, June 12, 1861.

Company E: Wounded Aug. 30, 1862 in battle of Bull Run, Va.; appointed Corporal Nov. 1, 1865; veteran.

Thomas D. Leasure, Corporal, age 28, entered service for period of 1 year, Oct. 1, 1864.

Company F: Appointed Corporal June 1, 1865; mustered out Oct. 1, 1865 on expiration of term of service.

John Lebold, Private, age 19, entered service for period of 3 years, June 14, 1861.

Company A: Wounded Aug. 30, 1862 in battle of Bull Run, Va. and July 2, 1863 in battle of Gettysburg, Pa.; mustered out July 16, 1864, on expiration of term of service.

Jason Lee, Private, age 18, entered service for period of 1 year, Oct. 3, 1864.

Company I: Mustered out Oct. 2, 1865 on expiration of term of service.

James P. Legin, Private, age 19, entered service for period of 1 year, Oct. 3, 1864.

Company D: no record given.

George W. Leohner, Corporal, age 32, entered service for period of 3 years, June 26, 1861.

Company H: Appointed Corporal Sept. 30, 1861; discharged July 12, 1862 at Washington, D.C. on Surgeon's certificate of disability.

Conrad Lesh, Private, age 18, entered service for period of 3 years, Feb. 15, 1864.

Company E: Wounded Dec. 6, 1864 in battle of Gregory's Landing, S.C.; discharged Aug. 21, 1865 by order of War Department.

Ephraim H. Lewis, Private, age 22, entered service for period of 3 years, April 3, 1862.

Company G: Wounded Aug. 29, 1862 in battle of Bull Run, Va.; died May 22, 1865 at Columbia, S.C.; veteran.

Lewis M. Lewis, Private, age 42, entered service for period of 3 years, June 8, 1861.

Company D: Transferred to 12th Battery O.L.A. March 12, 1862.

Morrison Lewis, Sergeant, age 20, entered service for period of 3 years, April 5, 1862.

Company K: Appointed Corporal April 1, 1864; Sergeant Nov. 5, 1864; mustered out with company June 18, 1866; veteran.

Morrison Lewis, Private, age..., entered service for period of 3 years, April 5, 1862.

Company K: Wounded May 3, 1863 in battle of Chancellorsville, Va..

Sheppard Lewis, Private, age 25, entered service for period of 3 years, June 24, 1861.

Company K: Wounded Dec. 1, 1863 in battle of Camp Alleghany, W. Va.; discharged Aug. 25, 1862 at Columbus, Ohio on Surgeon's certificate of disability.

Nicholas H. Licketer, Private, age 20, entered service for period of 3 years, June 8, 1861.

Company D: Transferred to 12th Battery O.L.A. March 12, 1862.

John Lightins, Private, age 18, entered service for period of 3 years, Dec. 25, 1863.

Company H: no record given.

Thomas Lincham, Private, age 18, entered service for period of 3 years, Feb. 29, 1864.

Company K: no record given.

George Lindeman, Private, age 35, entered service for period of 3 years, Feb. 23, 1864.

Company B: Mustered out with company June 18, 1866.

John P. Linden, Private, age 25, entered service for period of 3 years, Feb. 17, 1864.

Company K: Wounded Nov. 30, 1864 in battle of Honey Hill, S.C.; discharged May 13, 1865 at Columbus, Ohio on Surgeon's certificate of disability.

William Linder, Private, age 35, entered service for period of 3 years, June 5, 1861.

Company A: Mustered out July 16, 1864 on expiration of term of service.

Noah H. Lindsey, Private, age 33, entered service for period of 3 years, June 26, 1861.

Company I: Mustered out with company June 18, 1866; veteran.

Lyle Linford, Private, age 24, entered service for period of 3 years, April 1, 1862.

Company A: Mustered out April 1, 1865 on expiration of term of service.

James Lingafelter, Private, age 18, entered service for period of 1 year, Sept. 28, 1864.

Company G: Discharged Oct. 1, 1865 at Charleston, S.C. by order of War Department.

Archelus Lingo, Sergeant, age 21, entered service for period of 3 years, June 26, 1861.

Company I: Wounded July 1, 1863 in battle of Gettysburg, Pa.; appointed Corporal April 1, 1864; Sergeant, Aug. 1, 1865; discharged March 13, 1865 on Surgeon's certificate of disability.

Henry M. Link, Private, age 21, entered service for period of 3 years, June 10, 1861.

Company C: Transferred to Co. C 75th O.V.I. Jan. 16, 1864; from Co. C 75th O.V.I. May 6, 1864; mustered out July 16, 1864 at Camp Chase, Ohio on expiration of term of service.

Jacob Lips, Private, age 19, entered service for period of 3 years, June 10, 1861.

Company G: Mustered out with company June 18, 1866.

Jesse Little, Private, age 22, entered service for period of 3 years, June 12, 1861.

Company E: Killed June 8, 1862 in battle of Cross Keys, Virginia.

Oscar Little, Private, age 22, entered service for period of 3 years, June 10, 1861.

Company C: reduced from Corporal Mar. 1, 1862; discharged May 16, 1862 at Franklin, Va. on Surgeon's certificate of disability.

John C. Livensparger, 1st Lieutenant, age 22, entered service for period of 3 years, June 18, 1861.

Company F: Promoted from 2d Lieutenant Co. H Aug. 11, 1864; mustered out with company June 18, 1866.

Company G: Mustered as Corporal; appointed 1st Sergeant...; wounded May 2, 1863 in battle of Chancellorsville, Va.; promoted to 2d Lieutenant Co. H May 25, 1864; veteran.

Company H: Promoted from 1st Sergeant Co. G May 25, 1864; 1st Lieutenant Co. F Aug. 11, 1864; died Dec. 7, 1864 of wounds received in action.

Louis Livensparger, Corporal, age 18, entered service for period of 3 years, Feb. 20, 1864.

Company G: Wounded Dec. 6, 1864 in battle of Gregory's Landing, S.C.; appointed Corporal June 1, 1866; mustered out with company June 18, 1866.

Newton Livezey, Private, age 21, entered service for period of 3 years, July 9, 1861.

Company H: Wounded May 3, 1863 in battle of Chancellorsville, Va. and July 2, 1863 in battle of Gettysburg, Pa.; transferred to Veteran Reserve Corps May 15, 1864 by order of War Department.

Stephen Livezey, Private, age 22, entered service for period of 3 years, July 9, 1861.

Company H: Transferred to Co. C 75th O.V.I. Jan. 16, 1864; from Co. C 75th O.V.I. June 12, 1864; mustered out July 16, 1864 on expiration of term of service.

Joseph Livingston, Private, age 28, entered service for period of 3 years, Dec. 3, 1863.

Company G: no record given.

Andrew J. Lloyd, Private, age 25, entered service for period of 3 years, June 10, 1861.

Company B: Transferred to Co. H June 13, 1864.

Company H: Transferred from Co. B June 13, 1864; mustered out July 16, 1864 at Columbus, Ohio on expiration of term of service.

Lucius Lobdell, Private, age 28, entered service for period of 1 year, Sept. 2, 1864.

Company K: Discharged July 15, 1865 by order of War Department.

Albert Lockhart, Private, age 22, entered service for period of 1 year, Feb. 29, 1864.

Company B: no record given.

Charles H. Lockwood, Private, age 25, entered service for period of 1 year, Sept. 2, 1864.

Company C: Discharged May 23, 1865 at Hilton Head, S.C. on Surgeon's certificate of disability.

Frank D. Lockwood, Private, age 22, entered service for period of 3 years, June 8, 1861.

Company D: Transferred to 12th Battery O.L.A. March 12, 1862.

William T. Lockwood, Private, age 19, entered service for period of 3 years, June 5, 1861.

Company A: Wounded Dec. 12, 1861 in battle of Camp Alleghany, W. Va.; killed May 2, 1863 in battle of Chancellorsville.

Theodore E. Lodge, Private, age 25, entered service for period of 3 years, June 13, 1861.

Company F: Killed May 8, 1862 in battle of McDowell, Va..

David Logan, Private, age 22, entered service for period of 3 years, June 26, 1861.

Company I: Discharged March 20, 1863 on Surgeon's certificate o disability.

George Logan, Private, age 22, entered service for period of 3 years, June 8, 1861.

Company C: Transferred to 12th Battery O.L.A. March 12, 1862.

Franklin M. Long, Private, age 20, entered service for period of 3 years, June 10, 1861.

Company C: wounded May 2, 1863 in battle of Chancellorsville, Va.; transferred to Co. C 75th O.V.I. Jan. 16, 1864; from Co. C 75th O.V.I. May 6, 1864; mustered out July 16, 1864 at Camp Chase, Ohio on expiration of term of service.

Frederick Long, Private, age19, entered service for period of 3 years, Jan. 26, 1864.
Company C: Wounded May 2, 1863 at battle of Chancellorsville, Va.; transferred from Co. C 107th O.V.I. July 13, 1865; mustered out with company June 18, 1866.
George W. Long, Private, age 22, entered service for period of 1 year, Oct. 5, 1864.
Company D: Mustered out with company Oct. 20, 1865.
Henry L. Long, Private, age 19, entered service for period of 3 years, Feb. 29, 1864.
Company E: Discharged June 21, 1865 on Surgeon's certificate of disability.
Thomas Long, Sergeant, age 19, entered service for period of 3 years, June 20, 1861.
Company F: Appointed Corporal Aug. 1, 1864; Sergeant June 1, 1865; mustered out with company June 18, 1866; veteran.
William M. Long, Private, age 19, entered service for period of 3 years, June 10, 1861.
Company B: Wounded July 1, 1863 in battle of Gettysburg, Pa.; transferred to Co. C March 20, 1864; veteran.
Company C: Transferred from Co. B March 20, 1864; veteran.
Oliver C. Longmore, Corporal, age 19 entered service for period of 3 years, June 18, 1861.
Company G: Appointed Corporal…; wounded Nov. 30, 1864 in battle of Honey Hill, S.C.; discharged Aug. 8, 1865 at New York on surgeon's certificate of disability; veteran.
Robert Longmore, Private, age 20, entered service for period of 3 years, June 18, 1861.
Company G: Wounded July 1, 1863 in battle of Gettysburg, Pa.; mustered out July 16, 1864 on expiration of term of service.
George Longstreet, Private, age 26, entered service for period of 3 years, June 18, 1861.
Company G: Wounded June 8, 1862 in battle of Cross Keys, Va.; discharged Nov. 1, 1862 at Columbus, Ohio by order of War Department.
Benton Longwell, Private, age 19, entered service for period of 3 years, June 10, 1861.
Company B: Transferred to Co. H June 13, 1864.
Company H: Transferred from Co. H June 13, 1864; mustered out July 16, 1864 at Columbus, Ohio on expiration of term of service.

Robert Longwell, Private, age 23, entered service for period of 3 years, June 10, 1861.

Company C: wounded Aug. 29, 1862 in battle of Bull Run, Va.; discharged March 27, 1863 at Stafford C.H., Va. on Surgeon's certificate of disability.

Benton Longwell, Private, age 19, entered service for period of 3 years, June 10, 1861.

Company B: Transferred to Co. H June 13, 1864.

Company H: Transferred from Co. B June 13, 1864; mustered out July 16, 1864 at Columbus, Ohio on expiration of term of service.

Charles Loomis, Private, age 18, entered service for period of 1 year, Oct. 3, 1864.

Company I: Mustered out Oct. 2, 1865 on expiration of term of service.

Thomas Loonhardy, Private, age 25, entered service for period of 3 years, Jan. 1, 1864.

Company C: Transferred from Co. C 107th O.V.I. July 13, 1865; mustered out with company Jun1 18, 1866.

John Loose, Private, age 42, entered service for period of 3 years, June 12, 1861.

Company E: Discharged April 14, 1864 on Surgeon's certificate of disability.

Joseph Love, Private, age 18, entered service for period of 1 year, Sept. 30, 1864.

Company D: Mustered out July 15, 1865 by order of War Department.

Jacob H. Loveall, Private, age 20, entered service for period of 3 years, June 10, 1861.

Company C: Mustered out with company June 18, 1866; veteran.

Stephen Lovall, Private, age 20, entered service for period of 3 years, June 26, 1861.

Company I: discharged Sept. 8, 1863 for wounds received July 1, 1863 in battle of Gettysburg, Pa..

Edward T. Lovette, Corporal, age 19, entered service for period of 3 years, June 26, 1861.

Company I: Killed July 1, 1863 in battle of Gettysburg, Pa..

Nelson C. Lovette, Private, age 21, entered service for period of 3 years, June 26, 1861.

Company I: wounded Dec. 13, 1861 in battle of Camp Alleghany, W. Va. and Aug. 29, 1862 in battle of Bull Run, Va.; discharged Dec. 16, 1862 on Surgeon's certificate of disability.

Alexander W. Lowe, Private, age 19, entered service for period of 3 years, June..., 1861.

Company C; Wounded May 2, 1863 in battle of Chancellorsville, Va.; transferred to Co. C 75th O.V.I. Jan. 16, 1864; from Co. C 75th O.V.I. May 6, 1864; mustered out July 16, 1864 at Camp Chase, Ohio on expiration of term of service.

David Lowe, Private, age 18, entered service for period of 3 years, June 10, 1861.

Company B: Transferred to Co. H June 13, 1864.

Company H: Transferred from Co. B June 13, 1864; mustered out July 16, 1864 at Columbus, Ohio on expiration of term of service.

Flavius N. Lowery, Private, age 19, entered service for period of 3 years, May 16, 1862.

Company E: Discharged Oct. 31, 1862 for wounds received Aug. 31, 1862 in battle of Bull Run, Va.

Harrison Lowden, Private, age 22, entered service for period of 1 year, Sept. 6, 1864.

Company E: Discharged July 16, 1865 by order of War Department.

David Lowe, Private, age 19, entered service for period of 3 years, June 26, 1861.

Company H: Transferred from Co. B June 13, 1864; mustered out July 16, 1864 at Columbus, Ohio on expiration of term of service.

William J. Lowery, Private, age 22, entered service for period of 3 years, May 16, 1862.

Company E: Died Oct. 1, 1862 of wounds received Aug. 30, 1862 in battle of Bull Run, Va..

Elias Lowther, Private, age 18, entered service for period of 3 years, June 10, 1861.

Company B: Transferred to Co. H June 13, 1864.

Company H: Transferred from Co. B June 13, 1864; mustered out July 16, 1864 at Columbus, Ohio on expiration of term of service.

William M. Lowther, Private, age 21, entered service for period of 3 years, June 10, 1861.

Company B: Transferred to Co. C March 20, 1864; veteran.

Company C: Transferred from Co. B March 20, 1864; discharged Aug. 8, 1865 at Hilton Head, S.C. on Surgeon's certificate of disability.

John A. Luke, Private, age 18, entered service for period of 3 years, June 10, 1861.

Company C: Discharged Nov. 11, 1862 at Hopewell Gap, Va. on Surgeon's certificate of disability.

Francis A. Lumbar, 1st Sergeant, age 24, entered service for period of 3 years, June 18, 1861.

Company G: Wounded May 2, 1863 in battle of Chancellorsville, Va.; appointed Sergeant from private Aug. 1, 1864; 1st Sergeant Feb. 1, 1865; mustered out with company June 18, 1866; veteran.

Linford Lyle, Private, age 24, entered service for period of 3 years, April 1, 1862.
Company A: Mustered out April 1, 1865 on expiration of term of service.
Charles Lynes, Private, age 18, entered service for period of 1 year, Nov. 16, 1864.
Company G: transferred from Co. G 107th O.V.I. July 13, 1865; discharged Nov. 15, 1865 by order of War Department.
David H. Lynn, Private, age 18, entered service for period of 3 years, March 25, 1862.
Company K: no record given.

M

Andrew Machin, Private, age 19, entered service for period of 1 year, Oct. 4, 1864.
Company A; Mustered out Oct. 4, 1865 on expiration of term of service.
Jeremiah Mackey, Private, age 18, entered service for period of 3 years, Feb, 15, 1864.
Company C: Mustered out with company June 18, 1866.
Jeremiah Mackey, Private, age 23, entered service for period of 3 years, Feb, 22, 1864.
Company E: Killed Nov. 30, 1864 in battle of Honey Hill, South Carolina.
William Mackey, Private, age 29, entered service for period of 3 years, Sept. 22, 1864.
Company C: Died April 6, 1863 at Millett's Point, N.Y..
William H. Mackey, Sergeant, age 19, entered service for period of 3 years, June 112, 1861.
Company E: Appointed Corporal Nov. 2, 1864; Sergeant Nov. 1, 1865; discharged March 1, 1866 by order of War Department; veteran.
James Mackie, Private, age 28, entered service for period of 3 years, June 18, 1861.
Company G: no record given.
Uriah Magee, Private, age 27, entered service for period of 3 years, July 26, 1861.
Company G; Killed May 2, 1863 in battle of Chancellorsville, Va..
William T. Maher, Private, age 22, entered service for period of 3 years, June 18, 1861.
Company G: Killed Dec. 13, 1861 in battle of Camp Alleghany, W. Va..

David Mairoai, Private, age 22, entered service for period of 3 years, Feb. 23, 1864.

Company K: Discharged Aug. 11, 1865 at Hilton Head, S.C. on Surgeon's certificate of disability.

James Male, Private, age 28, entered service for period of 3 years, June 30, 1861. Company G; Discharged Dec. 27, 1862 at Washington, D.C. for wounds received Aug. 29, 1862 in battle of Bull Run, Va..

Charles Mallimus, Private, age 18, entered service for period of 3 years, Jan. 29, 1864.

Company E: Mustered out with company June 18, 1866.

Benjamin Mallory, Corporal, age 21, entered service for period of 3 years, June 8, 1861.

Company D: Transferred to 12th Battery O.L.A. March 12, 1862.

Michael Maloney, Private, age 18, entered service for period of 3 years, Nov. 13, 1863.

Company B: Transferred from Co. B 107th O.V.I. July 13, 1865; died Oct. 12, 1865 at Chester, S.C..

William Maloney, 2d Lieutenant, age 23, entered service for period of 3 years, June 20, 1861.

Company A: Promoted from Sergeant Co. F Oct. 20, 1862; transferred to Co. F April 9, 1863.

Company E: Promoted from 2d Lieutenant Co. H March 15, 1864; mustered out July 16, 1864 on expiration of term of service.

Company H: Transferred from Co. F April 16, 1863; promoted to 1st Lieutenant Co. E March 15, 1864.

Benjamin R. Manchester, Private, age 23, entered service for period of 1 year, Sept. 30, 1864.

Company I: Discharged July 15, 1865 by order of War Department.

John W. Mancil, Private, age 33, entered service for period of 3 years, August 30, 1864.

Company C: no record given.

Francis D. Manger, Corporal, age 28, entered service for period of 1 year, Oct. 3, 1864.

Company F: Appointed Corporal Nov. 5, 1864; discharged May 29, 1865 by order of War Department.

Thomas L. Manley, Private, age 31, entered service for period of year, Oct. 7, 1864.

Company D: Absent sick May 5, 1865 in hospital at Hilton Head, S.C.; mustered out with company Oct. 20, 1865.

Richard B. Manley, Private, age 26, entered service for period of year, Oct. 7, 1864.

Company D: Mustered out with company Oct. 20, 1865.

Mann Richard H., Private, age 19, entered service for period of year, Oct. 10, 1864.

Company D: Mustered out with company Oct. 20, 1865.

Nathaniel J. Manning, Captain, age 24, entered service for period of 3 years, June 10, 1861.

Company C: Promoted to 2d Lieutenant from 1st Sergeant Jan. 9, 1862; 1st Lieutenant March 12, 1862; Captain Co. K Jan. 1, 1864; mustered out July 16, 1864 at Columbus, Ohio on expiration of term of service.

William Manning II, Private, age 21, entered service for period of 3 years, Aug. 20, 1862.

Company F: Discharged Nov. 21, 1862 by order of War Department.

Robert Mariner, Private, age 40, entered service for period of 3 years, June 10, 1861.

Company B: Discharged April 14, 1863 at Burk's Station, Va. on Surgeon's certificate of disability.

George Markey, Private, age 18, entered service for period of 3 years, Feb, 20, 1864.

Company C; Discharged Aug. 7, 1865 at Hilton Head, S.C. on Surgeon's certificate of disability.

Jeremiah Markey, Private, age 18, entered service for period of 3 years, Feb. 15, 1864.

Company C: Mustered out with company June 18, 1866.

Henry S. Markley, Private, age 18, entered service for period of 3 years, Feb. 15, 1864.

Company K: no record given.

Dias N. Marlee, Corporal, age 19, entered service for period of 3 years, Feb. 15, 1864.

Company C: Appointed Corporal Aug. 1, 1865; mustered out with company June 18, 1866.

Christopher Marlo, Private, age 44, entered service for period of 3 years, Dec. 13, 1863.

Company G: Died Aug. 3, 1865 at Columbia, S.C..

Reuben B. Marquis, Private, age 24, entered service for period of nine months, Oct. 7, 1862.

Company H: Drafted; mustered out Aug. 31, 1863 on expiration of term of service.

Samuel B. Marquis, Private, age 26, entered service for period of 3 years, Oct. 7, 1862.

Company H: Drafted; mustered out Aug. 31, 1863 on expiration of term of service.

Eugene Marsh, Private, age 18, entered service for period of 3 years, Feb. 27, 1864.

Company B: Mustered out with company June 18, 1866.

Hardin D. Marsh, Private, age 43, entered service for period of 3 years, Feb., 25, 1864.

Company B: Wounded Dec. 6, 1864 in battle of Deveaux Neck, S.C.; discharged July 8, 1865 at DeCamp Hospital, New York on Surgeon's certificate of disability.

Lawrison Marsh, Private, age 20, entered service for period of 3 years, June 12, 1861.

Company E: Mustered out July 16, 1864 at Columbus, Ohio on expiration of term of service.

Lucius Marsh, Private, age 21, entered service for period of 3 years, June 12, 1861.

Company E: Wounded Aug. 30, 1862 in battle of Bull Run, Va.; mustered out July 16, 1864 at Columbus, Ohio on expiration of term of service, June 12, 1861.

Charles Martin, Private, age 45, entered service for period of 3 years, May 24, 1864.

Company G: Substitute; transferred from Co. A 107th O.V.I. July 13, 1865; mustered out with company June 18, 1866.

George W. Martin, 1st Lieutenant, age 23, entered service for period of 3 years, June 10, 1861.

Company B: Promoted from Sergeant July 30, 1862; wounded July 1, 1863 in battle of Gettysburg, Pa.; discharged Oct. 26, 1863 on Surgeon's certificate of disability.

James Martin, Private, age 23, entered service for period of 1 year, Oct. 7, 1864.
Company D: no record given.

James Martin, Private, age 25, entered service for period of 3 years, June 26, 1861.

Company H: Transferred to Veteran Reserve Corps Dec. 31, 1863 by order of War Department.

James Martin, Private, age 25, entered service for period of 3 years, June 26, 1861.

Company H: Transferred to Veteran Reserve Corps Dec. 31, 1863 by order of War Department.

Joseph Mason, Private, age 26, entered service for period of 3 years, May 24, 1864.
Company G: no record given.
Samuel Mason, Private, age 24, entered service for period of 3 years, June 26, 1861.
Company H: no record given.
Lewis Mason, Private, age 24, entered service for period of 3 years, June 10, 1861.
Company C; Mustered out July 16, 1864 at Camp Chase, Ohio on expiration of term of service.
Isaiah Masters, Corporal, age 22, entered service for period of 3 years, June 10, 1861.
Company C: appointed Corporal Aug. 1, 1864; discharged June 21, 1865 at Camp Chase, Ohio on Surgeon's certificate of disability; veteran.
Isaiah Masters, Private, age 20, entered service for period of 3 years, June 10, 1861.
Company C: Mustered out with company June 18, 1866.
John Masters, Private, age 19, entered service for period of 3 years, Feb. 15, 1864.
Company C: Wounded Dec. 6, 1864 in battle of Deveaux Neck, S.C.; mustered out with company June 18, 1866.
Joseph Masters, Private, age 18, entered service for period of 3 years, Feb. 15, 1864.
Company C: Mustered out with company June 18, 1866.
Thomas Masters, Sergeant, age 24, entered service for period of 3 years, June 18, 1861.
Company K: Transferred from Co. C April 1, 1864; mustered out July 16, 1864 on expiration of term of service.
Emil L. Marx, Private, age 35, entered service for period of 3 years, June 24, 1861.
Company K: Discharged May 20, 1863 at Brook's Station, Va. on surgeon's certificate of disability.
Lewis G. Mason, Private, age 24, entered service for period of 3 years, June 10, 1861.
Company C: Mustered out July 16, 1864 at Camp Chase, Ohio on expiration of term of service.
Samuel Mason, Private, age 24, entered service for period of 3 years, June 26, 1861.
Company H: no record given.

Isaiah Masters, Corporal, age 24, entered service for period of 3 years, June 10, 1861.
Company C: Appointed Corporal Aug. 1, 1864; discharged June 21, 1865 at Camp Chase, Ohio on Surgeon's certificate of disability; veteran.

Isaiah Masters, Private, age 20, entered service for period of 3 years, June 10, 1861.
Company C: Mustered out with company June 18, 1866.

John Masters, Private, age 19, entered service for period of 3 years, Feb. 15, 1864.
Company C: Wounded Dec. 6, 1864 in battle of Deveaux Neck, S.C.; mustered out with company June 18, 1866.

Joseph Masters, Private, age 18, entered service for period of 3 years, Feb. 15, 1864.
Company C: Mustered out with company June 18, 1866.

Thomas B. Masters, Sergeant, age 24, entered service for period of 3 years, June 10, 1861.
Company B: Wounded May 1, 1863 in battle of Chancellorsville, VA.; absent, sick…in U.S. General Hospital….; mustered out July 16, 1864 by order of War Department.

Thomas J. Masters, Private, age 21, entered service for period of 3 years, Feb. 15, 1864.
Company C: no record given.

Daniel W. Mathias, Private, age 20, entered service for period of 1 year, Oct. 5, 1864.
Company G: Mustered out Oct. 5, 1865 on expiration of term of service.

Peter Matthews, Private, age 19, entered service for period of 3 years, June 24, 1861.
Company K: Transferred to Co. C 75th O.V.I. Jan. 16, 1864; from Co. C 75th O.V.I. June 12, 1864; mustered out July 16, 1864 on expiration of term of service.

Alexander Mattison, 1st Lieutenant, age 29, entered service for period of 3 years, February 15, 1864.
Company B: Promoted from 2d Lieutenant March 25, 1864; to Captain Co. H Sept. 14, 1865.Company H: Promoted from 1st Lieutenant Co. B Sept. 14, 1865; mustered out with company June 18, 1866.

John C. Maxwell, Sergeant, age 21, entered service for period of 3 years, June 13, 1861.
Company F: Appointed Corporal April 16, 1863; Sergeant Oct. 14, 1863; mustered out July 16, 1864 on expiration of term of service.

Lyman May, Private, age 18, entered service for period of 3 years, June 8, 1861.
Company D: transferred to 12th Battery O.L.A. March 12, 1862.

John McAllister, Private, age 22, entered service for period of 3 years, June 10, 1861.

Company C: no record given

George W. McBride, Musician, age 21, entered service for period of 3 years, June 5, 1861.

Company A: Promoted to Principal Musician July 1, 1865; veteran.

James M. McBride, Private, age 18, entered service for period of 3 years, June 8, 1861.

Company D: transferred to 12th Battery O.L.A. March 12, 1862.

James H. McBride, Private, age 18, entered service for period of 3 years, June 26, 1861.

Company I: Promoted to Principal Musician July 15, 1865; veteran.

Thomas W. McBride, Corporal, age 39, entered service for period of 3 years, June 5, 1861,

Company A: Appointed Corporal April 1, 1864; discharged June 17, 1865 by order of the War Department; veteran.

William H. McBride, Private, age 19, entered service for period of 3 years, June 26, 1861.

Company I: Wounded May 8, 1862, in battle of McDowell, Va.; discharged July 18, 1862 on Surgeon's certificate of disability.

Jacob McCabe, Private, age 21, entered service for period of 3 years, June 5, 1861.

Company A: Detailed as scout July..., 1863; prisoner of war....; died....in Rebel prison at Richmond, Va.

Samuel W. McCauslen, Sergeant, age 32, entered service for period of 3 years, June 26, 1861.

Company H: discharged Dec. 4, 1862 at Philadelphia, Pa. on surgeon's certificate of disability

Frank McClain, Private, age 28 entered service for period of 1 year, March 13, 1865.

Company A: Mustered out March 13, 1865 on expiration of term of service.

Archibald McClelland, 2d Lieutenant, age 38 entered service for period of 3 years, June 4, 1861.

Company D: Transferred to 12th Battery O.L.A. March 12, 1862.

Samuel L. McClelland, Corporal, age 33, entered service for period of 3 years, Nov. 15, 1863.

Company A: Wounded Nov. 30, 1864 in battle of Honey Hill, S.C.; appointed Corporal April 1, 1865; mustered out with company June 18, 1866.

John G. McColly, Private, age 37, entered service for period of 3 years, Sept. 25, 1863.

Company A: Transferred from 107th O.V.I. July 13, 1865; mustered out with company June 18, 1866.

Burget McConnaughy, Sergeant, age 30, entered service for period of 3 years, June 5, 1861.

Company A: Appointed from Corporal Aug. 1, 18862; promoted to 1st Lieutenant Co. F May 25, 1864; veteran.

Company F: Promoted from Sergeant Co. A May 25, 1864; to Capt. Co. G Aug. 11, 1864.

Company G: Promoted from 1st Lieutenant Co. F Aug. 11, 1864; wounded Nov. 30, 1864 in battle of Honey Hill, S.C.; mustered out with company June 18, 1866.

James McConnell, Private, age 53, entered service for period of 3 years, Aug. 18, 1862.

Company F; Discharged Nov. 19, 1863 on Surgeon's certificate of disability.

John McConnell, Private, age 20, entered service for period of 3 years, June 5, 1861.

Company A: Mustered out with company July 18, 18666; veteran.

Wesley McConnell, Private, age 30, entered service for period of 3 years, June 26, 1861.

Company I: Reduced from Corporal...; discharged Jan. 25, 1863 on Surgeon's certificate of disability.

Hugh McConville, Corporal, age 21, entered service for period of 3 years, June 10, 1861.

Company B: Wounded Aug. 29, 1862 in battle of Bull Run, Va.; mustered out June 10, 1864 at Columbus, Ohio

Company C: Transferred from Co. B March 20, 1864; mustered out July 16, 1864 at Camp Chase, Ohio on expiration of term of service.

John McCord, Private, age 18, entered service for period of 3 years, Feb. 26, 1864.

Company B: Mustered out with company June 18, 1866.

George W. McCormick, Private, age 18, entered service for period of 1 year, Sept. 22, 1864.

Company C; Discharged July 15, 1865 by order of War Department.

James McCormick, Private, age 27, entered service for period of 1 year, Oct. 8, 1864.

Company A: Wounded Nov. 30, 1864 in battle of Honey Hill, S.C.; mustered out Oct. 8, 1865 on expiration of term of service.

John McCormick, Private, age 18, entered service for period of 3 years, Nov. 29, 1863.
Company G: Transferred from Co. B 107th O.V.I. July 13, 1865; mustered out with company June 18, 1866.
William McCormick, Private, age 21, entered service for period of 3 years, Dec. 30, 1863.
Company A: Transferred from 107th O.V.I. July 13, 1865; mustered out with company July 18, 1866.; veteran.
Samuel McCrum, Corporal, age 35, entered service for period of 3 years, June 5, 1861.
Company A: Appointed Corporal Sept. 15, 1863; transferred to 75th O.V.I. Jan 15, 1864 by order of the War Department. Wounded May 8, 1862 in battle of McDowell, Va. and July 1, 1863 in battle of Gettysburg, Pa.; transferred to.....; from 95th O.V.I. June 17, 1863; mustered out July 16, 1864 on expiration of service.
David McCullock, Private, age 19, entered service for period of 3 years, June 26, 1861.
Company I: Wounded June 8, 1862 in battle of McDowell, Va.; discharged Sept. 19, 1862 on Surgeon's certificate of disability.
David McDonald, Private, age 19 entered service for period of 3 years, June 26, 1861.
Company I: Transferred to Co. C 75th O.V.I. Jan. 16, 1864; from Co. C 75th O.V.I. June 12, 1864; mustered out July 16, 1864 on expiration of term of service.
James S. McDonald, Private, age 21, entered service for period of 1 year, Oct. 6, 1864.
Company G: Mustered out Oct. 6, 1865 on expiration of term of service.
Thoria McDonald, Corporal, age 18, entered service for period of 3 years, June 26, 1861.
Company I: Appointed Corporal June 1, 1866; mustered out with company June 18, 1866
Alfred A. McFadden, Private, age 18, entered service for period of 3 years, February 29, 1864.
Company A: Died April 6, 1864 in Carver Hospital at Washington, D.C..
Malcomb McFall, Private, age 18, entered service for period of 3 years, Oct. 12, 1864.
Company G: Discharged June 21, 1865 at Columbus, Ohio on Surgeon's certificate of disability.

William McFee, 2d Lieutenant, age 38 entered service for period of 1 year, Oct. 18, 1864.

Company D: Resigned July 6, 1865.

Lewis McGrath, Private, age 25 entered service for period of 3 years, July 21, 1861.

Company H: Discharged Aug. 30, 1862 at Frederick City, Md. on Surgeon's certificate of disability.

Morris McGregor, Private, age 18, entered service for period of 3 years, June 8, 1861.

Company D: Transferred to 12th Battery O.L.A. March 12, 1862.

Charles McGuckin, Private, age 18, entered service for period of 3 years, Feb. 19, 1864.

Company B; Mustered out with company June 18, 1866.

David McGuckin, 1st Sergeant, age 25, entered service for period of 3 years, June 10, 1861.

Company B: Appointed Sergeant from private March 16, 1864; 1st Sergeant Nov. 5, 1864; promoted to 2d Lieutenant Co. G Sept. 4, 1865.

Company G: Promoted from 1st Sergeant Co. B Sept. 4, 1865; mustered out with company June 18, 1866.

James McGuckin, 1st Sergeant, age 25, entered service for period of 3 years, Feb. 19, 1864.

Company B: Appointed Corporal March 16, 1864; Sergeant Nov. 5, 1864; 1st Sergeant Sept 28, 1865; discharged Jan. 25, 1866 at Columbus, Ohio by order of War Department.

Frank C. McKim, Private, age 19, entered service for period of 1 year, Oct. 3, 1864.

Company I: Mustered out Oct. 2, 1865 on expiration of term of service.

David S. McKinley, Corporal, age 18, entered service for period of 3 years, Aug. 4, 1862.

Company F: Appointed Corporal June 1, 1865; discharged July 15, 1865 by order of War Department.

John McKinley, Sergeant, age 20, entered service for period of 3 years, July 23, 1861.

Company F: Appointed from private Feb. 1, 1863; killed May 2, 1863 in battle of Chancellorsville, Virginia.

Isaac McKinney, Private, age 18, entered service for period of 3 years, Feb. 19, 1864.

Company K: Transferred from Co....107th O.V.I. July 13, 1865; mustered out with company June 18, 1866.

Jacob M. McKinney, Private, age 20, entered service for period of 3 years, Sept.. 28, 1862.

1865 on expiration of term of service.

Matthew F. McKirahan, Corporal, age 18, entered service for period of 3 years, Feb. 29, 1864.

Company A: Appointed Corporal Sept, 15, 1865; mustered out with company June 18, 1866.

John McKirhan, 1st Sergeant, age 21, entered service for period of 3 years, June 5, 1861.

Company A: Wounded Aug. 29, 1862 in battle of Bull Run, Va. and July 1, 1863 in battle of Gettysburg, Pa.; appointed Sergeant from private Aug. 1, 1864; 1st Sergeant March 9, 1866; discharged May 18, 1866; veteran.

James McKitrick, Private, age 22, entered service for period of 3 years, June 26, 1861.

Company I: Mustered out July 16, 1864 on expiration of term of service.

Bernard McLafferty, Private, age 36, entered service for period of 3 years, June 13, 1861.

Company F: discharged April 14, 1862 on Surgeon's certificate of disability.

Daniel McLargin, Private, age 37, entered service for period of 3 years, Feb. 26, 1864.

Company B: Discharged Dec. 16, 1865 at Columbia, S.C. by order of War Department.

James McLaughlin, Private, age 20, entered service for period of 9 months, Oct. 7, 1862.

Company K: Drafted; mustered out July 7, 1863 on expiration of term of service.

Thomas McLaughlin, Private, age 42, entered service for period of 3 years, Feb. 12, 1864.

Company B: Died June 25, 1865 in hospital at Hilton Head, South Carolina.

Levi McLaughlin, Private, age 21, entered service for period of 3 years, June 26, 1861.

Company H: Wounded July 2, 1863 in battle of Gettysburg, Pa.; discharged June 21, 1865 at Camp Dennison, Ohio by order of War Department; veteran.

Solomon McMillan, Corporal, age 30, entered service for period of 3 years, Feb. 25, 1864.

Company K: Appointed Corporal April 1, 1864; discharged March 29, 1866 at Columbus, Ohio by order of War Department.

John McMillin, Private, age 21, entered service for period of 3 years, June 5, 1861.

Company A: no record given

William McMillin, Private, age 42, entered service for period of 3 years, June 18, 1861.

Company G: Discharged Dec, 7, 1862 at Fairfax C.H., Va. on Surgeon's certificate of disability.

John McMonagle, Private, age 30, entered service for period of 3 years, Feb. 25, 1864.

Company K: no record given.

James McMullen, Private, age 21, entered service for period of 3 years, June 5, 1861.

Company A: Wounded Dec. 12, 1861 in Camp Alleghany, W. Va.; died Jan. 10, 1862 at Bridgeport, Ohio.

James D. McMune, Private, age 24, entered service for period of 3 years, June 10, 1861.

Company E: Transferred from Co. B June 13, 1864; mustered out July 10, 1864 at Columbus, Ohio on expiration of term of service.

David McMunn, Private, age 18, entered service for period of 3 years, Feb. 22, 1864.

Company I: Wounded Nov. 30, 1864 in battle of Honey Hill, S.C.; mustered out with company June 18, 1866.

James D. McMunn, Corporal, age 24, entered service for period of 3 years, June 10, 1861.

Company B: Wounded June 8, 1862 in battle of McDowell, Va.; transferred to Co. E June 13, 1864.

Company E: Transferred from Co. B June 13, 1864; mustered out July 10, 1864 at Columbus, Ohio on expiration of term of service.

Ezekiel McNutt, Private, age 25, entered service for period of 1 year, Aug. 20, 1864.

Company G: Discharged Oct. 1, 1865 at Charleston, S. C. by order of War Department.

James P. McPeak, Private, age 21, entered service for period of 3 years, June 10, 1861.

Company C: Killed May 8, 1862 in battle of McDowell, Va..

George D. W. McPherson, Private, 27, entered service for period of 3 years, June 5, 1861.

Company A: Discharged Oct. 28, 1862 at Alexandria, Va. on Surgeon's certificate of disability.

William F. McNichols, Private, age 18, entered service for period of 3 years, July 9, 1861.

Company H: Transferred to Co. B 75th O.V.I. Jan. 16, 1864; from Co. B 75th O.V.I. June 12, 1864; mustered out July 16, 1864 on expiration of term of service.

George McVicker, Private, age 21, entered service for period of 3 years, June 18, 1861.
Company G: Killed Aug. 30, 1862 in battle of Bull Run, Va..
James W. McWilliams, Sergeant, age 18, entered service for period of 3 years, June 26, 1861.
Company I: Appointed Corporal April 1, 1864; Sergeant Oct. 1, 1865; mustered out with company June 18, 1866; veteran.
Josiah A. Medley, Private, age 19, entered service for period of 3 years, Nov. 8, 1863.
Company C: Died Feb. 20, 1864 at Hilton Head, S.C..
Henry Meek, Private, age 30, Private, age 36, entered service for period of 3 years, June 5, 1861.
Company A: Wounded Dec. 12, 1861 in battle of Camp Alleghany, W. Va. and May 8, 1862 in battle of McDowell, Va.; discharged Dec. 24, 1862 at Wheeling, W.Va. on Surgeon's certificate of disability.
John Meeker, Private, age 24, entered service for period of 3 years, June 20, 1861.
Company F: Discharged Aug. 15, 1862 on Surgeon's certificate of disability.
James Mellor, Private, age 24, entered service for period of 3 years, June 5, 1861.
Company A: Reduced from Corporal...; mustered out July 18, 1864 on expiration of term of service.
William H. Mendinhall, Private, age 20, entered service for period of 3 years, June 26, 1861.
Company H: Discharged June 1, 1862 at Columbus, Ohio on Surgeon's certificate of disability.
George F. Mercer, Private, age38, entered service for period of 3 years, June 13, 1861.
Company F: Transferred to Veteran Reserve Corps Oct. 16,1863 by order of War Department.
Newlen Mercer, Private, age 28, entered service for period of 3 years, June 10, 1861.
Company B; Transferred to Co. C March 20, 1864; veteran.
Company C: Transferred from Co. B as Corporal March 20, 1864; mustered with company June 18, 1866.
Isaiah W. Meridith, Private, age 19, entered service for period of 3 years, June 20, 1861.
Company F: Transferred to 4th U.S. Cavalry Oct. 31, 1863.

Stephen Merrill, Private, age 35, entered service for period of 3 years, Nov. 9, 1863.

Company C: Died Jan. 8, 1864 at Hilton Head, S.C..

William F. Merrill, Private, age 18, entered service for period of 1 year, Sept. 30, 1864.

Company G: Discharged Oct. 1, 1865 in Charleston, S.C. by order of War Department.

John P. Merris, Private, age 28, entered service for period of 3 years, June 12, 1861.

Company E: Discharged Oct. 31, 1861 on Surgeon's certificate of disability.

John D. Merryman, 2d Lieutenant, age 23, entered service for period of 3 years, June 10, 1861.

Company B: Wounded Dec. 12, 1861 in battle of Camp Alleghany, W.Va.; promoted to 1st Lieutenant Co. I January 9, 1862.

Company I: Captain. Promoted from 2d Lieutenant Co. B Jan. 9, 1862; discharged Dec. 29, 1862 for wounds received Aug. 29, 1862 in battle of Bull Run, Virginia.

James A. Merwin, Private, age 19, entered service for period of 1 year, Oct. 5, 1864.

Company F: Mustered out..., 1865 on expiration of term of service.

Luther B. Mesnard, Captain, age 26, entered service for period of 3 years, March 17, 1864.

Company B: Mustered out with company June 18, 1866.

Joseph M. Metcalf, Private, age 18, entered service for period of 3 years, July 9, 1861.

Company H: Died March 8, 1863 at Brook's Station, Va.

William M. Metcalf, Private, age 26, entered service for period of 3 years, June 26, 1861.

Company H: Reduced from Sergeant Sept. 30, 1861; discharged July 29, 1862 at Camp Chase, Ohio on Surgeon's certificate of disability.

Daniel Metzer, 1st Sergeant, age 30, entered service for period of 3 years, June 18, 1861.

Company G: Mustered as Sergeant; appointed 1st Sergeant.....

James Metzgor, Private age 19, entered service for period of 3 years, June 24, 1861.

Company K: Discharged Nov. 27, 1861 at Cheat Mountain, W. Va. on Surgeon's certificate of disability.

William Meuser, Private, age 20, entered service for period of 3 years, June 12, 1861.

Company E: Died Nov. 20, 1862 at Fairfax C.H., Va..

Henry Meyer, Private, age 22, entered service for period of 3 years, Feb. 23, 1864.
Company K: Discharged Aug. 11, 1865 at Hilton Head, S.C. on Surgeon's certificate of disability.

Henry Mick, Private, age 18, entered service for period of 3 years, Jan. 2, 1864.
Company G: Transferred from Co. A 107th O.V.I. July 13, 1865; mustered out with company June 18, 1866.

Andrew Miller, Private, age 23, entered service for period of 1 year, Sept. 14, 1864.
Company K: Discharged July 15, 1865 by order of War Department.

David Miller, Private, age 22, entered service for period of 3 years, Nov. 10, 1863.
Company G: no record given.

Frances Miller, Private, age 41, entered service for period of 3 years, Feb. 20, 1864.
Company I: Mustered out with company June 18, 1866.

George Miller, Private, age 38, entered service for period of 3 years, March 15, 1864.
Company G: Transferred from Co. A 107th O.V.I. July 13, 1865; mustered out with company June 18, 1866.

Henry Miller, Private, age 20, entered service for period of 3 years, June 26, 1861.
Company I: no record given.

John W. Miller, age 28, entered service for period of 1 year, Oct. 1, 1864.
Company I: Mustered out Sept. 29, 1865 on expiration of term of service.

Israel Miller, Corporal, age 19, entered service for period of 3 years, June 20, 1861.
Company F: Appointed Corporal Nov. 5, 1864; reduced...; re-appointed July 1, 1865; mustered out with company June 18, 1866; veteran.

Jacob H. Miller, Private, age 22, entered service for period of 1 year, Oct. 5, 1864.
Company F: Mustered out...1865 on expiration of term of service.

Jerome Miller, Corporal, age 24, entered service for period of 3 years, June 13, 1861.
Company F: Appointed Corporal Sept. 15, 1861; discharged Nov. 5, 1862 on Surgeon's certificate of disability.

John Miller, Private, age 44, entered service for period of 1 year, Sept. 30, 1861.
Company D: Mustered out July 15, 1865 by order of War Department.

John Miller Private, age 36, entered service for period of 1 year, Oct. 3, 1864. Company A: Mustered out Oct. 3, 1865 on expiration of term of service.............................

John Miller, Private, age 18, entered service for period of 3 years, March 7, 1864. Company E: Wounded Nov. 30, 1864 in battle of Honey Hill, S.C.; mustered out with company June 18, 1866.

John R. Miller, Private, age 32, Private, age 36, entered service for period of 3 years, June 5, 1861. Company A: Discharged Aug. 19, 1861 at Grafton, Va. on Surgeon's certificate of disability.

John W. Miller, Private, age 28, entered service for period of 1 year, Sept 30, 1864. Company I: Mustered out Sept. 29, 1865 on expiration of term of service.

Joseph Miller, Private, age 30, entered service for period of 3 years, Sept. 23, 1863. Company G: Transferred from Co. A 107th O.V.I. July 13, 1865; mustered out with company June 18, 1866.

Jerome P. Miller, Corporal, age 24, entered service for period of 3 years, June 13, 1861. Company F: Appointed Corporal Sept. 15, 1861; discharged Nov. 5, 1862 on Surgeon's certificate of disability.

Lewis Miller, Private, age 18, entered service for period of 3 years, June 24, 1861. Company K: Transferred to 3d O.V. Cavalry....

Martin V. B. Miller, Private, age 21, entered service for period of 3 years, June 18, 1861. Company G: no record given.

Peter Miller, Private, age 19, entered service for period of 3 years, June 12, 1861. Company E: Mustered out with company June 18, 1866; veteran.

William Miller, Private, age 19, entered service for period of 3 years, June 18, 1861. Company G: Died July 12, 1863 of wounds received July 1, 1863 in battle of Gettysburg, Pa..

Robert H. Miller, Private, age 20, entered service for period of 3 years, June 5, 1861. Company A: Wounded May 8, 1862 in battle of McDowell, Va.; discharged July 31, 1863 at Columbus, Ohio on Surgeon's certificate of disability.

Joseph Millet, Private, age 24, entered service for period of 3 years, June 24, 1861.
Company K: no record given.
Charles T. Millhollan, Private, age 21, entered service for period of 3 years, June 24, 1861.
Company K: Wounded July 1, 1863 in battle of Gettysburg, Pa.; transferred to Co. C 75th O.V.IO. Jan. 16, 1864; from Co. C 75th O.V.I. June 12, 1864; mustered out July 16, 1864 on expiration of term of service.
John H. Milliman, 1st. Lieutenant, age 27, entered service for period of 3 years, June 18, 1861.
Company G: Appointed 1st Sergeant from Sergeant...; promoted to 2d Lieutenant July 30, 1862; 1st Lieutenant Feb. 1, 1863; wounded July 1, 1863 in battle of Gettysburg, Pa.; promoted to Captain Co. K March 15, 1865.
Company K: Promoted from 1st Lieutenant Co. G March 15, 1864; mustered out July 16, 1864 on expiration of term of service.
Wesley Milliman, Corporal, age 22, entered service for period of 3 years, June 18, 1861.
Company G: Died Oct. 8, 1861 at Cheat Mountain, Va..
Orlando S. Mills, Corporal, age 23, entered service for period of 3 years, June 12, 1861.
Company E: Appointed Corporal Aug. 20, 1861; wounded May 8, 1862 in battle of McDowell, Va.; discharged Feb. 18, 1862 on Surgeon's certificate of disability
William N. Mills, Private, age 18, entered service for period of 3 years, June 27, 1861.
Company H: Wounded May 3, 1863 in battle of Chancellorsville, Va.; discharged June 14, 1864 at Camp Chase, Ohio on Surgeon's certificate of disability.
Joel Millum, Private, age 26, entered service for period of 1 year, Oct. 3, 1864.
Company D: Mustered out with company Oct. 20, 1865
John Milton, Sergeant, age 21, entered service for period of 3 years, July 9, 1861.
Company H: Appointed Corporal Sept. 3, 1861; Sergeant Jan. 1, 1863; died Aug. 19, 1863 at Cincinnati, Ohio of wounds received July 1, 1863 in battle of Gettysburg, Pa..
Darius Minier, Private, age 23, entered service for period of 3 years, June 12, 1861.
Company E: Wounded Aug. 30, 1862 in Battle of Bull Run, Va..

John Minier, Private, age 18, entered service for period of 3 years, June 12, 1861.

Company E: Discharged Nov. 18, 1861 on Surgeon's certificate of disability.

Amos W. Minor, Private, age 19, entered service for period of 3 years, July 10, 1861.

Company K: Killed Aug. 30, 1862 in battle of Bull Run, Va..

Adam S. Miracle, Private, age 20, entered service for period of 3 years, June 26, 1861.

Company I: Transferred to Co. C 75th O.V.I. Jan. 16, 1864; from Co. C 75th O.V.I. June 12, 1864; mustered out July 16, 1864 on expiration of term of service.

Christian Mitchell, Private, age 28, entered service for period of 3 years, Dec. 23, 1863.

Company K: Transferred from Co C 75th O,V.I. June 12, 1864.

Joseph Mitchell, Private, age 18, entered service for period of 3 years, June 12, 1861.

Company E: Transferred to Co. C 75th O.V.I. Jan. 16, 1864; from Co. C 75th O.V.I. June 12, 1864; mustered out July 16, 1864 at Columbus, Ohio on expiration of term of service.

Andrew Moffatt, Private, age 25, entered service for period of 3 years, June 13, 1861.

Company F: no record given.

Perry Moffatt, Private, age 26, entered service for period of 3 years, June 10, 1861.

Company B: Discharged Jan. 12, 1863 on Surgeon's certificate of disability.

Thomas Moffatt, Private, 31, entered service for period of 3 years, June 10, 1861.

Company B: Discharged Oct. 15, 1862 on Surgeon's certificate of disability.

William Moffatt, Private, age 31, entered service for period of 3 years, June 10, 1861.

Company B: Died Dec. 8, 1862 at Fairfax Court House, Va..

Peter Molyette, Sergeant, age 18, entered service for period of 3 years, June 12, 1861.

Company E: Wounded July 1, 1863 in battle of Gettysburg, Pa.; appointed Corporal Nov. 5, 1864; Sergeant, March 17, 1866; mustered out with company June 18, 1866; veteran.

Elijah S. Monroe, Private, age 41, entered service for period of 1 year, Feb. 20, 1865.

Company C: no record given.

James W. Monroe, Private, age 18, entered service for period of 1 year, Feb. 29, 1864.
Company C: Discharged…at Columbus Ohio.
Edward Montgomery, Private, age 18, entered service for period of 1 year, Nov. 30, 1864.
Company K: Mustered out Nov. 30, 1865 on expiration of term of service.
Fred A. Montgomery, Private, age 18, entered service for period of 1 year, Oct. 18, 1864.
Company A: Mustered out Oct. 18, 1865 on expiration of term of service.
John G. Monz, Private, age 31, entered service for period of 1 year, Oct. 8, 1864.
Company K: Mustered out Oct. 8, 1865 on expiration of term of service.
Jacob Moog, Private, age 44, entered service for period of 1 year, Oct. 22, 1864.
Company G: Transferred from Co. .. 107th O.V.I. July 13, 1865; mustered out Oct. 22, 1865 on expiration of term of service.
James Mooney, Private, age 36, entered service for period of 3 years, June 13, 1861.
Company F: no record given.
Albert Moore, Private, age 32, entered service for period of 1 year, Oct. 7, 1864.
Company G: Mustered out Oct. 7, 1865 on expiration of term of service.
George Moore, Private, age 18, entered service for period of 3 years, Dec. 28, 1863.
Company G: no record given.
Harvey B. Moore, Sergeant, age 24, entered service for period of 1 year, Sept. 7, 1864.
Company F: Mustered as private; appointed Sergeant Nov. 5, 1864; discharged June 13, 1865 to accept promotion as 2d Lieutenant in 104th U.S. Colored Troops.
James T. Moore, Private, age 20, entered service for period of 3 years, June 27, 1861.
Company G: no record given.
James V. Moore, Private, age 27, entered service for period of year, Sept. 26, 1864.
Company I: Wounded Nov. 30, 1864 in battle of Honey Hill, S.C.; discharged July 15, 1865 by order of War Department.
Joseph Moore, Corporal, age 27, entered service for period of 3 years, Feb. 26, 1864.
Company K: Appointed Corporal Nov. 5, 1864; wounded Dec. 7, 1864 in battle of Deveaux Neck, S.C..
Lucius Moore, Private, age 28, entered service for period of 1 year, Oct. 7, 1864.
Company G: Mustered out Oct 7, 1865 on expiration of term of service.

Philander Moore, Private, age 18, entered service for period of 3 years, March 14, 1862.

Company K: no record given.

Lewis Moorer, Private, age 26, entered service for period of 3 years, June 12, 1861.

Company E: Mustered out on July 16, 1864 at Columbus, Ohio on expiration of term of service.

Henry H. Moose, Corporal, age 25, entered service for period of 3 years, June 10, 1861.

Company B: no record given.

John J. Moose, Private, age 19, entered service for period of 3 years, June 10, 1861.

Company B: Wounded July 1, 1863 in battle of Gettysburg, Pa.; discharged Feb. 15, 1864 on Surgeon's certificate of disability.

James Moran, Private, age 22, entered service for period of 3 years, June 24, 1861.

Company K: Killed (sic, Wounded}Aug. 30, 1862 in battle of Bull Run, Va.; discharged Jan. 24, 1863 at Alexandria, Va. on Surgeon's certificate of disability.

Joseph W. Moreland, Private, age 26, entered service for period of 3 years, Aug. 28, 1861.

Company I: Mustered out Aug. 28, 1864 on expiration of term of service.

George W. Morgan, Private, age 18, entered service for period of 3 years, March 5, 1864.

Company C: Wounded Dec. 6, 1864 in battle of Deveaux Neck, S.C..

Frederick Morrie, Corporal, age 18, entered service for period of 3 years, Dec. 23, 1863.

Company C: Transferred from Co. C 107th O.V. I. July 13, 1865; appointed Corporal Jan. 1, 1865; mustered out with company June 18, 1866.

Franklin Morris, Private, age 18, entered service for period of 1 year, Oct. 12, 1864.

Company G: Mustered Oct. 12, 1865 on expiration of term of service.

Lucius Morris, Private, age 28, entered service for period of 1 year, Oct. 7, 1864.

Company G: Mustered out Oct. 7, 1865 on expiration of term of service.

Nathan Morris, Private, age 19, entered service for period of 3 years, June 10, 1861.

Company B: Wounded May 8, 1862 in battle of McDowell, Va. and May 2, 1863 in battle of Chancellorsville, Va.; transferred to Co. C June 12, 1864.

Company C: Transferred from Co. B June 12, 1864; mustered out July 16, 1864 at Camp Chase, Ohio on expiration of term of service.

Omar D. Morris, Sergeant, age 22, entered service for period of 3 years, June 18, 1861.

Company G: Discharged Nov. 21, 1861 at Cheat Mountain, Va. on Surgeon's certificate of disability.

John Mortal, Private, age 24, entered service for period of 3 years, June 24, 1861.

Company K: Transferred to Co. C 75th O.V.I. Jan. 16, 1864; from Co. C 75th O.V.I. June 12, 1864; mustered out July 16, 1864 on expiration of term of service.

Henry H. Moseley, 1st Lieutenant, age 24, entered service for period of 3 years, June 20, 1861.

Company H: Promoted to 2d Lieutenant from 1st Sergeant Co. I Jan, 9, 1862; 1st Lieutenant June 30, 1862; Captain March 15, 1864, but not mustered; discharged March 20, 1865 by order of War Department.

Company I: Mustered as private; appointed 1st Sergeant July 26, 1861; promoted to 2d Lieutenant Co. H Jan. 9, 1862.

John M. Mosley, Captain, age 27, entered service for period of 3 years, June 4, 1871.

Company I: Died Sept. 27, 1861 at Cheat Mountain, Va..

George Motley, Private, age 24, entered service for period of 1 year, Sept. 20, 1864.

Company C: Discharged July 15, 1865 by order of War Department.

1864; Sergeant March 17, 1866; mustered out with company June 18, 1866; veteran.

Peter Moylette, Sergeant, age 18, entered service for period of three years, June 12, 1861.

Company E: Wounded July 1, 1863 in Battle of Gettysburg, Pa.; appointed Corporal, Nov. 5,

Michael Mulgrove, Private, age 44, entered service for period of 3 years, June 12, 1861.

Company E: Discharged July 15, 1862 on Surgeon's certificate of disability.

Harlow Muliken, 2d Lieutenant, age 44, entered service for period of 3 years, June 4, 1861.

Company K: Resigned Oct. 19, 1861.

Gottleib Muntz, Private, age 24, entered service for period of 3 years, Oct. 2, 1862.

Company K: Transferred from Co....107th O.V.I. July 13, 1865; mustered out Oct. 2, 1865 on expiration of term of service.

John Murphy, Private, age 18, Private, age 36, entered service for period of 1 year, March 7, 1864.

Company A: Discharged May 29, 1865 at Cincinnati, Ohio on Surgeon's certificate of disability.

Company A: Appointed Corporal April 1, 1862; wounded July 1, 1863 in battle of Gettysburg, Pa.; promoted to 1st Lieutenant Co. G. April 13, 1864; veteran.

Company E: Promoted from 1st Lieutenant Co. G, Oct. 17, 1864; mustered out July 16, 1864 on expiration of term of service.

Company G: Promoted from Corporal Co. A April 13, 1864; to Captain Co. E Oct. 17, 1864.

Michael Murray, 1st Lieutenant, age 24, entered service for period of 3 years, June 5, 1861.

Company G: Promoted from Company A April 13, 1864.

Company E: Promoted to Captain Oct. 17, 1864.

Artilius Musgrave, Corporal, age 22, entered service for period of 3 years, Feb. 11, 1864.

Company H: Appointed Corporal July 1, 1864; wounded Nov. 30, 1864 in battle of Honey Hill, S.C.; discharged March 21, 1865 by order of the War Department.

Delvan Myers, Private, age 18, entered service for period of 3 years, Feb. 29, 1864.

Company B: Mustered out with company June 18, 1866.

Godfrey Myer, Private, age 41, entered service for period of 3 years, Sept. 5, 1861.

Company D: Mustered out July 15, 1865 by order of War Department.

Adolpheus Myers, Private, age 21, entered service for period of 3 years, June 18, 1861,

Company G: Wounded June 8, 1862 in battle of Cross Keys, Va. and July 2, 1863 in battle of Gettysburg, Pa.; mustered out with company June 18, 1866; veteran.

Harrison J. Myers, Private, age 20, entered service for period of 3 years, June 12, 1861.

Company E: Discharged Aug. 16, 1861 on Surgeon's certificate of disability.

Louis G. Meyers, Surgeon, age 37, entered service for period of 3 years, July 26, 1861.

Mustered out July 16, 1864, on expiration of term of service.

Thomas J. Myers, Corporal, age 24, entered service for period of 3 years, June 18, 1861.

Company G: Appointed Corporal....; Died April 25, 1865 at Georgetown, D.C. of wounds received April 16, 1865 in battle of Red Hill, S.C.; veteran.

N

Fred Nave, Private, age 40, entered service for period of 3 years, Feb. 26, 1864.
Company K: Drowned June 27, 1864 at Jenkins' Island, S.C..

Simon Nedrow, Private, age 24, entered service for period of 1 year, Sept. 6, 1864.
Company E: Discharged July 15, 1865 on order of War Department.

Joshua B. Needs, Private, age 20, entered service for period of 3 years, Feb. 20, 1864.
Company I: Died April 8, 1864 at Camp Dennison, Ohio.

William Needs, Private, age 22, entered service for period of 3 years, Feb. 20, 1864.
Company I: no record given.

Derillo Nelson, Corporal, age 18, entered service for period of 3 years, June 24, 1861.
Company K: Appointed Corporal Dec. 1, 1865; discharged April 2, 1866 by order of War Department; veteran.

John R. Nelson, Corporal, age 28, entered service for period of 1 year, Oct. 4, 1864.
Company D: Appointed Corporal Aug. 1, 1864; mustered out with company Oct. 20, 1865.

James Nesbit, Private, age 23, entered service for period of 3 years, June 8, 1861.
Company D: Transferred to 12th Battery O.L.A. March 12, 1862.

John W. Nevill, Private, age 18, entered service for period of 3 years, Dec. 21, 1863.
Company A: Transferred from 75th O.V.I. June 13, 1864; mustered out with company June 18, 1866.

Eli Nevour, Private, age 20, entered service for period of 1 year, Oct. 6, 1864.
Company A: Wounded Nov. 30, 1864 in battle of Honey Hill, S.C.; mustered out Oct. 6, 1865 on expiration of term of service.

Isaac Newell, Corporal, age 18, entered service for period of 3 years, March 5, 1864.
Company G: no record given.

George Newman, Sergeant, age 33, entered service for period of 3 years, June 26, 1861.
Company H: Wounded May 3, 1863 in battle of Chancellorsville, Va.; transferred to Veteran Reserve Corps Dec. 18, 1863 by order of War Department.

George H. Newton, Sergeant, age 33, entered service for period of 3 years, June 26, 1861.

Company H: Wounded May 3, 1863 in battle of Chancellorsville, Va.; transferred to Veteran Reserve Corps Dec. 18, 1863 by order of War Department.

George H. Newton, Private age 20, entered service for period of 3 years, Feb. 29, 1864.

Company K: Mustered out with company June 18, 1864.

Michael R. Newton, Private, age 18, entered service for period of 3 years, Feb. 27, 1864.

Company B: Killed Nov. 30, 1864 in battle of Honey Hill, S.C..

Leonard K. Ney, Private, age 19, entered service for period of 3 years, June 18, 1861.

Company G: no record given.

Hiram Nicholl, Corporal, age 25, entered service for period of 3 years, June 5, 1861.

Company A: Transferred to 75th O.V.I. Jan. 15, 1864 by order of the War Department.

Joseph P. Neil, Private, age 26, entered service for period of 3 years, June 10, 1861.

Company B: Killed May 2, 1863 in battle of Chancellorsville, Va..

Michael R. Newton, Private, age 18, entered service for period of 3 years, Feb. 27, 1864.

Company B: Killed Nov. 30, 1864 in battle of Honey Hill, South Carolina.

Isaac R. Nicol, Private, age 43, entered service for period of 1 year, Sept. 29, 1864.

Company G: Discharged Oct. 1, 1865 at Charleston, S.C. by order of War Department.

Rudolph L. Niehus, Private, age 38, entered service for period of 3 years, Jan. 2, 1864.

Company K: Killed Feb. 8, 1865 in action at Combahee Ferry, S.C..

Alfred Noaker, Private, age 22, entered service for period of 3 years, June 8, 1861.

Company D: Transferred to 12th Battery O.L.A. March 12, 1862.

John Nolan, Private, age 27, entered service for period of 3 years, Jan. 5, 1864.
Company F: no record given.

Thomas Nolan, Private, age 28, entered service for period of 3 years, June 13, 1861.

Company F: Transferred to Co. C 75th O.V.I. Jan. 16, 1864; from Co. C 75th O.V.I. June 12, 1864; mustered out July 16, 1864 on expiration of term of service.

Aron Noland, Private, age 21, entered service for period of 3 years, June 10, 1861.
Company C: Died Jan. 21, 1863 at Woodsfield, Ohio.
Rule Noland, Private, age19, entered service for period of 3 years, Feb. 29, 1864.
Company H: Discharged Dec. 30, 1864 from hospital at Charleston, S.C. for wounds received Nov. 30, 1864 in battle of Honey Hill, S.C.
Silas Noland, Private, age 22, entered service for period of 3 years, June 26, 1861.
Company H: Discharged March 31, 1866 at Columbus, Ohio by order of War Department; veteran.
Joseph P. Noll, Private, age 26, entered service for period of 3 years, June 10, 1861.
Company C: Killed May 2, 1863 in battle of Chancellorsville, Va..
Daniel Y. Norfolk, Private, age 25, entered service for period of 3 years, June 10, 1861.
Company B: Transferred to Co. C March 20, 1864.
Company C: Transferred from Co. B March 20, 1864; mustered out July 16, 1864 at Camp Chase, Ohio on expiration of term of service.
Charles C. Norpel, Private, age 39, entered service for period of 3 years, June 18, 1861.
Company G: no record given.
William R. Norton, Private, age 18, entered service for period of 3 years, Feb. 22, 1864.
Company B: Mustered out with company June 18, 1866.
Henry Nunn, Private, age 18, entered service for period of 3 years, June 10, 1861.
Company C: Mustered out July 16, 1864 at Camp Chase, Ohio on expiration of term of service.
Isaac Nye, Private, age 18, entered service for period of 3 years, June 12, 1861.
Company E: Killed Dec. 13, 1861 in battle of Camp Alleghany, W. Va..

O

Cyrus Odell, Corporal, age 21, entered service for period of 3 years, June 12, 1861.
Company E: Wounded Aug. 30, 1862 in battle of Bull Run, Va.; discharged Oct. 4, 1862 on Surgeon's certificate of disability.

Bennager Odell, Private, age 18, entered service for period of 3 years, Aug. 4, 1862.

Company E: Wounded July 1, 1863 in battle of Gettysburg, Pa.; discharged July 21, 1865 on Surgeon's certificate of disability.

Dennis H. Odell, Corporal, age 30, entered service for period of 3 years, Feb. 27, 1864.

Company B: Appointed Corporal Nov. 5, 1864.

Hiram Odell, Private, age 23, entered service for period of 3 years, June 12, 1861.

Company E: Appointed Corporal June 6, 1864; Sergeant Aug. 1, 1865; 1st Sergeant March 19, 1866; mustered out with company June 18, 1866.

Charles Oechal, Private, age 25, entered service for period of 3 years, June 24, 1861.

Company K: Reduced from Corporal...; wounded July 1, 1863 in battle of Gettysburg, Pa.; transferred to Veteran Reserve Corps Nov. 30, 1863 by order of War Department.

Samuel Ogborn, Private, age 19, entered service for period of 3 years, June 18, 1861.

Company G: discharged Nov. 14, 1862 at Hopewell Gap, Va. on Surgeon's certificate of disability.

George S. Ogden, Corporal, age 19, entered service for period of 3 years, June 18, 1861.

Company G: Died Aug. 23, 1862 at Washington, D.C. of wounds received in battle of Camp Alleghany.

Gilbert J. Ogden, Corporal, age 19, entered service for period of 3 years, June 18, 1861.

Company G: Appointed Dorporal...; killed May 2, 1863 in battle of Chancellorsville, Va..

John F. Oliver, Captain, age 29, entered service for period of 3 years, June 4, 1861.

Company F: Resigned May 13, 1863; assigned to Provost Marshal's Bureau....

Joseph B. Oliver, Private, age 18, entered service for period of 3 years, June 26, 1861.

Company I: Veteran.

Lewis Olott, Private, age 44, entered service for period of 1 year, Oct. 4, 1864.

Company D: Mustered out with company Oct. 20, 1865.

John O'Neil, Private, age 25, entered service for period of 3 years, June 13, 1861.

Company F: Discharged March 25, 1863 on Surgeon's certificate of disability.

Thomas O'Neal, Private, age 20, entered service for period of 3 years, June 24, 1861.
Company K: Wounded May 8, 1862 in battle of McDowell, Va.; mustered out with company June 18, 1866.
George Osborn, Private, age 19, entered service for period of 3 years, Feb. 22, 1864.
Company B: no record given.
Gilbert Osborn, Private, age 36, entered service for period of 3 years, Feb. 24, 1864.
Company B: Discharged Feb. 24, 1866 at Columbia, S.C. by order of War Department.
John Osborn, Private, age 25, entered service for period of 3 years, June 10, 1861.
Company B; Transferred to Co. E June 13, 1864.
Company E: Transferred from Co. B June 13, 1864; mustered out July 16, 1864 at Columbus, Ohio on expiration of term of service.
Nathaniel C. Osborn, Private, age 19, entered service for period of 3 years, June 8, 1861.
Company D: Transferred to 12th Battery O.L.A. March 12, 1862.
Hiram Ostrander, Private, age 24, entered service for period of 3 years, June 12, 1861.
Company E: Discharged Nov. 18, 1861 on Surgeon's certificate of disability.
Jacob C. Ostrander, Private, age 41, entered service for period of 3 years, Dec. 29, 1863.
Company F: Died Sept. 4, 1865 in Regimental Hospital at Columbia, S.C.
Henry W. Outcalt, Private, age 21, entered service for period of 3 years, June 26, 1861.
Company H: Discharged July 16, 1862 at Camp Dennison, Ohio on Surgeon's certificate of disability.
Thomas J. Overman, Private, age 18, entered service for period of 3 years, Feb. 18, 1864.
Company E: Died Sept. 14, 1864 at Hilton Head, S.C..
Homer Overmeyer, Corporal, age 18, entered service for period of 3 years, Feb. 17, 1864.
Company E: Appointed Corporal Aug. 1, 1865; mustered out with company June 18, 1866.
John E. Oyer, Wagoner, age 21, entered service for period of 1 year, Sept. 26, 1864.
Company D: Discharged July 15, 1865 by order of the War Department.

P

Perry Panches, Private, age 22, entered service for period of 3 years, Sept. 16, 1864.
Company K: Discharged July 15, 1865 by order of War Department.

Harlan Page, Private, age 21, entered service for period of 3 years, June 24, 1864.
Company K: no record given.

John Page, Private, age 36, entered service for period of 3 years, July 1, 1861.
Company F: Drowned March 15, 1863 in Miami Canal at Delphos, Ohio.

Stephen Paint, Private, age 18, entered service for period of 3 years, June 20, 1861.
Company F: Discharged June 1, 1865 by order of War Department; veteran.

John T. Painter, Private, age 20, entered service for period of 3 years, June 26, 1861.
Company H: Wounded may 3, 1863 at battle of Chancellorsville, Va.; transferred to Co. C 75th O.V.I. Jan. 16, 1864; from Co. C 75th O.V.I. June 12, 1864; mustered out July 16, 1864 at Columbus, Ohio on expiration of term of service.

George H. Palmer, Sergeant, age 21, entered service for period of 3 years, June 24, 1861.
Company K: Appointed Corporal July 1, 1862; Sergeant May 28, 1863; wounded July 1, 1863 in battle of Gettysburg, Pa.; discharged Jan. 20, 1864 at Columbus, Ohio on Surgeon's certificate of disability.

Joseph A. Palm(er), Private, age…, entered service for a period of 3 years, June…,1861.
Company E: Resigned September, 1862; re-enlisted in Co. C, 54th Massachusetts Volunteer Infantry.

James Pancost, Private, age 18, entered service for period of 1 year, Sept. 22, 1864.
Company K: Discharged July 15, 1865 by order of War Department.

William Pancost, Private, age 21, entered service for period of 3 years, June 18, 1861.
Company G: Mustered out July 16, 1864 at Camp Chase, Ohio on expiration of term of service.

John W. Parish, 1st Sergeant, age 21, entered service for period of 3 years, Aug. 4, 1862.
Company F: Mustered as private; appointed Sergeant Jan. 25, 1864; 1st Sergeant Nov. 25, 1864; discharged July 15, 1865 by order of the War Department.

John P. Parrish, Private, age 35, entered service for period of 3 years, June 13, 1861.
Company F: Died Aug. 22, 1863 at Old Point Comfort, Va..
William P. Parrish. Private, age 22, entered service for period of 3 years, June13, 1861.
Company F: Mustered out July 16, 1864 on expiration of term of service.
David G. Parker, Private, age 21, entered service for period of 1 year, Nov. 30, 1864.
Company A: Mustered out Nov. 30, 1865 on expiration of term of service.
William D. Parker, Private, age 18, entered service for period of 1 year, Sept. 23, 1864.
Company A: Mustered out Sept. 23, 1865 on expiration of term of service.
Jacob Parmer, Private, age 27, entered service for period of 3 years, June 26, 1861.
Company H: no record given.
William P. Parrish, Private, age 22, entered service for period of 3 years, June 13, 1861.
Company F: Mustered out July 16, 1864 on expiration of term of service.
Frederick Passee, Private, age 20, entered service for period of 3 years, Oct. 9, 1862.
Company G: Transferred from Co...107th O.V.I. July 13, 1865; mustered out Oct. 9, 1865 on expiration of term of service.
James Paterson, Private, age 20, entered service for period of 1 year, Oct. 5, 1864.
Company F: no record given.
Jesse C. Patterson, Private, age 18 entered service for period of 3 years, June 5, 1861.
Company A: Mustered out July 16, 1864 on expiration of term of service.
William Patterson, Private, age 18, entered service for period of 1 year, Oct. 12, 1864.
Company D: Died Feb. 10, 1865 in hospital at Beaufort, S.C.
John Patten, Private, age 18, entered service for period of 3 years, July 10, 1861.
Company K: Discharged Feb. 12, 1863 on Surgeon's certificate of disability.
John L. Patton, Private, age 29, entered service for period of 3 years, June 10, 1861.
Company B: Wounded May 2, 1863 in battle of Chancellorsville, Va.; died July 20, 1864 on steamer enroute for New York.
George Peaver, Private, age 27, entered service for period of 1 year, Oct. 7, 1864.
Company D: Mustered out with company Oct. 20, 1865.

Edward Peck, Private, age 29, entered service for period of 3 years, July 18, 1861.

Company K: Killed Aug. 30, 1862 in battle of Bull Run, Va..

John F. Peck, Corporal, age 23, entered service for period of 3 years, June 5, 1861.

Company A: Wounded May 3, 1863 in battle of Chancellorsville, Va.; appointed Corporal...; transferred to 75th O.V.I. Jan. 15, 1864 by order of War Department.

Louis Pelleto, Private, age 42, entered service for period of 3 years, Feb. 29, 1864.

Company K: Wounded Dec. 6, 1864 in battle of Gregory's Landing, S.C.; discharged June 2, 1866 at Columbus, Ohio by order of War Department.

Elenander Pemberton, Sergeant, age 30, entered service for period of 3 years, June 12, 1861.

Company E: Appointed Corporal Nov. 1, 1861; Sergeant Sept. 1, 1862; discharged April 27, 1864 for wounds received July 1, 1863 in battle of Gettysburg, Pa.

James Pendleton, Private, age 45, entered service for period of 3 years, Jan. 4, 1864.

Company G: Transferred from Co. B 107th O.V.I. July 13, 1865; discharged Feb. 1, 1866 by order of War Department.

Greenberry Penn, Private, age 30, entered service for period of 3 years, June 26, 1861.

Company H: Discharged June 1, 1862 at Grafton, W. Va. on Surgeon's certificate of disability.

William Pentleton, Private, age 18, entered service for period of 3 years, Dec. 31, 1863.

Company G: Transferred from Co. B 107th O.V.I. July 13, 1865; mustered out with company June 18, 1866.

John Perdue, Private, age 20, entered service for period of 3 years, Feb. 23, 1864.

Company B: Wounded Nov. 30, 1864 in battle of Honey Hill, S.C.; died Dec. 17, 1864 in hospital at Hilton Head, S.C..

Henry Perkins, Private, age 26, entered service for period of 3 years, Feb. 12, 1862.

Company G: Died June 2, 1863 of wounds received May 2, 1863 in battle of Chancellorsville, Va..

Martin Perkins, Private, age 28, entered service for period of 1 year, Oct. 4, 1864.

Company D: Mustered out with company Oct. 20, 1865.

John A. Perkley, Private, age 22, entered service for period of 3 years, June 18, 1861.
Company G: Reduced from Sergeant...; transferred to Co. C 75th O.V.I. Jan. 16, 1864; from Co. C 75th O.V.I. June 12, 1864; mustered out July 16, 1864 on expiration of term of service.
Joseph S. Perry, 2d Lieutenant, age 24, entered service for period of 3 years, June 26, 1861.
Company I: Appointed 1st Sergeant from Corporal Feb. 1, 1862; wounded June 8, 1862 in battle of Cross Keys, Va.; promoted to 2d Lieutenant Sept. 5, 1862; discharged April 22, 1863 on Surgeon's certificate of disability.
Harris Peters, Private, age 34, entered service for period of 1 year, Aug. 24, 1864.
Company D: Mustered out July 15, 1865 by order of War Department.
Wilson H. Peterson, Private, age 21, entered service for period of 3 years, June 20, 1861.
Company F: Reduced from Corporal....; killed July 1, 1863 in battle of Gettysburg, Pa..
Robert A. Petrie, Private, age 20, entered service for period of 1 year, Sept 12, 1864.
Company K: Killed Feb. 8, 1865 in action at Combahee Ferry, S.C..
John Pettis, Private, age 18, entered service for period of 1 year, Sept. 12, 1864.
Company K: discharged July 15, 1865 by order of War Department.
James H. Petty, 1st. Lieutenant, age 30, entered service for period of 3 years, June 4, 1861.
Company I: Resigned Dec. 31, 1861.
Samuel Pfister, Private, age 18, entered service for period of 3 years, Dec. 31, 1863.
Company I: Transferred from Co. B 107th O.V.I. July 13, 1865; mustered out with company June 18, 1866.
Jacob Pheister, Private, age 20, entered service for period of 3 years, Feb. 22, 1864.
Company E: Mustered out with company June 18, 1866.
Abner J. Phelps, Private, age 42, entered service for period of 3 years, June 17, 1861.
Company D: Promoted to Q. M. Sergeant June 20, 1861.
Richard D. Phelps, 1st Sergeant, age 18, entered service for period of 3 years, June 12, 1861.
Company E: Wounded Dec. 13, 1861 in battle of Camp Alleghany, W. Va. and May 2, 1863 in battle of Chancellorsville, Va. and July 1, 1863 in battle of

Gettysburg, Pa; appointed Corporal Nov. 1, 1865; 1st Sergeant May 19, 1866; mustered out with company June 18, 1866; veteran.

David Phillip, Private, age 31, entered service for period of 1 year, Oct. 6, 1864.
Company F: Mustered out Oct. 6, 1865 on expiration of term of service.

Joseph Piccard, Private, age 18, entered service for period of 1 year, Oct. 7, 1864.
Company G: Mustered out Oct. 7, 1865 at Charleston, S.C. on expiration of term of service.

John Pierce, Sergeant, age 19, entered service for period of 3 years, June 10, 1861.
Company C: Appointed Corporal Nov. 19, 1861; Sergeant Jan. 1, 1863; killed July 3, 1863 in battle of Gettysburg, Pa..

William Pliss, Private, age 18, entered service for period of 3 years, Oct. 7, 1862.
Company G: no record given.

George M. Plummer, Private, age 26, entered service for period of 3 years, Feb. 22, 1864.
Company B: Wounded Dec. 9, 1864 in battle of Deveaux Neck, S.C.; died Feb. 5, 1865 in DeCamp Hospital, New York.

Cyrus Police, Private, age 20, entered service for period of 3 years, June 26, 1861.
Company H: no record given.

John Pool, Private, age 20, entered service for period of 3 years, June 13, 1861.
Company F: died Sept. 9, 1864 in U.S. Hospital, Philadelphia, Pa.; veteran.

Emit D. Porter, Private, age 18, entered service for period of 1 year, Sept. 26, 1864.
Company D: Mustered out July 15, 1865 by order of War Department.

Enoch Porter, Private, age 19, entered service for period of 3 years, Feb. 29, 1864.
Company B: Discharged June 15, 1865 at Hilton Head, S.C. by order of War Department.

William S. Porter, Corporal, age 19, entered service for period of 1 year, Sept. 24, 1864.
Company D: Appointed Corporal…; discharged July 15, 1865 by order of War Department.

Samuel B. Porterfield, Private, age 26, entered service for period of 3 years, June 5, 1861.
Company A: Discharged March 23, 1862 at Corryville, Md. on Surgeon's certificate disability.

David Potter, Corporal, age 21, entered service for period of 3 years, Feb. 23, 1864.

Company E: Wounded Nov. 30, 1864 in battle of Honey Hill, S.C. and April 15, 1865 in battle of Red Hill, S.C.; appointed Corporal June 1, 1866; mustered out with company June 18, 1866.

Barnibas Powell, Corporal, age 27, entered service for period of 3 years, June 10, 1861.

Company B: Discharged July 14, 1862 at Sperryville, Va. and promoted to 1st Lieutenant and Adjutant 3d Virginia Cavalry.

Isaac Powell, Private, age 30, entered service for period of 3 years, Feb. 27, 1864.

Company I: Mustered out with company June 18, 1864.

Isaac Powell, Private, age 28, entered service for period of 3 years, June 26, 1861.

Company I: Discharged March 18, 1863 on Surgeon's certificate of disability.

Albert Pratt, Private, age 19, entered service for period of 3 years, June 10, 1861.

Company C: Mustered out July 16, 1864 at Camp Chase, Ohio on expiration of term of service.

John L. Pratt, Private, age 23, entered service for period of 3 years, June 10, 1861.

Company B: Killed Sept. 13, 1861 in battle of Cheat Mountain, W. Va..

Samuel Prescott, Corporal, age 19, entered service for period of 3 years, June 10, 1861.

Company B: Appointed Corporal...; transferred to Co. C March 1, 1864; veteran.

Company C: Transferred from Co. B as Corporal March 20, 1864; appointed Sergeant Nov. 5, 1864; mustered out with company June 18, 1866; veteran.

Samuel Price, Corporal, age 43, entered service for period of 3 years, June 20, 1861.

Company F: Appointed Corporal Oct. 1, 1862; died Feb. 8, 1863 at Windmill Point, Va..

Christian Prister, Private, age 18, entered service for period of 3 years, Dec. 29, 1863.

Company I: no record given.

William Prouty, Private, age24, entered service for period of 1 year, Sept. 22, 1864.

Company C: Wounded Dec. 6, 1864 in battle of Deveaux Neck, S.C.; discharged July 15, 1865 by order of War Department.

Amida Province, Private, age 19, entered service for period of 3 years, June 10, 1861.

Company C: Wounded June 8, 1862 in battle of Cross Keys, Va.; discharged Oct. 25,1862 at Baltimore, Md. on Surgeon's certificate of disability.

James Province, Private, age 18, entered service for period of 3 years, June 10, 1861.

Company C: Wounded May 2, 1863 in battle of Chancellorsville, Va.; died June 6, 1863 at Brook's Station, Va..

Leander Province, Sergeant, age 21, entered service for period of 3 years, June 13, 1861.

Company F: Appointed from private July 13, 1862; died Jan. 18, 1863 at Bloomfield, Ohio.

Uriah Province, Private, age 23, entered service for period of 3 years, June 10, 1861.

Company C: Mustered out with company June 18, 1866; veteran.

James M . Pulver, Private, age 18, entered service for period of 3 years, June 8, 1861.

Company D: Transferred to 12th Battery O.L.A. March 12, 1862.

Eli Pyle, Corporal, age 28, entered service for period of 3 years, June 26, 1861.

Company H: Appointed Corporal April 1, 1864; killed Nov. 30, 1864 in battle of Honey Hill, S.C.; veteran.

Q

Michael Quinn, Private, age 19 entered service for period of 3 years, Dec. 30, 1863.

Company A: Transferred from 107th O.V.I. July 13, 1865; mustered out with company June 18, 1866

R

Jeremiah O. Ragan, Private, age 27, entered service for period of 3 years, Feb. 23, 1864.

Company B: Died Oct. 12, 1865 at Newberry, S.C..

John Ralston, Private, age 18, entered service for period of 1 year, Sept. 23, 1864.

Company D: Mustered out with company July 15, 1865.

George M. Ramsey, Private, age 31, entered service for period of 3 years, June 8, 1861.

Company D: Transferred to 12th Battery O.L.A. March 12, 1862.

Carrington E. Randall, Major, age 23, entered service for period of 3 years, June 12, 1861.

Promoted from Captain Co. G Aug. 11, 1864; died Dec. 16, 1864 or wounds received Nov. 30, 1864 in battle of Honey Hill, SC.

Company E: Appointed 1st Sergeant from Sergeant Sept. 1, 1861; promoted to 2d Lieutenant March 6, 1862; wounded May 2, 1863 in battle of Chancellorsville, Va.; promoted to 1st Lieutenant Co. G Oct 20, 1863.

Company G: Promoted to 1st Lieutenant from 2d Lieutenant Co. E Oct 20, 1862; Captain March 24, 1863; Major Aug. 11, 1864.

Campbell C. Rankin, Private, age 21, entered service for period of 3 years, June 5, 1861.

Company A: no record given.

Jonathan Ranney, Private, age 28, entered service for period of 9 months, Oct. 7, 1862.

Company K: Drafted; mustered out July 7, 1865 by order of War Department.

Fredoline Rantz, Private, age 43, entered service for period of 3 years, Dec. 19, 1863.

Company K: discharged June 18, 1865 by order of War Department.

George Raymond, Private, age 21, entered service for period of 3 years, June 26, 1861.

Company H: no record given.

William Reading, Private, age 18, entered service for period of 1 year, Sept. 26, 1864.

Company D: Mustered out July 15, 1865 by order of War Department.

John E. Rearick, Private, age 40, entered service for period of 3 years, June 12, 1861.

Company E: Wounded Dec. 13, 1861 in battle of Camp Alleghany, w. Va.; discharged March 14, 1864 on Surgeon's certificate of disability.

Isaac Reckner, Private, age 19, entered service for period of 3 years, Feb. 26, 1864.

Company B: Mustered out with company June 18, 1866.

John Reddicks, Private, age 21, entered service for period of 3 years, June 13, 1861.

Company F: Discharged June 25, 1861 on Surgeon's certificate of disability.

Albert Reed, Private, age 19, entered service for period of 1 year, Sept. 22, 1864.

Company C: Discharged July 15, 1865 by order of War Department.

George Reed, Private, age 26, entered service for period of 3 years, June 26, 1861.

Company H: Transferred to Co. C 75th O.V.I.; from Co. C 75th O.V.I. June 12, 1864; mustered out July 16, 1864 at Columbus, Ohio on expiration of term of service.

George W. Reed, Private, age 18, entered service for period of 3 years, June 26, 1861.

Company H: Transferred to Co. C 75th O.V.I.; from Co. C 75th O.V.I. June 12, 1864; mustered out July 16, 1864 at Columbus, Ohio on expiration of term of service.

Hines Reed, Private, age 20, entered service for period of 3 years, Feb. 27, 1862. Company G: Discharged Aug. 14, 1863 at Camp Convalescent, Va. on Surgeon's certificate of disability.

Samuel Reed, Private, age 24, entered service for period of 3 years, June 8, 1861.

Company D: Transferred to 12th Battery O.L.A. March 12, 1862.

Lowell Reese, Private, age 18, entered service for period of 3 years, Feb. 29, 1864.

Company B: Wounded Nov. 30, 1864 in battle of Honey Hill, S.C.; discharged June 16, 1865 at Camp Dennison, Ohio by order of the War Department.

Christian Resecker, Private, age 21, entered service for period of 3 years, June 10, 1861.

Company C: Transferred to Co. C 75th O.V.I. Jan. 16, 1864; from Co. C 75th O.V.I. May 6, 1864; mustered out July 16, 1864 at Camp Chase, Ohio on expiration of term of service.

Company E: Transferred to Co. C 75th O.V.I. Jan. 16, 1864; from Co. C 75th O.V.I. June 12, 1864; mustered out July 16, 1864 at Columbus, Ohio on expiration of term of service.

John M. Rhodes, Sergeant, age 22, entered service for period of 3 years, June 26, 1861.

Company I: Appointed Corporal June 1, 1862; wounded July 1, 1863 in battle of Gettysburg, Pa.; appointed Sergeant Aug. 6, 1864; promoted To Sergt. Major Sept. 1, 1865; veteran.

John S. Rhodes, Corporal, age 20, entered service for period of 3 years, June 26, 1861.

Company I: Appointed Corporal Aug. 1, 1865; discharged March 1, 1866 on Surgeon's certificate of disability.

Samuel N. Rhynard, Private, age 21, entered service for period of 3 years, June 10, 1861.

Company C: Transferred to Co. C 75th O.V.I. Jan. 16, 1864; from co. C 75th O.V.I. May 6, 1864; mustered out July 16, 1864 at Camp Chase, Ohio on expiration of term of service.

Josephus F. Rial, Private, age 25, entered service for period of 3 years, June 5, 1861.

Company A: Discharged May 10, 1862 at Huntersville, W. Va. on Surgeon's certificate of disability.

Emanuel Ribbetts, Private, age 35, entered service for period of 3 years, June 8, 1861.

Company D: Transferred to 12th Battery O.L.A. March 12, 1862.

George W. Rice, Private, age 18, entered service for period of 1 year, Oct. 11, 1864.

Company G: Mustered out Oct. 11, 1865 on expiration of term of service.

Joseph Rich, Private, age 19, entered service for period of 3 years, Feb. 1, 1864.

Company E: Mustered out with company June 18, 1866.

William H. Rich, Private, age 19, entered service for period of 1 year, Sept. 9, 1864.

Company I: discharged July 15, 1865 by order of War Department.

William H. Rich, Musician, age 18, entered service for period of 3 years, June 24, 1861.

Company K: Transferred to Co. C 75th O.V.I. Jan. 16, 1864; from Co. C 75th O.V.I. June 15, 1864; mustered out July 16, 1864 on expiration of term of service.

Allen Richards, Private, age 43, entered service for period of 3 years, Feb. 18, 1864.

Company K: discharged Aug. 11, 1865 on Surgeon's certificate of disability.

Frederick Richards, Private, age 27, entered service for period of 3 years, Feb. 15, 1864.

Company K: Wounded May (sic, Nov.) 30, 1864 in battle of Honey Hill, S.C.; discharged June 15, 1865 at Alexandria, Va. on Surgeon's certificate of disability.

John Richards, Private, age 23, entered service for period of 3 years, June 5, 1861.

Company A: Killed Dec. 13, 1861 in battle of Camp Alleghany, W. Va.

James L. Richardson, Private, age 18, entered service for period of 3 years, June 10, 1861.

Company C: Discharged April 29, 1863 at Chancellorsville, Va. to accept appointment as Cadet in West Point Military Academy.

William P. Richardson, Colonel, age 48, entered service for period of 3 years, June 22, 1861.

Field & Staff: Promoted from Lt. Col. May 16, 1862; wounded May 3, 1863 in battle of Chancellorsville, Va..breveted Brig. General, Dec. 7,1864; discharged May 9, 1866 by order of the War Department.

Joseph Richey, Private, age 22, entered service for period of 1 year, Sept. 5, 1864.

Company E: Discharged July 15, 1865 by order of War Department.

Matthias G. Richie, Private, age 42, entered service for period of 1 year, Oct. 1, 1864.

Company D: Mustered out with company Oct. 20, 1865.

William P. Richner, 1st Lieutenant, age22, entered service for period of 3 years, June 4, 1861.

Company C: Resigned Oct. 1, 1861.

Benjamin F. Rickey, Private, age 20, entered service for period of 3 years, June 26, 1861.

Company I: Discharged Oct. 21, 1862 for wounds received Aug. 29, 1862 in battle of Bull Run, Va..

Joseph Riddle, Private, age 22, entered service for period of 3 years, June 12, 1861.

Company E: Discharged July 2, 1862 on Surgeon's certificate of disability.

Thomas Riddle, Private, age 18, entered service for period of 1 year, Sept. 29, 1864.

Company D: Mustered out with company July 15, 1865 by order of War Department.

James Ridgeway, Corporal, age 18, entered service for period of 3 years, July 5, 1862.

Company C: Appointed Corporal March 1, 1864; died Jan. 4, 1865 at Hilton's Head, S.C. of wounds received Nov. 30, 1864 in battle of Honey Hill, South Carolina.

Benjamin Riglet, Private, age 18, entered service for period of 1 year, Oct. 8, 1864.

Company D: Mustered out with company Oct. 20, 1865.

Charles F. Riley, Private, age 19, entered service for period of 3 years, June 10, 1861.

Company C: Transferred to Co. C 75th O.V.I. Jan. 16, 1864; from Co. C 75th O.V.I. May 6, 1864; mustered out July 16, 1864 at Camp Chase, Ohio on expiration of term of service.

Charles T. Riley, Private, age 19, entered service for period of 3 years, June 26, 1861.

Company H: Transferred to Co. C 75th O.V.I. Jan. 16, 1864; from Co. C 75th O.V.I. June 12,1864; mustered out July 16, 1864 at Columbus, Ohio on expiration of term of service.

Emanuel L. Riley, Private, age 35, entered service for period of 3 years, June 5, 1861.

Company A: Wounded Aug. 30, 1862 at battle of Bull Run, Va.; discharged June 30, 1866 by order of the War Department; veteran.

Samuel N. Rinehard, Private, age 19, entered service for period of 3 years, June 10, 1861.
Company B: Wounded July 1, 1863 in battle of Gettysburg, Pa.; transferred to Co. C March 20, 1864; veteran.

Charles Ripkee, Private, age 40, entered service for period of 3 years, Jan. 4, 1864.
Company K: Transferred to Co. C 75th O.V.I. Jan. 16, 1864; from Co. C 75th O.V.I. June 15, 1864; mustered out with company June 18, 1866.

Joseph Ritchey, Private, age 22, entered service for period of 1 year, Sept. 5, 1864.
Company E: Discharged July 15, 1865 by order of War Department.

Elias M. Ritz, Private, age 18, entered service for period of 3 years, Jan. 4, 1864.
Company I: Transferred from Co. H 107th O.V.I. July 13, 1865; mustered out with company June 18, 1866.

John Ritz, Private, age 30, entered service for period of 3 years, June 10, 1861.
Company C: Transferred to Co. C 75th O.V.I. Jan. 16, 1864; from Co. C 75th O.V.I. May 6, 1864; mustered out July 16, 1864 at Camp Chase, Ohio on expiration of term of service

John Ritz, Private, age 30, entered service for period of 3 years, June 26, 1861.Company H: Transferred to Co. C 75th O.V.I. Jan. 16, 1864; from Co. C 75th O.V.I. June 12, 1864; mustered out July 16, 1864 at Columbus, Ohio on expiration of term of service.

James H. Roach, Private, age 24, entered service for period of 3 years, July 20, 1861.
Company H: discharged Aug. 27, 1862 at Fort McHenry, Va. on Surgeon's certificate of disability.

Zachariah T. Roach, Corporal, age 21, entered service for period of 3 years, June 26, 1861.
Company H: Died Nov, 7, 1881 in Huttonsville, W. Va..

Austin Robb, Private, age 17, entered service for period of 3 years, Aug. 16, 1862.
Company F: Discharged July 15, 1865 by order of War Department.

John E. Robb, Jr., Private, age 20, entered service for period of 1 year, August 18, 1864.
Company D: Mustered out July 15, 1865 by order of War Department.

Lewis Robber, Private, age 39, entered service for period of 3 years, June 12, 1861.
Company E: Discharged Feb. 9, 1863 on Surgeon's certificate of disability.

John J. Roberts, Private, age 25, entered service for period of 3 years, June 13, 1861.

Company F: Died Jan. 28, 1863 at Camp Parole Hospital, Annapolis, Md..

Peter Roberts, Private, age 21, entered service for period of 3 years, Feb. 22, 1864.

Company B: Mustered out with company June 18, 1866.

Henry B. Robins, Private, age 23, entered service for period of 3 years, February 15, 1864.

Company A: no record given.

Samuel M. Robinson, Private, age 21, entered service for period of 3 years, Feb. 29, 1864.

Company H: Wounded Dec. 6, 1864 in battle of Deveaux Neck, S.C.; discharged May 12, 1865 by order of War Department.

Charles F. Robison, Private, age 20, entered service for period of 3 years, June 18, 1861.

Company G: Mustered out July 16, 1864 at Camp Chase, Ohio on expiration of term of service.

Melvin O. Robison, Private, age 19, entered service for period of 3 years, June 27, 1861.

Company G: discharged June 25, 1862 at Alexandria, Va. for wounds received June 8, 1862 in battle of Cross Keys, Va..

Sanford E. Robison, Private, age 26, entered service for period of 1 year, Aug. 31. 1864.

Company C: discharged July 15, 1864 by order of War Department.

William Robison, Private, age 19, entered service for period of 3 years, June 27, 1861.

Company G: no record given.

Francis A. Rockafellow, Corporal, age 18, entered service for period of 3 years, Feb. 29, 1864.

Company G: Appointed Corporal Sept. 1, 1865; mustered out with company June 18, 1866.

Senaca C. Rodgers, Corporal, age 22, entered service for period of 3 years, June 26, 1861.

Company I: Wounded June 8, 1862 in battle of Cross Keys, Va.; appointed Corporal Jan. 1, 1866; mustered out with company June 18, 1866.

Charles C. Rodier, Private, age 18, entered service for period of 3 years, June 8, 1861.

Company D: Wounded Dec. 12, 1861 in battle of Camp Alleghany, W. Va.; transferred to 12th Battery O.L.A. March 12, 1862.

James A. Roland, Private, age 27, entered service for period of 3 years, June 26, 1861.

Company H: mustered out with company June 18, 1866; veteran.

George W. R. Rolf, Private, age 26, entered service for period of 1 year, Sept. 6, 1864.

Company E: Discharged July 16, 1865 by order of War Department.

Adam Romie, Private, age 18, entered service for period of 3 years, Feb. 19, 1864.

Company E: no record given.

James Romine, Private, age 17, entered service for period of 1 year, Sept. 12, 1864.

Company K: Discharged July 15, 1865 by order of War Department.

Christian Rosch, Private, age 34, entered service for period of 1 year, Sept. 13, 1863.

Company E: Discharged July 16, 1865 by order of War Department.

Frederick Rose, Private, age 21, entered service for period of 3 years, June 10, 1861.

Company B: Wounded May 2, 1863 in battle of Chancellorsville, Va.; transferred to Co. E June 13, 1864.

Company E: Transferred from Co. B June 13, 1864; mustered out July 16, 1864 at Columbus, Ohio on expiration of term of service.

Thomas Rose, Private, age 35, entered service for period of 3 years, June 24, 1861.

Company K: Wounded Aug. 30, 1862 in battle of Bull Run, Va.; discharged Dec. 5, 1862 at Alexandria, va. on Surgeon's certificate of disability.

August Rosina, Private, age 25, entered service for period of 1 year, Feb. 23, 1865.

Company C: Transferred from Co. F 107th O.V.I. July 13, 1865; mustered out Feb. 27, 1866 at Charleston, S.C. on expiration of term of service.

Eugene O. Ross, Corporal, age 18, entered service for period of 3 years, Feb. 19, 1864.

Company K: Appointed Corporal Feb. 1, 1864; discharged May 1, 1865 by order of War Department.

John W. Ross, 1st Lieutenant, age 33, entered service for period of 3 years, June 12, 1861.

Company F: Resigned April 21, 1862.

George Rouser, Private, age 30, entered service for period of 3 years, Jan. 22, 1864.

Company C: Transferred from Co. F 107th O.V.I. July 13, 1865; mustered out with company June18, 1866.

Lewis Row, Private, age 21, entered service for period of 1 year, Feb. 24, 1865.
Company C: Transferred from Co. F 107th O.V.I. July 13, 1865; mustered out
Feb. 26, 1866 at Charleston, S.C. on expiration of term of service.

Isaac Rucker, Private, age 22, entered service for period of 3 years, July 27,
1861.
Company E: Transferred to Co. C 75th O.V.I. Jan. 16, 1864; from Co. C 75th
O.V.I. June 12, 1864; mustered out July 16, 1864 at Columbus, Ohio on expiration of term of service.

John W. Rucker, Private, age 20, entered service for period of 3 years, June 26,
1861.
Company I: Died June 24, 1862 at Lynchburg, Va. while prisoner of war.

Gephard Rush, Private, age 20, entered service for period of 3 years, Feb. 20,
1864.
Company E: Mustered out with company June 18, 1866.

James Russel, Private, age 22, entered service for period of 3 years, June 5,
1861.
Company A: Wounded May 8, 1862 in battle of McDowell, Va. and July 1, 1863
in battle of Gettysburg, Pa.; transferred to 75th O.V.I. Jan. 13, 1864; from75th
O.V.I. June 15, 1864; mustered out July 16, 1864 on expiration of term of service.

John D. Russell, Private, age 24, entered service for period of 1 year, Oct. 7,
1864.
Company F: Mustered out Oct. 7, 1865 on expiration of term of service.

Robert S. Russell, Private, age 24, entered service for period of 3 years, June 26,
1861.
Company H: Reduced from Corporal Dec. 31, 1861; transferred to Co. C 75th
O.V.I. Jan. 16, 1864; from Co. C 75th O.V.I. June 12, 1864; mustered out July 16,
1864 at Columbus, Ohio on expiration of term of service.

James H. Rutherford, Private, age 20, entered service for period of 3 years, June
26, 1861.
Company I: no record given.

Robert Rutherford, Private, age 19, entered service for period of 3 years, June
10, 1861.
Company B: Transferred to Co. E June 13, 1864.
Company E: Transferred from Co. B June 13, 1864; mustered out July 16, 1864
at Columbus, Ohio on expiration of term of service.

Levi Ryan, Private, age 20, entered service for period of 3 years, June 5, 1861.
Company A: Wounded Dec. 12, 1861 in battle of Camp Alleghany, W. Va.;
veteran.

Peter Ryan, Private, age 38, entered service for period of 3 years, June 10, 1861. Company C: Transferred to Veteran Reserve Corps Aug. 1, 1863 by order of War Department.

S

Augustus Saltkied, Private, age 18, entered service for period of 3 years, Dec. 14, 1863.
Company H: Absent, sick Oct. 22, 1864; mustered out June 18, 1866 by order of War Department.
William Salts, Private, age 42, entered service for period of 1 year, Sept. 29, 1864.
Company F: no record given.
Benjamin F. Sanford, Corporal, age 21, entered service for period of 3 years, June 18, 1861.
Company G: no record given.
James W. Sanders, Private, age 18, entered service for period of 3 years, Aug. 16, 1862.
Company F: Wounded July 1, 1863 in battle of Gettysburg, Pa.; discharged July 15, 1865 by order of War Department.
Spencer Sanders, Private, age 18, entered service for period of 1 year, Oct. 8, 1864.
Company G: Mustered out Oct. 5, 1865 on expiration of term of service.
Senies Santer, Private, age 40, entered service for period of 3 years, Jan. 7, 1864.
Company K: Died Sept. 24, 1864 at David's Island, N.Y..
John H. Saunders, 1st Sergeant, age 28, entered service for period of 3 years, June 20, 1861.
Company F: Appointed Corporal Nov. 5, 1864; Sergeant June 1, 1865; 1st Sergeant July 15, 1865; mustered out with company June 18, 1866; veteran.
James Schallet, Private, age 21, entered service for period of 3 years, June 13, 1861.
Company F: Mustered out July 16, 1864 on expiration of term of service.
Ulric Schank, Private, age 21, entered service for period of 3 years, Dec. 15, 1863.
Company C: Transferred from Co. F 107th O.V.I. July 13, 1865; mustered out with company June 18, 1866.
Jacob Scharff, Private, age 29, entered service for period of 1 year, Feb. 24, 1865.
Company C: Transferred from Co. F 107th O.V.I......; mustered out Feb. 24, 1866 at Charleston, S.C. on expiration of term of service.

George Schaub, Private, age 21, entered service for period of 1 year, Sept. 29, 1864.

Company G: Discharged Oct. 1, 1865 by order of War Department.

George Schaulm, Private, age 30, entered service for period of 3 years, Jan. 4, 1864.

Company G: Transferred from Co. A 107th O.V.I. July 13, 1865; mustered out with company June 18, 1866.

Lorenzo Shecklee, Private, age 18, entered service for period of 3 years, June 26, 1861.

Company I: Killed Dec. 13, 1861 in battle of Camp Alleghany, W. Va..

Francis Schenhart, Private, age 38, entered service for period of 3 years, June 10, 1861.

Company C: Wounded Aug. 29, 1862 in battle of Bull Run, Va. and July 1, 1863 in battle of Gettysburg, Pa.; transferred to Co. C 75th O.V.I. Jan. 16, 1864; from So. C 75th O.V.I. May 6, 1864; mustered out July 16, 1864 at Camp Chase, Ohio on expiration of term of service.

John Schmale, Private, age 24, entered service for period of 3 years, Sept. 30, 1862.

Company I: Transferred from 107th O.V.I. July 13, 1865; mustered out Oct. 19, 1865 on expiration of term of service.

Fred Schmidt, Private, age 27, entered service for period of 3 years, Dec. 22, 1863.

Company K: Transferred to co. C 75th O.V.I. Jan. 16, 1864; from Co. C 75th O.V.I. June 15, 1864; mustered out with company June 13 (sic, 18), 1866.

Martin Schmidt, Private, age 35, entered service for period of 1 year, Oct. 1, 1864.

Company I: Wounded Dec. 6, 1864 in battle of Gregory's Landing, S.C.; mustered out Sept. 30, 1865 on expiration of term of service.

Fred Schnauffer, Private, age 20, entered service for period of 3 years, June 8, 1861.

Company D: Transferred to 12th Battery O.L.A. March 12, 1862.

Austen Schneider, Private, age 17, entered service for period of 3 years, Nov. 1, 1862.

Company K: Transferred form Co.....107th O.V.I. July 13, 1865; mustered out Nov. 1, 1865 on expiration of term of service.

LeRoy W. Schofield, Private, age 18, entered service for period of 1 year, Oct. 11, 1864.

Company A: Mustered out Oct. 11, 1865 on expiration of term of service.

Julius Schoneway, Private, age 26, entered service for period of 3 years, Feb. 24, 1864.
Company I: Transferred from co....107th O.V.I. July 13, 1865; mustered out with company June 18, 1866.
Francis Schonhart, Private, age 38, entered service for period of 3 years, June 26, 1861.
Company H: Transferred to Co. C 75th O.V.I. Jan. 16, 1864; from Co. C 75th O.V.I. June 12, 1864; mustered out July 16, 1864 at Columbus, Ohio on expiration of term of service.
Frederick Schonning, Private, age 27, entered service for period of 1 year, Sept. 23, 1864.
Company C: Discharged July 15, 1865 by order of War Department.
John Schorr, Private, age 25, entered service for period of 3 years, Nov. 1, 1862.
Company K: Transferred from Co. .. 107th O.V.I. July 13, 1865; mustered out Nov. 1, 1865 on expiration of term of service.
Joseph Schropp, Private, age 44, entered service for period of 3 years, Jan. 1, 1864.
Company K: Transferred to Co. C 75th O.V.I. Jan. 16, 1864; from Co. C 75th O.V.I. June 15, 1864; mustered out with company June 18, 1866.
George Schualm, Private, age 30, entered service for period of 3 years, Jan. 4, 1864.
Company G: Transferred from Co. A 107th O.V.I. July 13, 1865; mustered out with company June 18, 1866.
Christian Schultz, Private, age 27, entered service for period of 3 years, Dec. 23, 1863.
Company I: Transferred form Co....107th O.V.I. July 13, 1865.
Frederick Schultz, Corporal, age 22, entered service for period of 3 years, June 12, 1861.
Company E: Wounded July 1, 1863 in battle of Gettysburg, Pa.; appointed Corporal Nov. 1, 1864; veteran.
Charles S. Schupp, Private, age 41, entered service for period of 1 year, Oct. 4, 1864.
Company I: Wounded April 15, 1864 in Battle of Red Hill, S.C.; mustered out Sept. 30, 1865 on expiration of term of service.
Charles Schwarage, Private, age 19, entered service for period of 1 year, Sept. 20, 1864.
Company I: Discharged July 15, 1865 by order of War Department.

Gottleib Schwartz, Private, age 39, entered service for period of 3 years, Sept. 30, 1862.

Company I: Transferred from 107th O.V.I. July 13, 1865; mustered out Oct. 18, 1865 on expiration of term of service.

Alexander Scott, Private, age 19 entered service for period of 3 years, June 12, 1861.

Company E: Died Dec. 10, 1862 at Alexandria, Va..

David P. Scott, Sergeant, age 19, entered service for period of 3 years, June 13, 1861.

Company F; Appointed Corporal Oct. 4, 1862; Sergeant....16, 1863; transferred to Co. C 75th O.V.I. Jan. 16, 1864; from Co. C 75th O.V.I. June 12, 1864; mustered out July 16, 1864 on expiration of term of service.

Elbridge Scott, Private, age 18, entered service for period of 1 year, Oct. 12, 1864.

Company G: Died Dec. 28, 1865 at Hilton Head, S.C. of wounds received in battle of Honey Hill, S.C..

George A. Scott, Private, age 24, entered service for period of 1 year, Oct. 15, 1864.

Company E: Mustered out Oct. 15, 1865 on expiration of term of service.

Jefferson Scott, Musician, age 18, entered service for period of 1 year, Sept. 26, 1864.

Company D: Mustered out July 8, 1865 at Washington, D.C. by order of War Department.

William P. Scott, Captain, age 23, entered service for period of 3 years, June 24, 1861.

Company A: Promoted to 1st Lieutenant Co. K May 25, 1864; Captain February 10, 1864; wounded April 9, 1865 in action at Statesburg, S.C.; mustered out with company June 18, 1866; veteran.

Company K: Wounded May 3, 1863 in battle of Chancellorsville, Va.; appointed 1st Sergeant from Sergeant Jan. 1 1864; promoted to 2d Lieutenant March 16, 1864; 1st Lieutenant Co. A May 25, 1864; veteran.

Hugh Scullen, Private, age 19, entered service for period of 1 year, Oct. 2, 1864.

Company I: died Dec. 15, 1864 of wounds received Nov. 30, 1864 in battle of Honey Hill, S.C..

John Seagrist, Private, age35, entered service for period of 3 years, June 24, 1861.

Company K: discharged Nov. 27, 1861 at Cheat Mountain, W. Va. on surgeon's certificate of disability.

Jefferson Selot, Musician, age 18, entered service for period of 1 year, Sept. 26, 1864.
Company D: Mustered out July 8, 1865 at Washington D.C. by order of War Department.
John Serrells, Corporal, age 34, entered service for period of 3 years, June 20, 1861.
Company F: Appointed Corporal July 1, 1865; discharged May 4, 1866 by order of War Department.
Michael Sessing, Private, age 38, entered service for period of 3 years, Oct. 4, 1864.
Company I: Mustered out Sept. 30, 1865 on expiration of term of service.
Edward H. Severance, 1st Lieutenant, age 25, entered service for period of 3 years, June 24, 1861.
Company H: Promoted to 2d Lieutenant from 1st Sergeant Co. K May 16, 1862; 1st Lieutenant Sept. 11, 1862.
Company K: promoted to 2d Lieutenant Co. H May 16, 1862.
John Sey, Private, age 29, entered service for period of 3 years, Oct 11, 1862.
Company K: Transferred from Co....107th O.V.I. July 13, 1865; mustered out Oct. 11, 1865 on expiration of term of service.
Francis M. Shacklee, Corporal, age 31, entered service for period of 3 years, June 26, 1861.
Company I: Discharged Feb. 15, 1862 to accept promotion as Captain Co. I 20th O.V.I..
George W. Shafer, Private, age 22, entered service for period of 3 years, June 26, 1861.
Company I: Transferred to Co. C 75th O.V.I. Jan. 16, 1864; from Co. C 75th O.V.I. June 12, 1864; mustered out July 16, 1864 on expiration of term of service.
Michael Shaffer, Private, age 38, entered service for period of 1 year, Oct. 3, 1864.
Company D: Killed Nov. 30, 1864 in battle of Honey Hill, South Carolina.
Nelson H. Shaffer, Private, age 18, entered service for period of 3 years, June 24, 1861.
Company K: Transferred to Co. C 75th O.V.I. Jan. 16, 1864; from Co. C 75th O.V.I. June 1, 1864; mustered out July 16, 1864 on expiration of term of service.
William S. Shaner, Private, age 18, entered service for period of 3 years, June 5, 1861.
Company A: Mustered out July 16, 1864 at Columbus Ohio on expiration of term of service.
Company B: Musician. Transferred to Co. A June 16, 1864.

Alexander Shannon, Private, age 18, entered service for period of 3 years, June 20, 1861.
Company F: Died Nov. 11, 1862 in U.S. General Hospital at Fairfax Seminary, Va..
James S. Shannon, Private, age 35, entered service for period of 3 years, June 20, 1861.
Company F: Died Oct. 11, 1862 in hospital at Georgetown, District of Columbia.
Lewis F. Shannon, Sergeant, age 25, entered service for period of 3 years, June 24, 1861.
Company K: Killed Aug. 30, 1862 in battle of Bull Run, Virginia.
William F. Shannon, Private, age 20, entered service for period of 3 years, June 20, 1861.
Company F: Died March 2, 1865 at Hilton Head, S.C.; veteran.
Jesse Sharette, Private, age 24, entered service for period of 3 years, June 8, 1861.
Company D: Transferred to 12th Battery O.L.A. March 12, 1862.
John H. Sharette, Private, age 24, entered service for period of 3 years, June 8, 1861.
Company D: Transferred to 12th Battery O.L.A. March 12, 1862.
Edwin Sharp, Private, age 18, entered service for period of 3 years, Aug. 7, 1862.
Company E: Wounded Dec. 6, 1864 in battle of Gregory's Landing, S.C.; discharged July 15, 1865 by order of War Department.
John Shaub, Private, age 18, entered service for period of 3 years, Oct. 20, 1862.
Company I: Transferred from 107th O.V.I. July 13, 1865; mustered out Oct. 19, 1865 on expiration of term of service.
Harrison Shaw, Corporal, age 18, entered service for period of 3 years, June 26, 1861.
Company I: Wounded July 1, 1863 in battle of Gettysburg, Pa.; appointed Corporal April 1, 1865; mustered out with company June 18, 1866; veteran.
Henry C. Shaw, Private, age 19, entered service for period of 1 year, Oct. 19, 1864.
Company H; Mustered out Oct. 18, 1865 on expiration of term of service.
Samuel Shaw, Private, age 18, entered service for period of 3 years, Jan. 11, 1864.
Company F: Died Oct. 24, 1864 in hospital at Hilton Head, South Carolina.
William H. Shaw, Corporal, age 21, entered service for period of 3 years, June 26, 1861.
Company I: Appointed Corporal Dec. 1, 1863; died Nov. 28, 1864 at Hilton Head, S.C.; veteran.

Lorenzo Shecklee, Private, age 18, entered service for period of 3 years, June 26, 1861.
Company I: Killed Dec. 13, 1861, in battle of Camp Alleghany, W. Va..
Thomas B. Sheets, Private, age 18, entered service for period of 3 years, June 26, 1861.
Company H: Wounded May 3, 1863 in battle of Chancellorsville, Va. and Nov. 30, 1864 in battle of Honey Hill, S. C.; mustered out with company June 18, 1866; veteran.
Edward Shenewark, Private, age 22, entered service for period of 1 year, Oct. 12, 1864.
Company G: Muster out Oct. 12, 1865 on expiration of term of service.
William V. B. Shepler, Private, age 37, entered service for period of 1 year, Oct. 4, 1864.
Company H: Mustered out Oct. 7, 1865 on expiration of term of service.
Joseph Sheppard, Private, age 34, entered service for period of 3 years, Oct. 6, 1862.
Company I: Transferred from 107th O.V.I. July 13, 1865; mustered out Oct. 15, 1865 on expiration of term of service.
Aaron Shereman, Private, age 18, entered service for period of 3 years, Aug. 16, 1862.
Company F: no record given.
Hiram S. Sherman, Private, age 18, entered service for period of 3 years, Feb. 27, 1864.
Company B: Died April 2, 1865 at Carver Hospital, Washington, D.C..
Richard M. Sherman, Private, age 18, entered service for period of 3 years, June 24, 1861.
Company K: no record given.
Isaac Sherrick, Private, age 34, entered service for period of 1 year, Oct. 4, 1864.
Company F: Mustered out Oct. 4, 1865 on expiration of term of service.
Bazil C. Shields, Sergeant, age 20, entered service for period of 3 years, June 13, 1861.
Company F: Appointed from private Feb. 2, 1863; killed July 1, 1863 in battle of Gettysburg, Pa..
James I. Shields, Private, age 23, entered service for period of 3 years, Aug. 4, 1862.
Company F: Appointed Corporal Oct. 4, 1863; Sergeant Aug. 1, 1864; reduced to ranks June 1, 1865; discharged July 15, 1865 by order of War Department.

Samuel G. Shirk, 1st Sergeant, age 20, entered service for period of 3 years, June 26, 1861.

Company I: Wounded Aug. 19, 1862 in battle of Bull Run, Va. and July 1, 1863 in battle of Gettysburg, Pa.; appointed Sergeant from Corporal June 20, 1864; wounded Nov. 30, 1864 in battle of Honey Hill, S.C.; appointed 1st Sergeant April 1, 1865; mustered out with company June 18, 1866; veteran.

John W. Shirley, Private, age 27, entered service for period of 1 year, Oct. 6, 1864.

Company A: Mustered out Oct. 6, 1865 on expiration of term of service.

Stephen M. Shirely, Private, age 29, entered service for period of 1 year, Sept. 12, 1864.

Company K: Wounded April 15, 1865 in battle of Red Hill, S.C.; discharged Aug. 15, 1865 at Charleston, S.C. on Surgeon's certificate of disability.

Francis Shonhart, Private, age 38, entered service for period of 3 years, June 10, 1861.

Company C: Wounded Aug. 29, 1962 in battle of Bull Run, Va. and July 1, 1863 in battle of Gettysburg, Pa.; transferred to Co. C 75th O.V.I. Jan. 16, 1864; from Co. C 75th O.V.I. May 6, 1864; mustered out July 16, 1864 at Camp Chase, Ohio on expiration of term of service.

Frederick Shonning, Private, age 27, entered service for period of 1 year, Sept. 23, 1864.

Company C: Discharged July 15, 1865 by order of War Department.

John W. Shotwell, Private, age 18, entered service for period of 1 year, Oct. 5, 1864.

Company G: Wounded Nov. 30, 1864 in battle of Honey Hill, S. C.; mustered out Oct. 5, 1865 on expiration of term of service.

John Shoup, Private, age 18, entered service for period of 3 years, Feb. 29, 1864.
Company E: Discharged Oct. 11, 1865 for wounds received Nov. 30, 1864 in battle of Honey Hill, S.C..

John Shriver, Private, age 33, entered service for period of 1 year, Sept. 3, 1864.
Company C: Discharged July 15, 1865 by order of War Department.

Levi Shroyer, Private, age 20, entered service for period of 3 years, Feb. 29, 1864.

Company E: Wounded Dec. 6, 1864 in battle of Gregory's Landing, S.C..

William D. Shuman, Private, age 18, entered service for period of 3 years, Feb. 17, 1864.

Company E: Discharged July 21, 1865 by order of War Department.

George Shure, Private, age 39, entered service for period of 3 years, Feb. 26, 1864.

Company K: Killed Nov. 30, 1864 in battle of Honey Hill, South Carolina.

Nelson Shutt, Private, age 36, entered service for period of 3 years, Feb. 29, 1864.

Company B: Discharged March 12, 1866 at Charleston, S.C. by order of War Department.

Levi Shroyer, Private, age 20, entered service for period of 3 years, Feb. 29, 1864.

Company E: Wounded Dec. 6, 1864 in battle of Gregory's Landing, S.C..

Joseph Skinner, Private, age 21, entered service for period of 3 years, Feb. 27, 1864.

Company B: Died March 15, 1865 at DeCamp Hospital, New York.

Norton G. Skinner, Private, age 37, entered service for period of 3 years, June 12, 1861.

Company E: discharged Dec. 18, 1862 on Surgeon's certificate of disability.

Charles H. Silcox, Sergeant, age 22, entered service for period of 3 years, June 18, 1861.

Company G; Mustered as private; appointed Sergeant...; died Aug. 23, 1865 at Columbia, S.C. of wounds received...in action; veteran.

James W. Simpkins, Private, age 20, entered service for period of 3 years, July 7, 1861.

Company G: no record given.

William Simpson, Private, age 19, entered service for period of 3 years, July 14, 1862.

Company A: Discharged Sept. 16, 1863 at Washington, D.C. for wounds received May 3, 1863 in battle of Chancellorsville, Va.

Alexander Sinclair, 2d Lieutenant, age 28, entered service for period of 3 years, June 10, 1861.

Company C: Appointed 1st Sergeant from Sergeant Aug. 11, 1861; promoted to 2d Lieutenant March 12, 1862; 1st Lieutenant Co. K, July 30, 1862.

Company K: Promoted from 2d Lieutenant Co. C July 30, 1862; killed May 2, 1863 in battle of Chancellorsville, Va..

Francis M. Sinclair, 1st Lieutenant, age 22, entered service for period of 3 years, June 4, 1861.

Company C: Promoted from 2d Lieutenant Jan. 9, 1862; discharged March 6, 1862.

Robert C. Sisson, Musician, age 18, entered service for period of 3 years, Feb. 29, 1864.

Company K: Mustered out with company June 18, 1866.

Norton G. Skinner, Private, age 37, entered service for period of 3 years, June 12, 1861.

Company E: Discharged Dec. 18, 1862 on Surgeon's certificate of disability.

Charles Slaughterback, Private, age 41, entered service for period of 3 years, June 12, 1861.

Company E: Wounded June 8, 1862 in battle of Cross Keys, Va.; discharged Dec. 16, 1863 on Surgeon's certificate of disability.

Orlando Sline, Private, age 18, entered service for period of 1 year, Sept. 25, 1864.

Company D: Mustered out July 15, 1865 by order of War Department.

Charles Smith, Private, age 30, entered service for period of 3 years, June 5, 1861.

Company A: discharged Nov. 10, 1862 at Wheeling, W. Va. on Surgeon's certificate of disability.

Charles A. Smith, Musician, age 18, entered service for period of 1 year, Sept. 26, 1864.

Company H: Mustered out Sept. 26, 1865 on expiration of term of service.

Charles A. Smith, Corporal, age 24, entered service for period of 3 years, June 24, 1861.

Company K: Wounded June 8, 1862 in battle of Cross Keys, Va. and Nov. 30, 1864 in battle of Honey Hill, S.C.; appointed Corporal April 1, 1866; veteran.

Charles E. Smith, Private, age 24, entered service for period of 3 years, July 22, 1864.

Company C: Mustered out with company June 18, 1866.

Charles W. Smith, Private, age…, entered service for period of 3 years, Sept. 6, 1864.

Company K: Wounded April 15, 1865 in battle of Red Hill, S.C.; discharged May 1, 1865 on Surgeon's certificate of disability.

Conrad Smith, Private, age 43, entered service for period of 3 years, June 18, 1861.

Company G: Wounded June 8, 1862 in battle of Cross Keys, Va.; transferred to Veteran Reserve Corps…by order of War Department.

Dwight K. Smith, Private, age 18, entered service for period of 3 years, Feb. 22, 1864.

Company B: Mustered out June 18, 1866 by order of the War Department.

Florean Smith, Private, age 36, entered service for period of 3 years, June 12, 1861.

Company E: Discharged Dec. 18, 1862 on Surgeon's certificate of disability.

Isaac Smith, Private, age 36, entered service for period of 3 years, June 13, 1861.

Company F: Discharged Jan. 20, 1862 on Surgeon's certificate of disability.

James R. Smith, 1st Sergeant, age 20, entered service for period of 3 years, June 24, 1861.

Company K: Appointed Corporal Sept. 6, 1863; Sergeant April 1, 1864; 1st Sergeant Nov. 5, 1864; mustered out with company June 18, 1866; veteran.

John Smith, Private, age 39, entered service for period of 1 year, Sept. 14, 1864.

Company K: Discharged July 15, 1865 by order of War Department.

John J. Smith, Private, age 32, entered service for period of 3 years, June 26, 1861.

Company I: Mustered out July 16, 1864 on expiration of term of service.

John W. Smith, Private, age 18, entered service for period of 3 years, June 18, 1861.

Company G: Discharged Sept. 14, 1863 at Columbia Hospital, Washington, D.C. by order of War Department.

Joseph Smith, Private, age 34, entered service for period of 1 year, Sept. 24, 1864.

Company C; Discharged July 15, 1865 by order of War Department.

Joseph R. Smith, Private, age 38, entered service for period of 1 year, Sept. 8, 1864.

Company C: Discharged July 15, 1865 by order of War Department.

Joseph B. Smith, Private, age 35, entered service for period of 3 years, Feb. 29, 1864.

Company K: Discharged Aug. 2, 1865 at Hilton Head, S.C. on Surgeon's certificate of disability.

Joseph Smith, Private, age 34, entered service for period of 1 year, Sept. 24, 1864.

Company C: Discharged July 15, 1865 by order of War Department.

Joseph Smith, Private, age 43, entered service for period of 1 year, Sept. 26, 1864.

Company F: no record given.

Joseph R. Smith, Private, age 38, entered service for period of 1 year, Sept. 8, 1864.

Company C: Discharged July 15, 1865 by order of War Department.

Lem S. Smith, Private, age 18, entered service for period of 3 years, Feb. 24, 1864/

Company G: Mustered out with company June 18, 1866.

Mortimore Smith, Private, age 18, entered service for period of 3 years, June 10, 1861.
Company C: Died Nov. 30, 1861 at Huttonsville, W. Va..
Oliver P. Smith, Private, age 21, entered service for period of 3 years, June 10, 1861.
Company B: Wounded Aug. 29, 1862 in battle of Bull Run, Va.; discharged Jan. 7, 1863 at Columbus, Ohio on Surgeon's certificate of disability.
Peter Smith, Private, age 26, entered service for period of 3 years, June 26, 1861.
Company H: no record given.
William Smith, Private 26, entered service for period of 3 years, June 10, 1861.
Company B: Discharged May 7, 1862 on Surgeon's certificate of disability.
William S. Smith, Private, age 21, entered service for period of 3 years, June 26, 1861.
Company I: Mustered out with company June 18, 1866; veteran.
Zenas Smith, Sergeant, age 21, entered service for period of 3 years, June 5, 1861.
Company A: no record given
John R. Smithson, Private, age 20, entered service for period of 3 years, June 8, 1861.
Company D: Transferred to 12th Battery O.L.A. March 12, 1862.
James Smitzer, Private, age 18, entered service for period of 1 year, Sept. 29, 1864.
Company G: Died July 17, 1865 at Hilton Head, S.C..
William L Smoot, Private, age 21, entered service for period of 3 years, June 26, 1861.
Company H: Transferred to Co. C 75th O.V.I. Jan. 16, 1864; from Co. C 75th O.V.I. June 12, 1864; mustered out July 16, 1864 at Columbus, Ohio on expiration of term of service.
Henry Smuck, Private, age 23, entered service for period of 3 years, June 12, 1961.
Company E: Wounded May 2, 1863 in battle of Chancellorsville, Va. and July 1, 1863 in battle of Gettysburg, Pa.; transferred to Veteran Reserve Corps Jan. 15, 1864 by order of War Department.
Albert M. Snook, Private, age 17, entered service for period of 1 year, Feb. 26, 1865.
Company C: Mustered out Feb. 27, 1866 at Charleston, S.C. on expiration of term of service.

James Snyder, Private, age 18, entered service for period of 3 years, June 10, 1861.

Company B: Wounded July 1, 1863 in battle of Gettysburg, Pa.; transferred to Co. C. March 20, 1864.

Company C: Transferred from Co. B March 20, 1864; mustered out July 16, 1864 at Camp Chase, Ohio on expiration of term of service.

John S. Snyder, 2d Lieutenant, age 22, entered service for period of 3 years, June 26, 1861.

Company E: Promoted from 1st Sergeant Co. I May 25, 1864: mustered out July 16, 1864 on expiration of term of service.

Company I: (listed as John H. Snyder) Appointed from Sergeant Jan. 1, 1863; promoted to 2d Lieutenant Co. E May 25, 1865; veteran.

Jeremiah Snyder, Private, age 18, entered service for period of 3 years, June 8, 1861.

Company D: Transferred to 12th Battery O.L.A. March 12, 1862.

Edwin Soper, Private, age 18, entered service for period of 3 years, March 11, 1864.

Company B: no record given.

John G. Sparks, Private, age 33, entered service for period of 3 years, June 18, 1861.

Company G; Mustered out with company June 18, 1866; veteran.

John N. Sparks, Private, age 18, entered service for period of 3 years, June 8, 1861.

Company D; Transferred to 12th Battery O.L.A. March 12, 1862.

William H. Spear, Corporal, age 23, entered service for period of 3 years, June 5, 1861.

Company A: Died May 29, 1862 at Franklin Va. of wounds received May 8, 1862 in battle of McDowell, Virginia.

Benjamin H. Spelter, Private, age 19, entered service for period of 3 years, June 18, 1861.

Company G: Discharged June 30, 1861 by writ of habeas corpus.

Amos Spieglemiere, Private, age 18, entered service for period of 1 year, Sept. 22, 1864.

Company C: Discharged July 15, 1864 by order of War Department.

Joel Spohn, Private, age 22, entered service for period of 3 years, June 12, 1861.

Company E: Wounded June 8, 1862 in battle of Cross Keys, Va. and May 2, 1863 in battle of Chancellorsville, Va.; transferred to Co. C 75th O.V.I. Jan 12, 1864; from Co. C 75th O.V.I. July 12, 1864; mustered out July 16, 1864 at Columbus, Ohio on expiration of term of service.

Uriah Springer, Private, age 18, entered service for period of 3 years, Feb. 15, 1864.

Company C: nor record given.

William C. Springer, Private, age 21, entered service for period of 3 years, Feb. 15, 1864.

Company C; Discharged May 4, 1865 at New York City by order of War Department.

Robert W. Spurrier, Private, age 29, entered service for period of 3 years, June 26, 1861.

Company H: Wounded May 3, 1863 in battle of Chancellorsville, Va.; mustered out July 16, 1864 on expiration of term of service.

William Squire, Private, age 23, entered service for period of 1 year, Oct. 4, 1861.

Company F: Mustered out Oct, 4, 1865 on expiration of term of service.

William Stack, Private, age 21, entered service for period of 3 years, June 26, 1861.

Company H: no record given.

Lavander Stacy, Private, age 23, entered service for period of 1 year, Sept. 17, 1864.

Company C: Discharged July 15, 1865 by order of War Department.

William M. Stager, Private, age 22, entered service for period of 3 years, June 20, 1861.

Company F: Reduced from Corporal….; transferred to Co. C 75th O.V.I. Jan. 16, 1864; from Co. C 75th O.V.I. June 12, 1864; mustered out July 16, 1864 on expiration of term of service.

Benjamin Staley, Private, age 28, entered service for period of 3 years, June 12, 1861.

Company E: no record given.

Abraham Starkey, Private, age 18, entered service for period of 3 years, Feb. 26, 1864.

Company B: Wounded Nov. 30, 1864 in battle of Honey Hill, S.C.; mustered out with company June 18, 1866.

John W. Starkey, Private, age 18, entered service for period of 3 years, March 9, 1864.

Company B: Mustered out with company June 18, 1866.

Silas Starkey, Private, age 18, entered service for period of 3 years, June 18, 1861.

Company G: no record given.

Edward Stebbins, Private, age 18, entered service for period of 3 years, Feb. 17, 1864.

Company B: Mustered out with company June 18, 1866.

Henry Stedwell, Corporal, age 21, entered service for period of 3 years, June 8, 1861.

Company D: Transferred to 12th Battery O.L.A. March 12, 1862.

William H. Steed, Private, age 18, entered service for period of 3 years, Nov. 1, 1863.

Company C: Mustered out with company June 18, 1866.

John Steel, Private, age 33, entered service for period of 3 years, June 18, 8161.

Company G: Mustered out with company June 18, 1866; veteran.

William Steel, Private, age21, entered service for period of 3 years, June 18, 1861.

Company G: no record given.

Asbury C. Stephens, Private, age 21, entered service for period of 3 years, June 26, 1861.

Company I: Wounded May 8, 1862 in battle of McDowell, Va.; discharged July 10, 1862 on Surgeon's certificate of disability.

Henry Stephens, Private, age 39, entered service for period of 3 years, Feb. 17, 1864.

Company K: no record given.

Joseph R. Steunbaugh, Private, age 26, entered service for period of 3 years, Feb. 24, 1864.

Company I: Transferred from Co....107th O.V.I. July 13, 1865; mustered out with company June 18, 1866.

Abednego Stevens, Private, age 23, entered service for period of 3 years, June 12, 1861.

Company E: Wounded July 1, 1863 in battle of Gettysburg, Pa.; transferred to Veteran Reserve Corps Nov. 6, 1863 by order of War Department.

Emanuel Stevens, Corporal, age 18, entered service for period of 1 year, Sept. 20, 1864.

Company D: Appointed Corporal...; wounded Nov. 30, 1864 in battle of Honey Hill, S.C.; died Jan. 19, 1865 at Hilton Head Hospital, S.C..

George Stevens, Private, age 18, entered service for period of 3 years, March 9, 1864.

Company B: Mustered out with company June 18, 1866.

John W. Stevens, Private, age 19, entered service for period of 3 years, July 1, 1861.

Company H: Veteran.

Reuben Stevens, Private, age 26, entered service for period of 1 year, Oct. 7, 1864.

Company G: Mustered out Oct. 7, 1865 on expiration of term of service.

Thomas Stevenson, Musician, age 25, entered service for period of 3 years, July 8, 1861.

Company I: Promoted to Principal Musician July 26, 1861; reduced to ranks Sept. 1, 1862; discharged Oct. 1, 1862 on Surgeon's certificate of disability.

Alfred Stewart, Private, age 37, entered service for period of 1 year, Oct. 6, 1864.

Company F: Mustered out Oct. 6, 1865 on expiration of term of service.

Andrew D. Stewart, Sergeant, age 21, entered service for period of 3 years, June 18, 1861.

Company G: Mustered as Corporal; appointed Sergeant...; wounded July 1, 1863 in battle of Gettysburg, Pa.; mustered out July 16, 1864 at Camp Chase, Ohio on expiration of term of service.

Joseph Stewart, Private, age 21, entered service for period of 3 years, June 10, 1861.

Company B: Discharged March 28, 1863 at York, Pa. on Surgeon's certificate of disability.

Samuel R. Stewart, 2d. Lieutenant, age 23, entered service for period of 3 years, June 4, 1861.

Company A: Appointed Corporal Jan 6, 1862; wounded May 3, 1863 in battle of Chancellorsville, Va. and July 1, 1863 in battle of Gettysburg, Pa.; appointed Sergeant Sept. 1, 1863; 1st Sergeant May 1, 1864; promoted to 2d Lieutenant Oct. 17, 1864; 1st Lieutenant Co. G May 18, 1865; veteran.

Company G: Promoted from 2d lieutenant Co. A May 18, 1865; resigned July 18, 1865 at Columbus, Ohio.

Levi Stewart, Corporal, age 18, entered service for period of 3 years, June 12, 1861.

Company E: Appointed Corporal Sept. 1, 1861; killed Dec. 13, 1861 in battle of Camp Alleghany, W. Va..

Samuel R. Stewart, 2d Lieutenant, age 223, entered service for period of 3 years, June 4, 1861.

Company A: Appointed Corporal Jan. 6, 1862; wounded May 3, 1863 in battle of Chancellorsville, Va. and July 1, 1863 in battle of Gettysburg, Pa.; appointed Sergeant Sept. 1, 1863; 2d Lieutenant Oct. 17, 1864; 1st Lieutenant Co. G, May 18, 1865; veteran.

Company G: Promoted from 2d Lieutenant Co. A, May 18, 1865; resigned July 18, 1865 at Columbus, Ohio.

Chester T. Still, Private, age 24, entered service for period of 3 years, June 26, 1861.
Company I: Transferred to Co. C 75th O.V.I. Jan. 16, 1864; from Co. C 75th O.V.I. June 12, 1864; mustered out July 16, 1864 on expiration of term of service.

Joseph Still, Private, age 29, entered service for period of 3 years, June 10, 1861.
Company C: Wounded Aug. 29, 1862 in battle of Bull Run, Va.; transferred to Veteran Reserve Corps July 1, 1863 by order of War Department.

John Stillwell, Private, age 40, entered service for period of 1 year, Sept. 5, 1864.
Company K: Discharged July 15, 1865 by order of War Department.

William H. Stine, Private, age 20, entered service for period of 3 years, June 10, 1861.
Company B; Wounded May 2, 1863 in battle of Chancellorsville, Va.; transferred to Co. E June 13, 1864.
Company E: Transferred from Co. B June 13, 1864; mustered out July 16, 1864 at Columbus, Ohio on expiration of term of service.

Harrison Stitts, Wagoner, age 21, entered service for period of 3 years, June 10, 1861.
Company B: Transferred to Co. E June 13, 1864.
Company E: Transferred from Co. B June 13, 1864; mustered out July 16, 1864 at Columbus, Ohio on expiration of term of service.

John Stoecher, Private, age 21, entered service for period of 3 years, June 24, 1861.
Company K: Discharged Nov. 27, 1861 at Cheat Mountain, W. Va. on Surgeon's certificate of disability.

Lyman B. Stone, Private, age 18, entered service for period of 3 years, July 10, 1861.
Company K: Wounded May 2, 1863 in battle of Chancellorsville, Va.; transferred to Co. C. 75th O.V.I. Jan. 16, 1864; from Co. C 75th O.V.I. June 1, 1864; mustered out July 16, 1864 on expiration of term of service.

William T. Stradley, Private, age 18, entered service for period of 3 years, June 8, 1861.
Company D: Transferred to 12th Battery O.L.A. March 12, 1862.

William A. Sullivan Private, age 24, entered service for period of 3 years, June 26, 1861,
Company I: Died Oct. 4, 1861 on Cheat Mountain, W. Va.

Alfred F. Stump, 1st Sergeant, age 18, entered service for period of 3 years, June 12, 1861.
Company E: Wounded May 2, 1863 in battle of Chancellorsville, Va.; appointed Corporal April 1, 864; 1st Sergeant Nov. 5, 1864; wounded Dec. 6,

1864 in battle of Deveaux Neck, S.C.; discharged June 2, 1865 by order of War Department.

John A. Stump, Sergeant, age 22, entered service for period of 3 years, June 12, 1861.

Company E: Appointed Sergeant from Corporal March 1, 1862; discharged March 25, 1864 for wounds received May 2, 1863 in battle of Chancellorsville, Va..

Levi Stump, Private, age 18, entered service for period of 1 year, Oct. 4, 1864.

Company D: Mustered out with company Oct. 20, 1865.

Noah E. Stump, Sergeant, age 29, entered service for period of 3 years, Aug. 5, 1862.

Company E: Appointed Corporal Dec. 23, 1862; Sergeant April 1, 1864; discharged July 15, 1865 by order of War Department.

William R. Stump, Private, age 20, entered service for period of 3 years, June 12, 1861.

Company E: Wounded July 1, 1863 in battle of Gettysburg, Pa.; appointed Corporal Jan. 1, 1864; Sergeant Nov. 2, 1864; wounded Dec. 6, 1864 in battle of Gregory's Landing, S.C.; appointed 1st Sergeant July 1, 1865; reduced to ranks March 11, 1866; reappointed 1st Sergeant April 24, 1866; reduced to ranks May 18, 1866; mustered out with company June 18, 1866; veteran.

Ira B. Sturges, Corporal, age 19, entered service for period of 3 years, Feb. 27, 1864.

Company B: Appointed Corporal Aug. 1, 1865; mustered out with company June 18, 1866.

Nathan Sturges, Private, age 18, entered service for period of 3 years, Feb. 29, 1864.

Company B: Mustered out with company June 18, 1861.

Franklin Stutson, Private, age 26, entered service for period of 3 years, June 20, 1861.

Company F: no record given.

Eli Styles, Private, age 22, entered service for period of year, Aug. 16, 1864.

Company G: Wounded Nov. 30, 1864 in battle of Honey Hill, S.C.; discharged June 15, 1865 at Hilton Head, S.C. on Surgeon's certificate of disability.

William A. Sullivan, Private, age 24, entered service for period of 3 years, June 26, 1861.

Company I: died Oct. 4, 1861 on Cheat Mountain, W.Va..

James C. Sultzer, Private, age 19, entered service for period of 3 years, June 10, 1861.

Company B: Died April 6, 1863 at Brook's Station Va..

Sylvester Sultzer, Private, age 21, entered service for period of 3 years, June 10, 1861.

Company B: Transferred to Co. E June 13, 1864.

Wesley B. Sultzer, Private, age 24, entered service for period of 3 years, June 10, 1862.

Company B: Wounded May 8, 1862 in battle of McDowell, Va.; transferred to Co. C March 1, 1864.

Company C: Transferred from Company B March 1, 1864; mustered out July 16, 1864 at Columbus, Ohio on expiration of term of service.

George Sunholder, Private, age 18, entered service for period of 1 year, Sept. 24, 1864.

Company D: Mustered out July 15, 1865 by order of War Department.

John Suter, Private, age 27, entered service for period of 3 years, Dec. 1, 1863.

Company C: Died Nov. 26, 1864 at Hilton Head, S.C..

Solomon Suter, Private, age 19, entered service for period of 3 years, June 10, 1861.

Company C: Died Dec. 22, 1862 at Fairfax C.H., Va..

Samuel Sutler, Private, age 42, entered service for period of 3 years, June 8, 1861.

Company D: Transferred to 12th Battery O.L.A. March 12, 1862.

Henry H. Sutton, Private, age 32, entered service for period of 3 years, June 26, 1861.

Company H: Mustered out with company June 18, 1866; veteran.

Nathaniel Sutton, Private, age 22, entered service for period of 3 years, June 5, 1861.

Company A: Discharged May 6, 1863 at Wheeling, W. Va. on Surgeon's certificate of disability.

Sylvester Sutyzer, Private, age 21, entered service for period of 3 years, June 10, 1861.

Company B: Transferred to Co. E June 13, 1864.

Company E: Transferred from Co. B June 13, 1864; mustered out July 16, 1864 at Columbus, Ohio on expiration of term of service.

Washington M. Swallon, Private, age 36, entered service for period of 3 years, June 10, 1861.

Company C: Discharged Sept. 24, 1862 at Hopewell Gap, Va. on Surgeon's certificate of disability.

Thomas Swartwood, Private, age 23, entered service for period of 3 years, June 26, 1861.

Company I: Wounded May 8, 1862 in battle of McDowell, Va.; discharged Oct. 22, 1862 on Surgeon's certificate of disability.

Moses Sweeney, Private, age 30, entered service for period of 3 years, June 20, 1861.

Company F: Discharged Jan. 29, 1862 on Surgeon's certificate of disability.

Charles Swickert, Private, age 20, entered service for period of 1 year, Oct. 6, 1864.

Company F: no record given.

James W. Swift, Sergeant, age 18, entered service for period of 3 years, Dec. 4, 1863.

Company H: Appointed Corporal April 11, 1865; Sergeant Jan. 1, 1866; mustered out with company June 18, 1866.

George W. Swift, Corporal, age 30, entered service for period of 3 years, Feb. 17, 1864.

Company B: Appointed Corporal March 16, 1864; discharged June 22, 1865 at Camp Dennison, Ohio by order of the War Department.

William H. Swigert, Private, age 21, entered service for period of 3 years, July 16, 1861.

Company G: Discharged Aug. 8, 1862 at Fort McHenry, Md. on Surgeon's certificate of disability.

T

Leander Taber, Sergeant, age 22 entered service for period of 3 years, February 27, 1864.

Company B: Appointed Corporal March 16, 1864; Sergeant Feb. 1, 1865; mustered out with company June 18, 1866.

Samuel Talbert, Private, age 21, entered service for period of 3 years, June 5, 1861.

Company A: Died Nov. 21, 1861 on Cheat Mountain, Va.

William F. Talbert, Private, age 43, entered service for period of 3 years, June 5, 1861.

Company A: Discharged March 14, 1862 at Huttonsville, W. Va. on surgeon's certificate of disability.

George W. Talbot, Private, age 21, entered service for period of 1 year, Sept. 26, 1864.

Company I: Discharged July 15, 1865 by order of War Department.

John W. Tannal, Private, age 19, entered service for period of 9 months, Oct. 7, 1862.

Company K: Drafter: mustered out July 7, 1863 on expiration of term of service.

Francis M. Targer, Private, age 18, entered service for period of 3 years, Feb. 4, 1864.
Company K: Transferred from Co. C 75th O.V.I. June 15, 1864; mustered out with company June 18, 1866.
George W. Tauksbery, Private, age 18, entered service for period of 3 years, Feb., 1864.
Company B: Mustered out with company June 18, 1866.
Asa Taylor, Private, age 24, entered service for period of 3 years, June 5, 1861.
Company A: Mustered out July 16, 1864 on expiration of term of service.
George Taylor, Private, age 18, entered service for period of 3 years, June 18, 1861.
Company G: Wounded Aug. 30, 1862 in battle of Bull Run, Va. and May 2, 1863 in battle of Chancellorsville, Va.; mustered out July 16, 1864 on expiration of term of service.
Judson K. Taylor, Corporal, age 18, entered service for period of 1 year, Sept. 24, 1864.
Company D: Appointed Corporal...; discharged July 15, 1865 by order of War Department.
Walter B. Taylor, Corporal, age age 21, entered service for period of 3 years, Oct. 3, 1864.
Company D: Appointed Corporal July 1, 1865; mustered out with company Oct. 20, 1865.
Zachariah Taylor, Private, age 18, entered service for period of 3 years, Feb. 12, 1864.
Company K: Died May 10, 1866 in Charleston, S.C.
Matthew Teach, Corporal, age 19, entered service for period of 3 years, June 18, 1861.
Company G: Appointed Corporal June 1, 1866; mustered out with company June 18, 1861.
Adolphus Tebean, Private, age entered service for period of 3 years, June 24, 1861.
Company K: Discharged May 31, 1862 at Beverly, W.Va. on Surgeon's certificate of disability.
William Tedro, Private, age 21, entered service for period of 3 years, June 26, 1861.
Company H: no record given.
Edward J. Teeple, Corporal, age 25, entered service for period of 3 years, June 12, 1861.
Company E: Wounded Nov. 30, 1864 in battle of Honey Hill, S.C.; appointed Corporal June 1, 1866; mustered out with company June 18, 1866; veteran.

William G. Teese, Private, age 29, entered service for period of 3 years, June 10, 1861.
Company C: Transferred to Co. C 75th O.V.I. Jan. 16, 1864; from Co. C 75th O.V. I. May 6, 1864; mustered out July 16, 1864 at Camp Chase, Ohio on expiration of term of service.

Wilbert B. Teeters, Sergeant, age 24, entered service for period of 3 years, June 26, 1861.
Company I: Appointed Corporal Feb. 15, 1862; wounded May 8, 1862 in battle of McDowell, Va.; appointed Sergeant Aug. 19, 1862; promoted to Captain Co. H 116th O.V.I. Aug. 20, 1862.

Jonah Teflinger, Corporal, age 21, entered service for period of 1 year, Oct. 1, 1864.
Company D: Appointed Corporal Aug. 1, 1865; mustered out with company Oct. 20, 1865.

James Templeton, 1st Lieutenant, age 33, entered service for period of 3 years, June 4, 1861.
Company F: Promoted from 2d Lieutenant April 27, 1862; resigned Feb. 1, 1863.

Charles W. Terry, Private, age 20, entered service for period of 3 years, June 10, 1861.
Company C: Transferred to Co. C 75th O.V.I. Jan. 16, 1864; from Co. C 75th O.V.I. May 6, 1864; mustered out July 16, 1864 at Camp Chase, Ohio on expiration of term of service.
Company H: Transferred to Co. C 75th O.V.I. Jan. 16, 1864; from Co. C 75th O.V.I. June 12, 1864; mustered out July 16, 1864, 1864 at Columbus, Ohio on expiration of term of service.

John F. Thaenen, Private, age 24, entered service for period of 3 years, June 26, 1861.
Company H: Transferred to Co. C 75th O.V.I. Jan. 16, 1864; from Co. C 75th O.V.I. June 12, 1864; mustered out July 16, 1864, 1864 at Columbus, Ohio on expiration of term of service.

Christopher J. Thayer, Private, age 28, entered service for period of 3 years, June 12, 1861.
Company E: Killed Dec. 13, 1861 in battle of Camp Alleghany, W. Va.

John T. Thoman, Private, age 24, entered service for period of 3 years, June 10, 1861.
Company C: Transferred to Co. C 75th O.V.I. Jan. 16, 1864; from Co. C 75th O.V.I. May 6, 1864; mustered out July 16, 1864 at Camp Chase, Ohio on expiration of term of service.

Jacob D. Thomas, Corporal, age 21, entered service for period of 3 years, June 12, 1861.

Company E: discharged Oct. 30, 1861 on Surgeon's certificate of disability.

Hezkiah Thomas, Sergeant, age 24, entered service for period of 3 years, June 5, 1861.

Company A: Mustered as private; appointed Sergeant July 4, 1861; wounded Dec. 12, 1861 in battle of Camp Alleghany, W. Va.; 1st Sergeant Jan. 6, 1862; reduced to Sergeant July 15, 1862; promoted to Sergt. Major Sept. 1, 1862.

Company E: Promoted from Sergt. Major Aug. 11, 1864; mustered out with company June 18, 1866.

Charles R. Thompson, Private, age 18, entered service for period of 1 year, Sept. 27, 1864.

Company I: Discharged July 15, 1865.

Franklin Thompson, Private, age 27, entered service for period of 3 years, June 26, 1861.

Company H: Died March 27, 1862 at Beverly, W. Va..

Joan A. Thompson, Private, age 21, entered service for period of 9 months, Oct. 7, 1862.

Company K: Drafted; died July 26, 1863 at Baltimore, Md..

John F. Thompson, Private, age 42, entered service for period of 3 years, June 20, 1861.

Company F: Appointed Sergeant April 1, 1863; reduced Nov. 27, 1863; transferred to Co. C 75th O.V.I. Jan. 16, 1864; from Co. C 75th O.V.I. June 12, 1864; mustered out July 16, 1864 on expiration of term of service.

John W. Thompson, Private, age 18, entered service for period of 1 year, Sept. 28, 1864.

Company G: Discharged Oct. 1, 1865 by order of War Department.

Joseph M. Thompson, Private, age 19, entered service for period of 3 years, March 5, 1864.

Company C: Mustered out with company June 18, 1866.

Robert Thompson, Sergeant, age 38, entered service for period of 1 year, Oct. 7, 1864.

Company D: Mustered as private; appointed Sergeant...; discharged June 2, 1865 at Dennison U.S. General Hospital on Surgeon's certificate of disability.

Marion Y. Thornberry, Private, age 21, entered service for period of 3 years, June 10, 1861.

Company C: Wounded July 1, 1863 in battle of Gettysburg, Pa; transferred to Co. C 75th O.V.I. Jan. 16, 1864; from Co. C 75th O.V.I. May 6, 1864; mustered out July 16, 1864 at Camp Chase, Ohio on expiration of term of service.

Company H: Transferred to Co. C 75th O.V.I. Jan. 16,1864; from Co. C 75th O.V.I. June 12, 1864; mustered out July 16, 1864 at Columbus, Ohio on expiration of term of service.

Nelson Thorp, Private, age 18, entered service for period of 1 year, Oct. 6, 1864. Company G: Died Jan. 11, 1865 at Hilton Head, S.C. of wounds received Nov. 30, 1864 in battle of Honey Hill, S.C..

Charles Tiederman, Private, age 18, entered service for period of 3 years, Jan. 15, 1864. Company K: Died Aug. 12, 1864 at Hilton Head, S.C..

Christopher Tiederman, Private, age 18, entered service for period of 3 years, Dec. 23, 1863. Company K: Transferred from Co. C 75th O.V.I. June 15, 1864; mustered out with company June 18, 1866.

Ignatius Tillett, Private, age 19, entered service for period of 3 years, June 5, 1861. Company A: Mustered out with company June 18, 1866; veteran.

John E. Timberlaik, Private, age 22, entered service for period of 3 years, June 26, 1861. Company H: Wounded May 3, 1863 in battle of Chancellorsville, Va.; mustered out July 16, 1864 on expiration of term of service.

William H. Timberlaik, Private, age 21, entered service for period of nine months, Oct. 7, 1862. Company H: Drafted; mustered out Aug. 31, 1863 on expiration of term of service.

Theodore Timberlake, Corporal, age 18, entered service for period of 3 years, June 26, 1861. Company H: Appointed Corporal, April 1, 1864; died Dec. 19, 1864 at Hilton Head, S.C. of wounds received Nov. 30, 1864 in battle of Honey Hill, S.C.; veteran.

Thomas H. Timberlake, Sergeant, age 33, entered service for period of 3 years, June 26, 1861. Company I: Discharged June 20, 1862 on Surgeon's certificate of disability.

Abraham Tisher, Private, age 24, entered service for period of 3 years, June 10, 1861. Company C: Wounded May 2, 1863 in battle of Chancellorsville, Va.; transferred to Co. C 75th O.V.I. Jan. 16, 1864; from Co. C 75th O.V.I. May 6, 1864; mustered out July 16, 1864 at Camp Chase, Ohio on expiration of term of service.

Company H: Transferred to Co. C 75th O.V.I. Jan. 16, 1864; from Co. C 75th O.V.I. June 12, 1864; mustered out July 16, 1864 at Columbus, Ohio on expiration of term of service.

John Tisher, Private, age 23, entered service for period of 3 years, June 10, 1861.

Company C: Wounded May 2, 1862 in battle of McDowell, Va. and Aug. 29, 1862 in battle of Bull Run, Va.; transferred to Co. C 75th O.V.I. Jan. 16, 1864; from Co. C 75th O.V.I. May 6, 1864; mustered out July 16, 1864 at Camp Chase, Ohio on expiration of term of service.

Company H: Transferred to Co. C 75th O.V.I. Jan. 16, 1864; from Co. C 75th O.V.I. June 12, 1864; mustered out July 16, 1864 at Columbus, Ohio on expiration of term of service.

John W. Tompson, Private, age 18, entered service for period of 1 year, Sept. 28, 1864.

Company G: Discharged Oct. 1, 1865 by order of War Department.

Patrick O. Tool, Private, age 18, entered service for period of 1 year, Oct. 3, 1864.

Company I: Mustered Oct. 3, 1865 on expiration of term of service.

William I. Town, Private, age 25, entered service for period of 3 years, June 24, 1861.

Company K: Transferred to 18th U.S. Infantry....

Jonathan Townsend, Private, age 18, entered service for period of 1 year, Sept. 8, 1864.

Company G: Discharged Oct. 1, 1865 by order of War Department.

John Treedle, Private, age 21, entered service for period of 3 years, June 12, 1861.

Company E: Wounded Aug. 30, 1862 in battle of Bull Run; killed July 1, 1863 in battle of Gettysburg, Pa..

James Trigg, Private, age 27, entered service for period of 3 years, June 10, 1861.

Company B: Transferred to Co. C March 1, 1864.

Company C: Transferred from Co. B March 1, 1864; mustered out July 16, 1864 at Camp Chase, Ohio on expiration of term of service.

Samuel Trigg, Corporal, age 25, entered service for period of 3 years, June 10, 1861.

Company B: Wounded May 8, 1862 in battle of McDowell, Va.; discharged Aug. 13, 1863 at Convalescent Camp, Va. on Surgeon's certificate of disability.

Peter Triquart, 2d Lieutenant, age 25, entered service for period of 3 years, June 24, 1861.

Company K: Appointed Corporal Jan. 1, 1862; Sergeant May 1, 1863; wounded Aug. 30, 1862 in battle of Bull Run, Va.; appointed 1st Sergeant April 1, 1864; promoted to 2d Lieutenant Oct. 17, 1864; wounded Nov. 30, 1864 in battle of Honey Hill, S.C.; resigned July 20, 1865; veteran.

John Trowfelter, Private, age 43, entered service for period of 3 years, June 18, 1861.

Company G: Transferred to Veteran Reserve Corps...by order of War Department.

Isaac Troxel, Sergeant, age 21, entered service for period of 3 years, June 18, 1861.

Company G: Mustered as private; appointed Sergeant...; died Sept. 20, 1865 at Columbia, S.C..

John Troxel, Private, age 18, entered service for period of 3 years, Dec. 31, 1863. Company I: Transferred from Co. B 107th O.V.I. July 13, 1865; mustered out with company June 18, 1866.

Charles G. Troy, Private, age 21, entered service for period of 3 years, June 10, 1861.

Company B: Wounded May 8, 1862 in battle of McDowell, Va.; transferred to Co. H June 13, 1864.

Company E: Transferred from Co. B June 13, 1864; mustered out July 16, 1864 at Columbus, Ohio on expiration of term of service.

Henson W. True, Private, age 20, entered service for period of 3 years, June 26, 1861.

Company I: Wounded July 1, 1863 in battle of Gettysburg, Pa.; mustered out July 16, 1864 on expiration of term of service.

John Truxell, Private, age 25, entered service for period of 3 years, June 8, 1861. Company D;: Killed Sept. 17, 1861 in skirmish at Cheat Mountain, W. Va.

John Tucker, Sergeant, age 22, entered service for period of 3 years, June 20, 1861.

Company F: Appointed Corporal July 1, 1865; Sergeant Aug. 1, 1865; died Sept. 23, 1865 at Barnwell C.H., S.C.; veteran.

William Tucker, age 38, entered service for period of 1 year, Oct. 6, 1864. Company F: Mustered out Oct. 7, 1865 on expiration of term of service.

Henry Tudor, age 39, entered service for period of 1 year, Oct. 3, 1864. Company F: Mustered out Oct. 3, 1865 on expiration of term of service.

William G. Tuse, Private, age 29, entered service for period of 3 years, June 26, 1861.
Company H: Transferred to Co. C 75th O.V.I. Jan. 16, 1864; from Co. C 75th O.V.I. June 12, 1864; mustered out at Columbus, Ohio on expiration of term of service.

John H. Twaddle, Corporal, age 19, entered service for period of 3 years, June 10, 1861.
Company B: Appointed Corporal...; transferred to Co. C March 1, 1864; veteran.
Company C: Transferred from Co. B as Corporal March 20, 1864; appointed Sergeant Aug. 1, 1864; mustered out with company June 18, 1866; veteran.

Samuel Twaddle, Private, age 18, entered service for period of 3 years, Feb. 12, 1862.
Company E: Killed July 1, 1863 in battle of Gettysburg, Pa.

John Tucker, Sergeant, age 22, entered service for period of 3 years, June 20, 1861.
Company F: Appointed Corporal July 1, 1865; Sergeant Aug. 1, 1865; died Sept. 23, 1865 at Barnwell, C.H., S.C.; veteran.

William Tucker, Private, age 38, entered service for period of 1 year, Oct. 7, 1864.
Company F: Mustered out Oct. 7, 1865 on expiration of term of service.

Henry Tudor, Private, age 39, entered service for period of 1 year, Oct. 3, 1864.
Company F: Mustered out Oct. 3, 1865 on expiration of term of service.

William G. Tuse, Private, age 29, entered service for period of 3 years, June 26, 1861.
Company H: Transferred to Co. C 75th O.V.I. Jan. 16, 1864; from Co. C 75th O.V.I. June 12, 1864; mustered out July 16, 1864, at Columbus, Ohio on expiration of term of service.

Samuel Twaddle, Private, age 18, entered service for period of 3 years, Feb. 12, 1862.
Company E: Killed July 1, 1863 in battle of Gettysburg, Pa.

John Tweedle, Private, age 21, entered service for period of 3 years, June 12, 1861.
Company E: Wounded Aug. 30, 1862 in battle of Bull Run, Va.; killed July 1, 1863 in battle of Gettysburg, Pa.

Charles Twinem, Private, age 29, entered service for period of 3 years, June 10, 1861.
Company B: Wounded May 8, 1862 in battle of McDowell, Va.; transferred to Veteran Reserve Corps June 6, 1863; mustered out April 24, 1864 at Elyria, N.Y.

Daniel Tyrrell, Private, age 38, entered service for period of 3 years, Oct. 17, 1862.
Company A: Wounded July 2, 1863 in battle of Gettysburg, Pa.; mustered out Oct. 17, 1865 on expiration of term of service.
William S. Tyrrell, Musician, age 15, entered service for period of 3 years, Dec. 15, 1862.
Company A: Mustered out Dec. 14, 1865 on expiration of term of service.

U

Sylvanus Ullom, Private, age 19, entered service for period of 3 years, June 10, 1861.
Company B: Wounded July 1, 1863 in battle of Gettysburg, Pa; transferred to Co. C March 24, 1864; veteran.
Company C: Transferred from Co. B March 20, 1864; appointed Corporal Oct. 20, 1864; mustered out with company June 18, 1866; veteran.
William Underwood, Private, age 18, entered service for period of 3 years, June 8, 1861.
Company D: Transferred to 12th Battery O.L.A. March 12, 1862.
Martin Unger, Private, age 40, entered service for period of 1 year, Sept. 21, 1864.
Company C: Discharged July 15, 1865 by order of War Department.

V

Joseph Vallance, Private, age 24, entered service for period of 3 years, Feb. 22, 1864.
Company E: Died March 29, 1864 at Columbus, Ohio.
Alfred Vance, Private, age 18, entered service for period of 3 years, Oct. 20, 1863.
Company C: Mustered out with company June 18, 1866.
Robert H. Vance, Private, age 26 entered service for period of 3 years, Oct. 6, 1862.
Company A: Mustered out Oct. 6, 1865 on expiration of term of service.
Vance Vancurren, Private, age 25, entered service for period of 3 years, Nov. 18, 1863.
Company A: Transferred from Co. C June 25, 1864; mustered out with company June 18, 1866.
Company C: Transferred to Co. A June 25, 1864 by order of War Department.

Theodore Vangundy, Sergeant, age 28, entered service for period of 1 year, Oct. 3, 1864.

Company D: Mustered as private; appointed Sergeant...; wounded Nov. 30, 1864 in battle ofHoney Hill, S.C.; discharged June 2, 1865 at Dennison U.S. General Hospital on Surgeon's certificate of disability.

John Vaugh, Private, age 18, entered service for period of 3 years, June 8, 1861.

Company D: Transferred to 12th Battery O.L.A. March 121, 1862.

Joshua B. Vaughan, Private, age 26, entered service for period of 3 years, June 10, 1861.

Company B: Wounded May 3, 1863 in battle of Chancellorsville, Va.; transferred to Co. C March 20, 1864.

Company C: transferred from Co. B March 20, 1864; mustered out July 16, 1864 at Camp Chase, Ohio on expiration of term of service.

John H. Veite, Private, age 18, entered service for period of 3 years, June 13, 1861.

Company F: Reduced from Sergeant Jan. 24, 1864; mustered out with company June 18, 1866; veteran.

John Venrick, Private, age 34, entered service for period of 3 years, June 18, 1861.

Company G: Transferred to Co. C 75th O.V.I. Jan. 16, 1864; from Co. C 75th O.V.I. June 12, 1864; mustered out July 16, 1864 on expiration of term of service.

George W. Verbeck, Private, age 23, entered service for period of 3 years, June 5, 1861.

Company A: Died June 15, 1862 at Glenco, Ohio of wound received May 8, 1862 in battle of McDowell, Virginia.

William Vickory, Private, age 21, entered service for period of 3 years, July 10, 1861.

Company K: Wounded May 8, 1862 in battle of McDowell, Virginia.

David S. Viers, Private, age 24, entered service for period of 3 years, June 24, 1861.

Company K: Discharged Jan. 27, 1862 at Huttonsville, W. Va. on Surgeon's certificate of disability.

John B. Viers, Private, age 19, entered service for period of 3 years, June 24, 1861.

Company K: Reduced from Corporal...; discharged Jan. 24, 1862 at Alexandria, Va. on Surgeon's certificate of disability.

Lemuel Viers, Sergeant, age 18, entered service for period of 3 years, June 24, 1861.

Company K: Died May 21, 1863 at Division Hospital, Brook's Station, Va. of wounds received May 2, 1863 in battle of Chancellorsville, Va..

Robert M. Vickers, Private, age 18, entered service for period of 3 years, Oct. 20, 1863.
Company C: Mustered out with company June 8, 1866.
August Vierhelder, Private, age 21, entered service for period of 3 years, June 10, 1861.
Company C: Transferred from Co. B March 20, 1864; mustered out July 16, 1864 at Columbus, Ohio
Augustus Vierhelder, Private, age 21, entered service for period of 3 years, June 10, 1861.
Company B: Transferred to Co. C March 20, 1864; veteran.
Company C: Transferred from Co. B March 20, 1864; appointed Corporal Oct. 1, 1865; mustered out with company June 18, 1866; veteran.
Levi D. Vinson,. Corporal, age 20, entered service for period of 3 years, June 8, 1861.
 Company D: Transferred to 12th Battery O.L.A March 12, 1862.
John Veit, Private, age 23, entered service for period of 1 year, Feb. 24, 1865.
Company C: Transferred from Co. F. 107th O.V.I. July 13, 1865; mustered out Feb. 24, 1866 at Charleston, S.C. on expiration of term of service.
John Vogle, Private, age 30, entered service for period of 3 years, April 8, 1864.
Company I: Transferred for Co....107th O.V.I. July 13, 1865.
George Volks, Private, age 18, entered service for period of 3 years, Aug. 13, 1862.
Company A: Killed Dec. 6, 1864 in battle of Deveaux Neck, South Carolina.
Simon H. Vorhies, Corporal, age 27, entered service for period of 3 years, June 5, 1861.
Company A: Wounded July 1, 1863 in battle of Gettysburg, Pa.; appointed Corporal Nov. 5, 1864; mustered out with company June 18, 1866; veteran.

W

William F. Wade, Private, age 29, entered service for period of 3 years, July 2, 1861.
Company H: no record given.
James Wagner, Private, age 19, entered service for period of 1 year, Oct. 13, 1864.
Company G: Mustered out Oct. 13, 1865 on expiration of term of service.
William Wagner, Private, age 18, entered service for period of 1 year, Oct. 4, 1864.
Company K: Mustered out Oct. 4, 1865 on expiration of term of service.

John Wahl, Corporal, age 19, entered service for period of 3 years, Feb. 23, 1864.

Company B: Appointed Corporal May 19, 1866; mustered out with company June 18, 1866.

Lewis Wahl, Private, age 29, entered service for period of 3 years, Oct. 24, 1862.

Company C: Transferred from Co. F 107th O.V.I. July 13, 1865; mustered out Oct. 25, 1865 at Charleston, S.C. on expiration of term of service.

William Walker, Private, age 32, entered service for period of 3 years, June 18, 1861.

Company G: no record given.

Andrew W. Wallace, Private, age 22, entered service for period of 3 years, July 9, 1861.

Company H: Transferred to Co. C 75th O.V.I. Jan. 16, 1864; from Co. C 75th O.V.I. June 12, 1864; mustered out July 16, 1864 at Columbus, Ohio on expiration of term of service.

John N. Wallace, Private, age 33, entered service for period of 3 years, June 27, 1861.

Company G: no record given.

Nathaniel Wallace, Private, age 29, entered service for period of 3 years, Nov, 15, 1862.

Company A: Wounded July 1, 1863 in battle of Gettysburg, Pa.; mustered out Nov. 15, 1865 on expiration of term of service.

William Waller, Private, age 19, entered service for period of 1 year, Oct. 4, 1864.

Company D: Mustered out with company Oct. 29, 1865.

Elijah C. Walsworth, Private, age 18, entered service for period of 3 years, Feb. 22, 1864.

Company B: On detached service...; mustered out with company June 18, 1866.

Joel Walsworth, Private, age 18, entered service for period of 1 year, Sept. 26, 1864.

Company I: Discharged July 15, 1865 by order of the War Department.

Joseph M. Walters, Private, age 18, entered service for period of 3 years, Oct. 8, 1862.

Company A: Mustered Oct. 8, 1865 on expiration of term of service.

William Walter, Private, age 19, entered service for period of 1 year, Oct. 4, 1864.

Company D: Mustered out with company Oct. 20, 1864.

Clinton Walters, Wagoner, age 39, entered service for period of 3 years, June 12, 1861.

Company E: Discharged July 17, 1864 and turned over to civil authority.

Joseph Walters, Private, age 18, entered service for period of 3 years, Oct. 8, 1862.

Company A: Mustered out Oct. 8, 1865 on expiration of term of service.

Joseph N. Walters, Private, age 41, entered service for period of 3 years, Feb. 29, 1864.

Company B: Wounded Nov. 30, 1864 in battle of Honey Hill, S.C.; discharged June 2, 1865 at Camp Dennison, Ohio on Surgeon's certificate of disability.

Benjamin Walton, Private, age 27, entered service for period of 1 year, Oct. 3, 1864.

Company D: Mustered out with company Oct. 20, 1865.

John Walton, 1st Lieutenant, age 29, entered service for period of 3 years, June 10, 1861.

Company B: Promoted to 2d Lieutenant from Sergt. Major Feb. 10, 1864; to 1st Lieutenant Sept. 29, 1865; mustered out with company June 18, 1866.

John Walton, Private, age 20, entered service for period of 3 years, June 10, 1861.

Company C: Promoted to Sergt. Major Oct. 12, 1864; veteran.

William Walton, Surgeon, age…, entered service for period of 3 years, Oct. 7, 1862..

Promoted from Asst. Surgeon Aug. 8, 1864; mustered out with regiment June 18, 1866.

Jacob Wanzel, Private, age 21, entered service for period of 1 year, Sept. 28, 1864.

Company I: Wounded Nov. 30, 1864 in battle of Honey Hill, S.C.; discharged July 15, 1865 by order of War Department.

Hiram Ward, Sergeant, age 22, entered service for period of 3 years, June 8, 1861.

Company D: Transferred to 12th Battery O.L.A. March 12, 1862.

John B. Ward, Corporal, age 24, entered service for period of 3 years, June 8, 1861.

Company D: Wounded Dec. 12, 1861 in battle of Camp Alleghany, W. Va.; transferred to 12th Battery O.L.A. March 12, 1862.

John J. Warts, Private, age 23, entered service for period of 3 years, June 24, 1861.

Company K: Transferred to Co. C 75th O.V.I. Jan. 16, 1864; from Co. C 75th O.V.I. June 1, 1864; mustered out July 16, 1864 on expiration of term of service.

James Washburn, Captain, age 39, entered service for period of 3 years, June 4, 1861.

Company B: Promoted to Colonel 116th O.V.I. July 7, 1862.

George Wasnur, Sergeant, age 20, entered service for period of 1 year, Sept 24, 1864.

Company D: Mustered as private; appointed Sergeant...; discharged July 15, 1865 by order of War Department.

John M. Watkins, Corporal, age 18, entered service for period of 3 years, May 25, 1864.

Company A: Appointed Corporal May 1, 1866; mustered out with company June 18, 1866.

Asa Way, Captain, age 54, entered service for period of 3 years, June 4, 1861.

Company G: Resigned Oct. 27, 1862 at Brook's Station, Va..

Charles A. Way, Sergeant, age 29, entered service for period of 3 years, Aug. 9, 1862.

Company G: Mustered as Private; appointed Sergeant...; discharged July 15, 1865 at Columbia, S.C. by order of War Department

Edgar A. Way, Corporal, age 19, entered service for period of 3 years, June 18, 1861.

Company G: Appointed Corporal...; killed May 2, 1863 in battle of Chancellorsville, Va..

Walter A. Way, Private, age 27, entered service for period of 3 years, Aug. 9, 1862.

Company G: Transferred to Co. C 75th O.V.I. Jan. 16, 1864; from Co. C 75th O.V.I. June 12, 1862; mustered out July 16, 1864 on expiration of term of service.

Albert Way, Corporal, age 21, entered service for period of 3 years, Feb. 4, 1864.

Company A: Appointed Corporal Aug, 1, 1865; mustered out with company June 18, 1866.

Washington Weaver, Private, age 38, entered service for period of 1 year, Sept. 30, 1864.

Company A: Discharged July 15, 1863 by order of the War Department.

Matthew Webber, Private, age 18, entered service for period of 1 year, Sept. 29, 1864.

Company G: Discharged...by order of War Department.

Miran Webber, Corporal, age 23, entered service for period of 3 years, June 8, 1861.

Company D: Transferred to 12th Battery O.L.A. March 12, 1862.

George Webster, Lt. Col, age 36, entered service for period of 3 years, June 28, 1861.

Promoted from Major May 16, 1862; resigned July 30, 1862 to accept commission as Colonel of 98th O.V.I..

George R. Weeks, Asst. Surgeon, age 35, entered service for period of 3 years, July 2, 1861. Promoted to Surgeon 24th O.V.I. July 23, 1861.

Michael Weeler, Private, age 31, entered service for period of 3 years, Dec. 19, 1863.

Company K: Transferred from Co....107th O.V.I. July 13, 1865; discharged Feb. 21, 1866 on Surgeon's certificate of disability.

Herman Wehagen, Private, age 18, entered service for period of 3 years, Jan. 6, 1864.

Company I: Transferred from Co. B 107th O.V.I. July 13, 1865; mustered out with company June 18, 1866.

Gottleib Weidenkaup, Private, age 36, entered service for period of 3 years, Oct. 16, 1862.

Company I: Transferred from 107th O.V.I. July 13, 1865; mustered out Oct. 15, 1865 by order of War Department.

Jacob Weidkrhr, Private age 29, entered service for period of 1 year, Feb. 24, 1865.

Company C: Transferred from Co. F 107th O.V.I. July 13, 1865; mustered out Feb. 24, 1866 at Charleston, S.C. on expiration of term of service.

Charles Weinstine, Private, age 18, entered service for period of 3 years, June 26, 1861.

Company I: Wounded Aug. 29, 1862 in battle of Bull Run, Va.; discharged April 27, 1863 on Surgeon's certificate of disability.

Benjamin F. Welch, 1st Sergeant, age 23, entered service for period of 3 years, June 10, 1861.

Company B: Appointed Corporal March 16, 1864; Sergeant Feb. 1, 1865; 1st Sergeant Jan. 25, 1866; mustered out with company June 18, 1866; veteran.

Jacob Welch, Private, age 34, entered service for period of 1 year, Sept. 29, 1864.
Company G: Discharged...by order of War Department.

James S. Welch, Private, age 18, entered service for period of 3 years, June 26, 1861.
Company H: no record given.

John B. Welch, Sergeant, age 25, entered service for period of 1 year, Sept. 27, 1864.

Company F: Appointed from private Nov. 5, 1864; discharged June 22, 1865 to accept promotion as 2d Lieutenant in 104th U.S. Colored Troops.

Adolph Weldabusch, Private, age 18, entered service for period of 3 years, Nov. 24, 1862.

Company A: Wounded July 1, 1863 in battle of Gettysburg, Pa.; mustered out Nov. 24, 1865 on expiration of term of service.

Apollo Wells, Private, age 23, entered service for period of 3 years, June 10, 1861.

Company B: Transferred to Co. H June 13, 1864.

Company H: Transferred from Co. B June 13, 1864; mustered out July 16, 1864 at Columbus, Ohio on expiration of term of service.

John B. Wells, Musician, age 24, entered service for period of 3 years, June 8, 1861.

Company D: Transferred to 12th Battery O.L.A. March 12, 1862.

Christian Wenger, Private, age 18, entered service for period of 3 years, Dec. 29, 1863.

Company I: Transferred from Co. B 107th O.V.I. July 13, 1865; mustered out with company June 18, 1866.

John Wenger, Private, age 18, entered service for period of 3 years, Dec. 31,1863.

Company I: Transferred from Co. b 107th O.V.I. July 13, 1865; mustered out with company June 18, 1866.

John A. Wenrick, Private, age 19, entered service for period of 1 year, Oct. 25, 1864.

Company C: Mustered out Oct. 24, 1865 at Charleston, S.C. on expiration of term of service.

George Wenzen, Private, age June 24, 1861.

Company K: no record given.

John A. West, Private, age 18, entered service for period of 1 year, Oct. 5, 1864.

Company G: Discharged…at Hilton Head, S.C. on Surgeon's certificate of disability.

William S. West, Corporal, age 22, entered service for period of 3 years, June 26, 1861.

Company I: Appointed Corporal July 20, 1861; discharged Feb. 28, 1862 on Surgeon's certificate of disability.

David Westfall, Private, age 42, entered service for period of 1 year, April 16, 1864.

Company F: Discharged June 15, 1865 on Surgeon's certificate of disability.

Eli Westfall, Private, age 19, entered service for period of 3 years, Feb. 19, 1864.

Company F: Mustered out with company June 18, 1866.

John Weyer, Sergeant, age 23, entered service for period of 3 years, June 5, 1861.

Company A: Wounded May 3, 1863 in battle of Chancellorsville, Va.; appointed Corporal April 1, 1864; Sergeant Aug. 1, 1864; wounded Nov. 30, 1864 in battle of Honey Hill, S.C.; promoted to Hospital Steward March 19, 1865; veteran.

Abner Whaley, Private, age 30, entered service for period of 1 year, Sept. 27, 1864.

Company K: Drafted; mustered out Oct. 5, 1865 on expiration of term of service.

Arthur Wharton, Private, age 19, entered service for period of 3 years, June 26, 1861.

Company I: Wounded Nov. 30, 1864 in battle of Honey Hill, S.C. ; discharged Dec. 31, 1863 to re-enlist as veteran. No further record found.

George I. Wharton, Private, age 20, entered service for period of 3 years, Jan. 21, 1862.

Company I: Died June 8, 1862 at Staunton, Va..

William H. Wharton, Private, age 21, entered service for period of 3 years, June 26, 1861.

Company I: Wounded June 8, 1862 in battle of Cross Keys, Va.; discharged Sept. 16, 1862 on Surgeon's certificate of disability.

John Wheeler, Private, age 26, entered service for period of 3 years, February 17, 1864.

Company B: Died April 15, 1865 at Wright's Bluff, S.C..

Anthony Wheeler, Private, age 25, entered service for period of 3 years, June 10, 1861.

Company B; Wounded July 1, 1863 in battle of Chancellorsville, Va.; transferred to Co. C March 20, 1864.

Company C: Transferred from Co. B March 20, 1864; mustered out July 16, 1864 at Camp Chase, Ohio on expiration of term of service.

Orin Wheeler, Private, age 22, entered service for period of 3 years, June 26, 1861.

Company H: Died Nov. 16, 1861 at Huttonsville, W. Va..

Eli Westfall, Private, age 19, entered service for period of 3 years, Feb. 19, 1864.
Company F: Musterd out with company June 18, 1866.

Nicholas Whitmore, Private, age 28, entered service for period of 3 years, Feb. 18, 1864.

Company K: no record given.

Newton Whetstone, Private, age 18, entered service for period of 1 year, Sept. 23, 1864.

Company D: Mustered out July 15, 1865 by order of War Department.

Edward Whileford, Private, age 37, entered service for period of 1 year, Sept. 27, 1864.
Company I: Wounded Dec. 6, 1864 in battle of Gregory's Landing, S.C.; discharged July 15, 1865 by order of War Department.
William A. Whitcraft, 1st Lieutenant, age 22, entered service for period of 3 years, March 12, 1862.
Company A: Promoted from 2d Lieutenant Sept. 5, 1862; died May 25, 1863 of wounds received May 3, 1863 in battle of Chancellorsville, Va..
George White, Private, age 34, entered service for period of 3 years, June 18, 1861.
Company G: Transferred to Veteran Reserve Corps...by order of War Department.
Henry C. White, Private, age 21, entered service for period of 3 years, June 5, 1861.
Company A: Wounded May 8, 1862 in battle of McDowell, Va.; died May 15, 1862 at Washington, D.C.
Israel White, 1st Lieutenant, age 36, entered service for period of 3 years, June 5, 1861
Company A: Appointed 1st Sergeant from Sergeant July 1, 1862; promoted to 2d Lieutenant March 6, 1863; wounded June 8, 1862 in the battle of Cross Keys, Va., and May 3, 1863 in the battle of Chancellorsville, Va.; promoted to 1st Lieutenant June 1, 1863; Captain Co. I May 25, 1864.
Company I: Captain. Promoted from 1st Lieutenant Co. A May 23, 1864; wounded Nov. 30, 1864 in battle of Honey Hill, S.C.; mustered out with company June 18, 1866.
John T. White, Private, age 19, entered service for period of 3 years, June 10, 1861.
Company B: Discharged Aug. 9, 1862 at Fort McHenry, Md. on Surgeon's certificate of disability.
John W. White, Corporal, age 36, entered service for period of 3 years, Sept. 27, 1864.
Company F: Appointed Corporal Nov. 5, 1864; discharged July 15, 1865 by order of War Department.
Samuel White, Private, age 22, entered service for period of 3 years, June 10, 1861.
Company B: Wounded June 8, 1862 in battle of Cross Keys, Va.; discharged Oct. 30, 1862 on Surgeon's certificate of disability.
Thomas G. White, Private, age 18, entered service for period of 3 years, February 9, 1864.
Company A: Killed Nov. 30, 1864 in battle of Honey Hill, South Carolina.

William White, Private, age 20, entered service for period of 3 years, June 8, 1861.

Company D: Wounded Dec. 2, 1861 in battle of Camp Alleghany, W. Va.; transferred to 12th Battery O.L.A. March 12, 1862.

William H. White, Private, age 19, entered service for period of 3 years, June 5, 1861.

Company A: Wounded July 3, 1863 in battle of Gettysburg, Pa; absent…in hospital; mustered out July 16, 1864 by order of War Department.

Levi Whiteman, Private, age 18, entered service for period of 3 years, Feb. 29, 1864.

Company B: On detached service…; mustered out with company June 18, 1866.

George Whitson, Private, age 39, entered service for period of 3 years, June 18, 1861.

Company G: Killed June 8, 1862 in battle of Cross Keys, Va..

Joseph H. Whitten, Private, age 26, entered service for period of 3 years, June 20, 1861.

Company F: Discharged April 15, 1863 on Surgeon's certificate of disability.

Amon M. Whitney, Private, age 19, entered service for period of 1 year, Oct. 8, 1864.

Company A: Mustered Oct. 8, 1865 on expiration of term of service.

Decatur Whitney, Private, age 29, entered service for period of 3 years, June 12, 1861.

Company E: Transferred to Veteran Reserve Corps Aug. 1, 1863 by order of War Department.

James C. Whittle, Private, age 21, entered service for period of 3 years, June 5, 1861.

Company A: Wounded May 3, 1863 in battle of Chancellorsville, Va. and July 1, 1863 n battle of Gettysburg, Pa.; absent…in hospital at Washington, D.C.; discharged April 19, 1864 on Surgeon's certificate of disability.

Jacob Wiedrkrhr, Private, age29, entered service for period of 1 year, Feb. 29, 1865.

Company C: Transferred from Co. F 107th O.V.I. July 13, 1865; mustered out Feb. 24, 1866 at Charleston, S.C. on expiration of term of service.

Jacob Wike, Private, age 18, entered service for period of 1 year, Oct. 11, 1864.

Company K: Transferred from Co….107th O.V.I. July 13, 1865; mustered out Oct. 11, 1865 on expiration of term of service.

Amos Wilcox, Private, age 223, entered service for period of 3 years, June 26, 1861.

Company H: no record given.

Edward P. Wilcox, Private, age 38, entered service for period of 3 years, June 18, 1861.
Company G: Mustered out July 16, 1864 on expiration of term of service.
Samuel A. Wildman, Sergeant, age 18, entered service for period of 3 years, Feb. 24, 1864.
Company B; Appointed Corporal Nov. 5, 1864; Sergeant Jan. 25, 1866; mustered out with company June 18, 1866.
Archibald Wiley, Private, age 25, entered service for period of 3 years, June 26, 1861.
Company I: Wounded July 1, 1863 in battle of Gettysburg, Pa.; mustered out July 16, 1864 on expiration of term of service.
James S. Wiley, Private, age 21, entered service for period of 3 years, June 26, 1861.
Company H: Reduced from Corporal Jan. 15, 1864; transferred to Co. C 75th O.V.I. Jan. 16, 1864; from Co. C 75th O.V.I. June 12, 1864; mustered out July 16, 1864 at Columbus, Ohio on expiration of term of service.
William F. Wiley, Sergeant, age 21, entered service for period of 3 years, June 26, 1861.Company I: Wounded July 1, 1863 in battle of Gettysburg, Pa.; appointed Corporal Feb. 1, 1865; mustered out with company June 18, 1866; veteran.
Edmond Wilkison, Private, age 30, entered service for period of 1 year, Oct. 6, 1864.
Company F: Discharged July 6, 1865 on Surgeon's certificate of disability.
Bodi William, no record available.
David Williams, Private, age 34, entered service for period of 3 years, Aug. 9, 1862.
Company F: Wounded July 1, 1863 in battle of Gettysburg, Pa.; transferred to Veteran Reserve Corps Nov. 1, 1863; by order of War Department.
James Williams, Private, age 22, entered service for period of 3 years, July 17, 1861.
Company H: no record given.
James T. Williams, Private, age 19, entered service for period of 3 years, June 18, 1861.
Company G: Appointed Corporal Nov. 5, 1864; Sergeant Feb. 1, 1865; reduced to ranks Sept. 1, 1865; mustered out with company June 18, 1866; veteran.
John Williams, Private, age 17, entered service for period of 3 years, Aug. 9, 1862.
Company F: Discharged July 15, 1865 by order of War Department.

Jeremiah Williams, Lt. Col., age 29, entered service for period of 3 years, June 10, 1861.

Promoted to Major from Captain Co. C July 30, 1862; Lt. Col. May 3, 1863; wounded and captured July 1, 1863 at battle of Gettysburg, Pa.; prisoner of war in Libby Rebel Prison at Richmond, Va. eleven months; discharged June 21, 1864 by order of War Department.

Oliver W. Williams, 1st Lieutenant, age 19, entered service for period of 3 years, June 18, 1861.

Company C: Promoted to 2d Lieutenant from Hospital Steward May 25, 1865; 1st Lieutenant Aug. 11, 1864; wounded Nov. 30, 1864 in battle of Honey Hill, S.C.; discharged April 26, 1865.

Sylvanus Williams, Private, age 20, entered service for period of 3 years, June 10, 1861.Company C: Died June 1, 1862 at New Creek, Va. of wound received May 8, 1862 in battle of McDowell, Va..

Theodore S. Williams, Sergeant, age 26, entered service for period of 3 years, Feb. 24, 1864.

Company B: Appointed Corporal May 9, 1864; wounded Nov. 30, 1864 in battle of Honey Hill, S.C.; appointed Sergeant Sept. 28, 1865; mustered out with company June 18, 1866.

John Willie, Private, age 32, entered service for period of 3 years, December 18, 1863.

Company C: Transferred from Co. C 107th O.V.I. July 13, 1865; mustered out with company June 18, 1866.

Henry J. Willing, Sergeant, age 22, entered service for period of 3 years, June 24, 1861.

Company K: Appointed Corporal April 1, 1864; Sergeant April 1, 1866; mustered out with company June 18, 1866; veteran.

Levi M. Wills, Private, age 20, entered service for period of 3 years, June 20, 1861.

Company F: Mustered out July 16, 1864 on expiration of term of service.

Eli M. Wilson, Asst. Surgeon, age…, entered service for period of 3 years, Aug. 8, 1864. Mustered out with regiment June 18, 1866.

Friend P. Wilson, Corporal, age 20, entered service for period of 3 years, June 26, 1861.

Company I: Killed June 8, 1862 in battle of Cross Keys, Va..

Harrison Wilson, Corporal, age 21, entered service for period of 3 years, June 26, 1861.

Company I: Discharged Feb. 11, 1862 to accept promotion as 1st Lieutenant Co. I, 20th O.V.I..

Hugh Wilson, Private, age 25, entered service for period of 3 years, June 20, 1861.
Company F: Wounded Dec. 13, 1861 in battle of Camp Alleghany, W. Va. and July 1, 1863 in battle of Gettysburg, Pa. and Nov. 30, 1864 in battle of Honey Hill, S.C.; reduced from Sergeant Jan. 1, 1866; mustered out with company June 18, 1866; veteran.

Isaac Wilson, Private, age 21, entered service for period of 3 years, June 26, 1861.
Company I: Mustered out with company June 18, 1866; veteran.

Lewis E. Wilson, 1st Sergeant, age 18, entered service for period of 3 years, June 10, 1861.
Company C: Appointed Sergeant from private Oct. 1, 1861; 1st Sergeant March 12, 1862; promoted to 2d Lieutenant Co. K Sept. 19, 1862.

Joseph H. Wilson, Sergeant, age 23, entered service for period of 3 years, June 26, 1861.
Company I: Appointed Corporal Sept. 30, 1862; Sergeant Nov. 5, 1864; wounded Nov. 30, 1864 in battle of Honey Hill, S.C.; discharged March 11, 1866 on Surgeon's certificate of disability; veteran.

Lewis E. Wilson, 2d Lieutenant, age 18, entered service for period of 3 years, June 10, 1861.
Company K: Promoted from 1st Sergeant Co. I Sept. 19, 1862; to 1st Lieutenant July 1, 1863 but not mustered; killed July 1, 1863 in battle of Gettysburg, Pa.

Robert S. Wilson, Private, age 18, entered service for period of 3 years, Feb. 26, 1864.
Company I: Died June 28, 1865 at Hilton Head, S.C.

Jacob H. Wilt, Private, age 34, entered service for period of 1 year, Oct. 1, 1864.
Company F: Died March 26, 1865 at Beaufort, S.C.

Alfred Weinestine, Corporal, age 27, entered service for period of 3 years, Feb. 26, 1864.
Company I: Appointed Corporal Sept. 1, 1865; mustered out with company June 18, 1866.

William F. Wire, Corporal, age 19, entered service for period of 3 years, Feb. 22, 1864.
Company I: Appointed Corporal Aug. 1, 1865, mustered out with company June 18, 1866.

John Wise, Corporal, age 18, entered service for period of 3 years, Feb. 22, 1864.
Company E: Appointed Corporal May 19, 1866; mustered out with company June 18, 1866.

Samuel Wise, Private, age 23, entered service for period of 3 years, Feb. 22, 1864.

Company E: Mustered out with company June 18, 1866.

George Wisener, Private, age 18, entered service for period of 3 years, June 10, 1861.

Company C: Transferred to Co. C 75th O.V.I. Jan. 16, 1864; from Co. C 75th O.V.I. May 6, 1864; mustered out July 16, 1864 at Camp Chase, Ohio on expiration of term of service.

Philip D. Wiser, Private, age 19, entered service for period of 3 years, June 26, 1861.

Company H: no record given.

George W. Wisner, Private, age 18, entered service for period of 3 years, June 10, 1861.

Company C: Transferred to Co. C 75th O.V.I. Jan. 16, 1864; from Co. C 75th O.V.I. May 6, 1864; mustered out July 16, 1864 at Camp Chase, Ohio on expiration of term of service.

Company H: Transferred to Co. C 75th O.V.I. Jan. 16, 1864; from Co. C 75th O.V.I. June 12, 1864; mustered out July 16, 1864 at Columbus, Ohio on expiration of term of service.

Henry Wolf, Private, age 43, entered service for period of 1 year, Jan. 20, 1864.
Company C: Transferred from Co. F 107th O.V.I. July 13, 1864; discharged March 5, 1866 at Charleston, S.C. by order of War Department.

Martin V. B. Wolf, Private, age 19, entered service for period of 3 years, June 18, 1861.

Company G: Discharged Aug. 14, 1863 at Convalescent Camp, Va. by order of War Department.

Harvey Wood, Private, age 23, entered service for period of 1 year, Oct 6, 1864.
Company A: Wounded Dec. 6, 1864 in battle of Deveaux Neck, S.C.; mustered out Oct. 6, 1865 on expiration of term of service.

John T. Wood, Captain, age 29, entered service for period of 3 years, June 4, 1861.

Company E: Promoted to 1st Lieutenant from 2d Lieutenant Co. G May 16, 1862; wounded July 1, 1863 in battle of Gettysburg, Pa.; promoted to Captain Sept. 20, 1863; resigned Aug 31, 1864. Re-enlisted as Major of 180th Ohio Volunteer Infantry.

Company H: Promoted to 1st. Lieutenant Co. E May 16, 1862.

Stephen Wood, Private, age 18, entered service for period of 1 year, Oct. 6, 1864.

Company A: Mustered out Oct. 6, 1865 on expiration of term of service.

Thomas C. Woodburn, Private, age 20, entered service for period of 3 years, Feb. 20, 1862.
Company E: no record given.
Frederick Woodley, Private, age 24, entered service for period of 3 years, June 10, 1861.
Company C: Died July 9, 1862 at Alleghany City, Pa. of wounds received May 8, 1862 in battle of McDowell, Va..
James T. Woodman, Private, age 21, entered service for period of 3 years, June 26, 1861.
Company H: no record given.
John Woodward, Private, age 26, entered service for period of 3 years, June 26, 1861.
Company H: Transferred to Co. C 75th O.V.I. Jan. 16, 1864; from Co. C. 75th O.V.I. June 12, 1864; mustered out July 16, 1864 at Columbus, Ohio on expiration of term of service.
Company H: Appointed Corporal April 1, 1864; veteran.
J. Workman, Private, age 30, entered service for period of 3 years, Feb. 12, 1863.
Company G: no record given.
Solomon Workman, Private, age 37, entered service for period of 3 years, Oct. 8, 1862.
Company A: no record given.
George D. Wormwood, Private, age 26, entered service for period of 3 years, June 12, 1861.
Company E: Discharged Dec. 17, 1861 on Surgeon's certificate of disability.
Thomas Worthington, Private, age 21, entered service for period of 1 year, Sept. 27, 1864.
Company D: Mustered out July 15, 1865 by order of War Department.
Charles T. Wright, Private, age 18, entered service for period of 3 years, June 8, 1861.
Company D: Transferred to 12th Battery O.L.A. March 12, 1862.
Franklin Wright, Private, age 19, entered service for period of 3 years, Aug. 7, 1862.
Company E: Wounded Dec. 6, 1864 in battle of Gregory's Landing, S.C.; discharged July 15, 1865 by order of War Department.
George Wright, Private, age 18, entered service for period of 1 year, Oct. 14, 1864.
Company C: Killed Nov. 30, 1864 in battle of Honey Hill, South Carolina.
Joseph Wright, Private, age 21, entered service for period of 3 years, June 12, 1861.
Company E: Killed May 2, 1863 in battle of Chancellorsville, Va.

Robert Wright, Private, age 27, entered service for period of 3 years, June 5, 1861.

Company A: Mustered out July 16, 1864 on expiration of term of service. Transferred to Co..., 75th O.V.I. Jan. 15, 1864.

William B. Wright, Sergeant, age 23, entered service for period of 3 years, June 5, 1861.

Company A: Appointed 1st Sergeant from Sergeant April 1, 1863; reduced to Sergeant April 30, 1863; mustered out July 18, 1864, on expiration of term of service.

Levi Wyman, Private, age 18, entered service for period of 3 years, Feb. 29, 1864.

Company B: On detached service...; mustered out with company June 18, 1866.

John D. Wymer, Private, age 21, entered service for period of 3 years, June 26, 1861.

Company H: no record given.

X none listed

Y

Jonathan H. Yarnall, Private, age 19, entered service for period of 9 months, Oct. 7, 1862.

Company K: Drafted; mustered out July 8, 1863 on expiration of term of service.

Peter Yarnall, Private, age 38, entered service for period of 3 years, June 13, 1861.

Company F: Transferred to Co. C 75th O.V.I. Jan. 16, 1864; from Co. C 75th O.V.I. June 12, 1864; mustered out July 16, 1864 on expiration of term of service.

William T. Yaton, Private, age 20, entered service for period of 3 years, June 26, 1861.

Company H: no record given.

Peter Yoho, Private, age 18, entered service for period of 3 years, June 18, 1861.

Company C: Discharged Dec. 2, 1864 at Camp Dennison, Ohio on Surgeon's certificate of disability.

David Yonly, Private, age 33, entered service for period of 3 years, Oct. 6, 1862.

Company A: Mustered out Oct. 6, 1865 on expiration of term of service.

Elihu Young, Private, age 27, entered service for period of 3 years, Feb. 3, 1863.

Company A: Transferred to Veteran Reserve Corps Aug. 1, 1863 by order of War Department.

Isaac N. Young, Private, age 19, entered service for period of 3 years, June 26, 1861.
Company H: Transferred to Co. C 75th O.V.I. Jan. 16, 1864; from Co. C 75th O.V.I. June 12, 1864; mustered out July 16, 1864 at Columbus, Ohio on expiration of term of service.

Z

John Zane, Private, age 25, entered service for period of 3 years, June 5, 1861.
Company A: Discharged Dec. 24, 1864 at Wheeling, W. Va. by order of War Department.
Jacob Zeller, Private, age 18, entered service for period of 1 year, Oct. 5, 1864.
Company D: Mustered out with company Oct. 20, 1865.
Lewis Zeigler, Private, age 24, entered service for period of 3 years, June 12, 1861.
Company E: Wounded May 2, 1863 in battle of Cahncellorsville, Va. and July 1, 1863 in battle of Gettysburg, Pa.; transferred to Veteran Reserve Corps March 15, 1864 by order of War Department.
Lewis Zimmerman, Private, age 44, entered service for period of 3 years, Jan. 29, 1864.
Company E: Wounded Dec. 6, 1864 in battle of Gregory's Landing, S.C.; discharged June 21,
1865 by order of War Department.
Martin Zimmerman, Private, age 26, entered service for period of 1 year, Sept. 27, 1864.
Company F: Died Jan. 13, 1865 at Hilton Head, S.C. of wounds received Nov. 30, 1864 in battle of Honey Hill, S.C.

About the Author

Tom J. Edwards holds an MBA and has nearly thirty years experience in positions of business management and college administration, currently working with South Carolina Technical Education system. Edwards' research skills won two successful National Register Historic District nominations. He is past president of the South Carolina Archeological Society.

INDEX

0-595-27608-3

DEB
Lakeside Ohio
7/06

Printed in the United States
31935LVS00004B/115-120

9 780595 276080